15-Minute WATERCOLOR FLORALS

Create Exquisite Paintings with 30 Beginner-Friendly Tutorials

Joly Poa

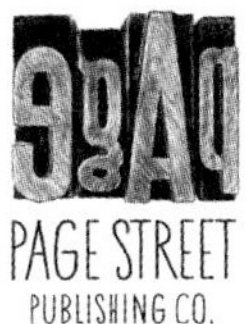

PAGE STREET
PUBLISHING CO.

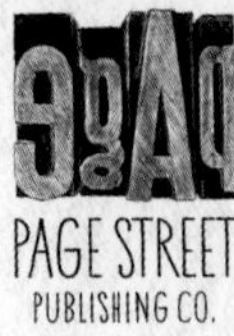

PAGE STREET
PUBLISHING CO.

First published in 2026 by
Page Street Publishing Co.
27 Congress Street, Suite 1511
Salem, MA 01970
www.pagestreetpublishing.com

Distributed by Macmillan, sales in Canada by The Canadian Manda Group.

30   29   28   27   26   1   2   3   4   5

ISBN-13: 979-8-89003-464-9

Library of Congress Control Number: 2025948340

Edited by Krystle Green
Cover and book design by Elena van Horn for Page Street Publishing Co.
Artwork by Joly Poa

Printed and bound in the United States of America

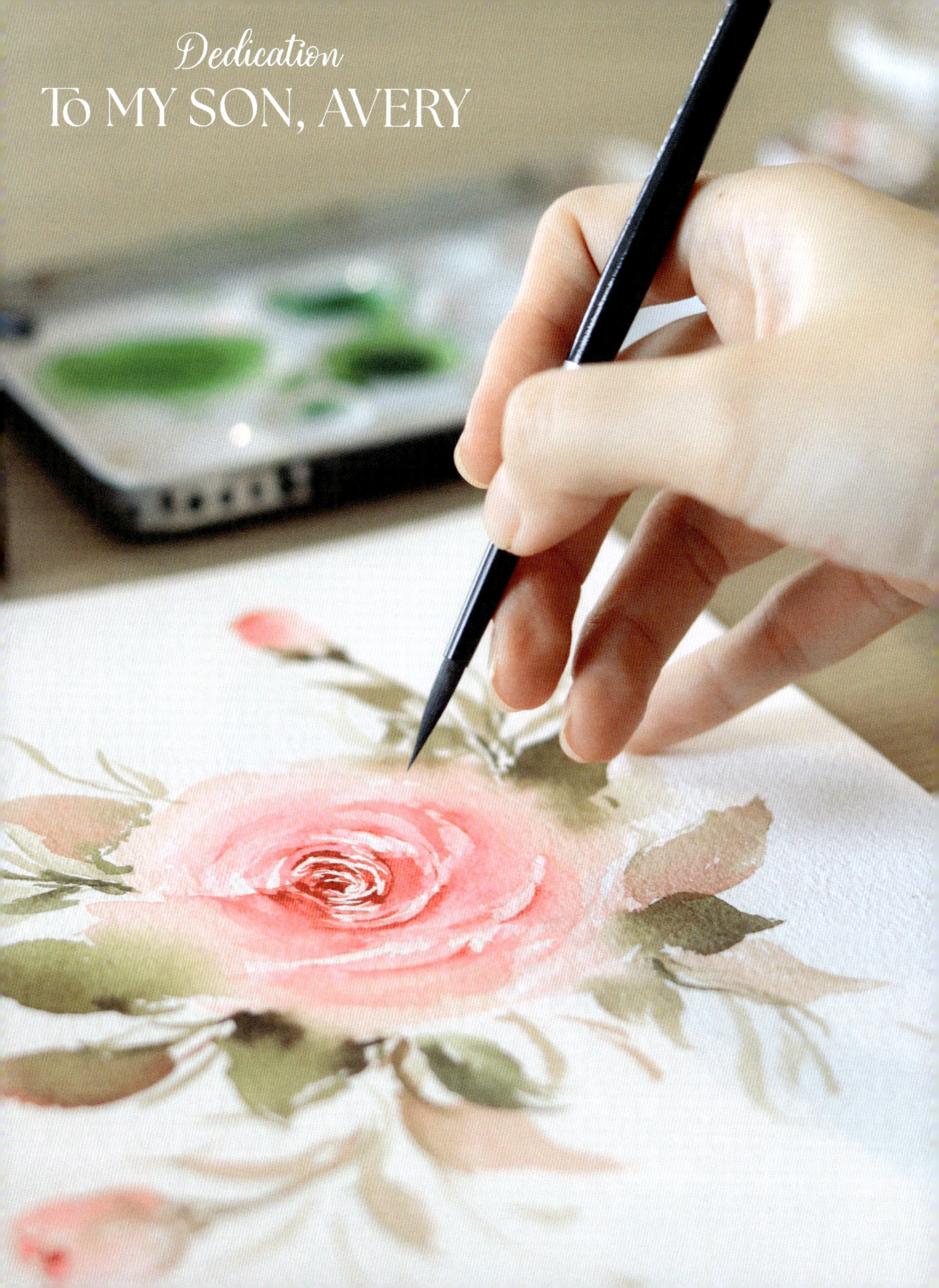

Dedication
To MY SON, AVERY

Table of CONTENTS

Romantic Pink Rose | 37

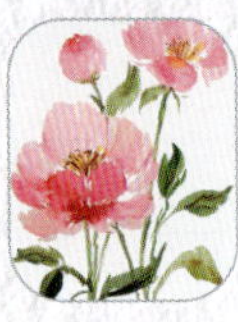

Lush Pink Peony | 43

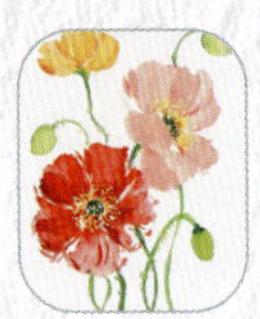

Fiery Icelandic Poppy | 47

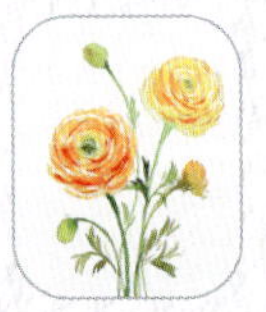

Sunlit Yellow Orange Ranunculus | 53

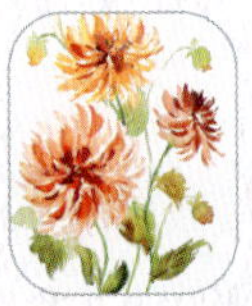

Soft Coral Dahlia | 57

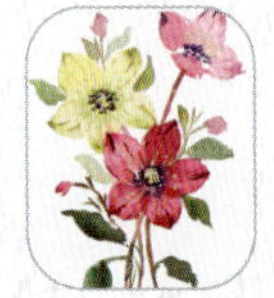

Moody Mauve Hellebore | 63

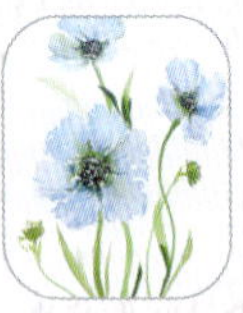

Dusty Blue Scabiosa | 69

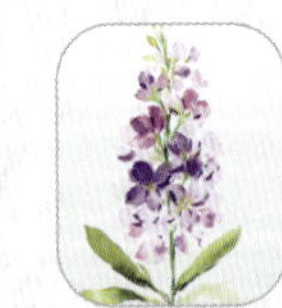

Stormy Violet Stock | 73

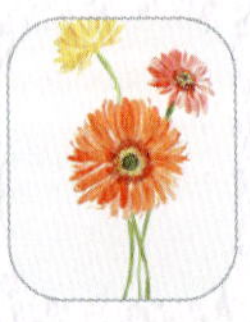

Sunset Orange Gerbera | 79

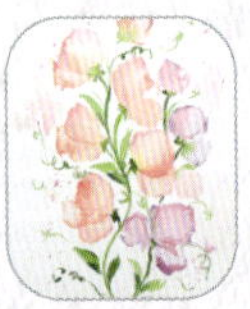

Blush Sweet Pea | 83

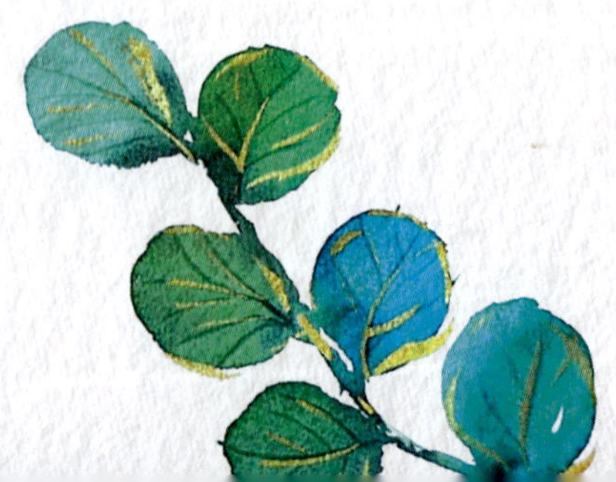

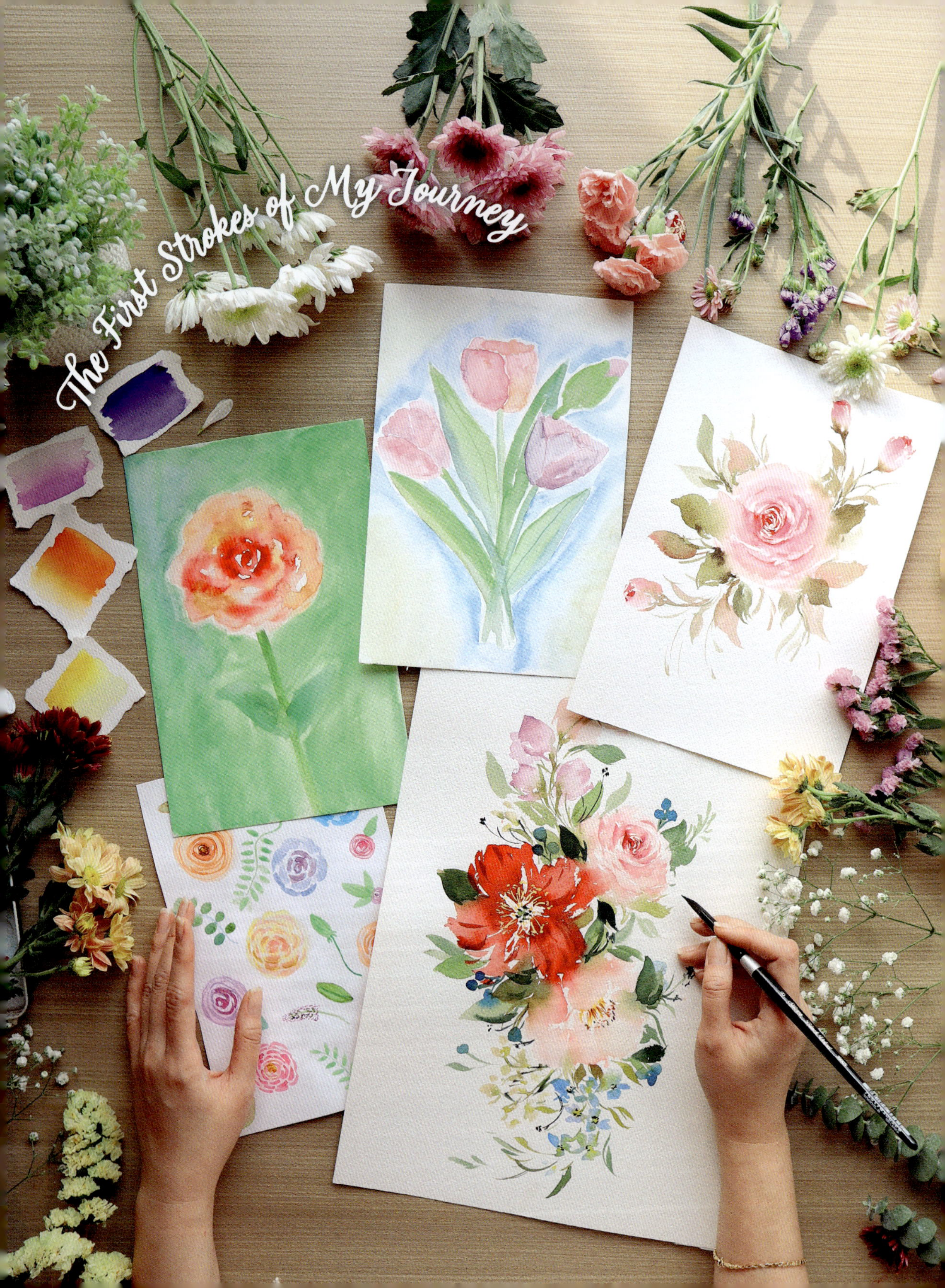
The First Strokes of My Journey

INTRODUCTION

Welcome to *15-Minute Watercolor Florals*! This book was born to show you how small pockets of creativity can lead to big bursts of joy.

There's something truly special about painting loose watercolor florals. It gives you the creative freedom to explore and capture the essence of a flower through color, movement, and expressive brushstrokes.

For me, it feels like dancing with my brush. Each stroke has its own rhythm, and together they create something beautiful on paper.

I know how intimidating watercolor can feel at first because I've been there. When I was just starting out, many of my paintings looked like colorful blobs of paint. But with daily practice, patience, and plenty of trial and error, I slowly found my way into painting florals that felt light and loose.

Before becoming an artist, I was actually a baker. My husband and I ran a small cake shop together. In 2013, I tried watercolor as a hobby and fell in love with it. It became a wonderful way to de-stress and fill my creative cup. Around the same time, I began documenting my journey on Instagram. I would share short tutorial videos and photos of my progress like a digital diary. Many people resonated with the experience of starting from scratch, and my page slowly grew into a supportive and inspiring community.

Since then, I have had the opportunity to do live stage demos for art brands at big events, teach workshops in the Philippines and abroad, and publish my first online watercolor class on Skillshare by the end of 2018. Teaching thousands of students on Skillshare taught me how to break down watercolor into simple and approachable steps for beginners. It also taught me to anticipate students' challenges and demonstrate or give tips on how to troubleshoot common "oops!" moments.

When I was starting out, resources on loose watercolor florals were limited. That inspired me to create this book, one I wrote with my beginner self in mind so learning would feel joyful, less intimidating, and accessible for anyone beginning their watercolor journey.

One thing that helped me stay consistent in my artistic journey was learning how to paint in small pockets of time. I found that by simplifying shapes, painting on smaller sheets of paper, and using a hairdryer to speed up drying time, I could make 15-minute paintings doable and enjoyable.

In this book, I'll guide you through 30 beginner-friendly projects designed to help you explore watercolor florals at your own pace. We'll start with the basics like art supplies, how to hold a brush, essential floral strokes, watercolor techniques, and composition tips before moving on to painting individual flowers. In the second half of the book, we'll bring those flowers together into compositions like bouquets, wreaths, and other creative projects.

By the end, you'll feel more confident with your brush and comfortable with creating your own loose watercolor florals.

Over the years, painting florals has become my source of joy and creative outlet. My hope is that you'll move through these pages discovering the joy of slowing down, letting go of perfection, and embracing your unique style.

So grab your brush, and let's start painting together!

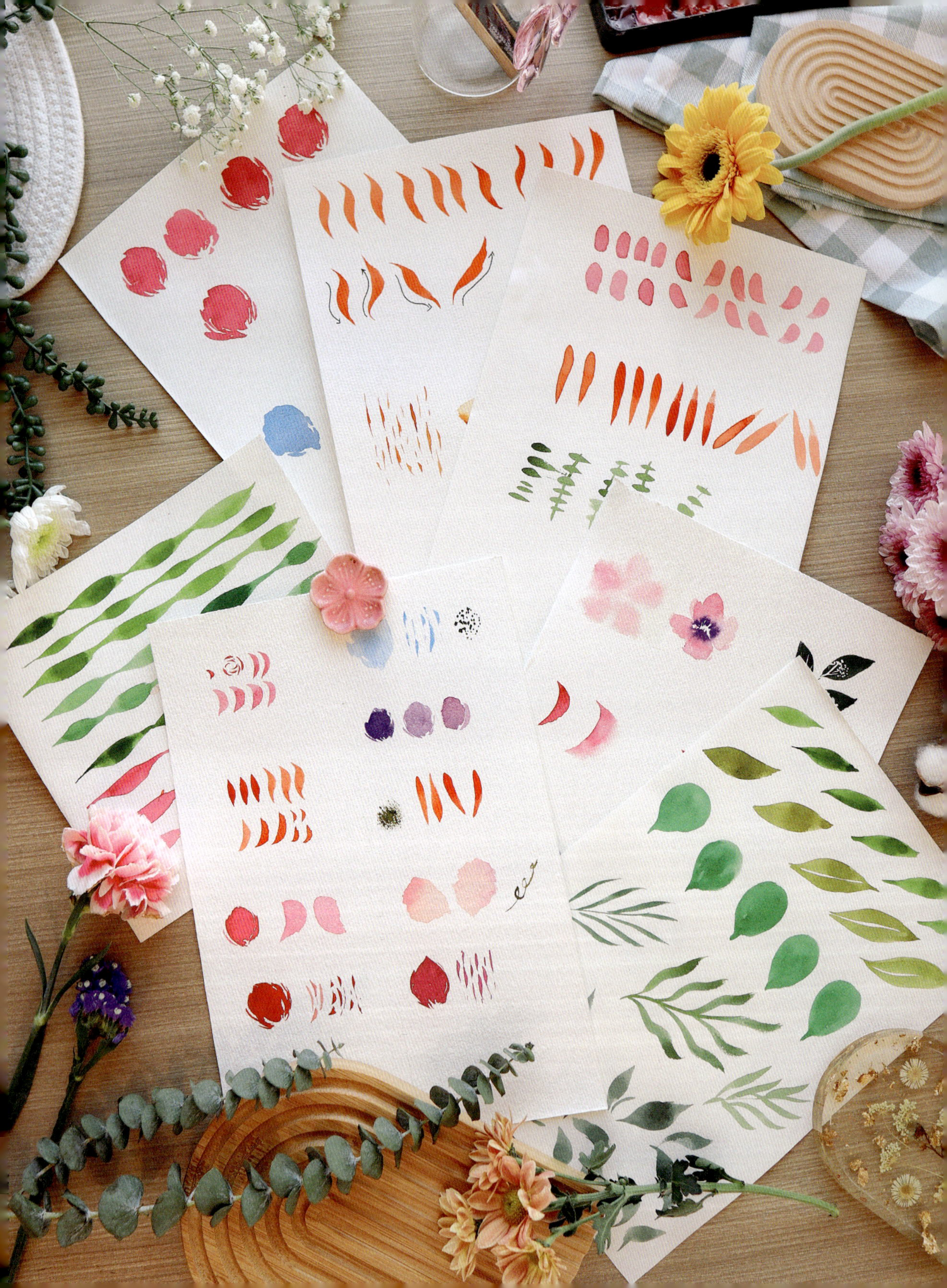

Bloom
BASICS
Your Watercolor Floral Toolkit

Every beautiful flower starts with the basics. In this chapter, I'll share my top ten tips for painting loose watercolor florals. We'll learn about how water and pigment work together, and how understanding your brush can make a huge difference in your strokes. You'll get to try simple brushwork drills to loosen up.

I'm also excited to share with you a set of essential floral strokes that I often use so you can use them as a guide when painting different flowers.

Finally, we'll explore a handful of watercolor techniques that will help you understand this medium better and several floral composition tips to help you combine your flowers beautifully. Think of this as a little warm-up before you begin to paint full florals. Enjoy the process and have fun experimenting. Trust that your unique style will bloom!

MY TOP TEN TIPS FOR PAINTING LOOSE FLORALS

One of the joys of painting loose florals is capturing the essence of a flower without getting caught up in every detail. Here are some helpful tips to guide you:

Focus on a Distinct Characteristic

You don't need to paint every petal and vein. Instead, choose one or two traits that make the flower unique, like the center, the tight petals, or the overall silhouette. Let those details suggest the flower. Loose painting is all about impression, not perfection.

Use Contrast to Make Flowers Pop

Adding a darker center or dropping in a deeper value while the flower is still wet instantly creates contrast. A simple five-petal flower suddenly comes to life and feels more dimensional.

Frame with Leaves

Placing leaves near the main flowers helps define the flowers' shapes. This is especially effective for lighter colored flowers, which might look washed out in a bouquet. Placing darker leaves around light flowers makes them pop. Leaves can also add movement and direct the viewer's eye around the painting.

Leave White Spaces

Throughout this book, you will often see me mention leaving white spaces to let the flowers breathe. These gaps keep the painting light and airy, while also separating the petals so they don't merge into a single blob of color. Remember, negative space is an important part of the composition too.

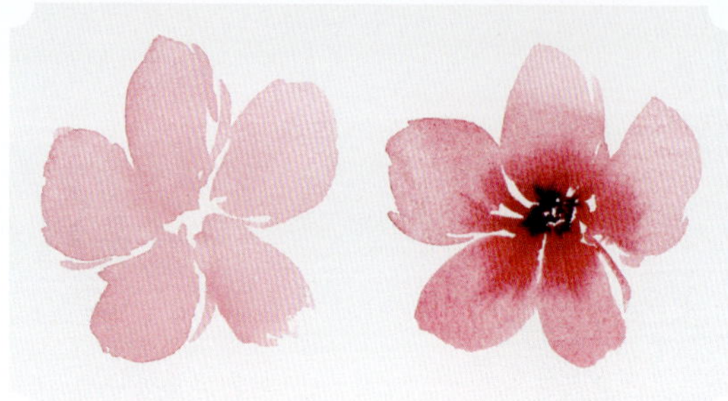

Use Contrast to Make Flowers Pop

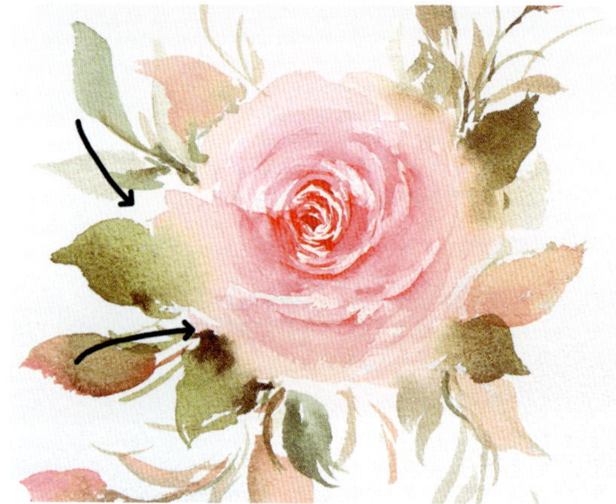

Frame with Leaves

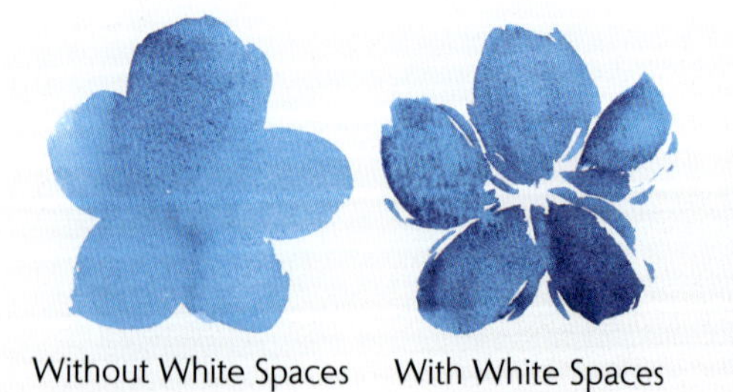

Leave White Spaces

Don't Be Afraid of Pressure

Many beginners hesitate to press their brush down when painting, but varying the pressure is key to creating expressive strokes. Experiment with light and heavy pressure to discover the full range of marks your brush can make. A great way to practice is on regular printer paper, so you can freely explore without worrying about wasting your watercolor paper.

Embrace Water and Flow

Let the water do some of the work for you. Try wetting an area, then dropping in color, and watch how the pigments spread naturally. This will give you an idea of how to create soft, dreamy petals.

Don't Be Afraid of Pressure

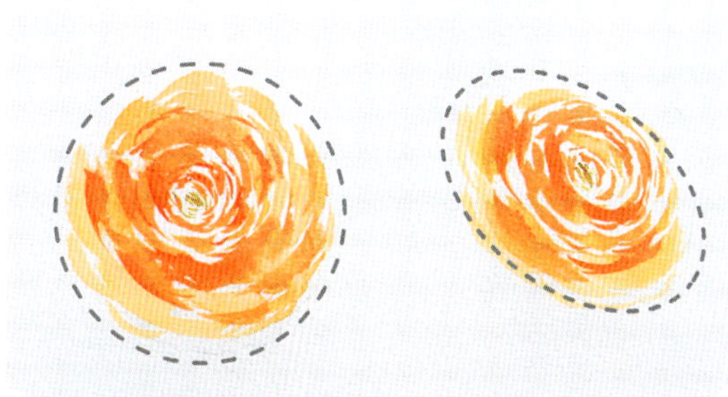

Observe Flowers from Different Perspectives

Choose a Safe Color to Start With

If mixing colors feels overwhelming, start with a single familiar shade. When I was beginning, I painted all my flowers in my favorite pink. Using a safe, go-to color takes the pressure off inventing something new. It allows you to focus on practicing brushstrokes and shapes. Once you feel more confident, you can experiment with mixing or layering colors for variety.

Blot Your Brush

In my early days, I hesitated to blot my brush on tissue paper because it felt like wasting paint. But I soon realized how important this step is. Blotting removes the excess moisture, giving you the right balance of water and pigment. With that better control, your brush glides smoothly across the paper without creating puddles, and you can drop in another color on a damp petal without it spreading uncontrollably.

Observe Flowers from Different Perspectives

Front-facing flowers usually appear round because you look directly into the bloom. On the other hand, side-facing flowers are oval in shape because you are viewing them at an angle. Mixing these perspectives in your arrangement prevents it from looking flat and creates interest.

Use a Hairdryer or Fan to Speed Up Painting Time

Since this book focuses on 15-minute projects, a hairdryer or fan can be your best friend. It helps dry layers quickly so you don't have to wait too long to add second-layer details that bring depth to your florals, like veins. This also keeps your momentum going and lets you finish your painting in just a few minutes. So don't hesitate to use these shortcuts—they help make each painting session feel doable.

ART SUPPLIES

One of the best things about watercolor is that you don't need a lot to get started. The materials are light, portable, and easy to clean up.

When I was just beginning, I worked with student-grade paints, papers, and brushes. Art supplies can be costly, so don't hesitate to use what fits your budget. I still remember using both sides of my student-grade paper to make the most out of it. Those early days of practicing with student-grade materials were valuable. I learned how to control the amount of water in my brush and observe how the paint behaved.

That said, I still recommend switching to artist-grade materials when you can. It allows for a wider range of watercolor techniques and brings out the best in your colors.

Watercolor Paper

Paper makes a big difference in how your painting turns out. Here are some things that you can take note of:

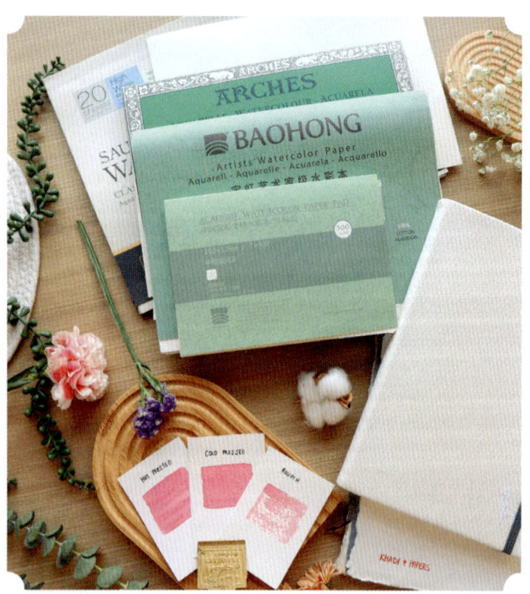

Quality

Student-grade papers are usually made of cellulose. They are affordable and great for practicing. However, sometimes the paints may look dull, and water tends to sit on the surface, creating hard edges. Wet-on-wet techniques can also be tricky on this paper. My current favorite student-grade paper, which performs almost like artist-grade, is Baohong Academy. You may also try Canson XL® or Strathmore® 400 series.

Artist-grade papers, on the other hand, are made of 100% cotton. The paint stays wet longer, allowing for beautiful blends, richer colors, and more depth in your work. Throughout the book, I will be using Baohong Artist-Grade Watercolor Paper: Cold Pressed. I also recommend brands such as Arches®, Fabriano Artistico, Saunders Waterford®, and Winsor & Newton. For sketchbooks, I like the Khadi sketchbook and Etchr Lab.

Texture

Watercolor paper texture plays a huge role in how your paint moves and settles. Each texture creates a slightly different look and feel in your painting.

Cold-Pressed

This is my favorite texture for a loose watercolor style. It has right amount of tooth.

Hot-Pressed

Smooth and ideal for fine details. If you love painting realistic watercolor botanicals, this paper is perfect.

Rough

More textured than cold pressed, which can make floral strokes look jagged, rough paper works beautifully for landscapes and expressive textures.

Weight

I recommend 300 gsm (140 lb) paper. It's thick enough to handle wet washes without warping. For lighter washes or projects that need folding like envelopes, 200 gsm can be good enough. It's also a more affordable choice.

Format

Watercolor papers come in blocks, loose sheets, pads, and sketchbooks.

Blocks

These are my go-to, as the sheets are glued on all sides except for one, keeping the paper flat while you paint. Just slide a spatula or ruler under the unglued side to release the sheet once it's dry.

Loose Sheets

Cost-effective since large sheets are affordable, you can cut loose sheets down to any size you like.

Sketchbooks

Sketchbooks are a good way to see your progress, since they keep all your paintings together in one place.

Brushes

When it comes to watercolor flowers, I find that brushes are important because they help shape the petals and give character to your strokes.

Choosing a brush is a very personal preference. Some artists prefer dense brushes for bolder marks, while others lean toward softer ones for fluid and expressive strokes. You'll discover what works best for you as you experiment.

For me, a good brush holds plenty of water yet keeps its point. It should follow my flow with every movement, small or big. Here are some of my favorites:

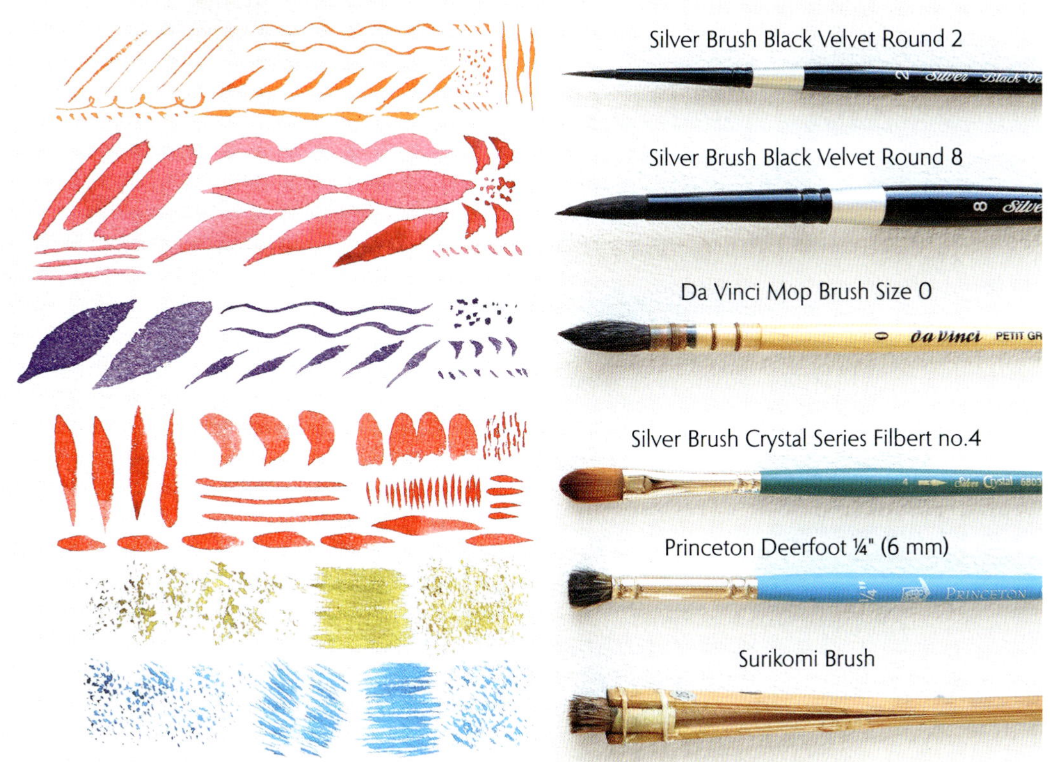

Round Brush

My everyday go-to brush is the Silver Brush Black Velvet round brush in size 8. It's perfect for medium-sized paintings, and I often pair it with a size 6. For fine details, you may use a size 2. This brush is a blend of natural and synthetic hair, which gives both softness and the right amount of bounce. You can also find good round brushes from the Princeton Neptune and Princeton Velvetouch series.

Mop or Quill Brush

Though it may look intimidating at first, the mop brush is wonderful for painting loose, expressive strokes. Most mop brushes are made of natural hair, which is incredibly soft and holds a lot water. I love the Da Vinci mop brush in size 0.

With today's brush technology, some brands now produce excellent synthetic mop brushes that mimic natural hair, like Tintoretto.

Filbert Brush

Using a filbert brush makes painting petals feel effortless. It has a curved edge that creates a rounded petal shape. I love using a ¾-inch (2-cm) size for big, fluffy, loose petals. For smaller petals and rounded leaves, a size ³⁄₈ inch (1 cm) is perfect.

Surikomi Brush and Deerfoot Brush

One of my signature tools is the surikomi brush, which I discovered in an art shop in Japan. It has a bamboo handle and a unique structure originally designed for stenciling. The size I use is 2.5; the smaller the number, the smaller the brush size. When pressed lightly on the paper, it creates a delicate dotted or speckled texture that's perfect for adding details to your flower center. An alternative is the Princeton deerfoot brush. The size ¼ inch (6 mm) works well for adding dotted texture in small areas, or you can use it to suggest grass by dragging the brush lightly and flicking it for a more natural effect.

You can also achieve a similar dotted texture with an old toothbrush. Just make sure to use a thicker paint mixture so the tiny dots appear clearly rather than forming a small blob.

Paints

When it comes to watercolor paint, I prefer artist-grade paints because they are more pigmented and they blend beautifully on paper. However, there are now many good student-grade options that are great starting points. You can always upgrade to artist-grade paints when you are comfortable with the medium.

Watercolors may come in tubes or pans. Tubes are convenient if you often work on larger paintings, while pans are perfect for medium-sized paintings and when you're travelling. Both are the same in terms of quality.

One fun option is the Japanese brand Kuretake Gansai Tambi™ which offers sets in premixed colors.

Personally, I love using the brand ShinHan PWC, which comes in tubes. I pour them into empty half pans, let them dry, and then store them in a metal tin. When I'm about to paint, I simply spray a little water over the pans and let them soften for a minute before using. Other good brands that I have tried are Holbein, Sennelier, Schmincke, Winsor & Newton, QoR® watercolor, and A. Gallo Colors.

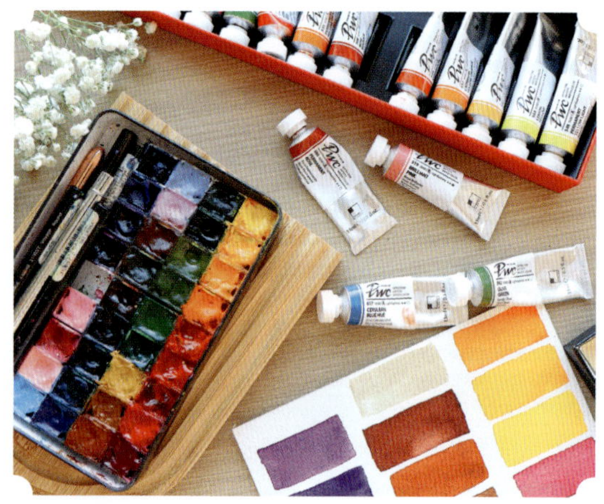

The colors below are some of my go-to shades. You don't need to have these exact colors. Since I mostly paint florals, my palette is filled with happy shades of pinks, purples, oranges, and greens. I also like to include a deep color for contrast such as Indigo or Sepia. Recently, I've added some pastel tones to bring extra softness to my work, along with Buff Titanium from the QoR brand—a beautiful creamy beige that I love!

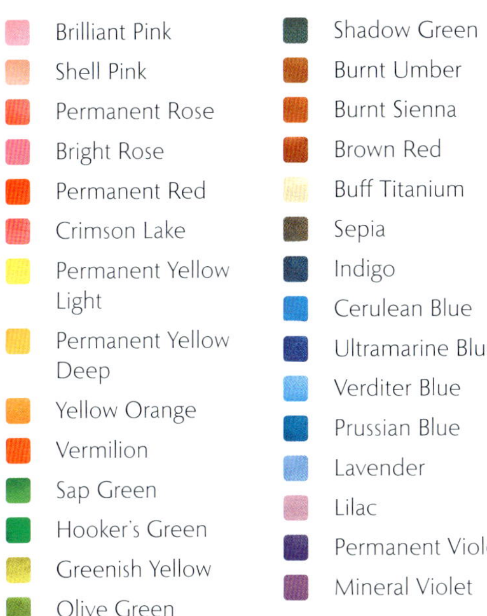

Other Materials

Along with your usual paint, paper, and brushes, these extra supplies will come in handy as you paint. Have a mixing palette, a jar of water, and some tissue paper ready because they'll be useful for every project.

Mixing Palette

I use the lid of my watercolor tin as my mixing palette. But I also enjoy collecting ceramic palettes in different designs. They make painting more enjoyable and brighten up my workspace.

Washi Tape

For some projects, we will use tape to create clean borders. Washi tape is my favorite because it's gentle on paper. Just remember to peel it off at an angle to avoid tearing the surface. I have found lovely washi tapes in art stores in Japan, but any regular printed washi tape will work too.

Pencil

I usually reach for a mechanical pencil to sketch light guidelines. Nothing fancy is needed here, just something comfortable to use.

Eraser

A kneaded eraser is such a game changer. Instead of rubbing, you can gently roll it across the paper to lift and erase the pencil lines without damaging the surface.

White

To add highlights or white details, I like using Holbein gouache in Permanent White. You may also use a POSCA® acrylic pen or a Uniball™ Signo white pen for fine details.

Gold

Adding gold details gives a nice touch of elegance to your paintings. I personally like Kuretake Gold Mica and Kuretake Starry Colors.

Jar of Water

Keep a jar or two of clean water, one for rinsing your brush and another for picking up clean water for painting.

Tissue Paper

Prepare a few sheets of tissue paper or a small towel to help blot off the excess water in your brush.

UNDERSTANDING COLOR AND WATER RATIO

One of the most important skills to learn in watercolor is learning how to control water and paint. Watercolor is a transparent and fluid medium. It changes depending on how much water and pigment you use. Let's learn more about this:

How to Control Water in Your Brush

Your brush can hold a lot of water, a little water, or just the right amount. Let me demonstrate what these look like.

Too Wet

Dip your brush in the water jar and lift. Observe how the bristles well up with water and water is dripping off the brush. This means your brush is too wet. This is okay if you want to paint backgrounds on larger areas. If you try to paint flowers, you will end up with large puddles.

Just Right

Dip your brush in the water jar, then tap the brush on the rim of jar. Notice how some of the water drips back in the jar. When you lift your brush, it's still wet but not dripping. You may also lightly dab your brush on a tissue paper to get rid of excess moisture.

Dry

After dipping your brush in the jar, blot out all the moisture in your brush. This will result in a dry brush. You will see the bristles separate. This can be used to create texture that looks like subtle streaks.

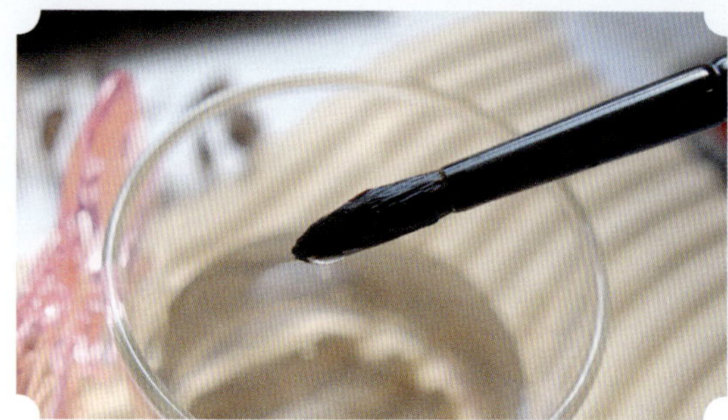

Too Wet

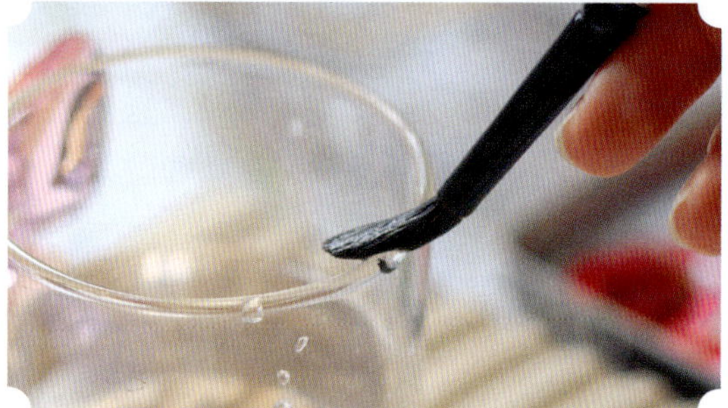

Just Right

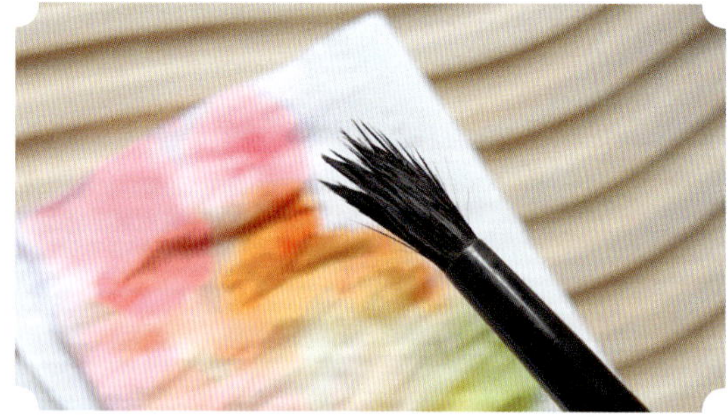

Dry

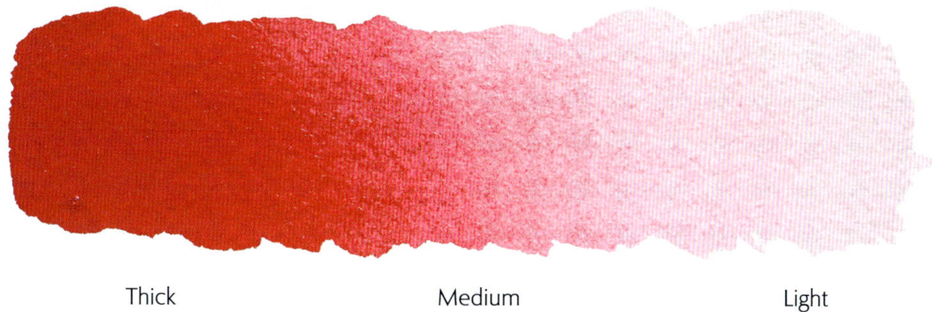

Thick   Medium   Light

Color Value

Value is the relative lightness or darkness of a color. To make a color lighter, we can add more water. To make a color darker, add more pigment. Throughout the book, you will see me talk about paint consistencies. Here, I'll talk about three primary consistencies, but you can definitely work between them.

Thick Consistency

Load your brush with very little water and more pigment. The result is an opaque mixture.

Medium Consistency

This is a balanced mixture of water and pigment, perfect for soft strokes like we use for leaves and petals.

Light Consistency

Load your brush with lots of water and a little bit of pigment. This creates a translucent tone which may be used for layering, subtle details, or softening the edges of flowers.

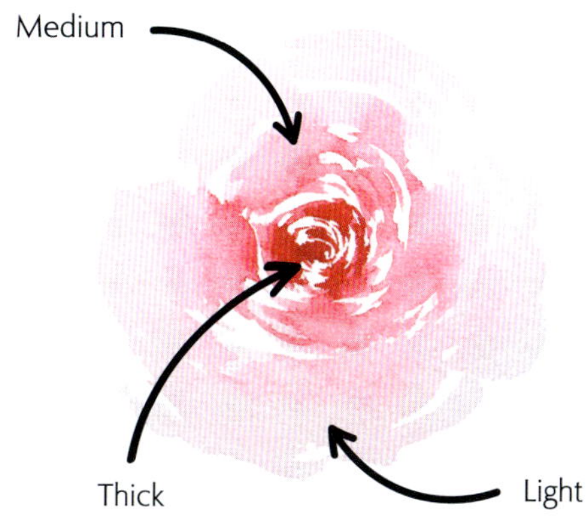

In the rose example, you will see that the center is almost opaque because I used a thick-consistency paint. The petals around the center were painted with medium-consistency paint, and the outermost petals were painted with light-consistency paint. We use light consistency to add softness to loose florals.

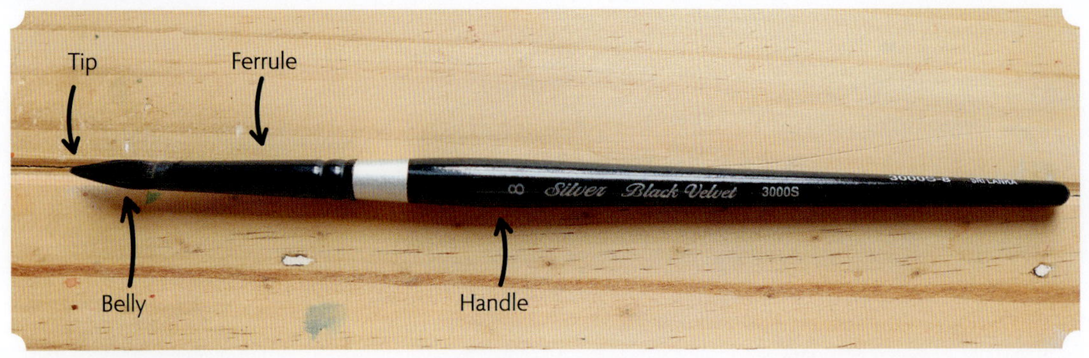

GET TO KNOW YOUR BRUSH

Before we paint flowers, it's important to become comfortable with the tool that you will use the most: your brush. When used with intention, you can create expressive strokes that capture the softness and flow of petals and leaves.

Let's check out the parts of the brush and how each contributes to your painting experience.

Parts of the Brush

Understanding the anatomy of the brush helps you handle it with confidence.

Tip

This is referring to the very end of the bristles, used for painting fine details like veins, tiny stems, and delicate dots.

Belly

This is the middle and thickest part of the bristles, where the brush holds the most water and pigment. It is ideal for broader strokes like petals and leaves or for covering larger areas.

Ferrule

This is the metal part that connects the bristles to the handle. It keeps the brush secure.

Handle

This is the part you hold, which is usually made of wood or acrylic. They may have different lengths and weights.

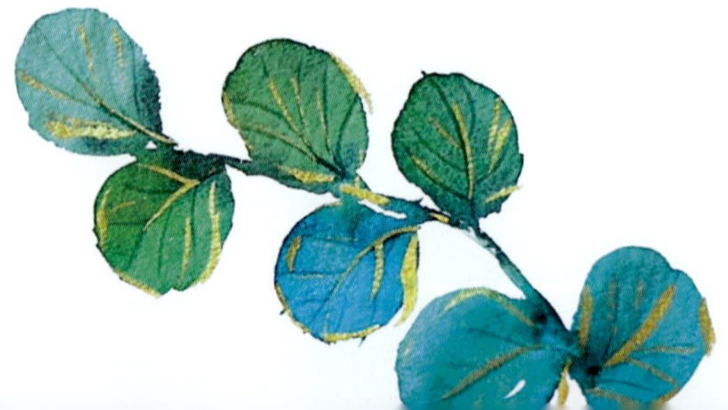

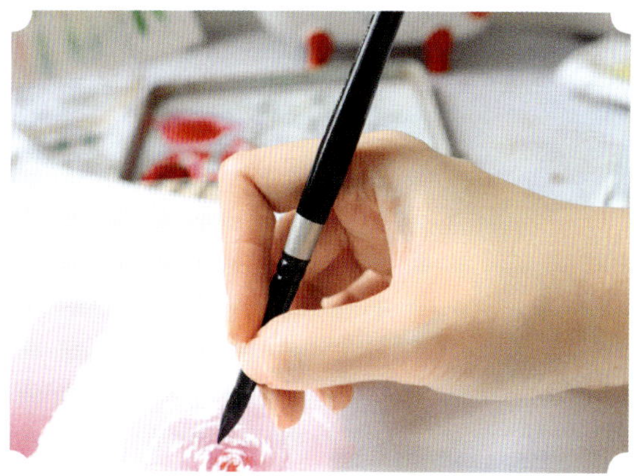

Near the Ferrule

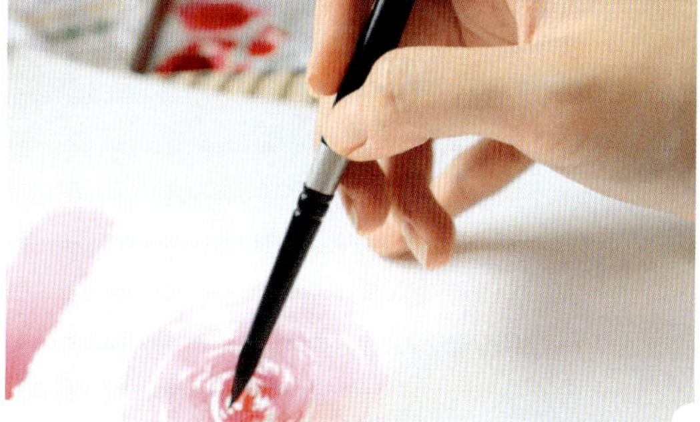

Middle of the Handle

How to Hold Your Brush

There is no single correct grip, but how you hold the brush affects how your strokes appear on paper. I recommend starting around the middle of the handle so you can get a natural feel for the brush, then adjusting as you grow more comfortable.

Avoid gripping your brush tightly as the stiffness will show in your strokes.

Near the Ferrule

Holding your brush close to the bristles gives you more control, which is useful for painting fine details.

Middle of the Handle

Holding your brush around the middle is a nice balance. You have control, but there is enough freedom for loose strokes.

Toward the End of the Handle

Holding your brush farther back encourages looser and more expressive strokes, as if you are dancing with your brush and letting it move freely across the paper.

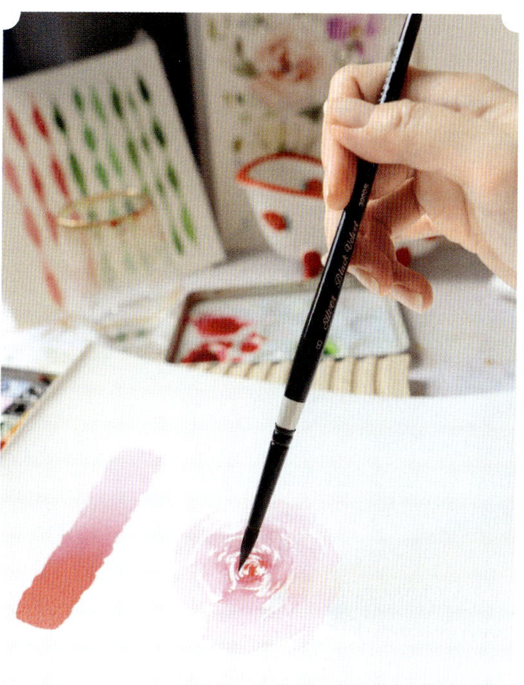

Toward the End of the Handle

Brushstroke Drills

Now that we have learned how to hold a brush, let's explore how pressure and movement affect your strokes. Practicing these drills will help you build muscle memory, improve dexterity, and help you paint with confidence. Notice how painting slowly gives you more controlled strokes while painting faster can result in looser strokes. Even with just a size 8 round brush, you'll be surprised at how many different strokes and shapes you can make.

Tip Strokes

Use the very tip of your brush and glide across the paper to create fine lines. Tilt your brush to almost 90 degrees. Create gentle curves, dots, and even tiny leaves by slightly flicking your brush.

Half Stroke

Press the brush down until about half of the bristles are flat on the paper. This creates medium-width strokes perfect for small flower petals and leaves. Try to experiment by stamping your brush, swaying, and flicking.

Full Belly Stroke

Press the brush down so that the full belly touches the paper. You will see the bristles fan out as you move your brush sideways. This is ideal for creating broad petals.

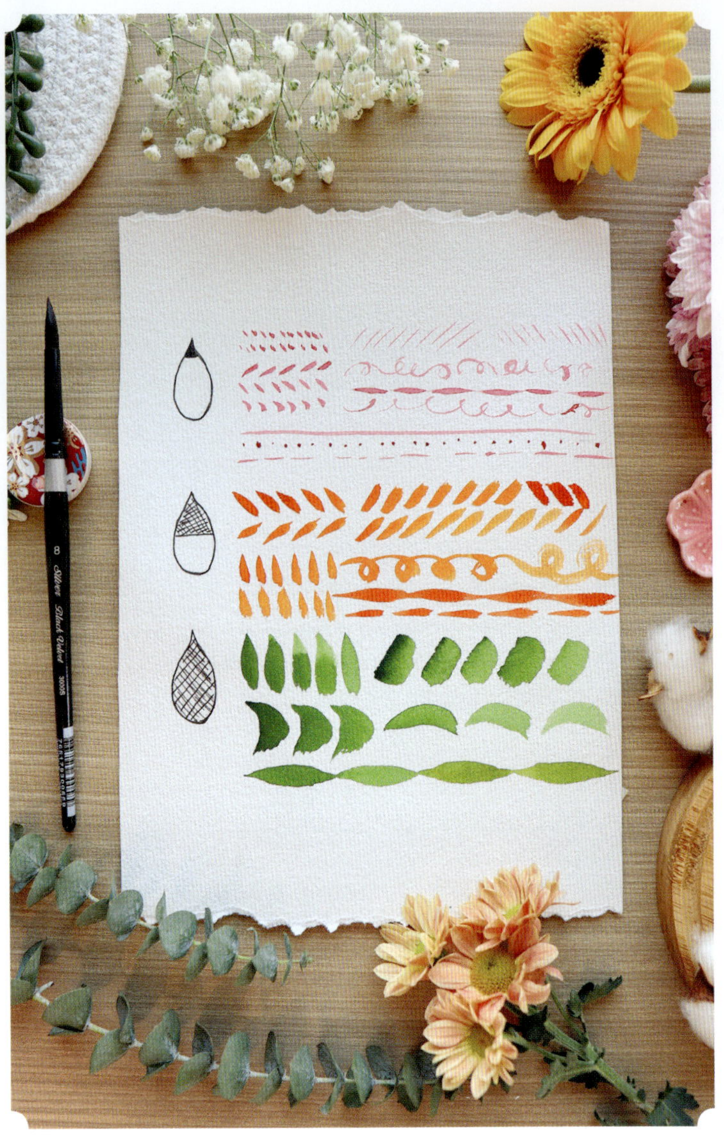

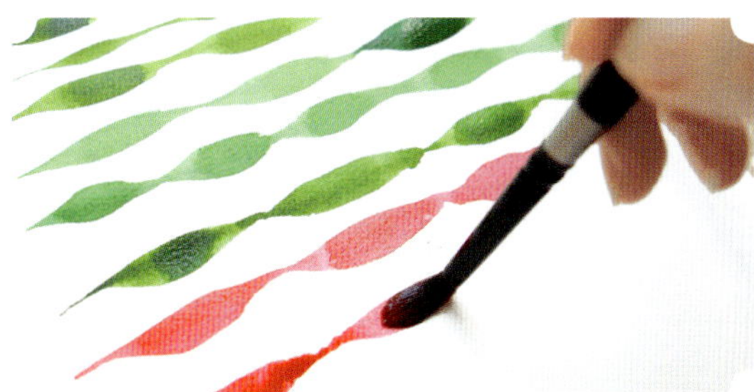

Thin and Thick Strokes

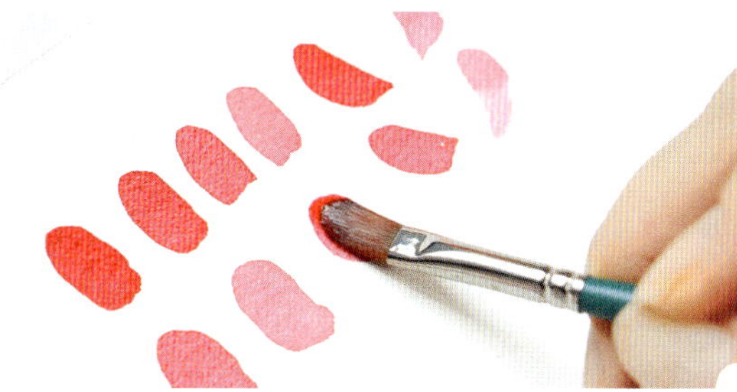

Filbert Stroke: Flat Side

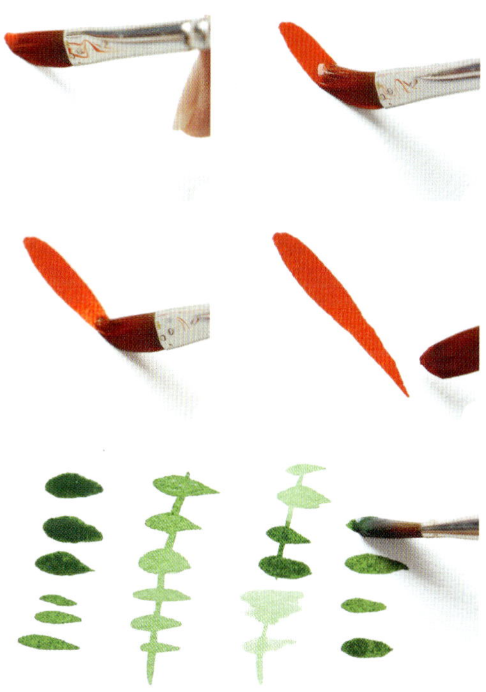

Side Brush

Thin and Thick Strokes

This is a classic drill in watercolor, but it is so useful. Start with the tip of the brush and begin with light pressure. Toward the middle of the stroke, press your brush down to gradually widen the stroke, then lift to taper it back to a fine line. You may do this in one continuous stroke for practice.

Filbert Stroke

There are two ways to use the filbert brush when painting flowers and leaves:

Flat Side

Load your brush with paint and lightly stamp the flat side of your brush on the paper. You will notice how you can effortlessly paint a natural petal shape with a soft, curved edge. Try to explore more strokes by painting in different directions and adding movement to create a variety of petal strokes.

Side Brush

Load your brush with paint and use the thin side of the brush to stamp on the paper. Using this stroke will create thin, elongated petals. Apply more pressure at the start, then gradually lift to a fine tip. This is helpful for painting long and slender petals like those of a Gerbera (page **79**). You can also use this stroke to create eucalyptus leaves.

Building Dexterity and Muscle Memory

Set aside a few minutes before each painting session to practice these drills. Vary your speed, angle, and pressure as you paint. Practice both slow strokes for more control and quick strokes to encourage fluidity. Over time, your brush will feel like an extension of your arm. Painting will become more intuitive, with a natural rhythm, as if you're dancing with your brush. And you will be able to create more spontaneous and expressive strokes.

ESSENTIAL FLORAL STROKES

The next step is to learn the basic strokes that form the foundation of loose watercolor florals. These are techniques that I have developed over the years, and I'm so excited to share them with you. With practice, you'll naturally develop your own rhythm and style.

Comma Stroke

I often use this small stroke when painting my roses, especially for creating the centers.

Hold your brush at a 45-degree angle, place the tip on the paper, and gently press down about a quarter of the brush as you move in a soft curve. Then, lift your brush at the end to create a fine tip. Each stroke may look a little different, and that's perfectly okay.

Comma Stroke

C Stroke

C strokes are used in circular florals like Romantic Pink Roses (page 37) and Sunlit Yellow Orange Ranunculus (page 53). We will vary the thickness depending on the size of the petal.

Start at the top of the stroke and slowly move in a curved manner while pressing your brush, then lift at the end with a flick to get a pointy tip. It doesn't have to be an exact C shape; just a resemblance. It could be a bit more elongated too. Practice this facing in different directions and lengths.

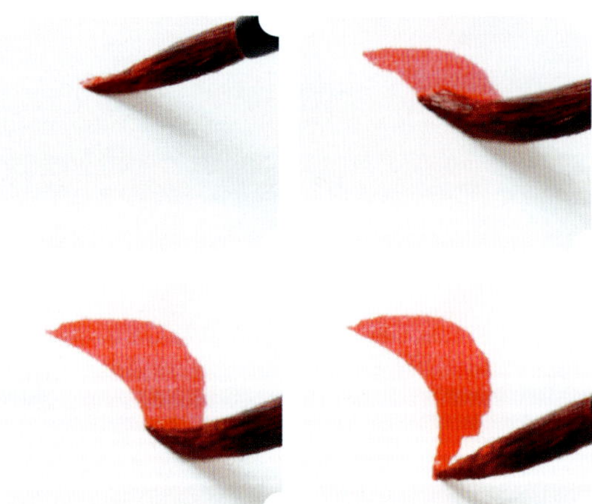

C Stroke

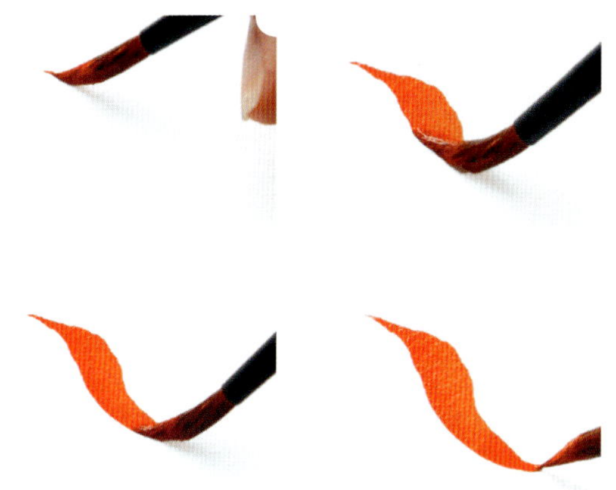

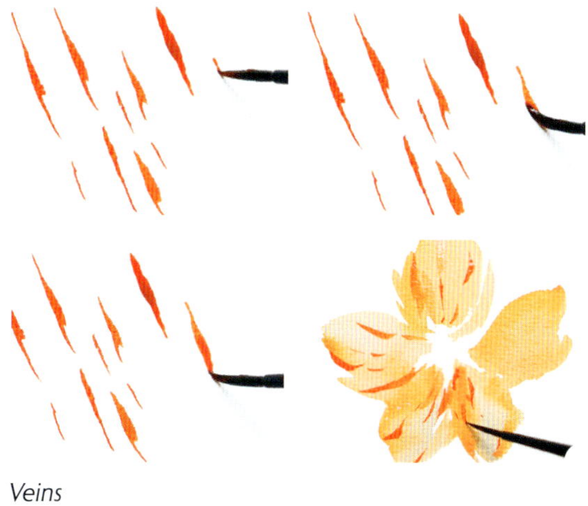

S Stroke

S strokes work well with curling petals and leaves. We will be using this stroke for the petals of the Soft Coral Dahlia (page 57).

Move your brush in an S curve, starting thin, widening through the curve, then tapering off again. You can work from the top to the bottom or vice versa.

S Stroke

Veins

Veins on petals and leaves are a great way to add depth and character.

Use a size 2 round brush and load it with paint. Start with light pressure and slowly press your brush toward the middle of the stroke, then lift at the end. Instead of a straight line, you have a more natural-looking vein. Play around with pressure and think of these veins as lines and dots.

Veins

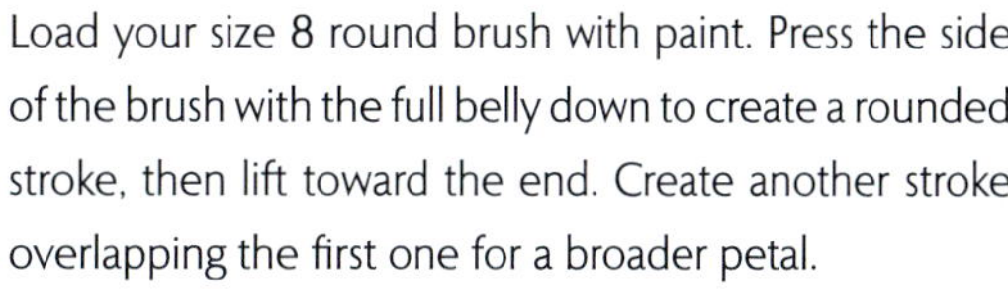

Rounded Petals

Rounded petals are very versatile for painting loose watercolor flowers. We can create so many different petals like those of the Lush Pink Peony (page 43) and many more.

Load your size 8 round brush with paint. Press the side of the brush with the full belly down to create a rounded stroke, then lift toward the end. Create another stroke overlapping the first one for a broader petal.

Add thin strokes using the tip of the brush to add character. Leave white spaces in between strokes.

Rounded Petals

Ruffled Petals

Some flowers have ruffled edges such as the Dusty Blue Scabiosa (page 69) and Blush Sweet Pea (page 83). Load your size 8 round brush very well with paint and press it down on the paper with the tip facing away from you. Gently move your brush up and down while moving to the left side of the petal. Do the same for the right side for a broad petal. Then, press your brush in the center of the petal, drag, and lift to create a pointy tip. You can come back in and add fine lines on the sides for character.

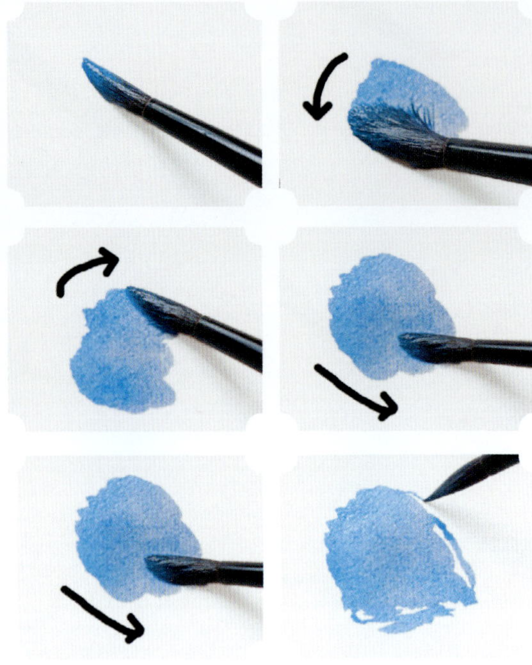

Ruffled Petals

Stamping

Stamping is one of the easiest ways to paint a petal. We are simply making the shape of the brush work for us. With a round brush, we'll get a pointed-tip petal by pressing it onto the paper. You may stamp individual petals or repeat this motion several times to form a larger shape like a cluster of petals that resembles a hydrangea or other grouped flowers.

We will be using this technique on the Sunset Orange Gerbera (page 79), using a deerfoot brush or surikomi brush to create a dotted texture from bristles.

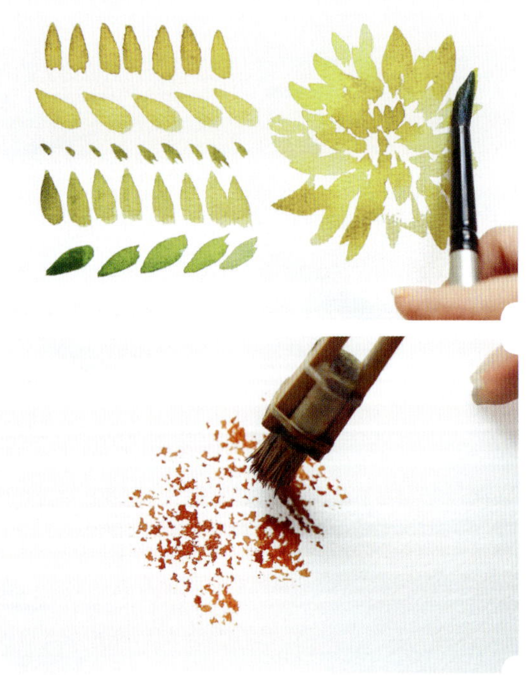

Stamping

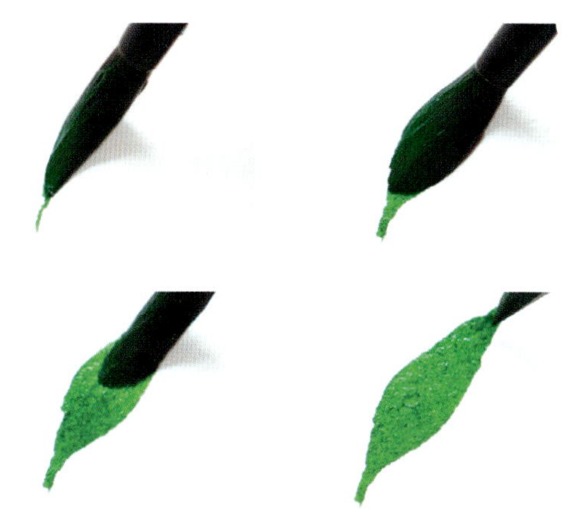

Leaf Strokes

Leaves and fillers add balance and movement to your composition. With a few simple strokes, we can create a variety of shapes.

One-Stroke Leaf

Load your brush with green paint, start at the tip, press down to widen the stroke, then lift back up to a fine point.

One-Stroke Leaf

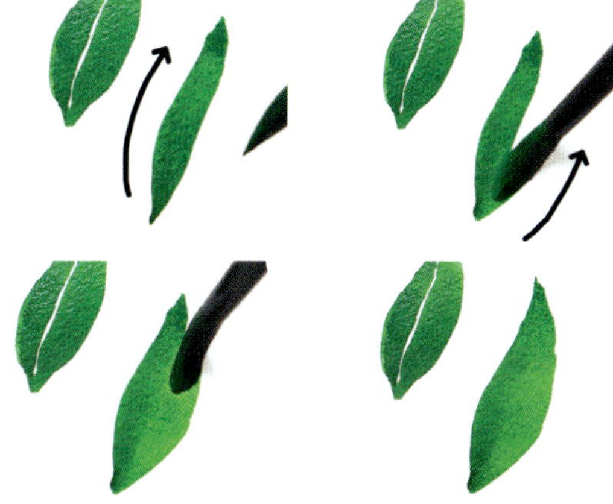

Two-Stroke Leaf

Start with the left side of the leaf. Load your brush with green paint, start at the tip, press down to widen the stroke, then lift back up to a fine point. Move to the right side of the leaf and do the same. You may combine the two strokes in the center or leave a white space.

Two-Stroke Leaf

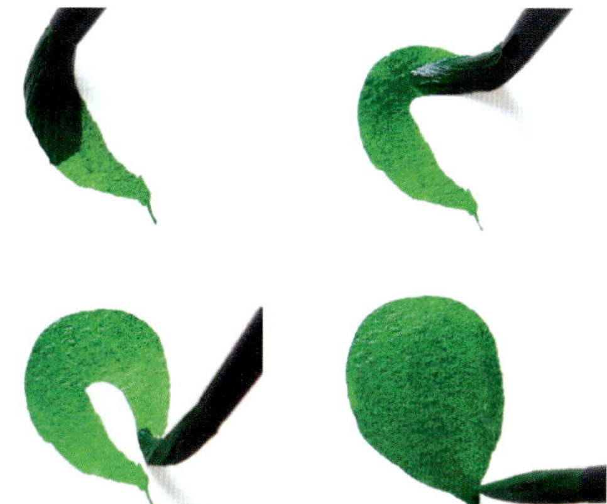

Rounded Leaf

Point the tip of your brush at the base of the leaf. As you move upward, press the belly of the brush to create a rounded curve, guiding it in a loop shape.

Then lift the pressure as you return to the base.

Rounded Leaf

Elongated Leaf

Start with the tip of the brush, press until about half of the bristles are flat on the paper, and then drag your brush to a fine point. You may add movement by making wavy curves. For larger leaves, press the full belly of the brush onto the paper instead of only half, then drag and lift.

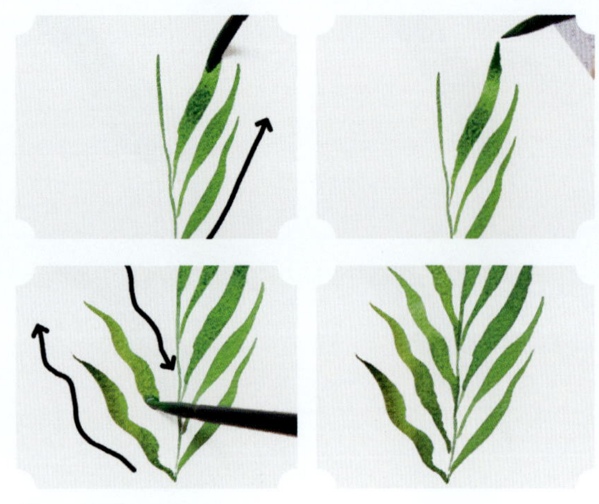

Elongated Leaf

Expressive Leaf

This leaf starts like the one-stroke leaf. Load your brush with green paint and start at the tip. When you press down to widen the stroke toward the middle, wiggle your stroke to create a rough edge, then drag and lift your brush at the end of the stroke. Play around with the direction of the leaves.

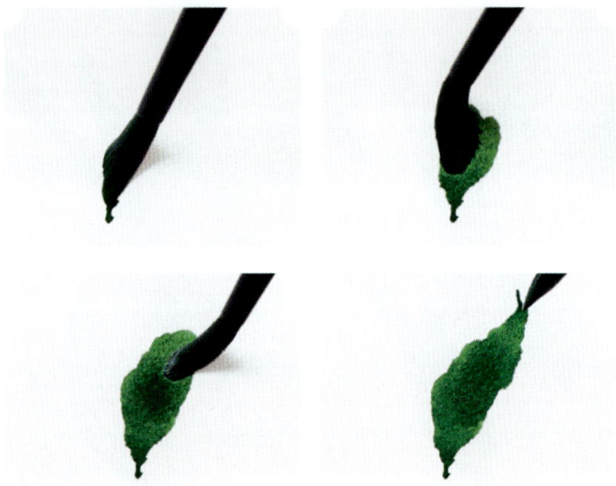

Expressive Leaf

Textural Elements

Filler textures help balance your floral compositions and make them feel more lush or loose. Use a size 2 round brush and try quick flicks for the leaves in different directions. Paint a cluster of tiny dots with thin stems, small berries, or dark sprigs for contrast.

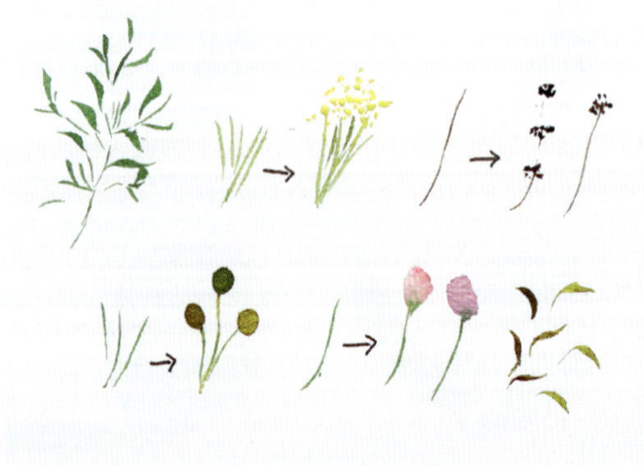

WATERCOLOR TECHNIQUES

Wet on Dry

Think of these techniques as making up your water-color toolbox. You don't need to use every one of them in a single painting, but knowing what's possible will give you the freedom to explore this medium to its fullest potential.

Wet on Dry

Applying wet paint onto dry paper gives you sharp, defined edges and vibrant colors. You'll also have more control over your brushstrokes. In this book, we'll use this technique often for base flowers and fine details.

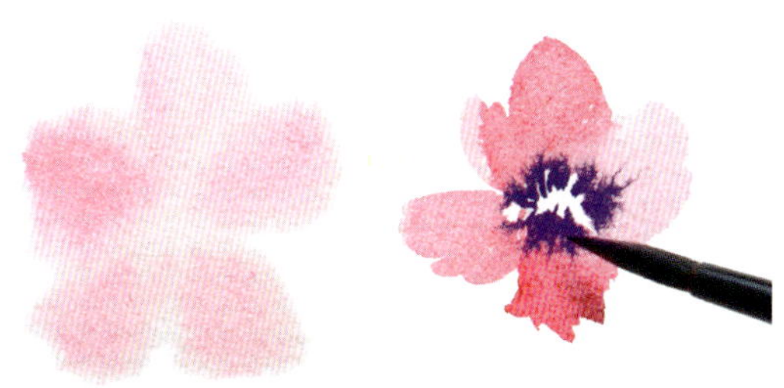

Wet on Wet

Wet on Wet

This is when you apply wet paint on a wet surface. It creates soft blooms and transitions. In loose florals, I often use this when dropping darker pigments into a damp flower center to create contrast. Keep in mind that a watery mixture spreads quickly on wet paper, while a thicker mixture stays in place and moves less.

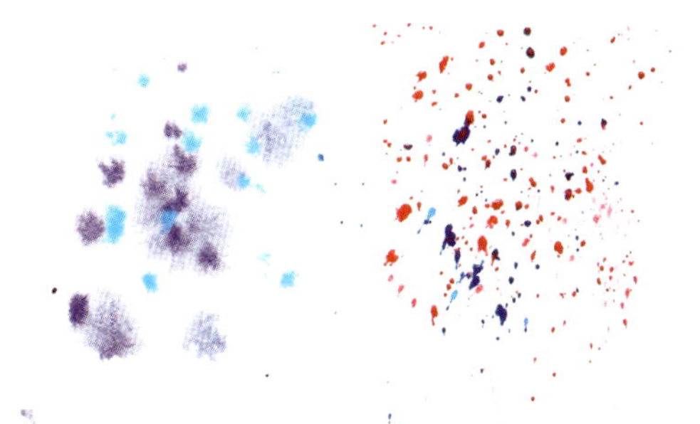

Splattering

Splattering

Splattering, also known as flicking, adds character to your painting. Load your brush with paint, then start tapping the brush on your finger or against another brush.

On dry paper, the splatters will look crisp. On wet paper, they spread softly like little blooms, which is great for backgrounds.

Fading

Fading or blurring is when you soften one side of a stroke. This is a technique that I use for my signature roses.

- Paint a petal stroke.

- Rinse your brush and blot off the excess water.

- Gently swipe the clean brush along the edge of the stroke. The pigment will flow into the damp area, leaving a soft edge on one side of the stroke.

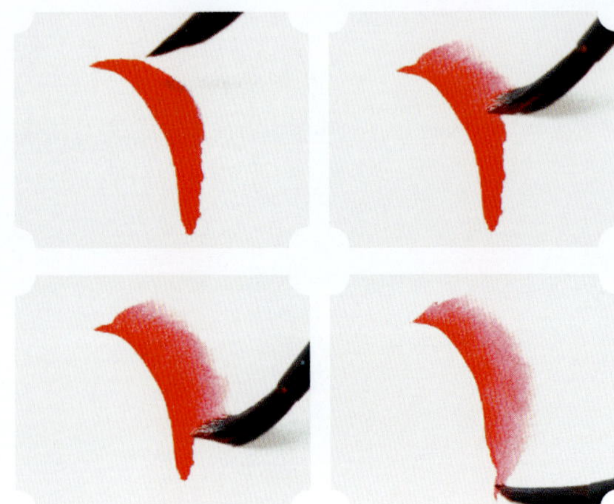

Fading

Bleeding

Bleeding happens when two wet colors touch, creating a soft transition. Paint one petal with medium-consistency pigment, then place a lighter petal beside it so their edges touch. The colors will naturally flow into each other. This works beautifully for petals and leaves.

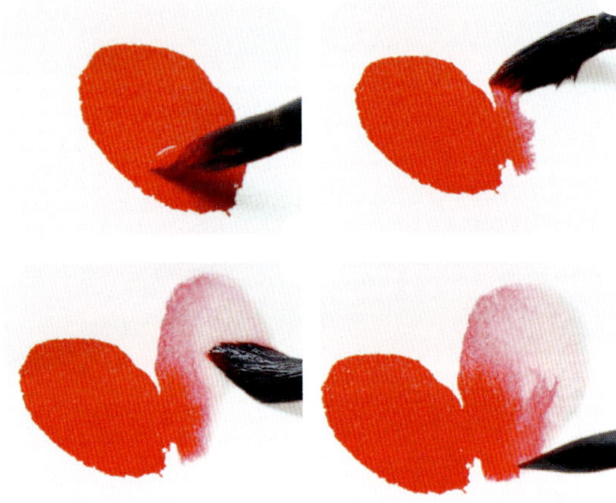

Bleeding

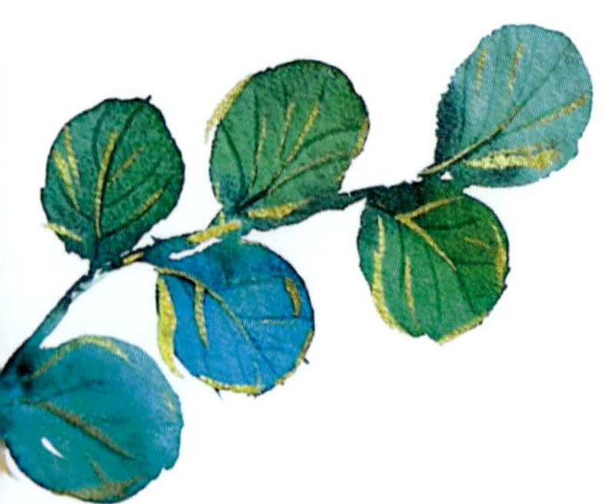

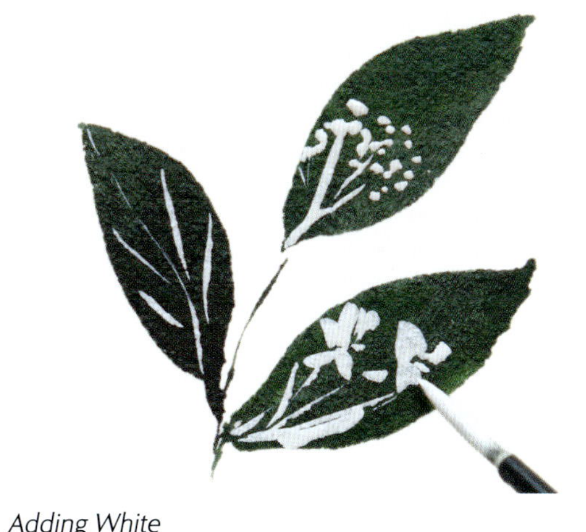

Adding White

Adding White

Highlights and details in white bring extra dimension. Make sure to add the white on top of a darker background to make the details pop. You may use a gel pen or acrylic marker for fine lines or dots.

I personally like using white gouache as it is opaque. Mix it with a little water to get a creamy consistency.

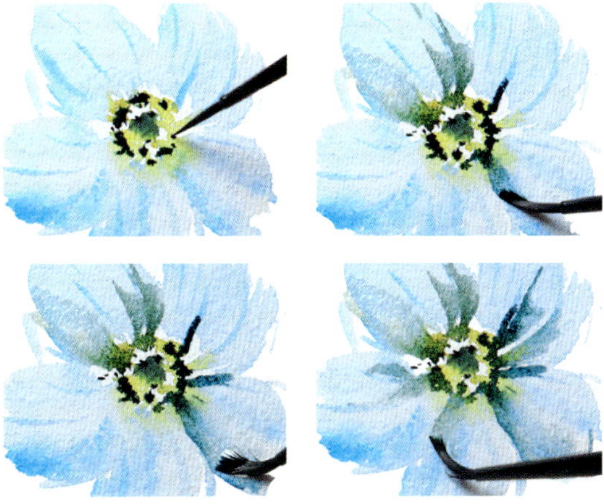

Pulling

Pulling

This technique creates a dramatic effect in flower centers and helps define petals. Once a Five-Petal Flower (page 111) is dry, add small dots of dark pigment like Indigo in the center. Get a clean, damp brush and lightly pull the pigment outward into the spaces between the petals.

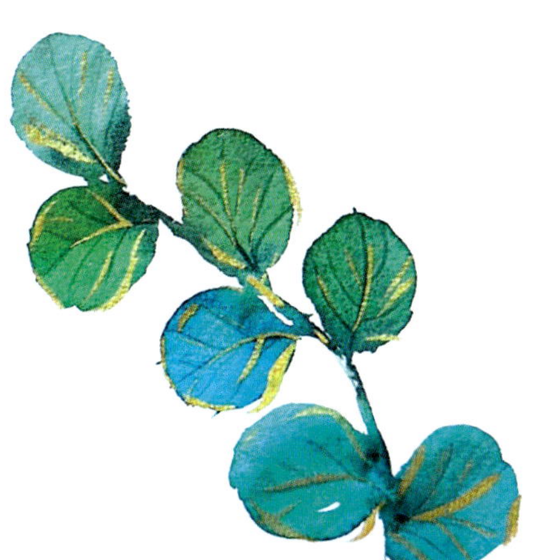

FLORAL COMPOSITION TIPS

Composition is what makes your painting feel balanced and pleasing to the eye. For loose watercolor florals, this is important as we want our work to have movement. The good news is that it doesn't need to be complicated. I'll walk you through my favorite tips and tricks to help you build your own floral arrangement. Think of these as guidelines rather than strict rules. With practice, arranging flowers on paper will feel as natural as a well-trained chef cooking without a recipe.

Choose Bloom Weights

Every flower carries a different visual weight. Some flowers are big and look too heavy when placed at the top of a bouquet. Knowing how to balance flower sizes will help your composition feel more harmonious. Let's check out the floral ingredient chart.

Focal Flowers

Focal flowers are the star of the show. They are big and bold flowers that grab your attention.

Secondary Flowers

Secondary flowers support the focal flower and are medium-sized.

Fillers

Fillers like small buds, sprigs, berries, and other textural elements add movement and help tie everything together.

Foliage

Foliage is made up of leaves of different shapes and sizes that provide structure and support to the flowers.

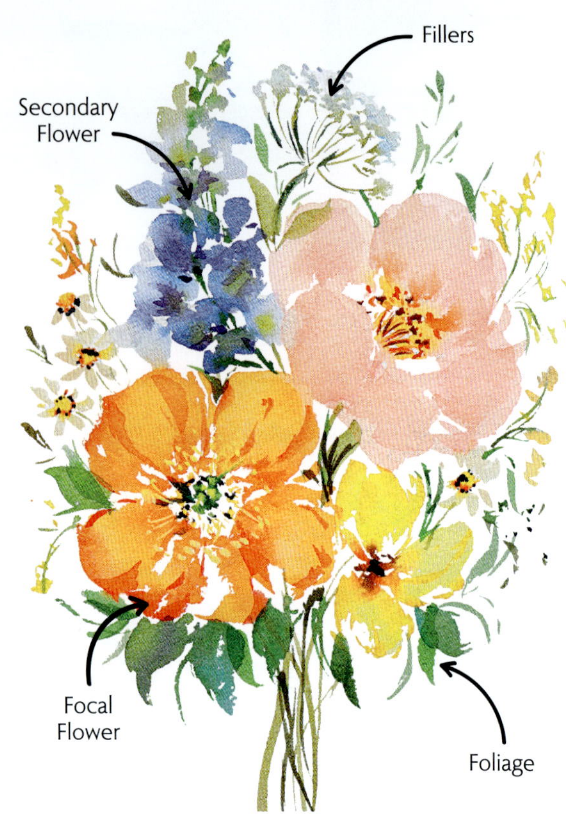

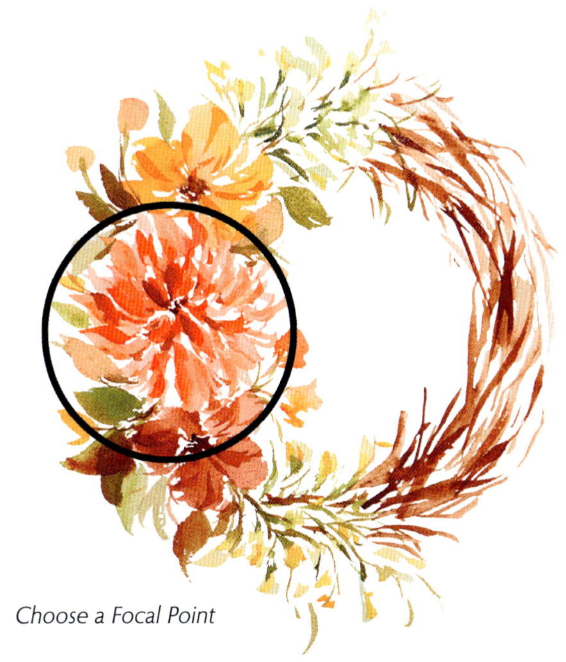

Choose a Focal Point

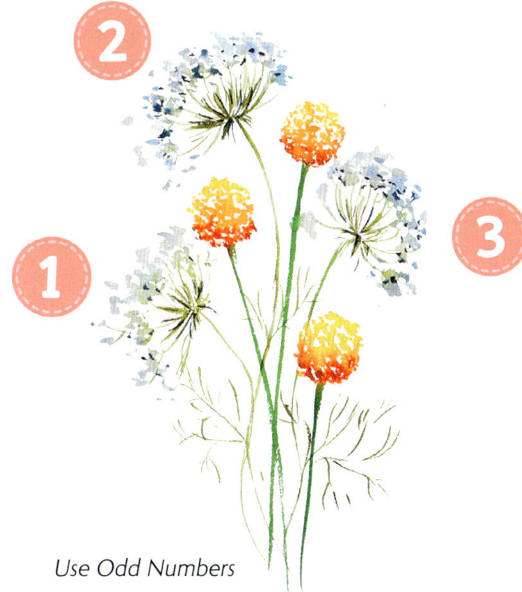

Use Odd Numbers

Choose a Focal Point

When planning your composition, you could start by choosing a focal point where you want your viewer's eye to land first. I usually choose a big fluffy flower and put it on one side of a wreath. This acts like an anchor. I build around it with secondary flowers, fillers, and foliage.

Use Odd Numbers

Arranging flowers in odd numbers—such as sets of three, five, or seven—creates a natural look. I often use this as a guide when creating wreaths and bouquets, and it's especially helpful if you are just starting out. That said, don't feel like you must count every flower in a bouquet. Sometimes, two roses can work beautifully if the rest of the elements balance the piece.

Think of Flowers and Leaves as Shapes

Simplify botanicals into shapes like circles, ovals, triangles, and so on. This makes it easier to plan spacing and overall visual flow. You can also mix the shapes in different sizes for variety. I use this technique often. For example, when painting the Personalized Floral Monogram (page 167), I start by sketching circles for the main flowers before adding details.

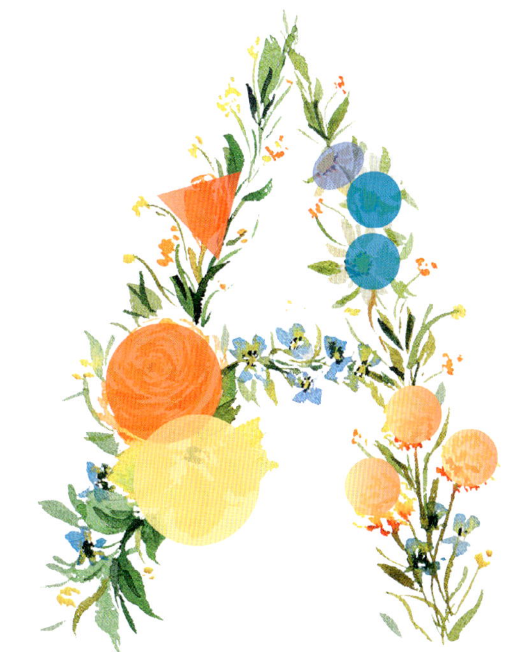

Think of Flowers and Leaves as Shapes

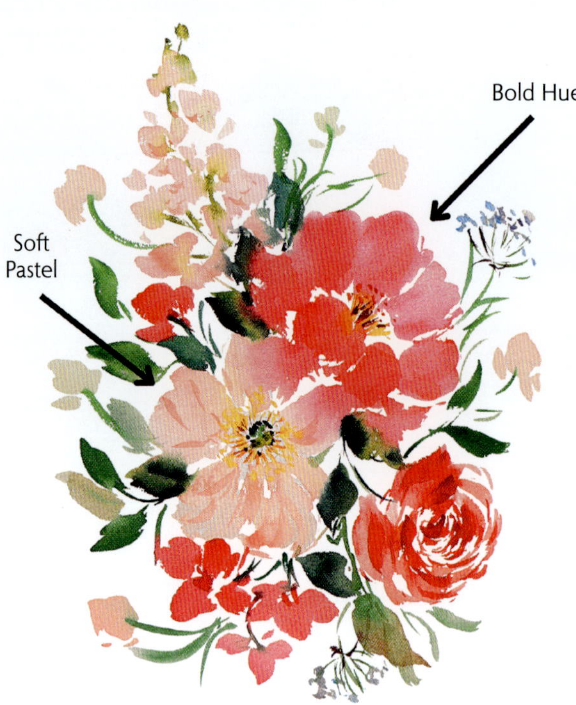

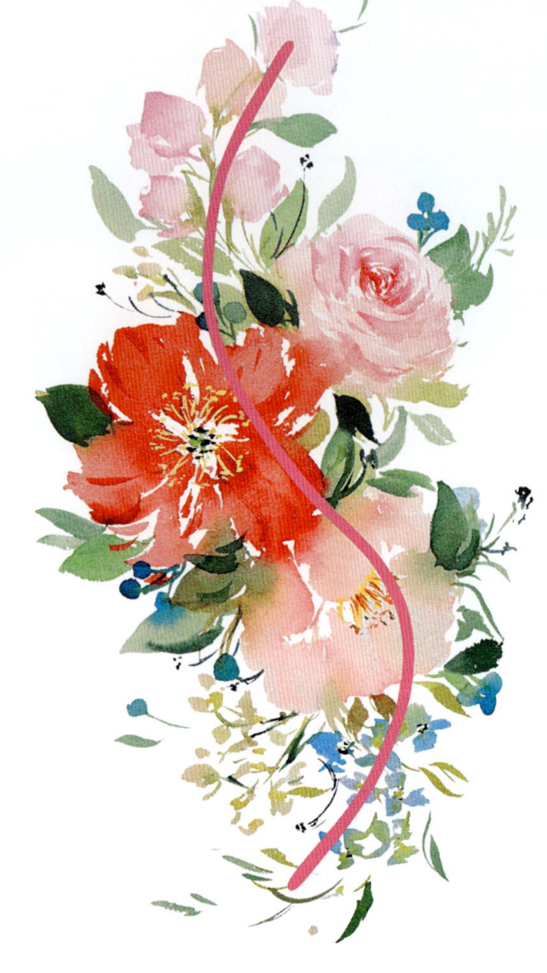

Play with Contrast

Contrast brings life to a painting. You can create this through color and value.

Color

Pair soft pastels with bold hues, add a bright accent, or pair complementary colors.

Value

Mix light and dark tones. Use darker fillers alongside softer florals.

Use Flow and Movement

Play with the direction of your composition, for example by making an S-shaped curve, a diagonal, or a triangle. Place the flowers along this path so your viewer's eyes will travel smoothly across the page instead of getting stuck in one spot.

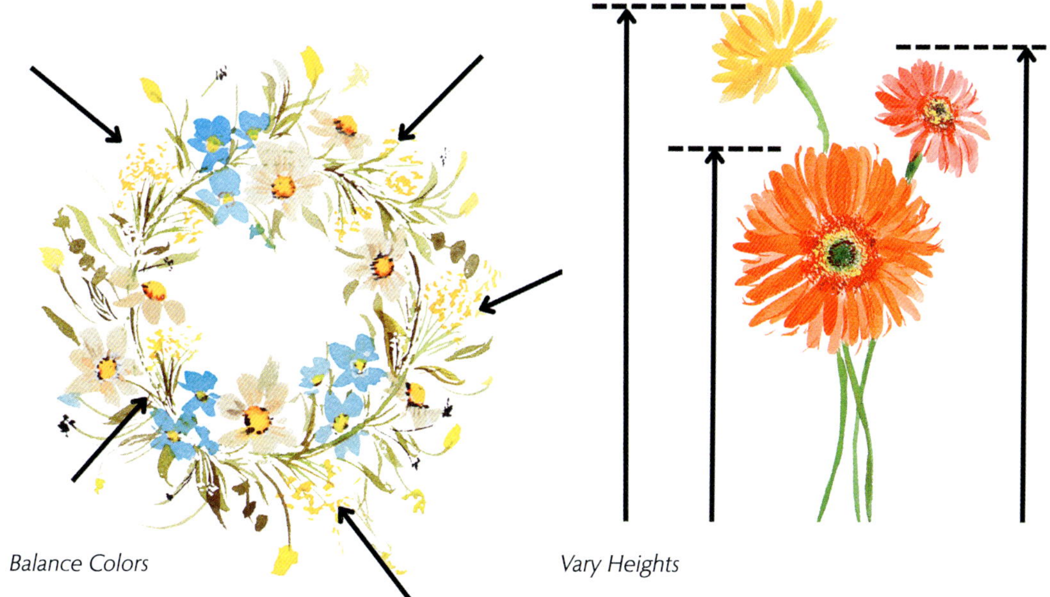

Balance Colors

Vary Heights

Balance Colors

Repeat colors throughout the painting so they don't feel isolated. For example, in this wreath, if you have yellow Buttercups (page 95), scatter touches of yellow in smaller fillers to unify the arrangement. You may also add the color of the main flower on the leaves for added harmony.

Vary Heights

Avoid placing flowers all at the same level, as it will make the composition look flat. Instead, stagger heights by placing some florals higher and some lower. This variation creates a sense of movement, as if the flowers are dancing across the page.

Add Shadow Leaves

Leaves and stems do more than add foliage. They connect flowers and fillers, and direct the eye across the page. We can also use them to add height or add a sense of looseness by painting wispy leaves.

Try placing what I call shadow leaves or faded greens in the background to add depth and make your flowers stand out.

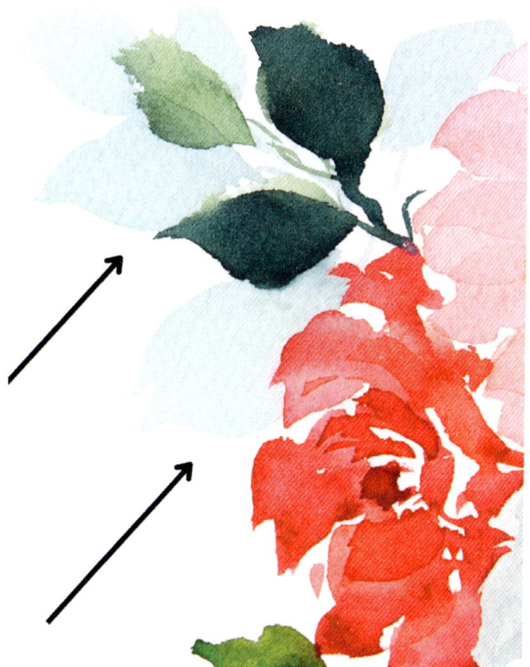

Add Shadow Leaves

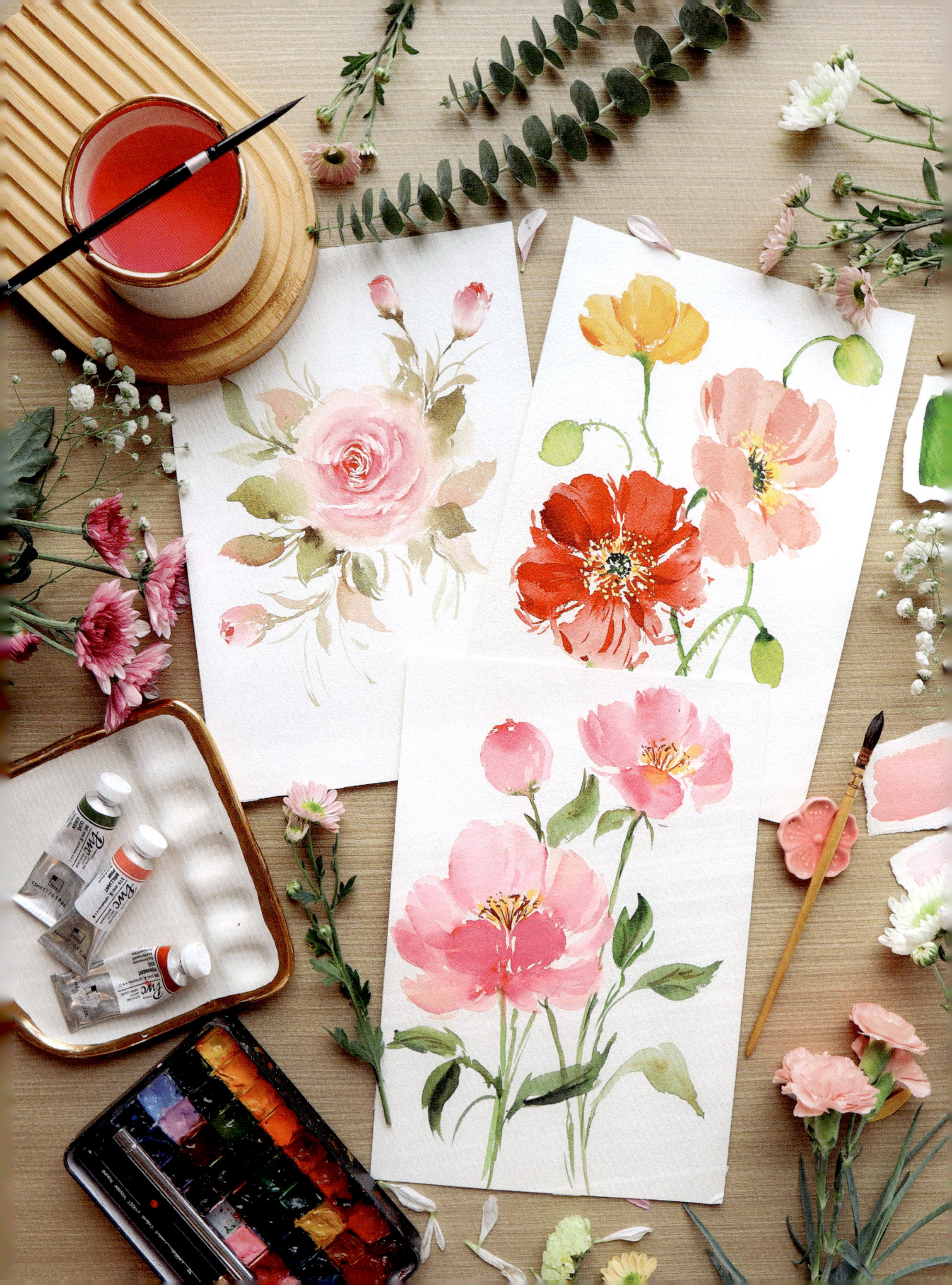

Stunning STATEMENT FLOWERS

Welcome to my favorite chapter! These flowers are bold, eye-catching, and full of personality. They are the kinds of blooms that naturally draw your attention. Their striking forms make them lovely subjects to paint loosely, allowing you to play with the petal shapes and express your unique artistic style.

The Romantic Pink Rose (page 37), in particular, is very special to me. It was one of the first few flowers that I tried painting loosely, and one that I struggled a lot with in the beginning. What started out as a few frustrating blobs eventually turned into one of my signature styles. Practicing every day taught me to be patient, and eventually it helped hone the muscle memory in my hand. I'm excited for you to try this tutorial!

In this chapter, you'll also learn to paint a Lush Pink Peony (page 43) with soft, fluffy petals, and explore the bold, vibrant charm of a Fiery Icelandic Poppy (page 47).

As we go through the flowers in this chapter, you'll learn how to dance with your brush to create expressive petals and leaves.

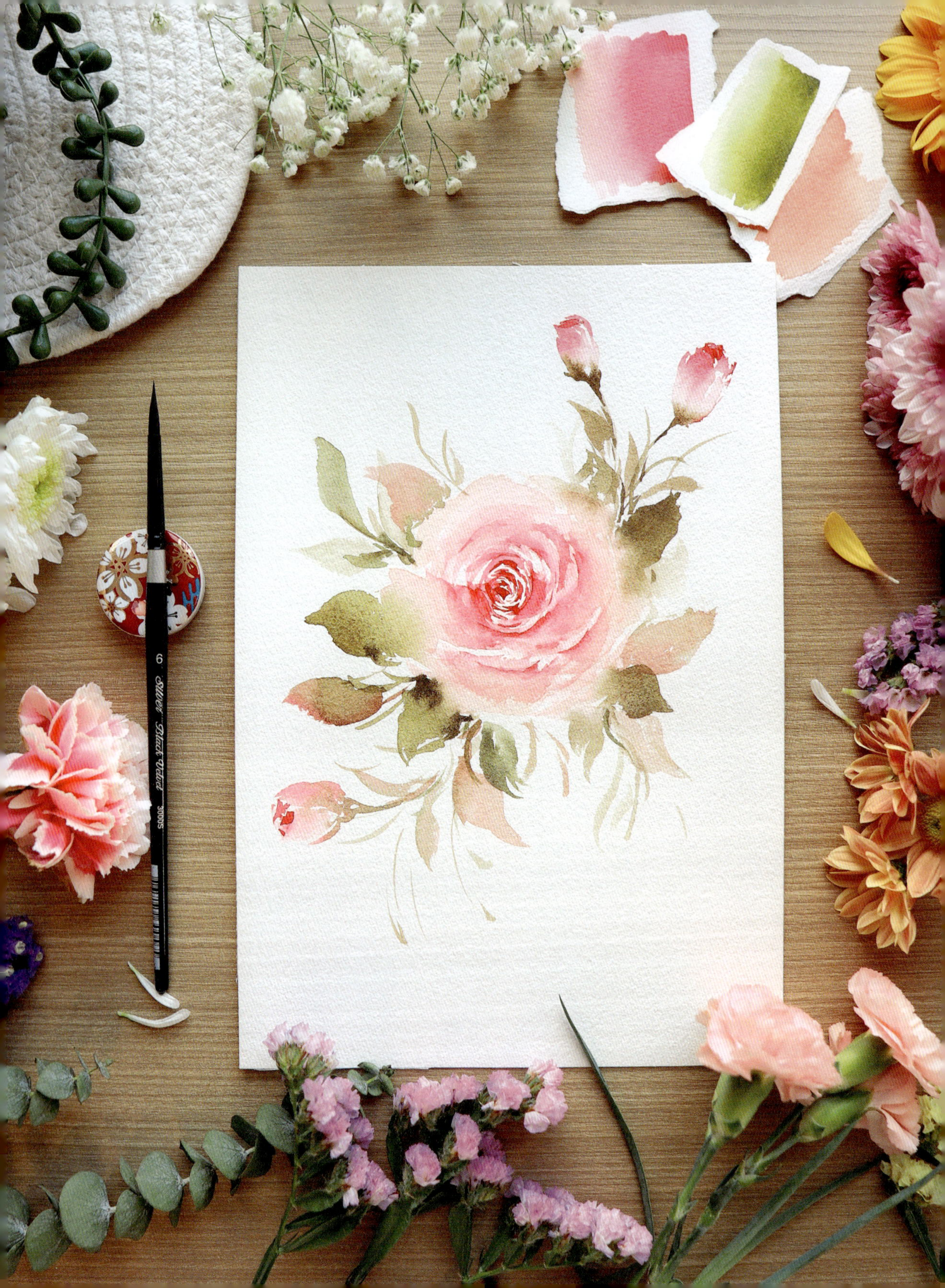

ROMANTIC PINK ROSE

I still can't believe that my roses will be part of this book! Roses have always held a special place in my watercolor journey.

Over time, these once-frustrating flowers grew to become a signature part of my work and now, I'm so excited to share everything I've learned with you.

In this tutorial, I'll walk you step-by-step from painting thin and tight C-shaped strokes in the center of the flower to painting bigger and more expressive strokes as we move further away from the center. You'll also learn how to add a second layer to build depth, though you're always welcome to stop after the first layer if you love the result.

Painting roses can be challenging, but don't let that stop you. Every rose you paint is one-of-a-kind and carries your unique touch, and that's what makes it beautiful.

Colors

- ■ Permanent Rose
- ■ Permanent Yellow Light
- ■ Burnt Umber
- ■ Sap Green

Brush

- Size 6 round brush

Floral Strokes

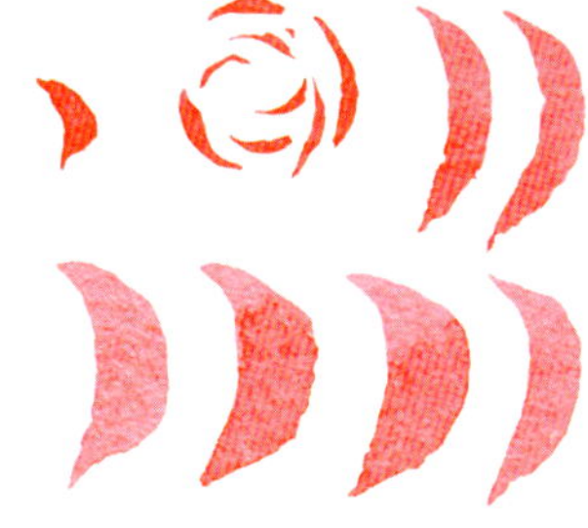

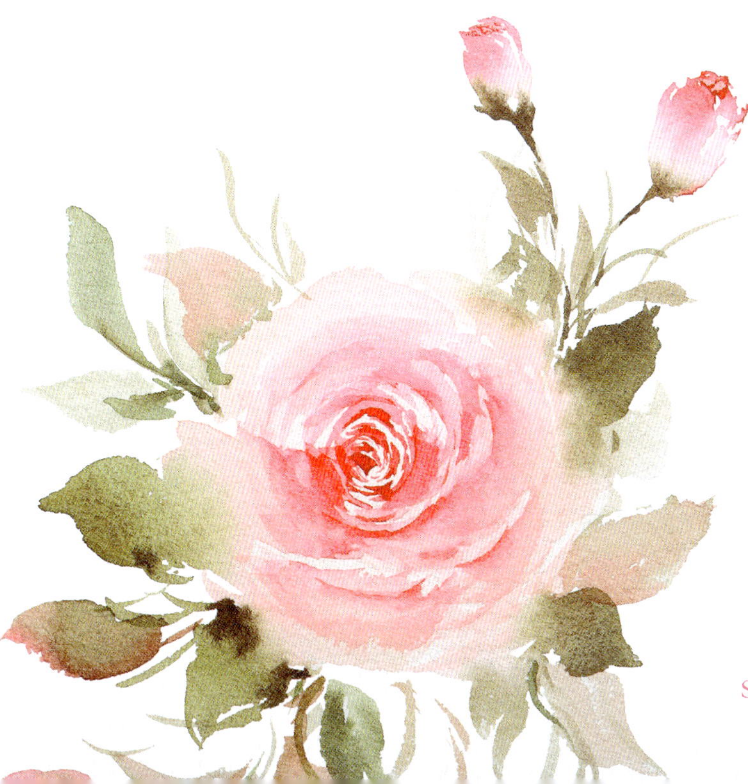

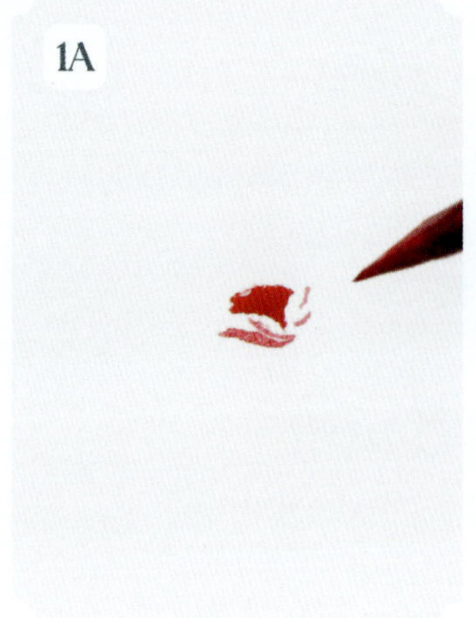

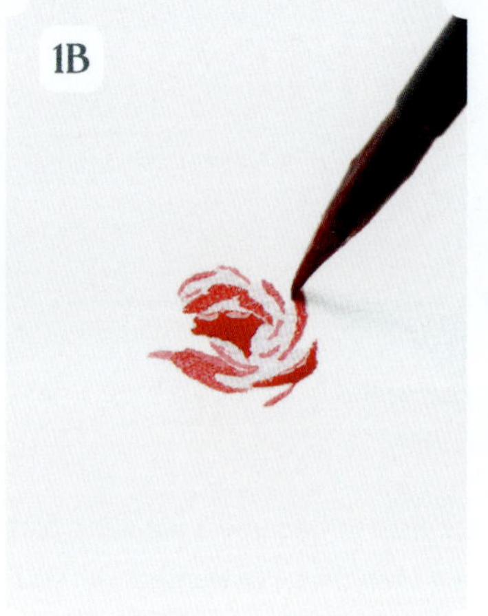

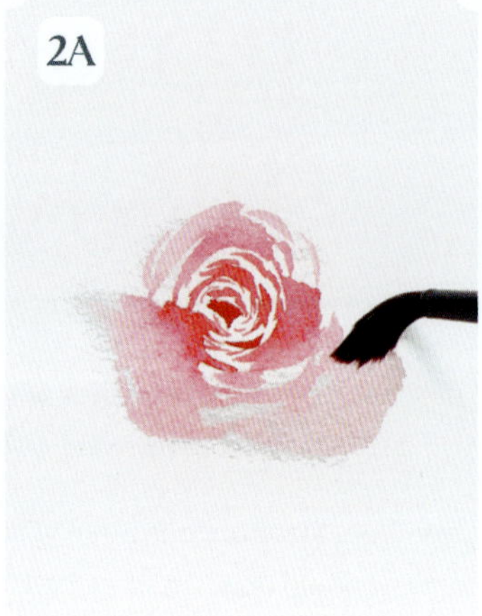

1. Start with the Center

Grab your size 6 round brush. Load it with a thick consistency of Permanent Rose. Using the tip of the brush, lightly press your brush to paint a comma stroke. Around this, add several thin C strokes with varying lengths. Leave small white gaps between the petals and allow some of the strokes to overlap or touch the center. This helps create the illusion that the petals are interconnected, not floating separately.

2. Build the Next Layer

As we move further away from the center, the petals will get bigger. Without rinsing your brush, dip it in water and tap off the excess on the rim of your jar. This will produce a lighter pink color for the next layer of petals. Press about half the belly of your brush to create curved C shapes, each one gently hugging the shape of the rose center.

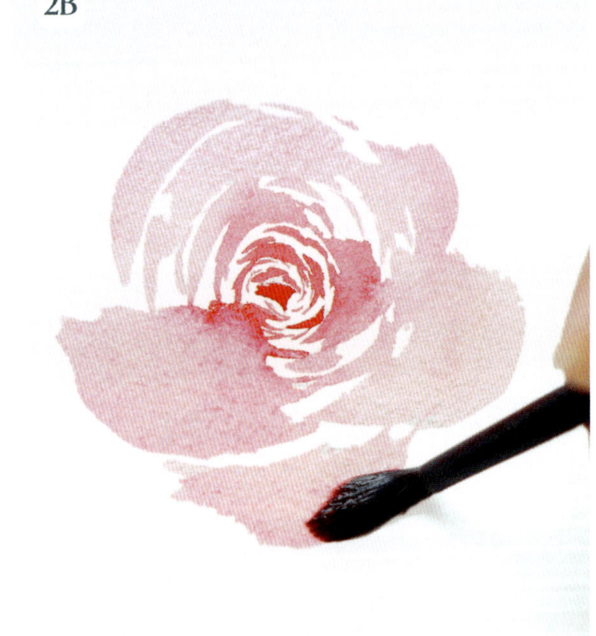

When you are about two-thirds done with the rose petals (again, working out from the center), begin to paint even broader strokes. Mix a light consistency of Permanent Rose color. Press the full belly of the brush to create a wide C-shaped petal. Do this in a curved motion and slowly lift toward the end of the brush to create a soft taper, allowing the petals to touch each other naturally.

3

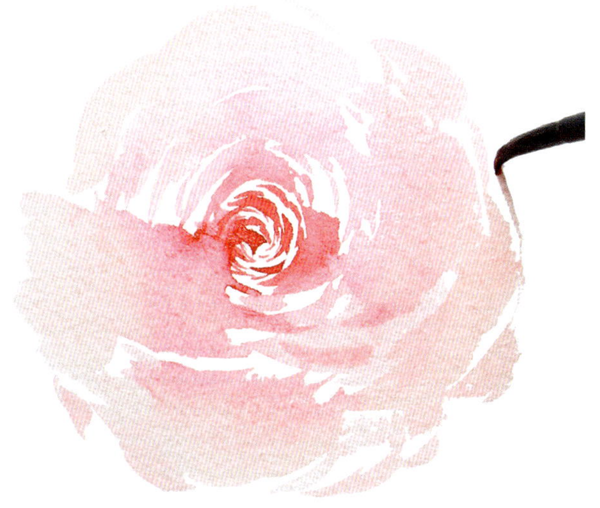

3. Add Another Color

For a touch of variety, mix one part Permanent Yellow Light and two parts Permanent Rose into a very light watery consistency. Use this watery mix to add a few more C-shaped petals at the edges of the rose. You can lightly wiggle the brush to suggest a ruffled texture. Fill in any noticeable gaps with thin lines using just the tip of your brush.

4. Add Soft Leaves with a Gentle Bleed

Mix one part Burnt Umber and two parts Sap Green into a medium consistency. While the petals are still damp, lightly press the side of the brush on the outermost petal and drag your brush to paint a leaf. This will create leaves that gently bleed into the rose.

Add more leaves and stems around the rose. Drop in a deeper green on the damp leaves for more depth.

4A   4B

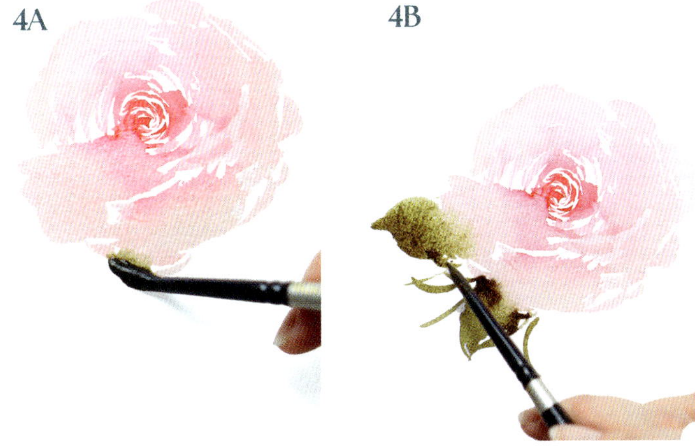

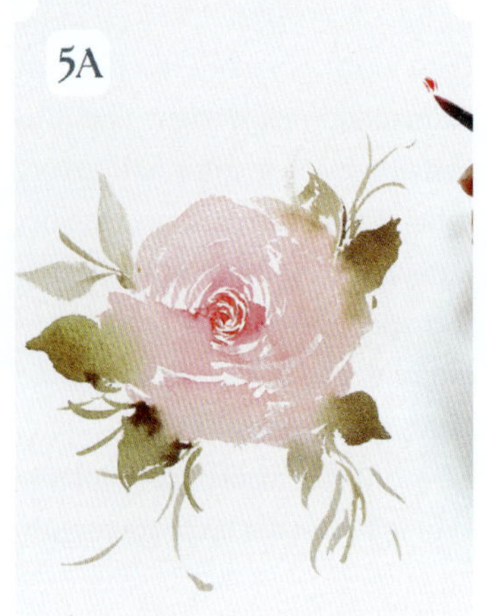

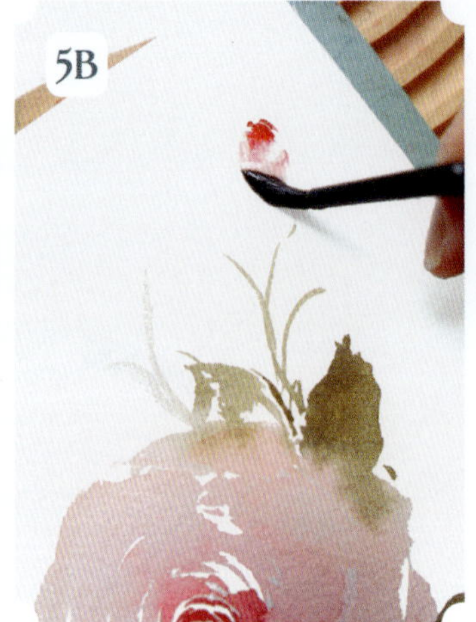

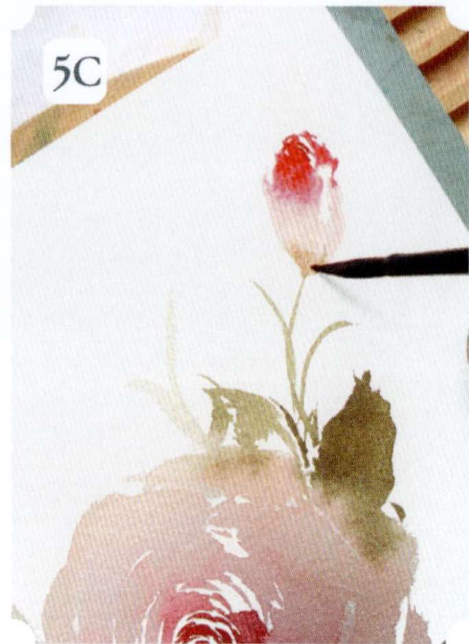

5. Make Quick Rosebuds

Using a thick consistency of Permanent Rose, paint a comma stroke and a few thin and short curvy lines to form the top of a rosebud. These should be lightly wet. Now, rinse your brush and tap the excess water on the rim of the jar.

Gently touch the base of the comma and pull the color downward using the side of your brush to form a soft, bulb-like shape. The pigment will follow the water from your brush, creating a beautiful gradient. You can shape the bud with the tip of your brush and add a touch of green at the base to connect it to a stem. Feel free to paint a few more.

Each bud will turn out slightly different and that's what makes them special!

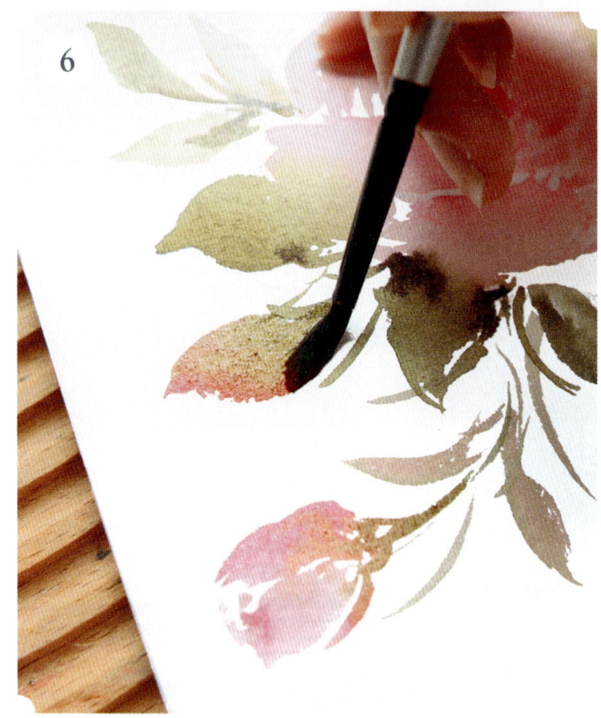

6. Use a Two-Tone Leaf Technique

Add the color of the flower into the leaves. Mix a light to medium consistency of Sap Green and load your brush. Next, dip the tip of the same brush in a medium consistency of Permanent Rose (the main color of the rose). With two colors in your brush, you may start painting leaves that come out with a beautiful gradient.

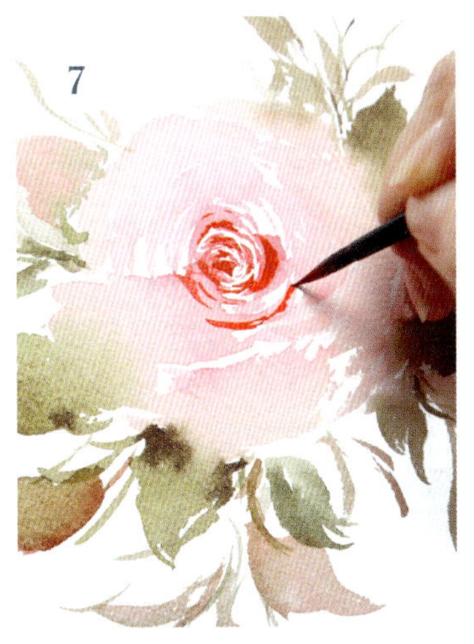

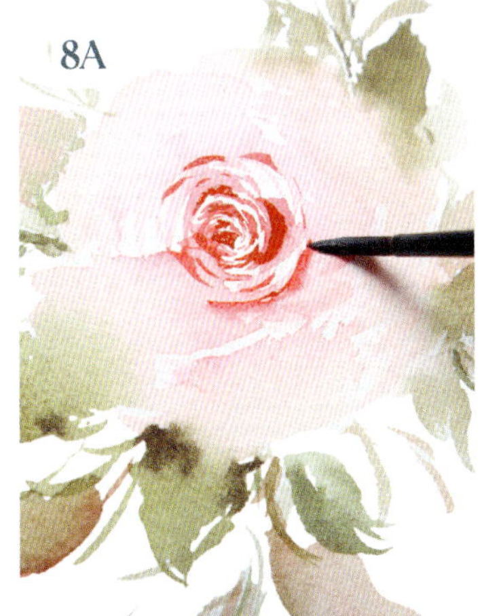

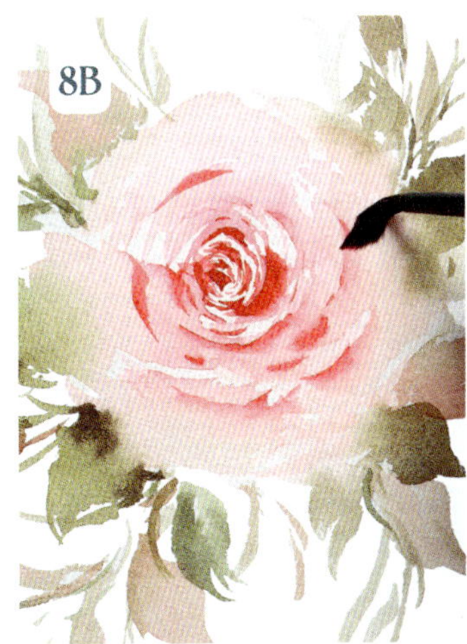

7. Add a Second Layer for Depth

If you are happy with this rose, you can stop here. But if you would like to add a second layer, make sure that the first layer is already dry.

Then, mix a thick consistency of Permanent Rose. Using your size 6 round brush, paint the same comma stroke in the center along with the thin curvy lines on top of the first layer. This will help add contrast to the center of the flower.

8. Blend and Soften

About one-third of the way out from the center, add more delicate C-shaped strokes using the tip of your brush. Work quickly while the paint is still damp. Rinse your brush, tap off excess moisture, and use the clean tip to softly blur one side of each stroke. This is called the fading technique, and it creates a dreamy, diffused effect. Be mindful not to overwork this layer. Leave enough space between strokes to keep the rose looking light and airy. Look at that! Your rose is blooming beautifully.

TIP: You may practice this rose in a different color too. Don't stress about perfection. You've got this!

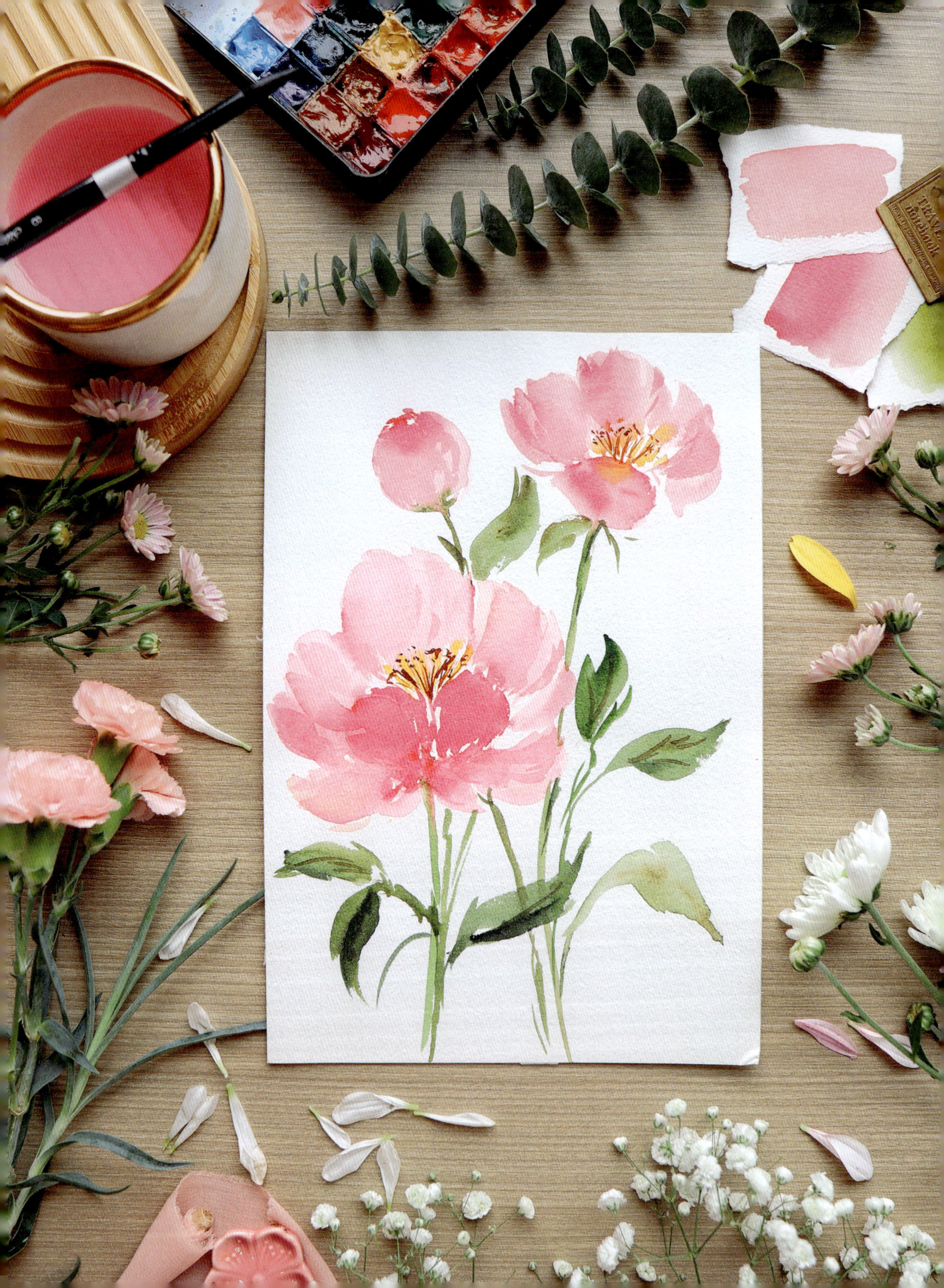

LUSH PINK PEONY

Watercolor peonies are incredibly popular. Their lush and delicate petals give a romantic feel, which makes them a favorite flower to paint among artists.

In this lesson, I'll show you my own easy-to-understand approach to painting this flower. It's a soft and simple technique that focuses on building layers with curved strokes. Think of the overall shape of the peony as a cup to guide you as you add each petal. We'll focus on building up the form with gentle, curved strokes, and you'll see how changing your brush angle creates expressive, organic shapes.

Feel free to use this tutorial as a guide and eventually add your own creative spin to it. Let's enjoy painting this elegant bloom one soft layer at a time.

Colors

- Bright Rose
- Permanent Rose
- Permanent Yellow Light
- Sap Green
- Burnt Umber
- Burnt Sienna

Brushes

- Size 8 round brush
- Size 2 round brush

Other Materials

- Pencil, optional

Floral Strokes

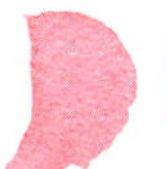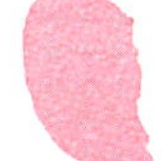

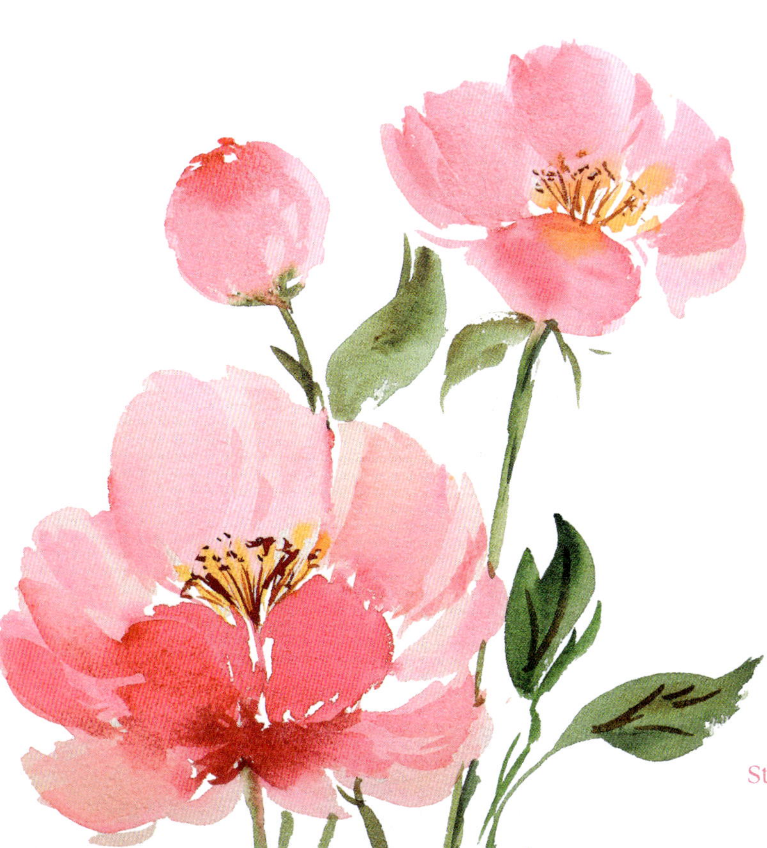

1. Paint the First Petals

When painting a peony, think of the flower as a cup. You may use a pencil to lightly sketch a semicircle as a guide.

Mix equal parts of Bright Rose and Permanent Rose into a medium consistency, or you may use your favorite pink. Load a size 8 round brush with this juicy mixture, then paint a rounded petal shape (see rounded petals stroke on page 23) by pressing the side of your brush and slowly lifting toward the end.

Paint another petal beside it so the two form a V shape. Don't worry about making the petals uniform. They look more natural with slight variations.

2. Paint the Remaining Petals

Begin with the top petal. Mix a light consistency of Permanent Rose and load your brush generously to make it easier to glide on the paper. You may optionally add a touch of Permanent Yellow Light to the light-consistency Permanent Rose to warm up the color. From the top of the flower, press the side of the brush and lift at the end to create a pointy tip. Overlap a few strokes and slightly wiggle your brush to build volume and to create ruffled edges. Be sure to leave a white space at the center for the stamen later on.

Continue painting along the sides of the flower. Start from the tip of each petal and drag your brush following the arrow in the image. Vary the angle and direction to suggest petals viewed from different sides. Let some petals touch and softly blend for a loose effect. Remember to leave white spaces between certain petals to keep the flower airy.

> **TIP:** As you build out the flower, always bring your strokes back toward the center base, where all the petals meet.

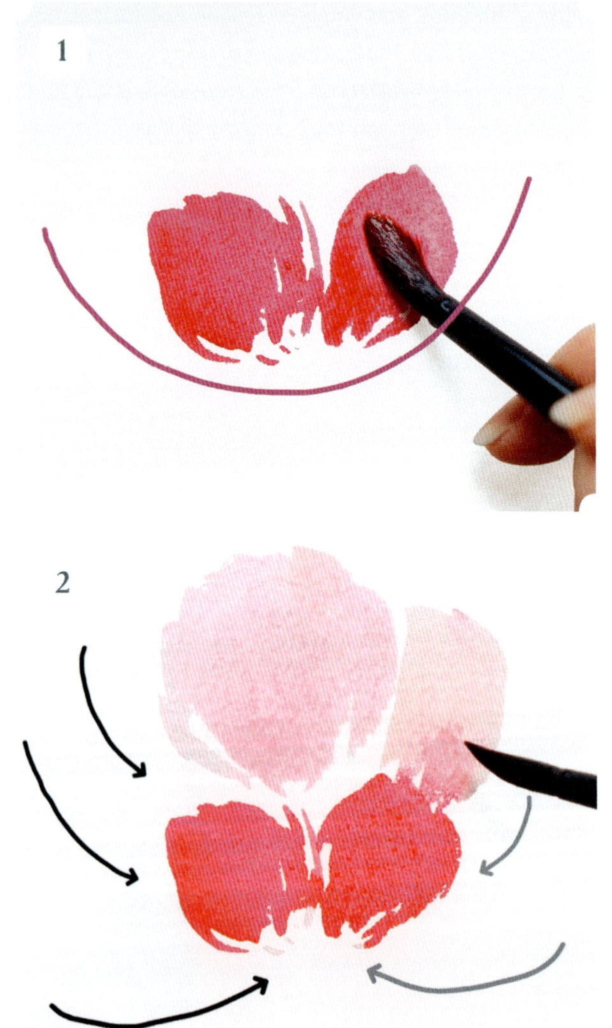

3. Add Contrast

While the peony flower is still wet, drop in a thick consistency of Permanent Rose at the base where the petals meet. This creates a natural shadow and brings the center forward.

For more depth, add more color between the petals while they are still damp. Load your brush with a medium consistency of Permanent Rose and tap it on a tissue paper first. This prevents adding too much water, which may cause patchy areas.

Now, paint the stamen by adding short, thin strokes in the center of the flower using a medium consistency of Permanent Yellow Light. Do this while the petals are still wet so the yellow bleeds softly into the pink petals. Finally, paint a thin stem using Sap Green.

4. Paint a Side-Facing Flower

Let's paint a peony at an angle. Load your size 8 round brush with a medium consistency of Permanent Rose.

Begin with the base petal. Press the side of your brush and slowly move it to the right to form an oval-shaped petal in a horizontal position. This will suggest a folded petal seen from the side.

Next, mix a lighter pink consistency and add three or four smaller petals along the top using the same press-drag-and-lift technique. Vary the size of the petals. Be sure to leave space in the center for the stamen.

Paint the same short, thin yellow strokes in the stamen and complete the flower with a green stem.

3

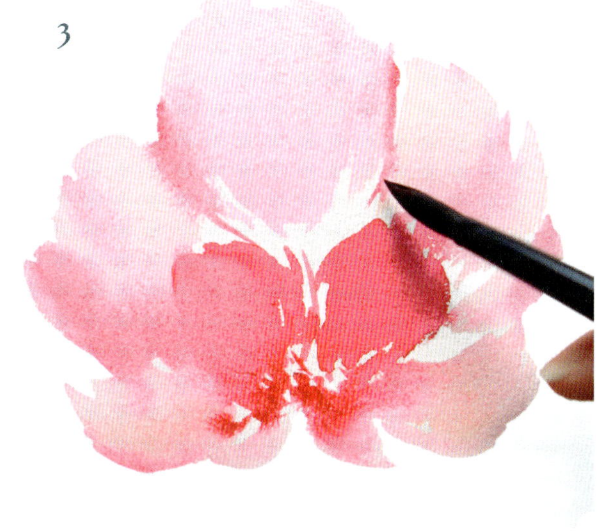

4

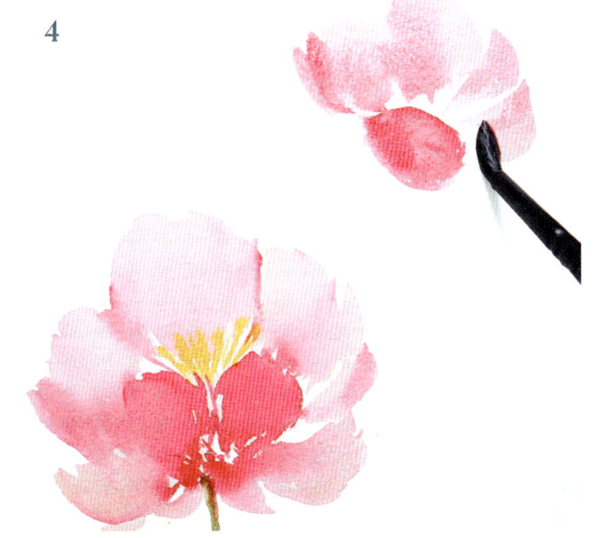

5. Add Buds and Leaves

To bring variety to your composition, let's paint a peony bud. Start with a thick mixture of Permanent Rose and paint a cluster of small C strokes to suggest the top of the bud. Rinse your brush and lightly touch the base of the strokes to pull the color and form a rounded bud. Add a Sap Green stem to complete it.

For the leaves, mix two parts Sap Green and one part Burnt Umber for an earthy green tone. Using your size 8 round brush, paint elongated leaves by pressing down, dragging the brush, then flicking it to form a pointy tip. Peony leaves are slightly curved and tapered at the ends, so aim for flowing strokes. Vary your greens for a more natural effect.

6. Add Finishing Touches

Deepen the stamen by mixing equal parts Burnt Sienna and Burnt Umber. Use a size 2 round brush to paint short, thin strokes and some dots over the yellow stamen to create contrast.

To make the petals look fuller, add a second layer on top of the existing flower. Mix a light consistency of Permanent Rose or Bright Rose, then use your size 8 round brush to paint a few curved strokes. Keep

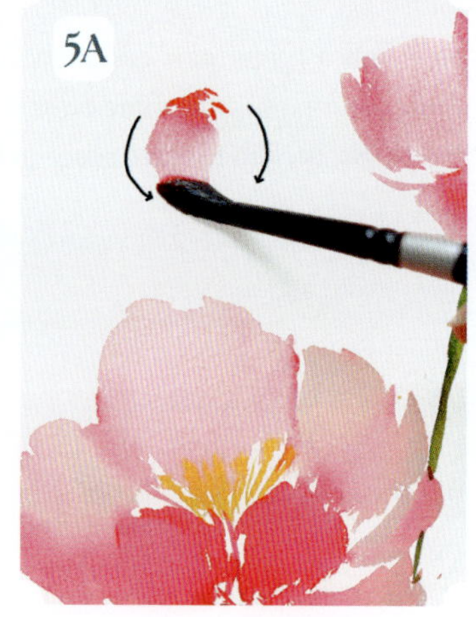

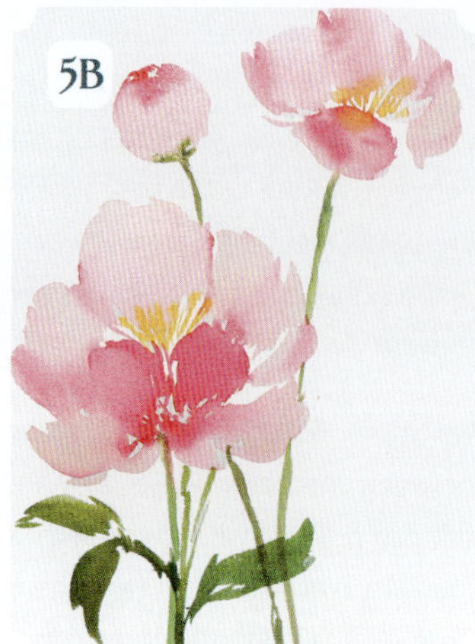

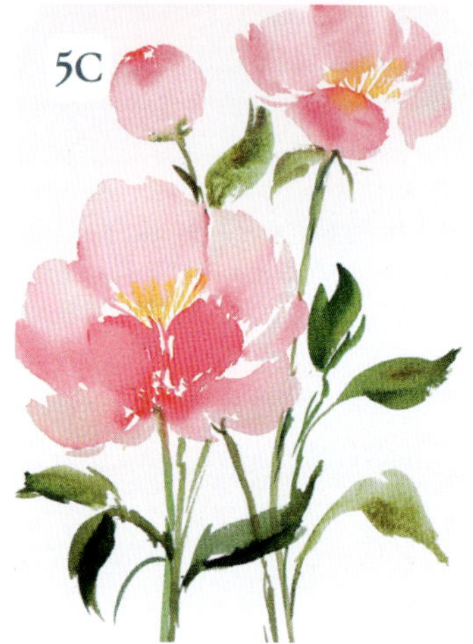

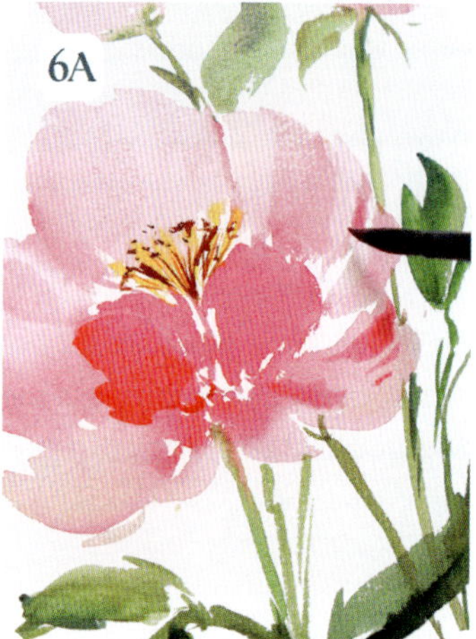

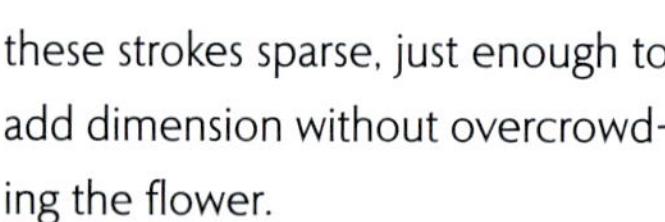

these strokes sparse, just enough to add dimension without overcrowding the flower.

Optionally, you may paint thin, dark veins on the leaves using a thick-consistency mixture of two parts Sap Green and one part Burnt Umber for extra detail.

Step back and admire your lush and radiant peony!

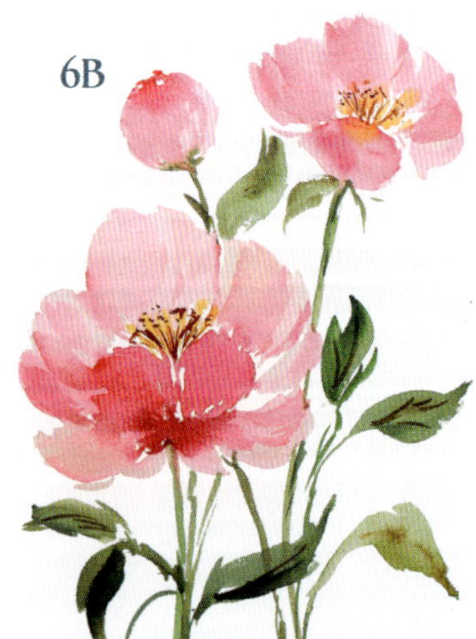

FIERY ICELANDIC POPPY

Icelandic poppies are known for their paper-thin petals and beautifully ruffled edges. Their large, airy petals make them perfect for practicing loose, broad strokes, which is why I chose a mop brush for this project. This brush allows you to experiment with varying pressure, creating strokes that feel natural and full of movement.

In this lesson, you'll learn how to let the pigments flow, how to embrace the natural bleeds, and how to create depth without losing lightness. We'll paint a full, open flower, a side-angled bloom, and delicate buds to complete a balanced composition. I'll also show you a secret way to make the center pop.

Colors

- Permanent Yellow Light
- Permanent Red
- Hooker's Green
- Shell Pink, or any light pink
- Yellow Orange
- Sap Green
- Greenish Yellow
- Indigo

Brushes

- Size 2 round brush
- Size 0 mop brush

Other Materials

- Pencil, optional
- White gouache

Floral Strokes

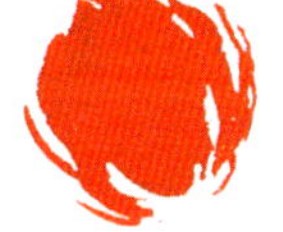
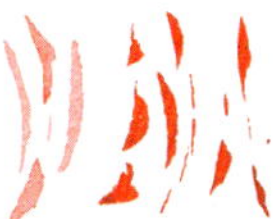

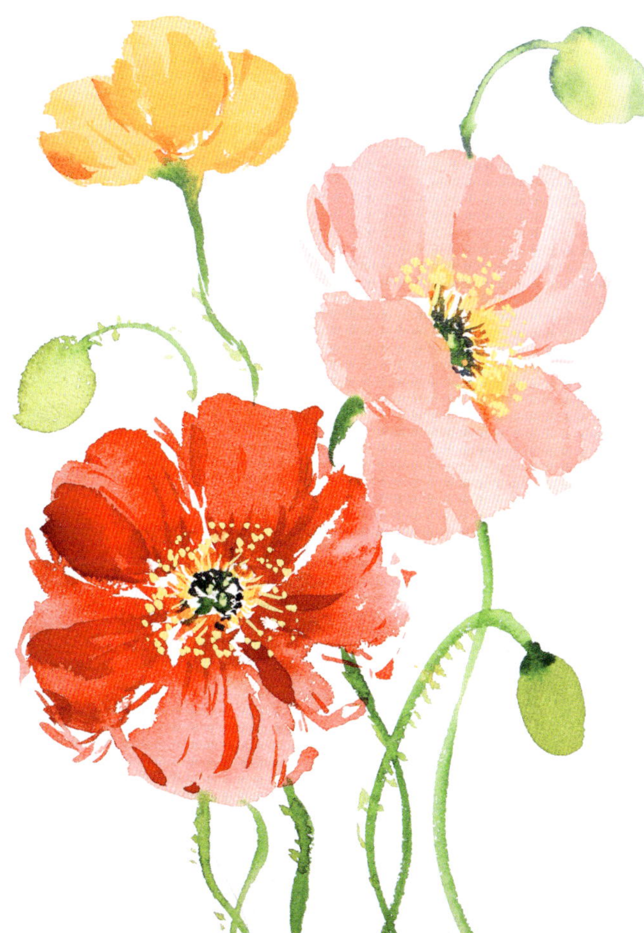

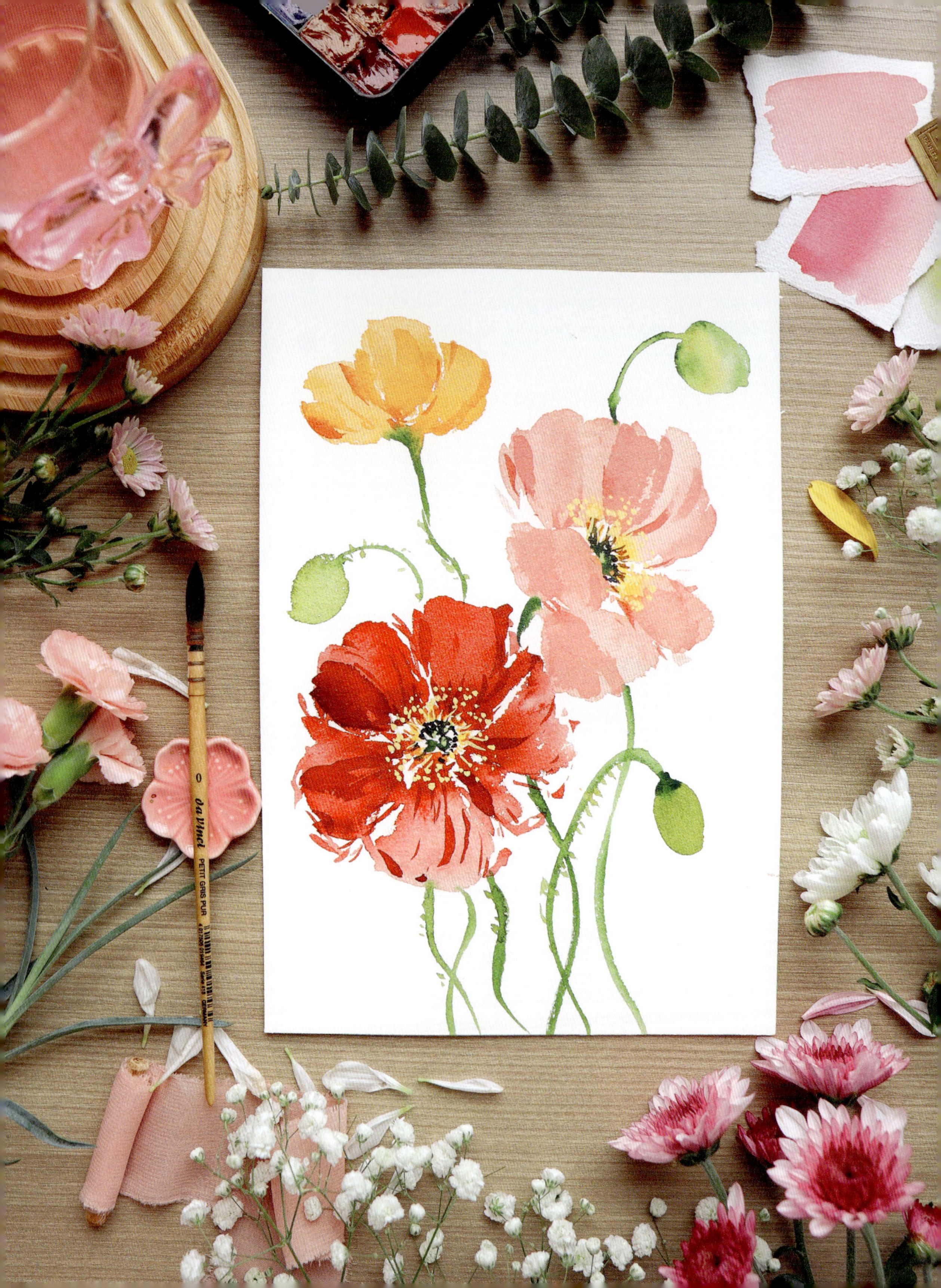

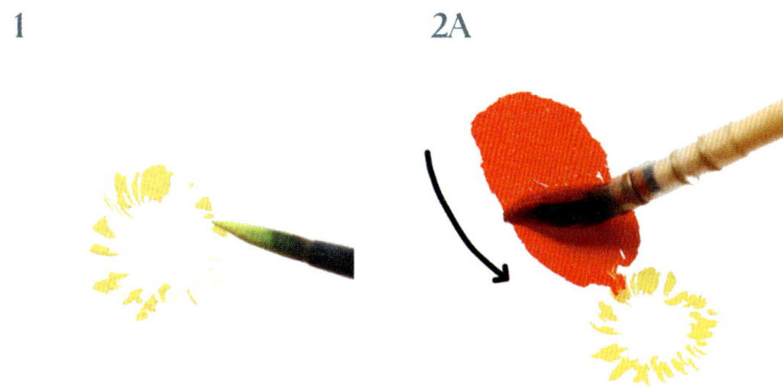

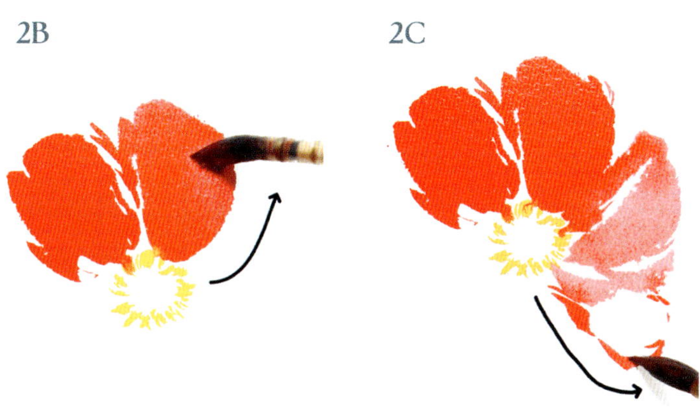

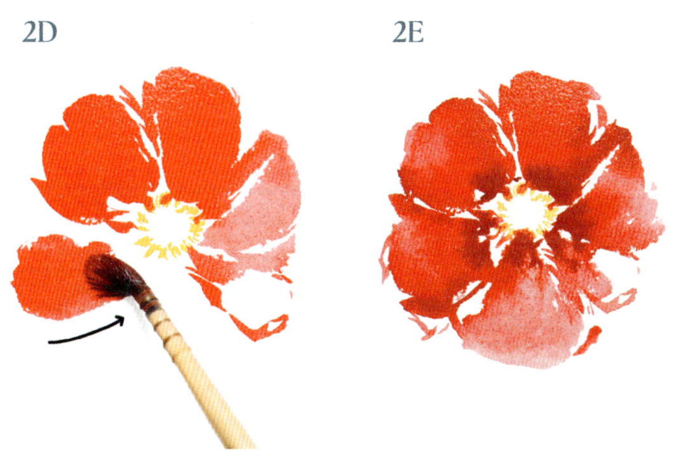

1. Paint the Center

Using a size 2 round brush, mix a medium consistency of Permanent Yellow Light. You may lightly draw a small dot with a pencil to help guide where the center will be. Using the tip of your brush, paint short, radiating strokes forming a loose circle. Keep an open space in the middle and vary the thickness of your strokes.

2. Add the Petals

While the yellow center is still wet, mix a medium consistency of Permanent Red and load your size 0 mop brush with lots of juicy paint. Starting about 2 inches (5 cm) from the center, press the side of your brush and drag it toward the center, lifting at the end. Add a few thin, curvy strokes with the tip of the mop brush beside it for character.

Paint the next petal from the center outward, letting the yellow and red bleed into each other. Slightly wiggle your brush to get ruffled edges. Leave some white gaps between petals to let the paper breathe. Alternate the saturation by adding more water to some petals for softness and let some part of the petals touch each other.

While the petals are damp, mix three parts Permanent Red and one part Hooker's Green to create a deeper red color. Drop this into the base of the petals where they meet to create depth.

3. Paint a Side-Angled Flower

Let's paint a flower on its side. We'll start with a petal that looks like it's folded. Mix a medium consistency of Shell Pink or any light pink. Load your size 0 mop brush then press and drag your brush to create an oval shape. Next, rinse your brush and mix a light consistency of Shell Pink. Press and drag your brush to create a broad stroke and slightly wiggle to create ruffled edges. Alternate with thinner strokes to suggest overlapping petals. Make three or four petals, leaving white gaps between them.

Using a size 2 round brush with medium-consistency Permanent Yellow Light, paint short strokes in the center while the petals are still wet. Watch the beautiful soft bleed!

Add contrast by mixing Shell Pink with a touch of Permanent Red to create a deeper pink. Drop this in between the petals to create subtle shadows.

4. Add Small Buds and Flowers

To make this composition more balanced, let's add smaller flowers and buds. Mix a medium consistency of Yellow Orange and load it in your size 0 mop brush. Paint three rounded petals beside each other, creating a fan shape. Connect them to a base using Sap Green and add a thin stem.

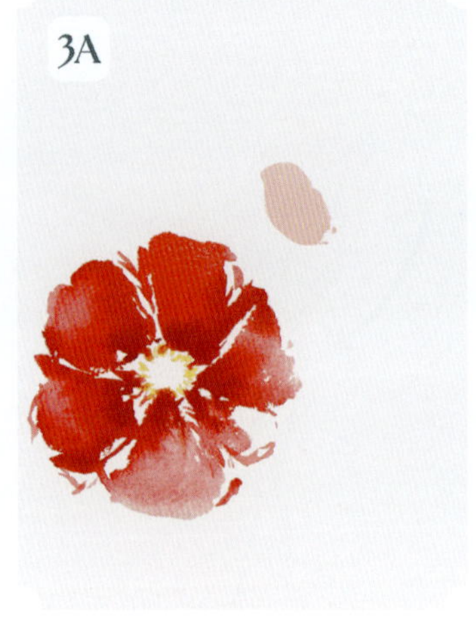

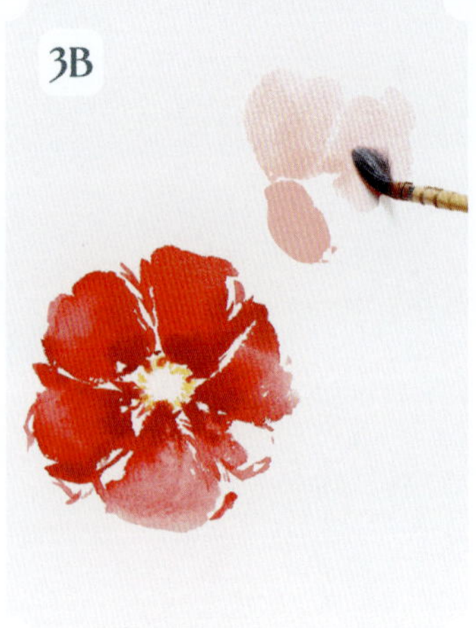

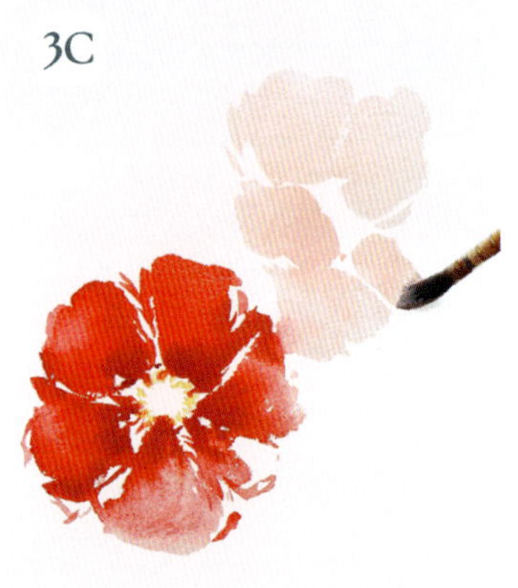

For the buds, mix a medium consistency of Greenish Yellow and paint oval shapes. Use a medium-consistency Sap Green to create wavy stems. Poppy stems have a subtle hairy texture. You can create this by lightly flicking your size 2 round brush with a light consistency of Sap Green along the stem edges. Add these sparingly to keep the main focus on the blooms.

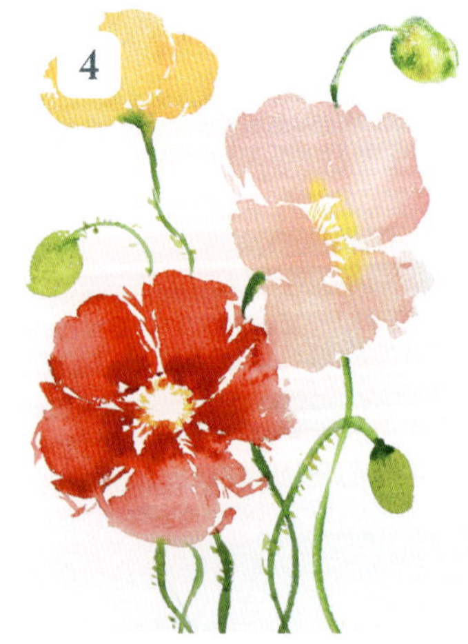

5. Add a Second Layer

When the first layer of petals is already dry, begin adding depth by painting stronger strokes. Mix three parts Permanent Red and one part Hooker's Green to create a deep red medium consistency. Using a size 2 round brush, paint thin and thick strokes throughout the petals. Lightly press the tip of the brush for fine lines. Add more pressure for thicker strokes and play with lengths. Some can be just tiny dots. Keep the overall effect loose and expressive, making sure you still see the first layer.

For the pink and orange flowers, create slightly darker mixes (add a touch of Permanent Red to Shell Pink and Yellow Orange). Use these to deepen the spaces between petals and add gentle contrast.

6. Add Finishing Touches

Using Sap Green, dab your brush to create a round center at the hearts of the flowers. Then mix a medium consistency of Indigo and add tiny dots around it for depth.

To make the center pop, let's add an opaque yellow. Use about one part white gouache and one part Permanent Yellow Light—feel free to adjust the ratio. Using your size 2 round brush, add short thin lines and dots radiating from the center to form the stamen. This touch of opaque yellow brings the flower to life. Your painting now shines with so much charm!

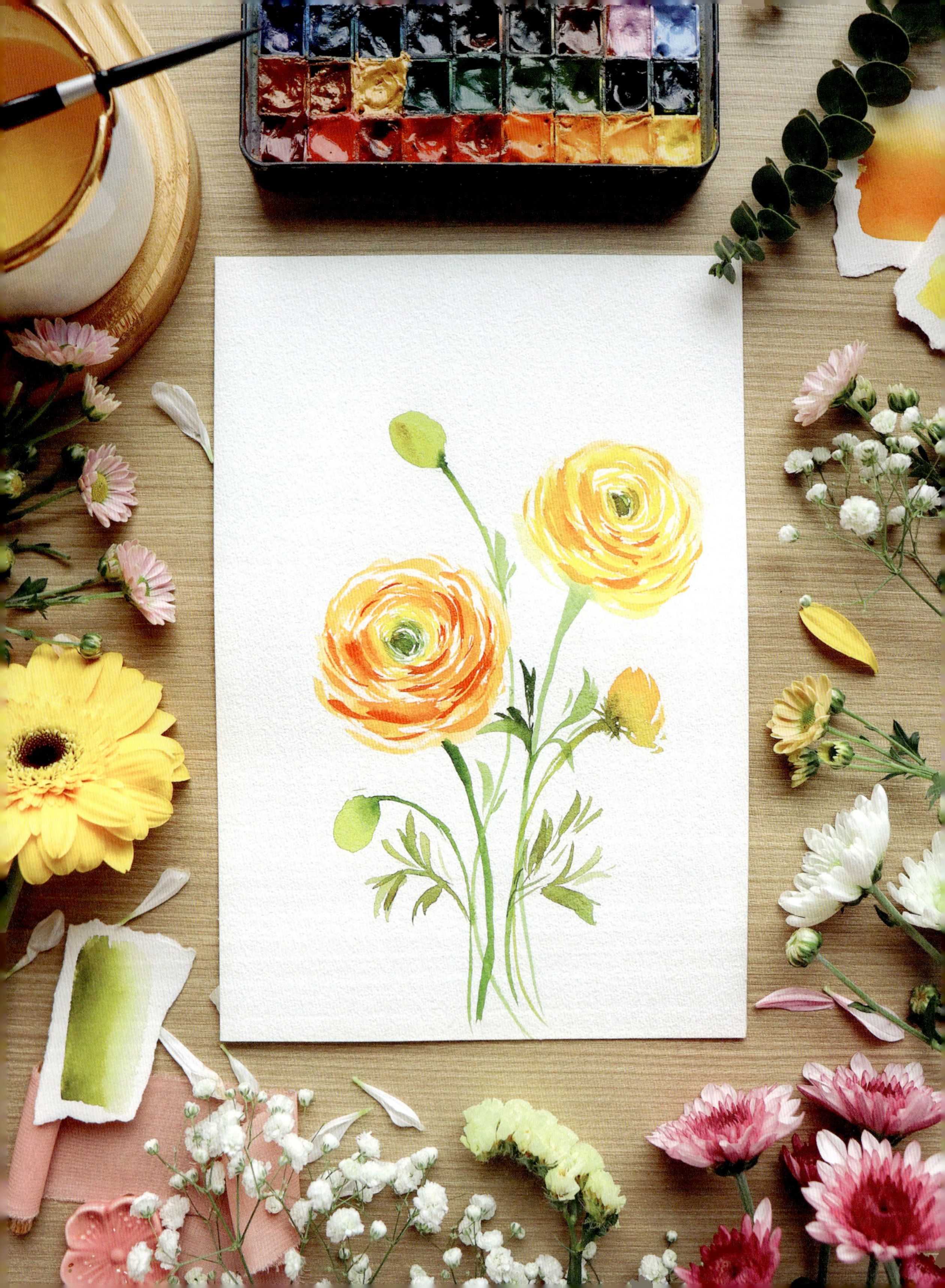

SUNLIT YELLOW ORANGE RANUNCULUS

- Sap Green
- Permanent Yellow Light
- Yellow Orange
- Greenish Yellow
- Permanent Yellow Deep
- Burnt Umber
- Permanent Red, optional

I especially love painting ranunculus in yellow and orange tones. They instantly brighten up a painting and give a sense of warmth. While striking on their own, they make perfect secondary flowers in a bouquet, balancing out the bolder blooms.

In this lesson, we will paint this flower from different angles and explore how to layer petals using thin C strokes. While the technique is somewhat similar to painting a rose, we'll keep the strokes much finer to capture the tightly packed petals that give a ranunculus its signature look. You'll also learn how to keep the flower looking soft and round while keeping your brushwork light and loose.

Brushes

- Size 4 round brush
- Size 6 round brush

Floral Strokes

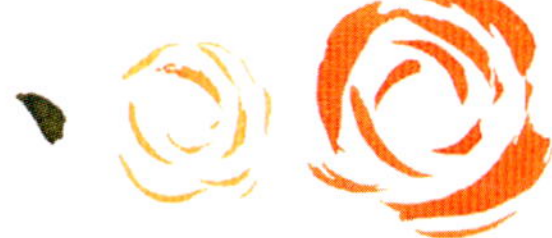

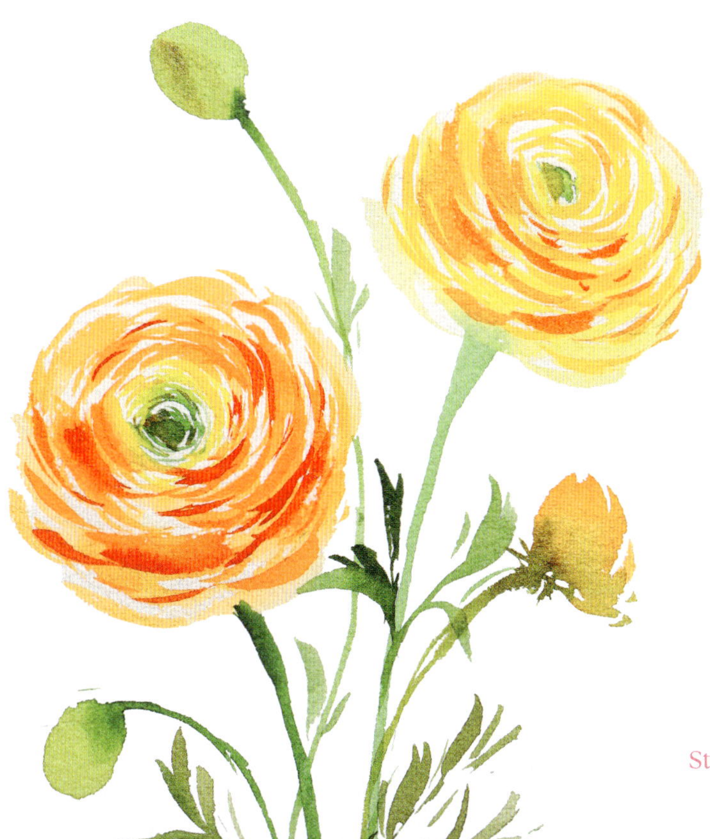

1. Start with the Center

Grab your size 4 round brush and load it in a medium-consistency Sap Green. Paint a comma stroke that will serve as the center of the flower.

Tilt your brush upright and paint very thin C strokes around the center. Keep the strokes as fine as you can, and remember to leave white spaces between them to keep it airy and light.

Next, rinse your brush and load it with a medium-consistency Permanent Yellow Light. Paint slightly larger thin C strokes around the green center. Let some of the yellow strokes blend into the green. This soft transition will help the center feel more natural.

2. Paint the Main Flower

Now let's bring the flower to life! Load your brush with a medium consistency of Yellow Orange. Continue adding longer C strokes around the yellow layer. The finer the strokes you add, the more this flower will look lush and full.

For the outermost layer of petals, use a lighter consistency of Yellow Orange to soften the edges. This creates a nice contrast and keeps the flower from looking too heavy.

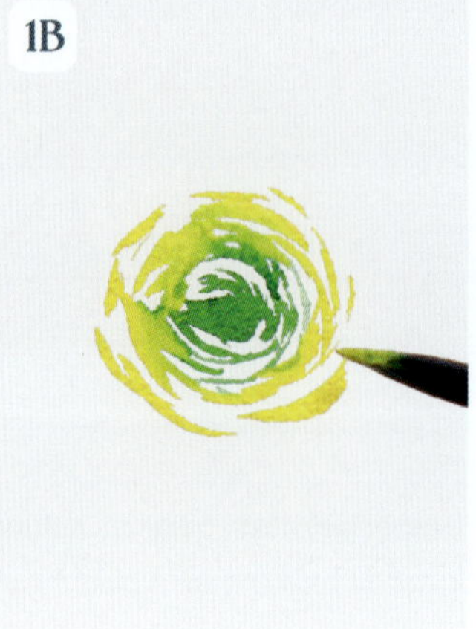

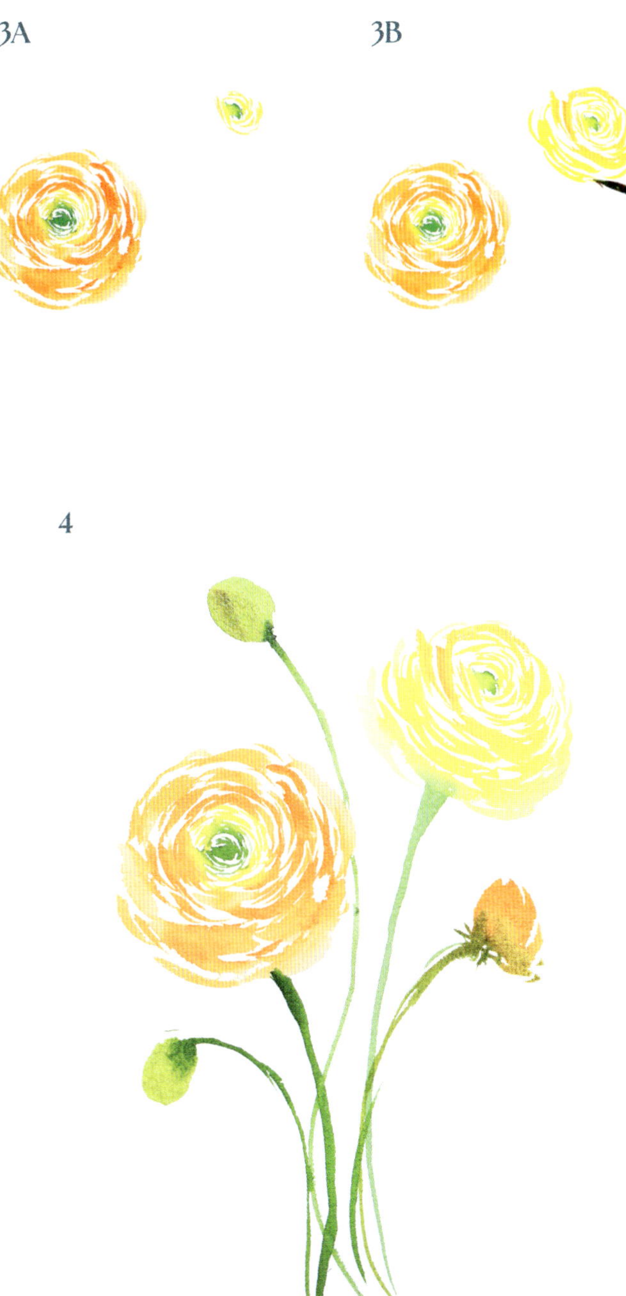

3. Add a Side-Facing Flower

Let's add variation by painting a flower from the side. A side-facing ranunculus has a slightly oval shape, with more volume on the bottom. Use a size 6 round brush and load it with a medium consistency of Sap Green. Start with a comma stroke, then add thin C strokes around it to form the green center.

Rinse your brush, then switch to a medium consistency of Permanent Yellow Light. Paint more thin C strokes around the center, letting some blend slightly with the green.

Remember to build more volume toward the bottom half of the flower to help show its angle. Finish with a few outer petals, using a lighter yellow wash for a soft edge.

4. Add Buds and Stems

Ranunculus stems are long, slender, and slightly curved. Use a medium-consistency Sap Green and add stems attached to the bases of the flowers.

To paint the buds, use a light consistency of Greenish Yellow and add small oval shapes facing in different directions. These buds bring variety to your composition.

You can also paint a small flower about to bloom by creating two to three overlapping petal shapes. Use the same colors as your main flower to keep everything harmonious.

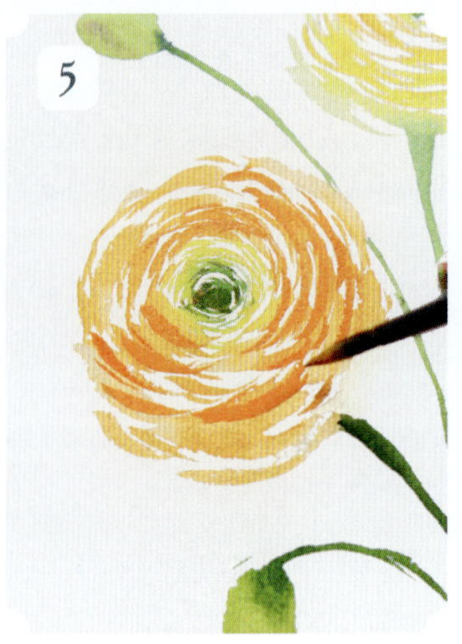

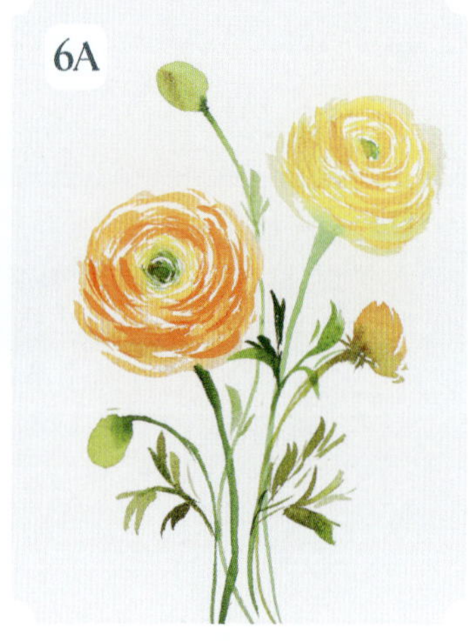

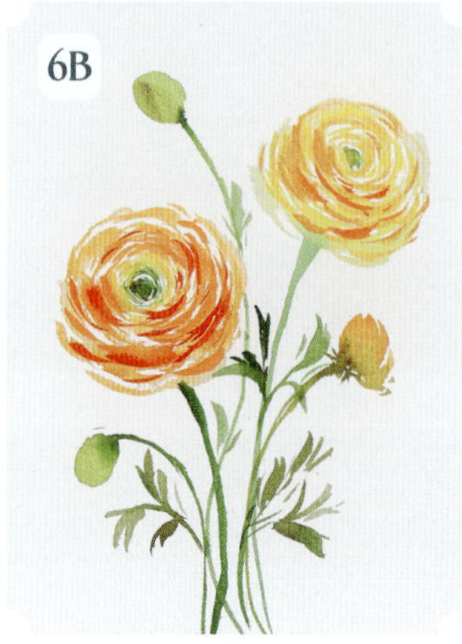

5. Add a Second Layer of Petals

Let's add more depth to this flower. Make sure that the flowers are already dry before continuing. Use a hairdryer to speed up the drying process.

Load your brush with a thick consistency of Yellow Orange. Paint another round of thin C strokes around the middle and outer edges of the first flower. Keep your hand light as you add the strokes. We're adding a subtle shadow to make the flower look more dimensional.

For the yellow ranunculus, mix a thick consistency of Permanent Yellow Deep or add a thick consistency of two parts Sap Green and one part Burnt Umber to the yellow mixture. Focus the second layer of C strokes more toward the bottom half. This second layer is where the flower gains character.

6. Add Leaves and Finishing Touches

The leaves of a ranunculus are light, feathery, and slightly jagged. Mix two parts Sap Green and one part Burnt Umber for an earthy green color. Paint very thin stems and then flick your brush outward to create wispy leaves. Some strokes might merge and others might look like broken strokes. Embrace the looseness and let your brush dance a little! You can also vary the green color and add a little Yellow Orange to Permanent Yellow Deep to make it look interesting.

Optionally, if you wish to add more depth to the ranunculus petals, mix one part Permanent Red and one part Yellow Orange. Add a third layer of C strokes focusing more on the bottom part of the flower to suggest a subtle shadow.

You did it! All those strokes came together into a gorgeous ranunculus.

> **TIP:** Ranunculus come in different colors. Experiment with pastels using the colors Brilliant Pink or Shell Pink.

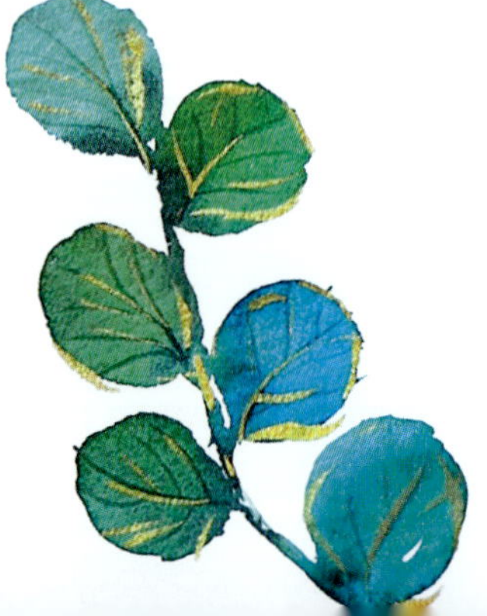

SOFT CORAL DAHLIA

Dahlias are truly captivating flowers. They have a bold structure and yet can be painted in a loose and expressive manner. The layered petals radiate outward and look like they are dancing. I find it so relaxing to add each curvy petal, one layer at a time.

In this lesson, we will explore how to paint this flower from different angles. You will learn how to build the petals layer by layer in a circular formation while keeping the painting loose. We will also go over how to add depth and contrast to make the flower pop.

Take your time and enjoy each brushstroke!

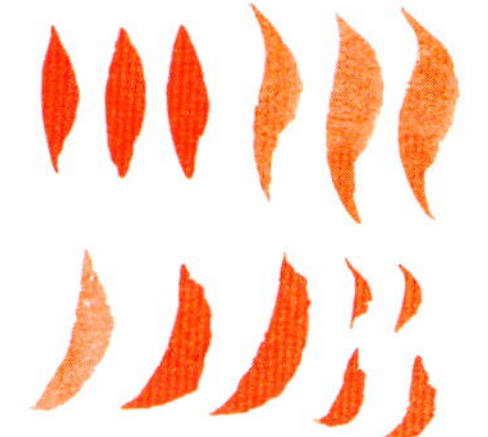

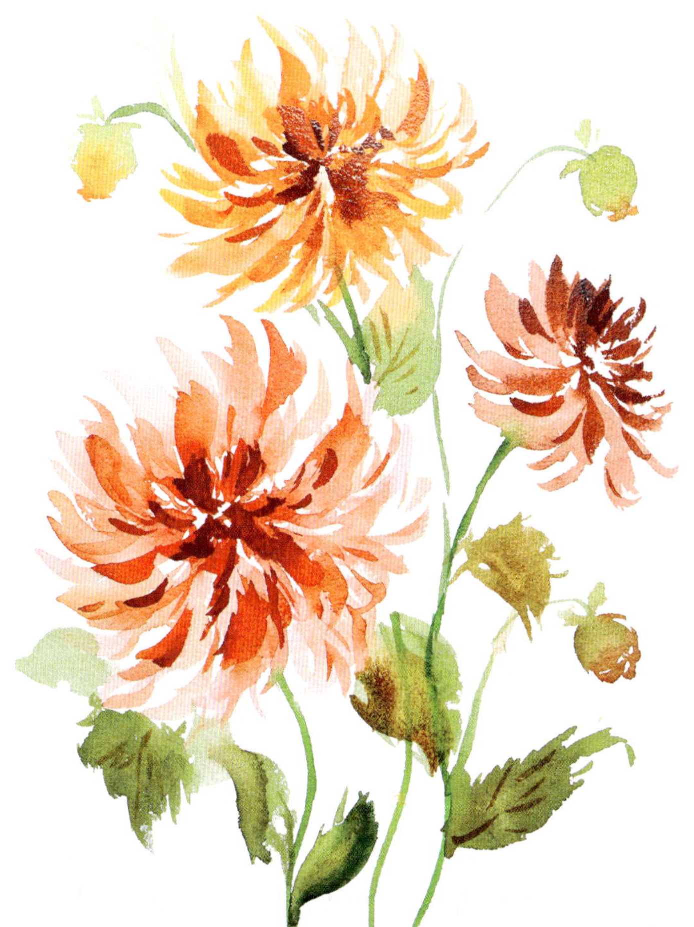

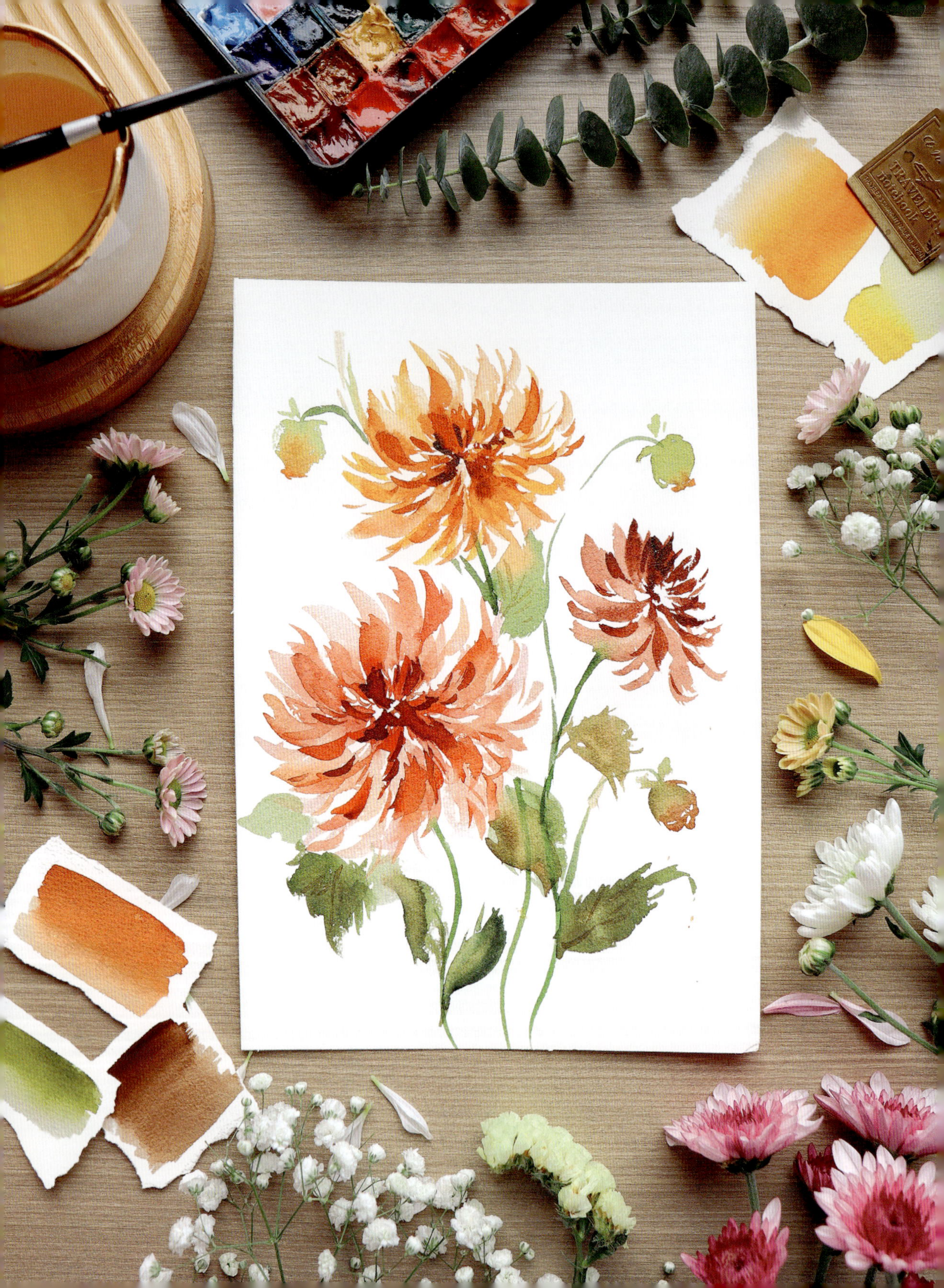

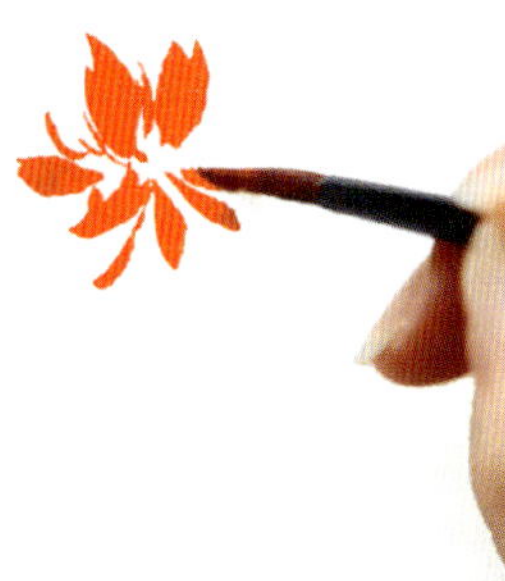

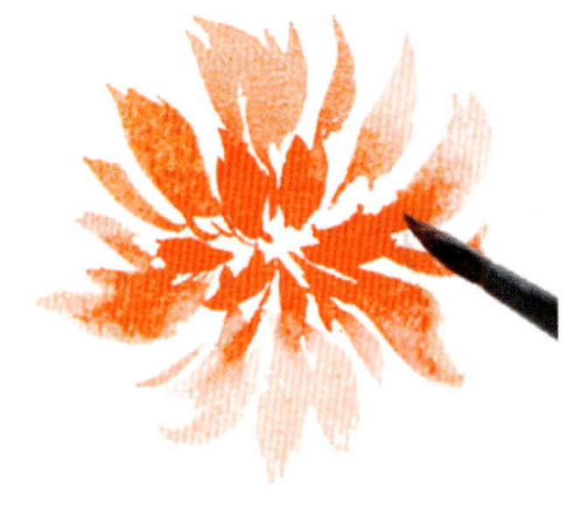

1. Start with the Center

Mix a thick consistency of Permanent Rose and Burnt Sienna. Load your size 6 round brush with this color. Begin by painting small, short petal strokes in a circular formation. Press your brush onto the paper and gently lift at the end of each stroke to create pointy tips. Vary the thickness of your strokes to keep the look loose and natural. Keep your hand light and the strokes slightly curved to suggest soft, delicate petals.

Next, mix a lighter value of the same coral mixture and paint another layer of petals around the center. These petals should be longer than the ones in the center and should resemble an S curve. Then, add a third round of petals using the same light mixture, but this time keep the strokes even

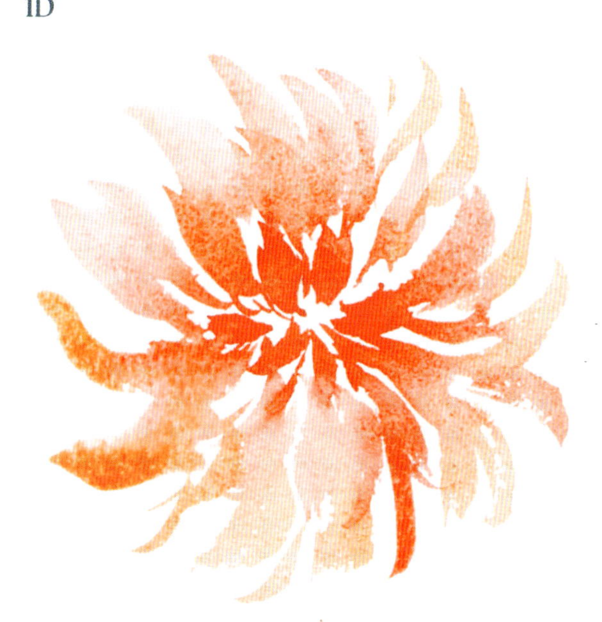

lighter and curvier. It's okay if some petals touch or merge. We don't want perfectly uniform shapes. Our goal is a loose and organic look. To add interest, drop in a very light wash of Permanent Rose on a few petals for a soft pop of pink.

2. Paint a Side-Angled Flower

Once the first flower is finished, use a medium consistency of Sap Green to paint a curved stem beneath the flower.

Now, let's paint a flower at an angle. The overall shape will be oval. Load your brush with a thick consistency of Brown Red. Paint a cluster of small, wispy strokes that form a semicircle. This will be the top half of the flower. Vary the stroke thickness and leave some space between each one. Rinse your brush and mix a light consistency of Brown Red. Paint pointy and curvy petals along the bottom half of the flower. I like making the petals face in different directions to give the flower a natural feel.

3. Paint a Third Flower

The third flower is front facing but slightly smaller than the first one. Start by loading your size 6 round brush with a thick consistency of Yellow Orange. Paint short petal strokes in a circular formation. Add a second and third layer of petals in a lighter consistency of Yellow Orange. Be sure to keep white spaces in between the petals. We want the flower to appear round but not perfect. Some petals can be longer or face slightly outward in different directions.

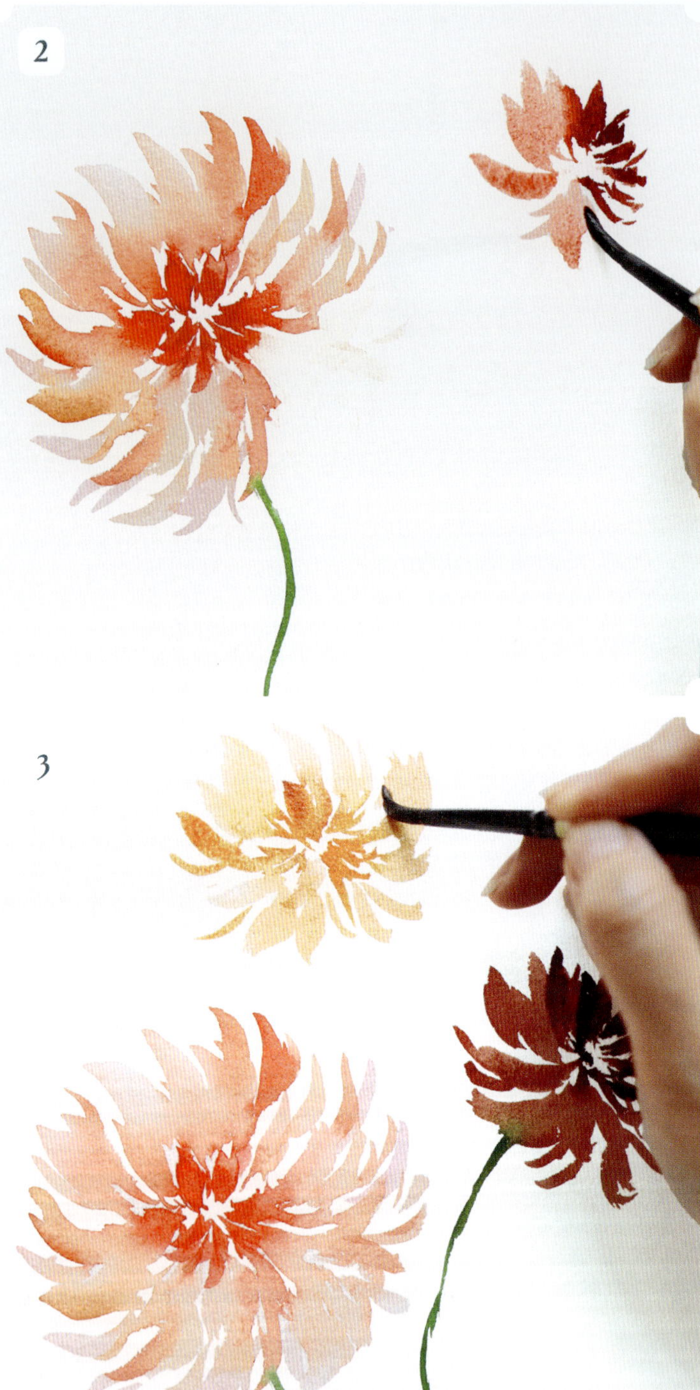

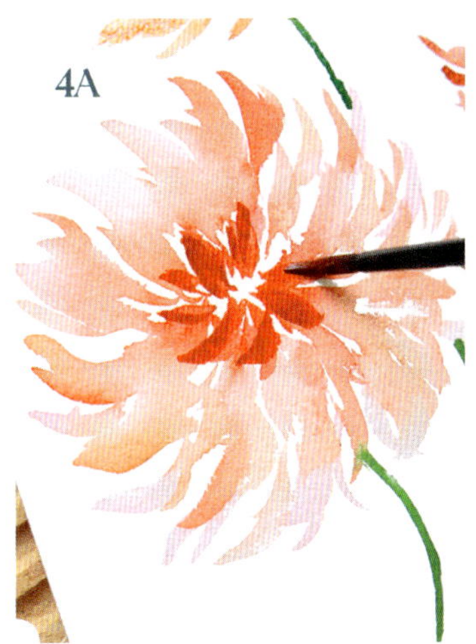

4A

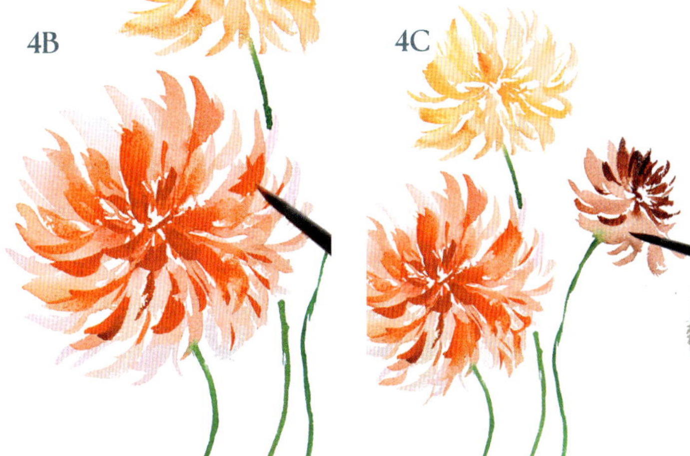

4B 4C

4. Add Contrast

This step is key to giving your flowers more depth. Make sure the petals are completely dry. For the first flower (bottom left), mix a thick consistency of Permanent Rose and Burnt Sienna. Paint a new layer of center petals in a circular formation, leaving gaps so the previous layers remain visible. As you work outward, paint larger petals (a mix of C and S shapes) by pressing the side of the brush down and flicking toward the tip to form pointy ends. For the side-angled flower, use a thicker consistency of Brown Red.

Do the same for the Yellow Orange dahlia, using a thick mix of Yellow Orange and Burnt Sienna.

For the side-angled flower, use a thicker consistency of Brown Red to deepen the top cluster.

4D

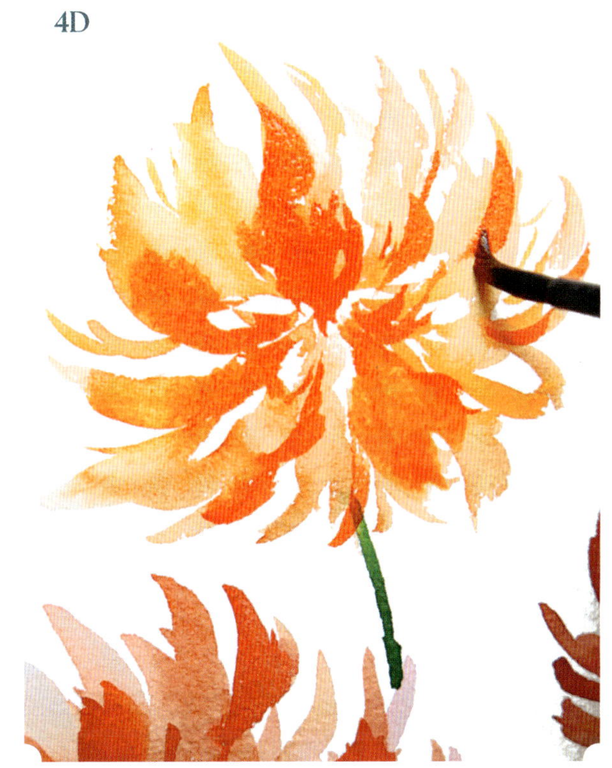

5. Add Leaves and Buds

Using a medium consistency of two parts Sap Green and one part Burnt Umber, paint the leaves and some stems sticking out. For the flower buds, use Greenish Yellow and paint oval shapes. While the green buds are wet, drop in a bit of Yellow Orange at the tip of the bud to suggest that it's starting to bloom.

6. Finishing Touches

Adding a dark center can help your loose flower really stand out. Mix equal parts of Permanent Rose, Burnt Sienna, and Brown Red to create a deeper shade. Feel free to adjust the ratio to your liking. Load your size 6 brush and use the tip to paint thin, curvy strokes, concentrating more in the center of the flower. Soften some of the strokes gently by fading them with a clean, damp brush. Be careful not to overdo this step as we still want the flower to be loose.

Repeat the same technique with the Yellow Orange flower but add a touch of Brown Red to deepen the center color.

Good job! Your florals look full and expressive.

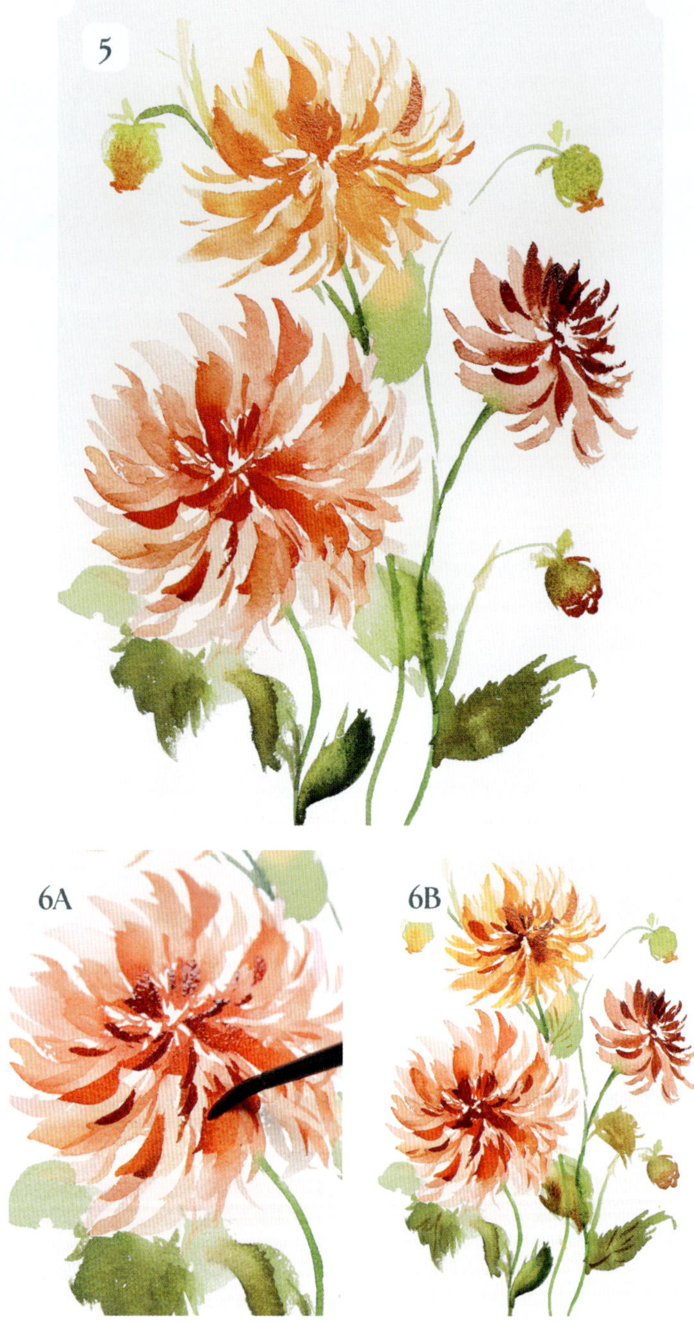

MOODY MAUVE HELLEBORE

Painting hellebores is a refreshing change from painting the usual bright florals. They have soft velvety petals with deep moody colors that bring a different character to your bouquet. I love how unique they are, with some varieties showing hints of Greenish Yellow, which is one of my favorite greens.

In this lesson, we'll explore muted tones and use a wet-on-wet technique for the petals. I'll show you how to add veins and how to make the center stand out with a simple gouache detail.

Colors

- Crimson Lake
- Permanent Violet
- Burnt Umber
- Greenish Yellow
- Olive Green
- Sap Green
- Hooker's Green
- Indigo

Brushes

- Size 8 round brush
- Size 2 round brush

Other Materials

- White gouache

Floral Strokes

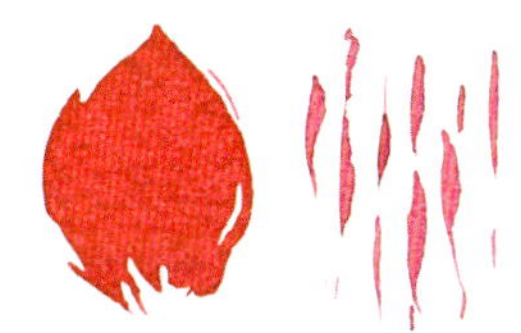

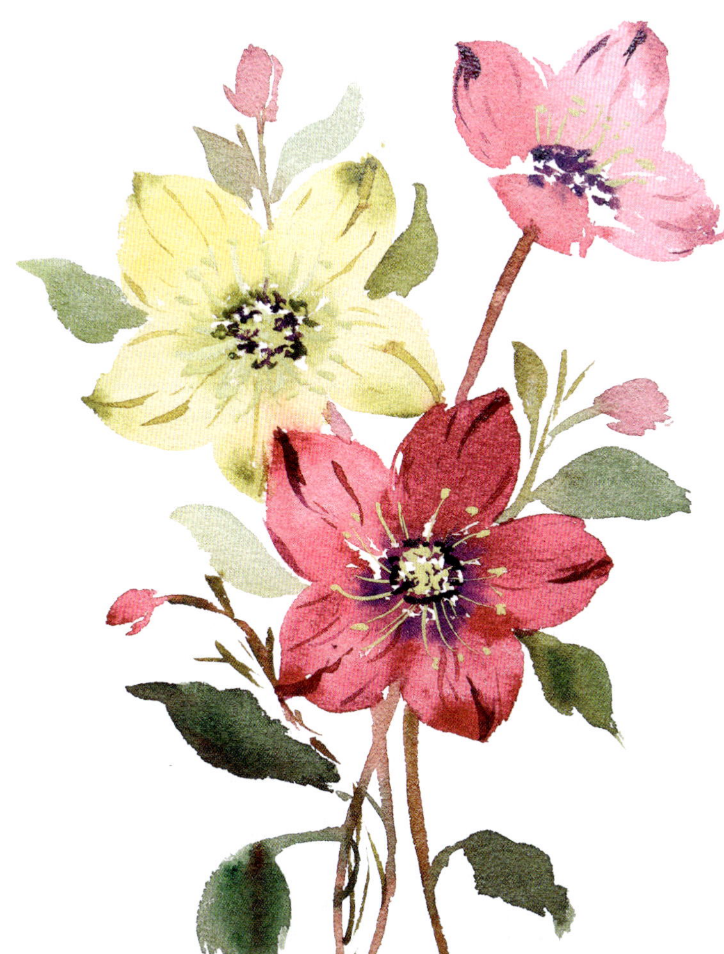

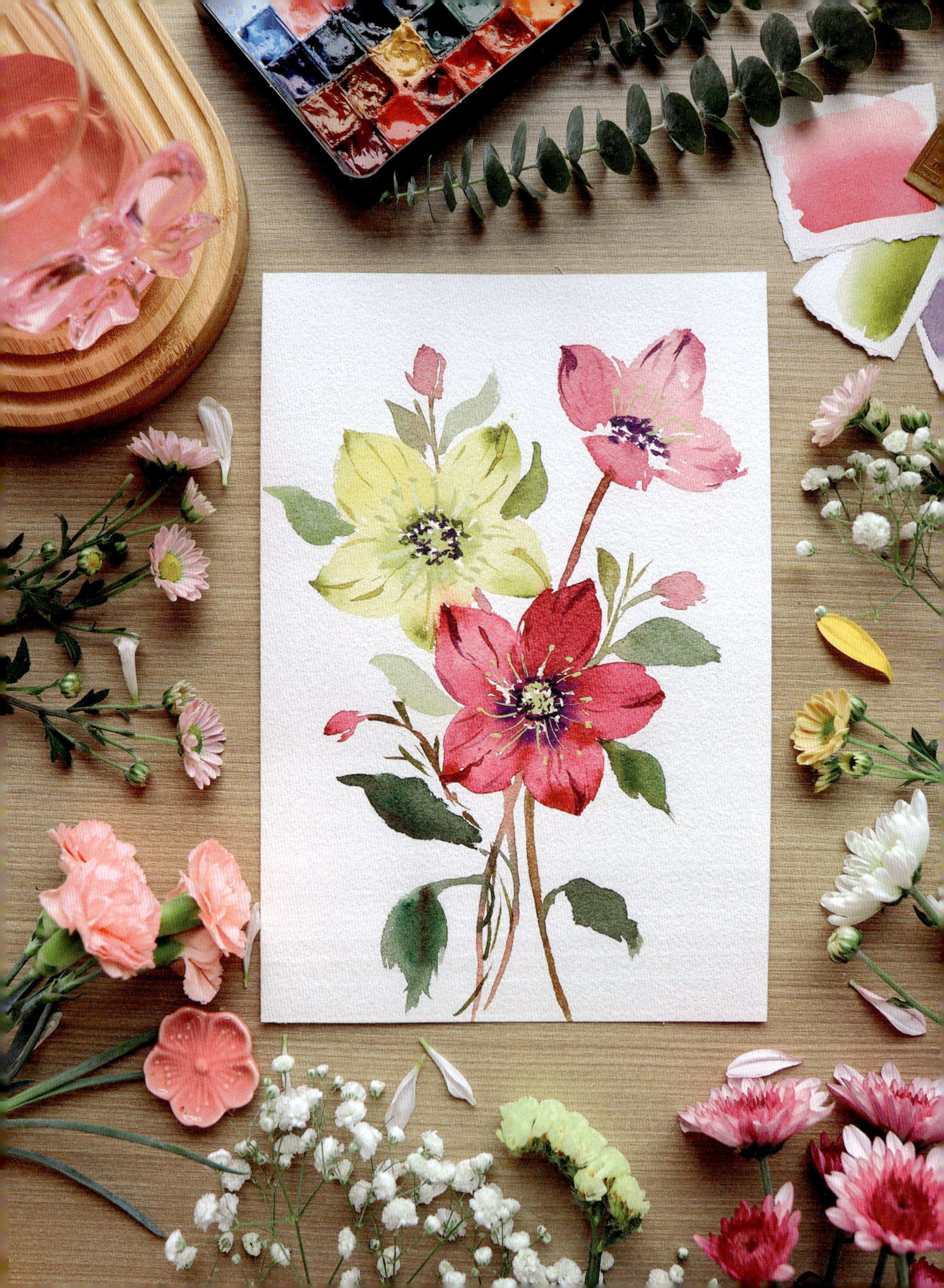

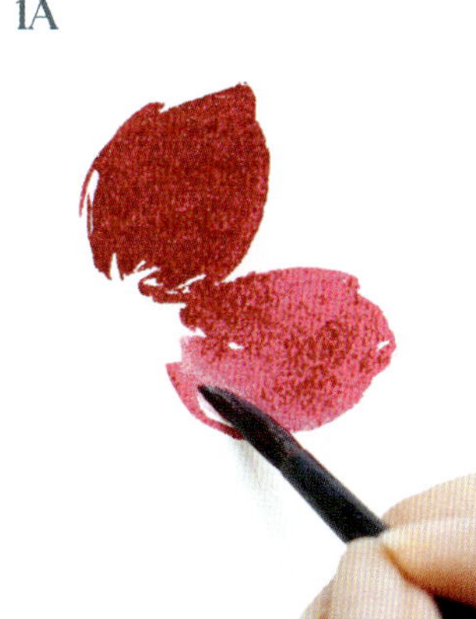

1A

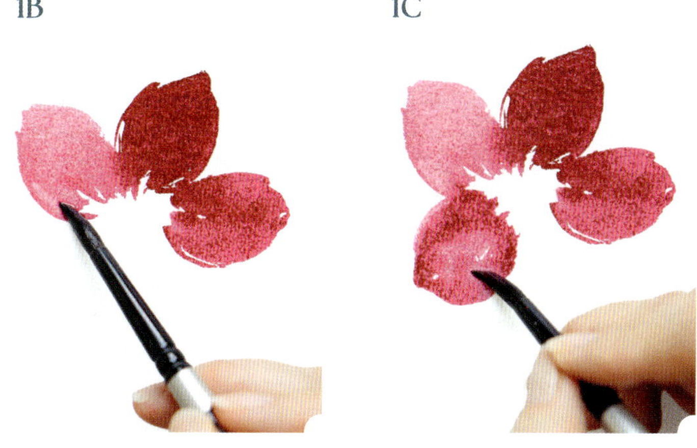

1B

1C

1. Paint the Mauve Petals

Mix equal parts of Crimson Lake and Permanent Violet into a medium consistency. Adjust the ratio as you like or add a hint of Burnt Umber for a more muted color.

Using a size 8 round brush, paint a Five-Petal Flower (page 111) with pointed tips. Stamp your brush with the tip away from you, drag with a slight curve, then lift. Overlap with a similar stroke to form each petal. Leave the center open.

While the petals are still damp, drop in a more pigmented mix of Crimson Lake and Permanent Violet at the tips and in between the petals.

Add a dark center using thick-consistency Permanent Violet.

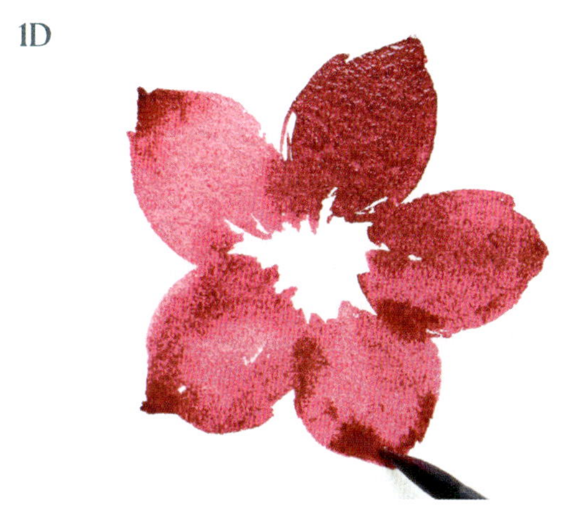

1D

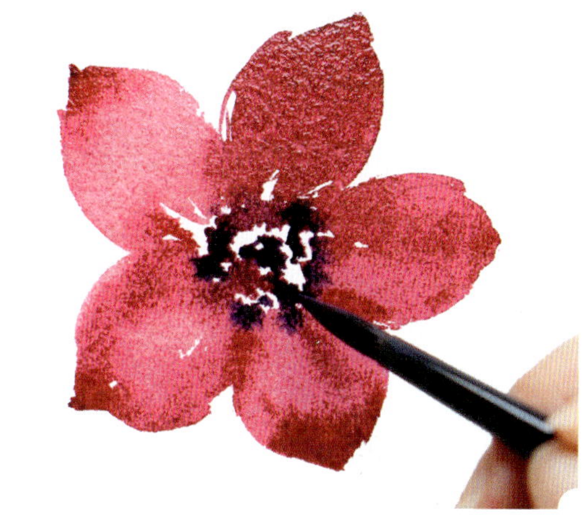

1E

2. Paint the Remaining Flowers

Using a light consistency of Greenish Yellow, paint a similar Five-Petal Flower diagonally across the first one. It's fine if the petals touch the first flower. Deepen the center and petal tips with Olive Green.

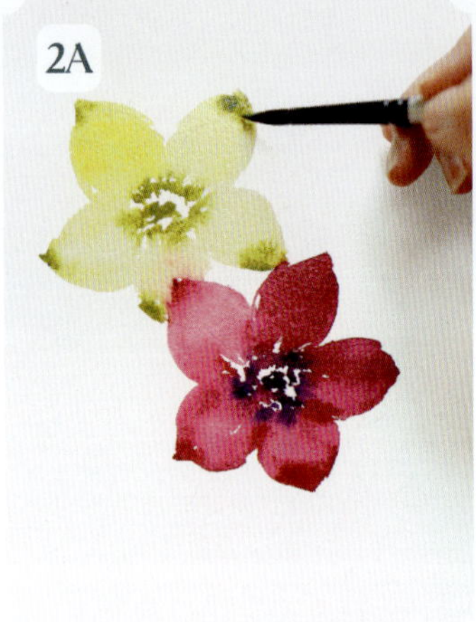

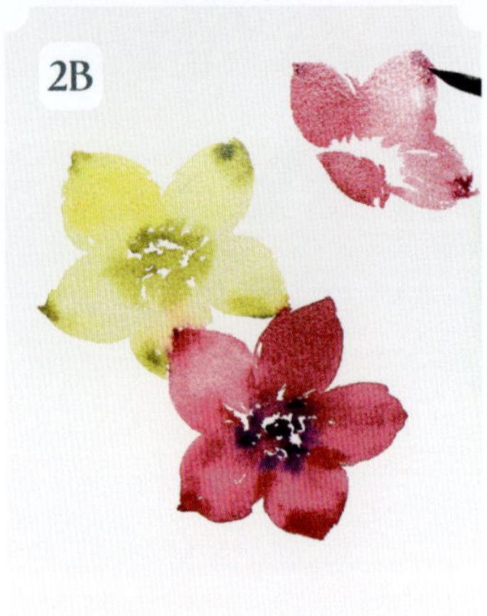

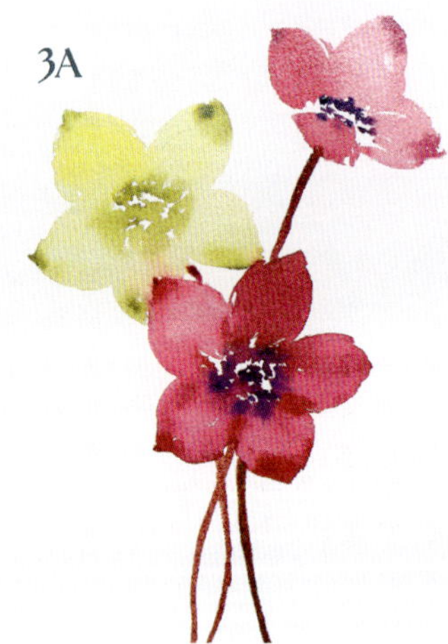

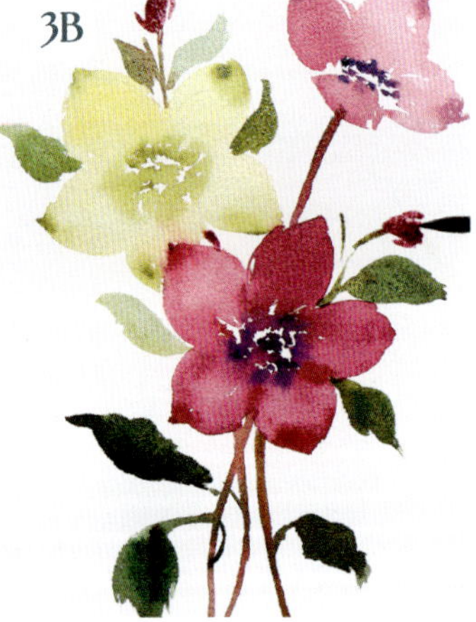

For the side-facing flower, mix a medium-consistency Crimson Lake and Permanent Violet. Start with a horizontal stroke and paint three petals above it. Add deeper tones along the tips and near the center while the petals are still damp.

3. Add the Stems and Leaves

The hellebore stems have a slight purplish undertone. Mix Sap Green with the same color of the mauve petals (equal parts Crimson Lake and Permanent Violet) for better color harmony. Connect the slightly curved stems to the flowers.

Using medium-consistency Hooker's Green, paint jagged leaves. Press your brush, then wiggle and drag to create a fine tip. Let the leaves face different ways. Drop in a touch of Indigo toward the base of the leaves for more depth. Vary the green tones and add it near the flowers to make them pop.

For the buds, use the color of the main mauve petals (equal parts Crimson Lake and Permanent Violet) and load it into your brush. Look for a loose stem and stamp your brush to create a petal-like shape. Feel free to add a few thin strokes beside it.

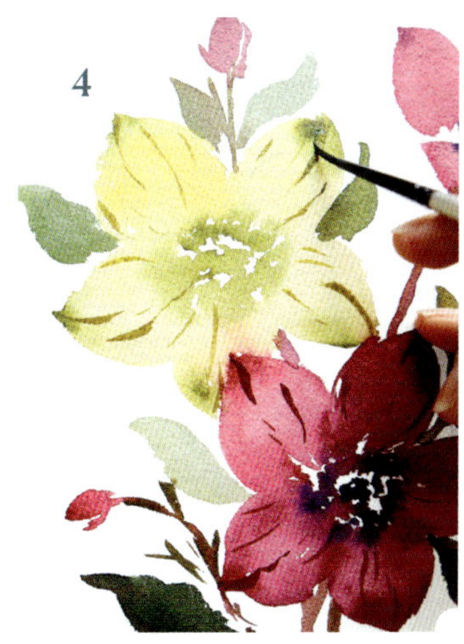

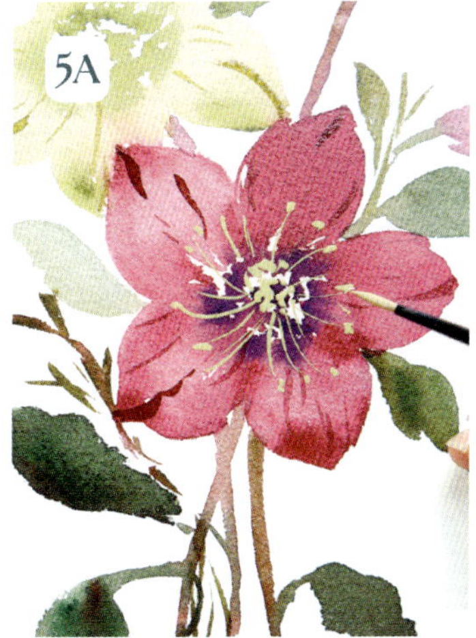

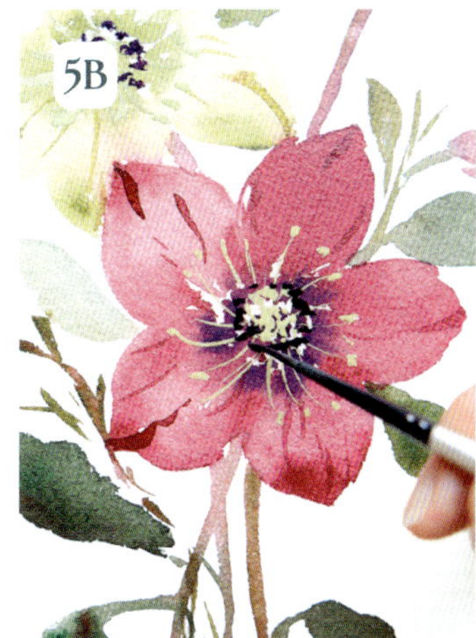

4. Add Veins

Mix a shade or two darker than the petal color. With a size 2 round brush, add fine details by dragging the tip of the brush on the paper to suggest veins. Keep it subtle because too many veins can make the flower look busy. Repeat for the other flowers.

5. Add the Center

Mix equal parts of white gouache and Greenish Yellow. Add more yellow if you want more color. With a size 2 round brush, stamp your brush in the center to add texture.

Then, add the stamen. Use the brush tip to create fine lines with dots at the end. Add this to all the flowers.

For more depth, mix a medium-consistency Permanent Violet. Paint a ring of small dots in the center to add depth. All done! Your hellebore centers look delicate and beautifully textured.

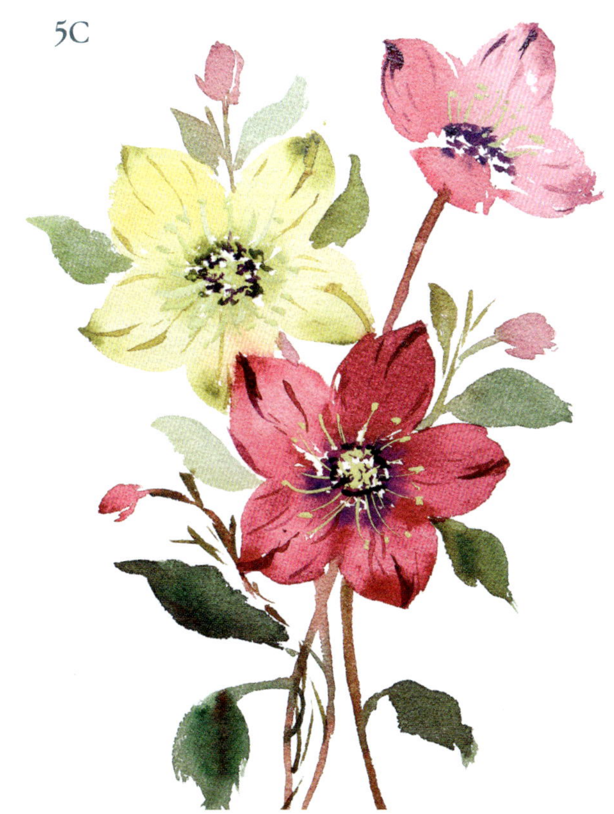

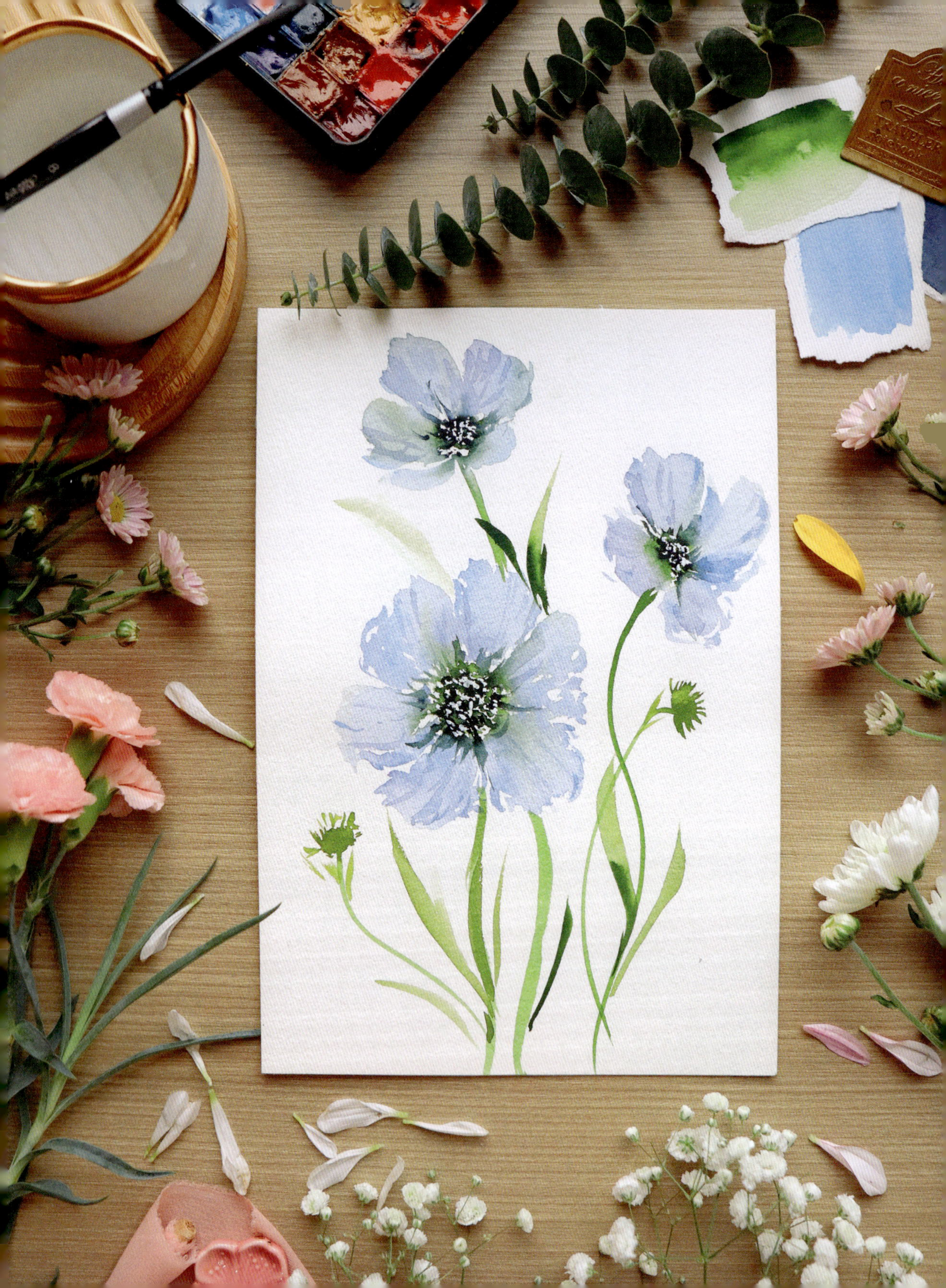

DUSTY BLUE SCABIOSA

Scabiosa, also known as the pincushion flower, has such a sweet and whimsical look. It has a round, textured center with soft ruffled petals and almost feels like it's floating on the stem. This makes it such a fun flower to paint. The loose nature of the petals gives you room to play and wiggle your brush to create the ruffled edges. No need to stress about perfect shapes.

In this lesson, you'll get to practice creating soft colors, adding subtle folds to the petals, and using texture to make the center stand out.

Colors

- ■ Sap Green
- ■ Indigo
- ■ Verditer Blue
- ■ Permanent Violet

Brushes

- Size 2 round brush
- Size 6 round brush

Other Materials

- Pencil
- White gouache, optional

Floral Strokes

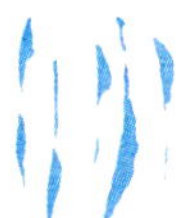

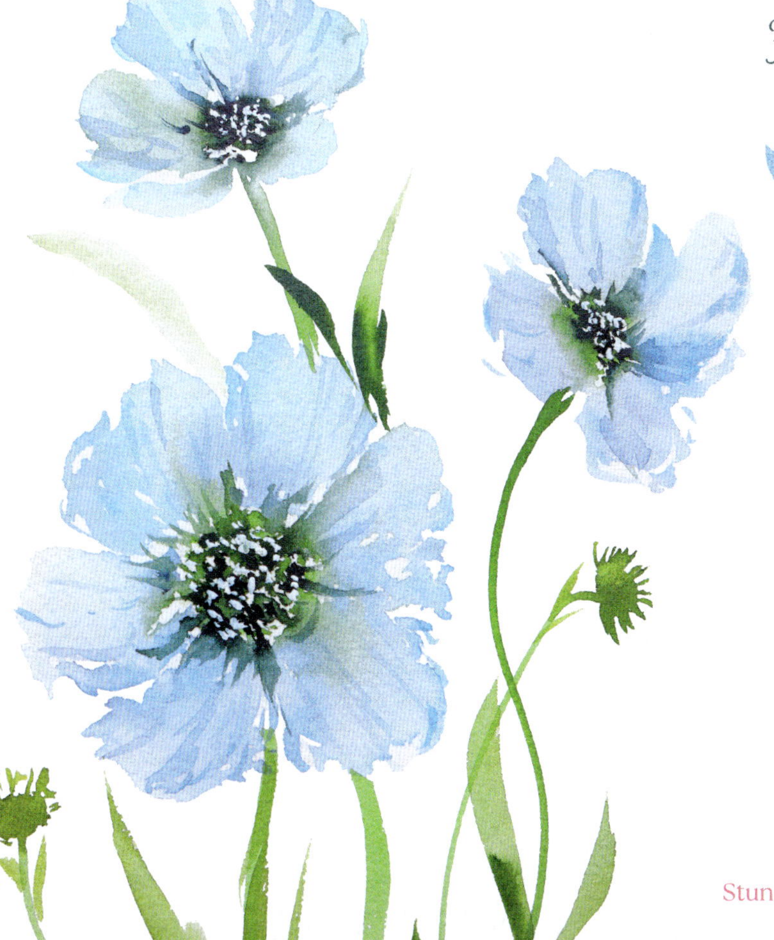

1. Start with the Center

Lightly draw a 1-inch (2.5-cm) circle using a pencil as a guide for the flower center. Load your size 2 round brush with a medium-consistency Sap Green. Paint tiny clustered dots to form the textured center. Rinse your brush and pick up a lighter consistency of Sap Green to soften a few areas around the edges. While it's still damp, drop in a few dots of medium-consistency Indigo to add depth.

2. Add the Petals

Mix a very light consistency of Verditer Blue. It should be almost translucent as we want the petals to be light and fluffy. Add a touch of Permanent Violet if you want a hint of lavender.

Using a size 6 round brush, load it with juicy paint. Press the brush on the paper with the point facing outward, wiggle slightly to create ruffled edges, then drag it toward the center.

Overlap the strokes if you want fuller petals. Don't worry if the green center bleeds into the petals. It will add a more expressive look.

Continue painting petals around the center. You can also add some curvy, thin strokes to add character to the petals. Make sure to leave some white spaces to let your petals breathe.

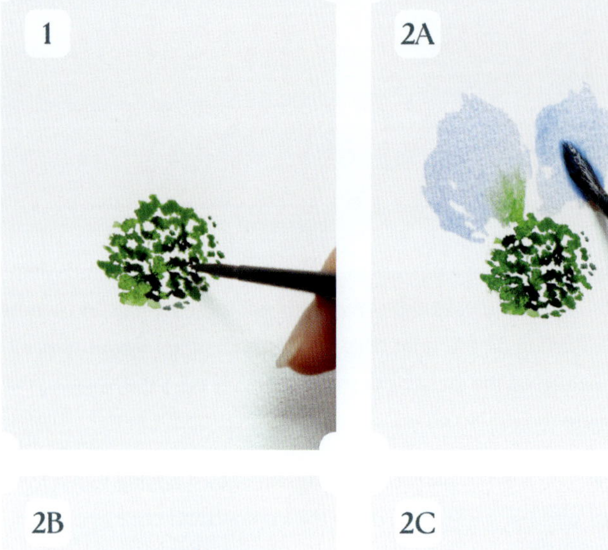

For more depth, mix a more concentrated Verditer Blue and Permanent Violet. Drop it in between the petals and at the base where the petals meet and along the edges while they are still damp.

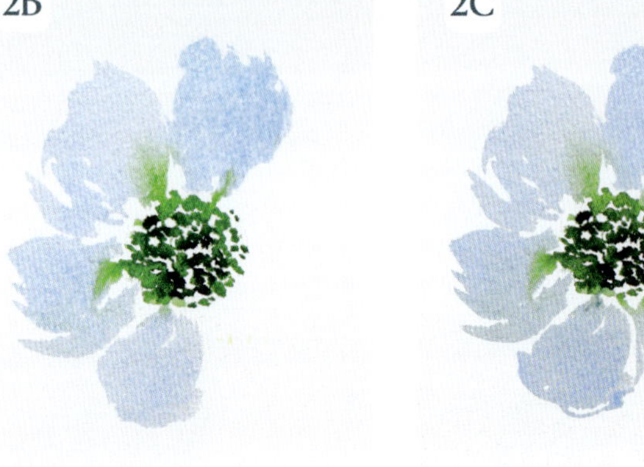

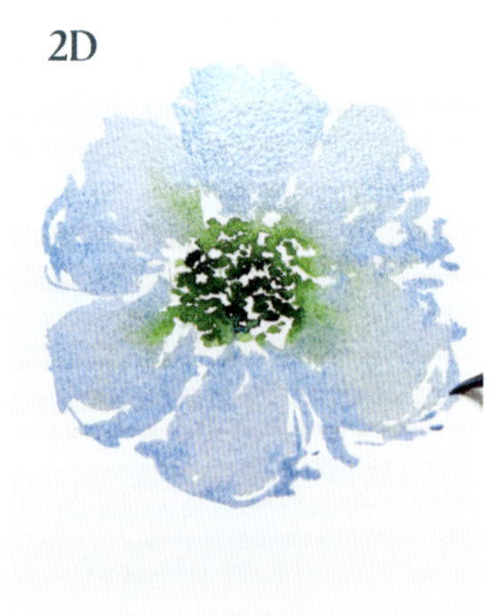

3. Paint a Side-Facing Flower

Using a size 2 round brush, mix a medium consistency of Sap Green and paint a cluster of tiny dots forming an oval to suggest that a second flower is at an angle. You may drop in a few dots of medium-consistency Indigo while the center is wet. Just add a few dots as we still want to see the green center.

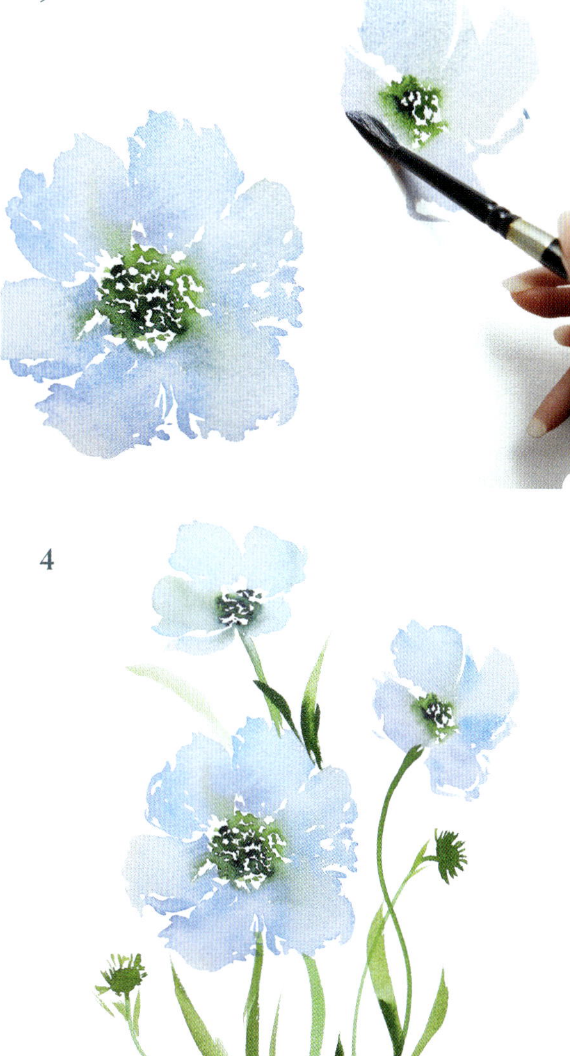

Switch to a very light consistency of Verditer Blue with your size 6 round brush. Press, wiggle, and drag your brush to the center. Create three petals beside each other on the top half of the flower. Watch how the green center softly bleeds into the petals. Next, lightly press and drag your brush on the bottom part of the center to create an oval shape.

Bring more depth by mixing three parts Verditer Blue and one part Permanent Violet and adding it in between the petals. Make another side-angled flower toward the top to create a more balanced composition.

4. Add Leaves and Buds

Using a medium-consistency Sap Green, get your size 6 round brush and paint long, slender stems with graceful curves.

Add the small buds by painting horizontal oval shapes. Use the tip of the brush to add some tiny spikes on top of them. Connect them with thin stems.

Paint the elongated leaves using varied shades of green. Press and drag your size 6 round brush and lift toward the end to create a pointy tip. While the leaves are wet, you may drop in a medium-consistency Indigo toward the base of the leaves to add depth.

5. Add Petal Details

Scabiosa petals have gentle folds and ruffles. Mix a light consistency of Verditer Blue with Permanent Violet and adjust the ratio of water to paint. We want the color to be one to two shades darker than your base petals. Using a size 2 round brush, drag the tip to create thin and thick curvy lines on the petals to suggest the veins and folds.

Add a few dots of medium-consistency Indigo in the center. With a damp brush, pull some of the pigment into the veins to create a soft, dramatic effect. Just be careful not to overdo it to keep the petals light and airy. Do the same for the other flowers.

6. Add White Gouache for Texture

This step will make a more textured center, but you can opt to skip it if you are happy with your painting. Mix a creamy consistency of white gouache by adding a few drops of water to your gouache. Using a size 2 round brush, paint tiny dots in the dry center. This detail really makes the center pop, especially against darker backgrounds. That's it! You've just finished painting this beautiful flower!

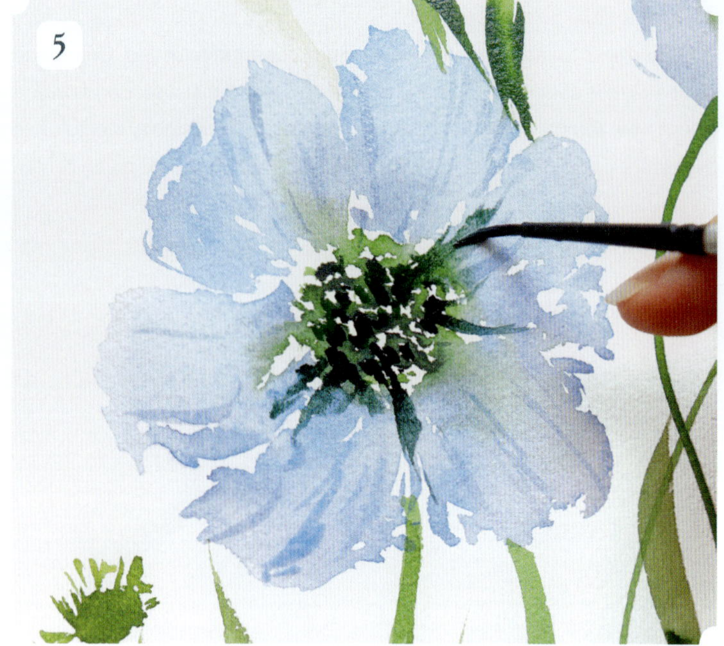

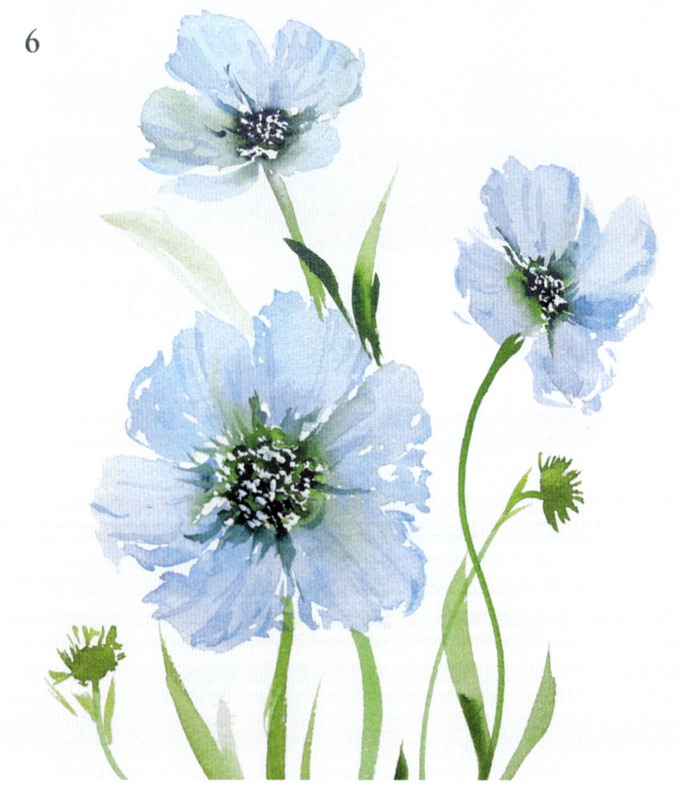

STORMY VIOLET STOCK

Stock flowers are known for their tall, elegant spikes with clusters of delicate blooms. Larger flowers sit at the base while the smaller ones taper toward the top. For this project, we'll use a rich violet to make the petals pop, but feel free to play around with blush pinks and pastel yellows too.

In this lesson, you'll learn how to layer the petals to create depth without overthinking each stroke. We'll explore how to vary the tones, blending bold, saturated petals with loose, almost watery washes. We'll embrace unexpected blooms and blends that will add charm to your painting!

Brushes

- Size 6 round brush
- Size 8 round brush

Floral Strokes

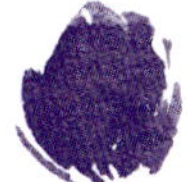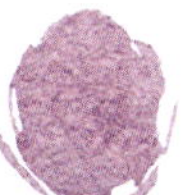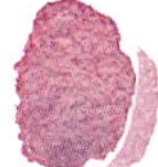

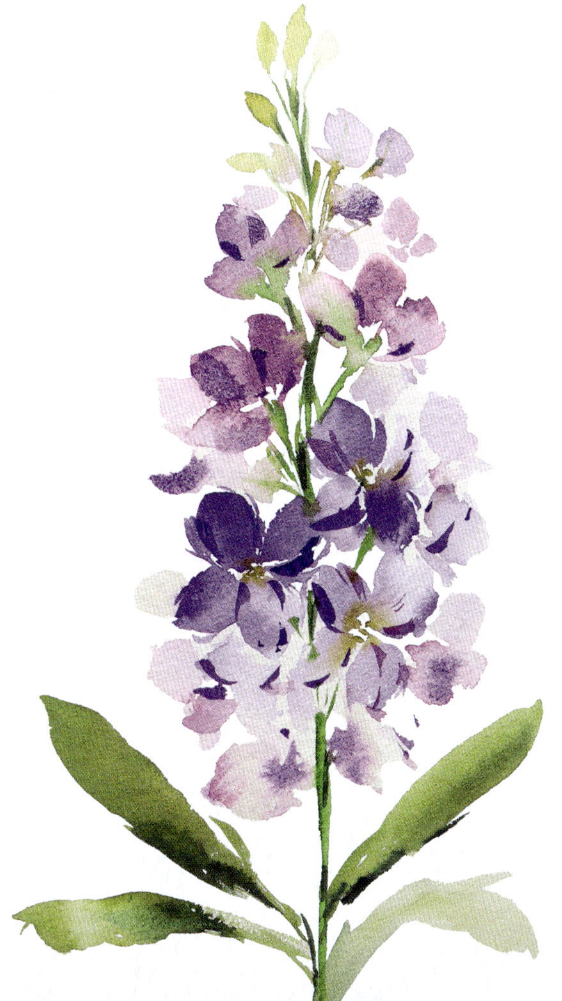

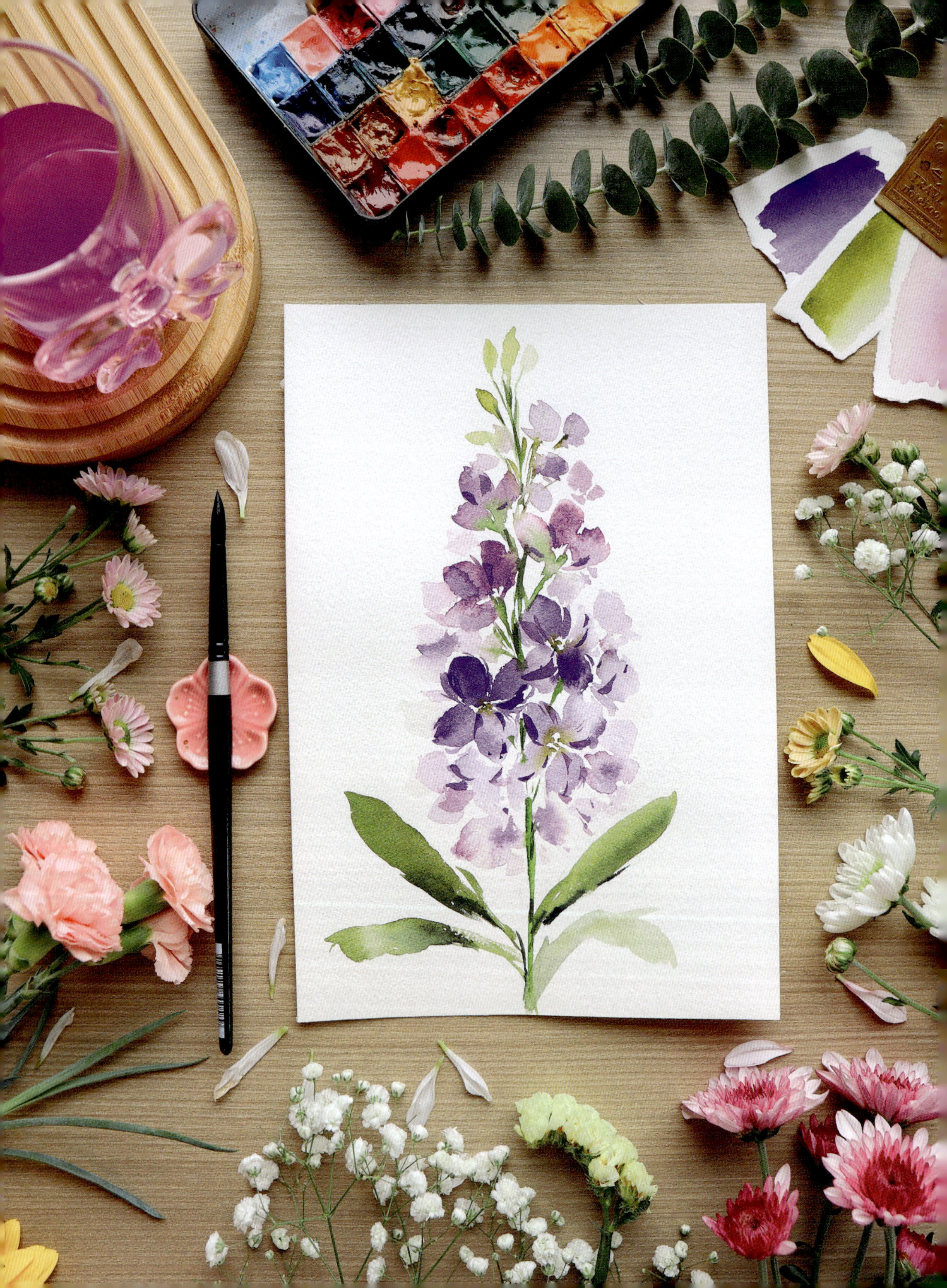

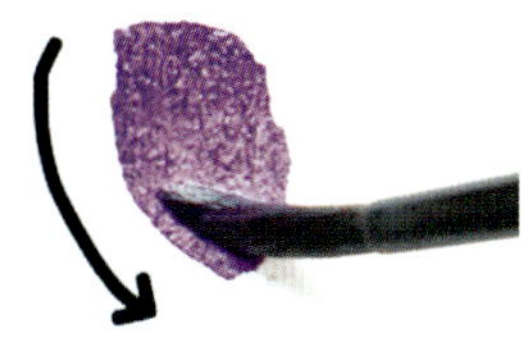

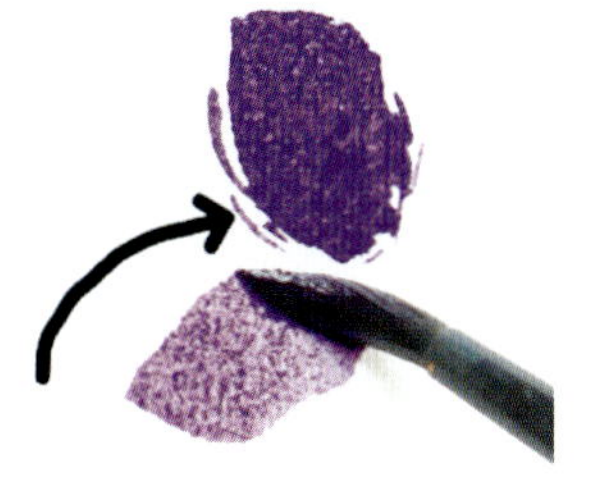

1. Paint the First Cluster of Flowers

Let's start with a simple five-petal flower. Load your size 6 round brush with a medium-consistency Permanent Violet. Press and slowly drag your brush toward the center of the flower to create rounded petals. Add a few thin, curvy strokes around some petals for some flair. Paint a few more petals to form this small flower. Allow some petals to overlap slightly and leave white gaps between others.

Add at least two more flowers. Feel free to add more if you like. Vary the values, using a lighter wash for some petals to create contrast. Place very light petals near saturated ones to keep the cluster visually interesting.

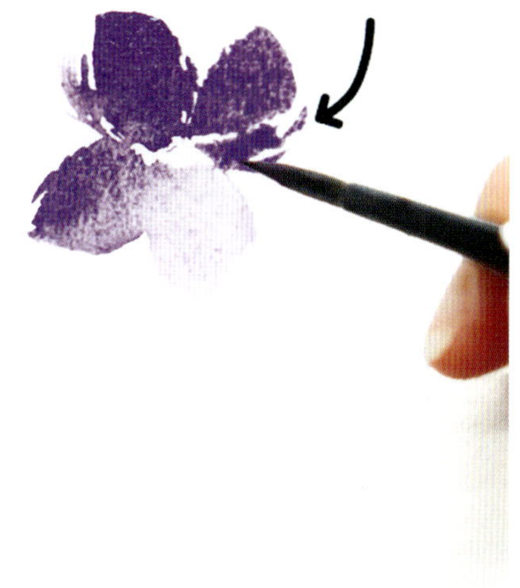

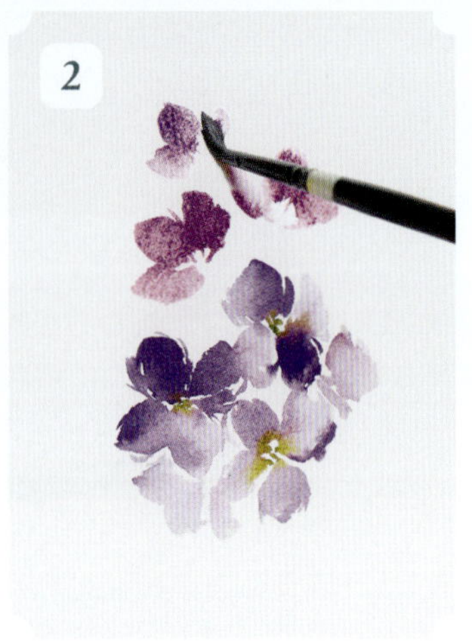

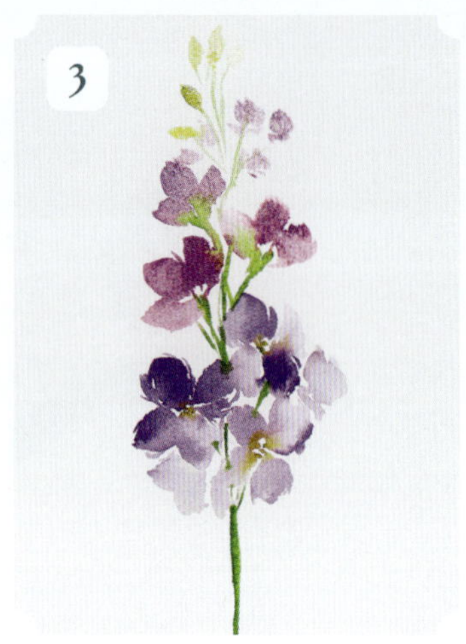

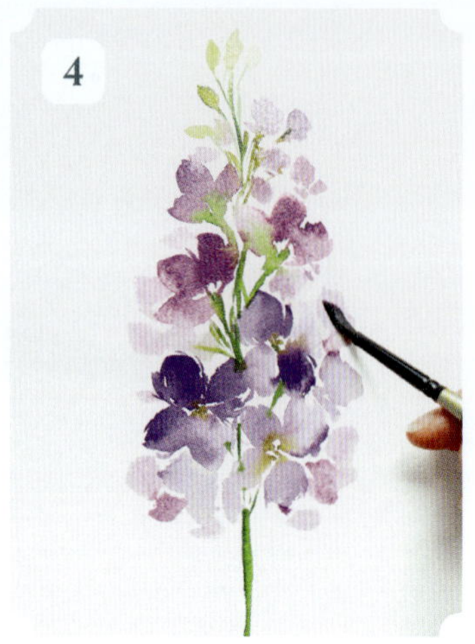

2. Build Up the Flower Spike

While the flowers are damp, drop a little bit of Greenish Yellow in the center. Use a brush that isn't too wet to keep the green from spreading too far.

Continue painting clusters above the first group to form the spike. Paint three round petals side by side to suggest flowers at different angles. Include some petals with a very watery wash too, for a looser look. We want to mix the bold and soft tones.

TIP: For variation, switch to Mineral Violet or mix a hint of Permanent Rose into your violet.

3. Add Stem and Buds

While the flowers are still damp, paint a slender stem running through the center using Sap Green. Add smaller stems branching out to connect the blooms. Keep the lines slightly uneven and curved to add movement.

At the top, paint small oval-shaped buds using a mix of medium-consistency Greenish Yellow. For variety, add a few tiny buds with a soft wash of Mineral Violet.

4. Add Volume

To make this flower look lush, fill in the white gaps with additional loose petals. Load your size 6 round brush with a very light consistency of Mineral Violet. Press lightly and wiggle your brush to create soft oval shapes. Scatter these randomly to give the impression of more blooms in the background.

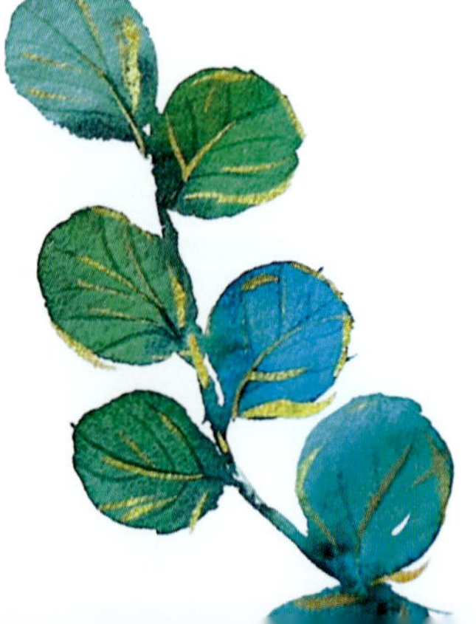

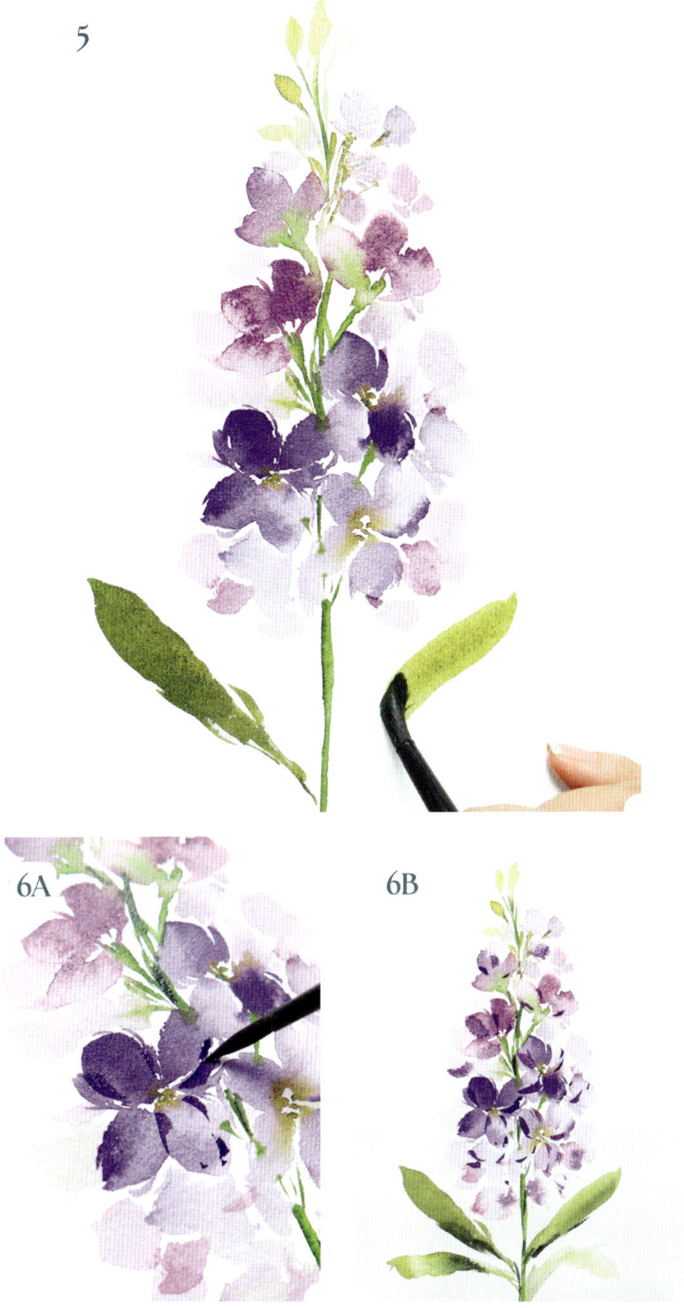

5. Add Leaves

For the leaves, mix two parts Sap Green and one part Burnt Umber into a medium consistency. With a size 8 round brush, load a juicy amount of paint. Start at the tip of the leaf, press down, drag the brush, and lift toward the stem. Vary the greens. You may drop in Indigo on the bottom part of the leaves to add contrast.

6. Finishing Touches

For the final touch, use a thicker mix of Permanent Violet to add subtle details. Paint thin C strokes and dots in between the petals. Add these accents lightly to avoid overcrowding the petals.

If some paint lands on wet petals, that's okay! Embrace the bleed as it often creates the most beautiful organic effect! If you prefer crisp and sharp details, use a hairdryer to dry the first layer quickly before adding your second layer.

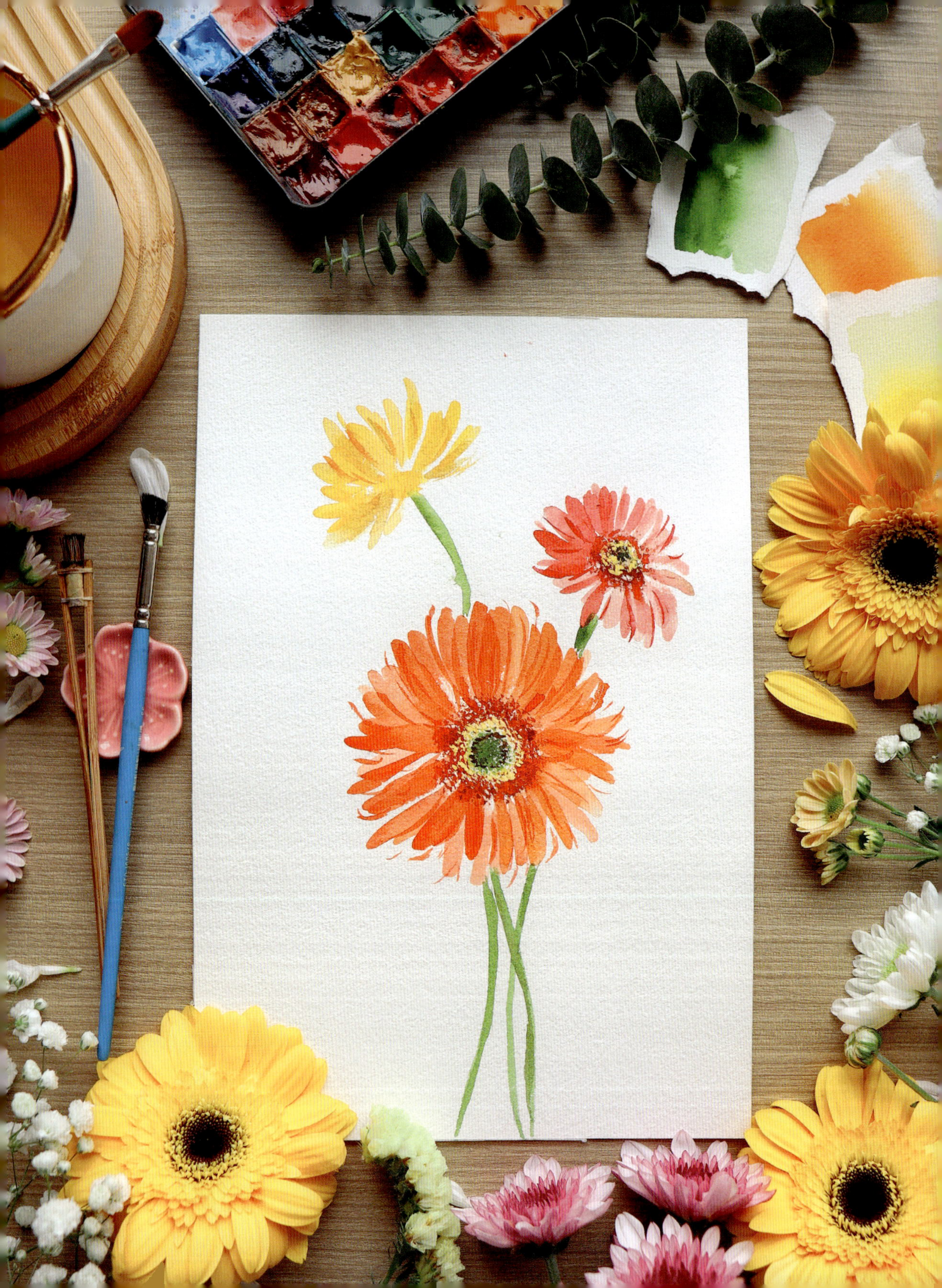

SUNSET ORANGE GERBERA

Gerbera daisies are cheerful flowers with bold, elongated petals radiating from a round center. Their petals can be slightly pointed or have rounded tips.

For this project, we will be using a small filbert brush to achieve the rounded tip petals. If you don't have this specific type of brush, don't worry—a small round brush will work perfectly fine for painting tiny dots in the flower's center, or you can even use an old toothbrush.

In this lesson, you will learn how to layer petals to build volume and add subtle details that make your Gerbera come alive on paper!

Colors

- ■ Sap Green
- ■ Permanent Yellow Light
- ■ Vermilion
- ■ Burnt Sienna
- ■ Permanent Rose

Brushes

- ¼-inch (6-mm) deerfoot brush
- ⅜-inch (1-cm) filbert brush
- Size 2 round brush

Other Materials

- Pencil
- White gouache, optional

Floral Strokes

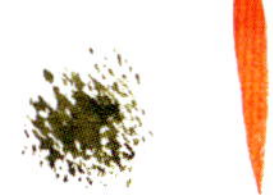
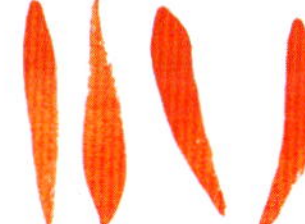

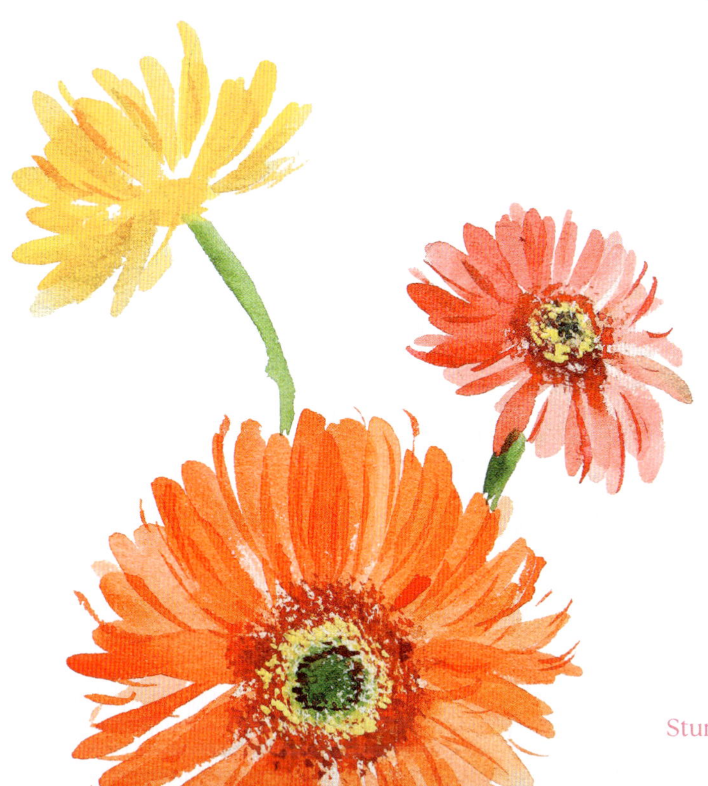

1. Paint the Center

Load your deerfoot brush with a medium-consistency Sap Green. Dab the excess paint on a tissue paper. Stipple the brush on the paper to form a textured circle. Rinse your brush and switch to a Permanent Yellow Light color. Stipple around the green center to create a yellow ring, allowing some yellow and green dots to blend naturally.

Note: No deerfoot brush? Use a small round bush and dab the tip to create tiny dots for a similar effect, or use an old toothbrush to stipple.

2. Add the First Layer of Petals

Prepare two puddles of Vermilion on your palette—one light and one medium consistency. Using a ³⁄₈-inch (1-cm) filbert brush, paint elongated petals starting from the tip and pulling toward the center. Alternate between the flat side of the brush for broad strokes and the edge for thinner ones. Let your brush sway slightly to create movement in your strokes. Leave some spaces in between your petals. We will fill them in during the next step.

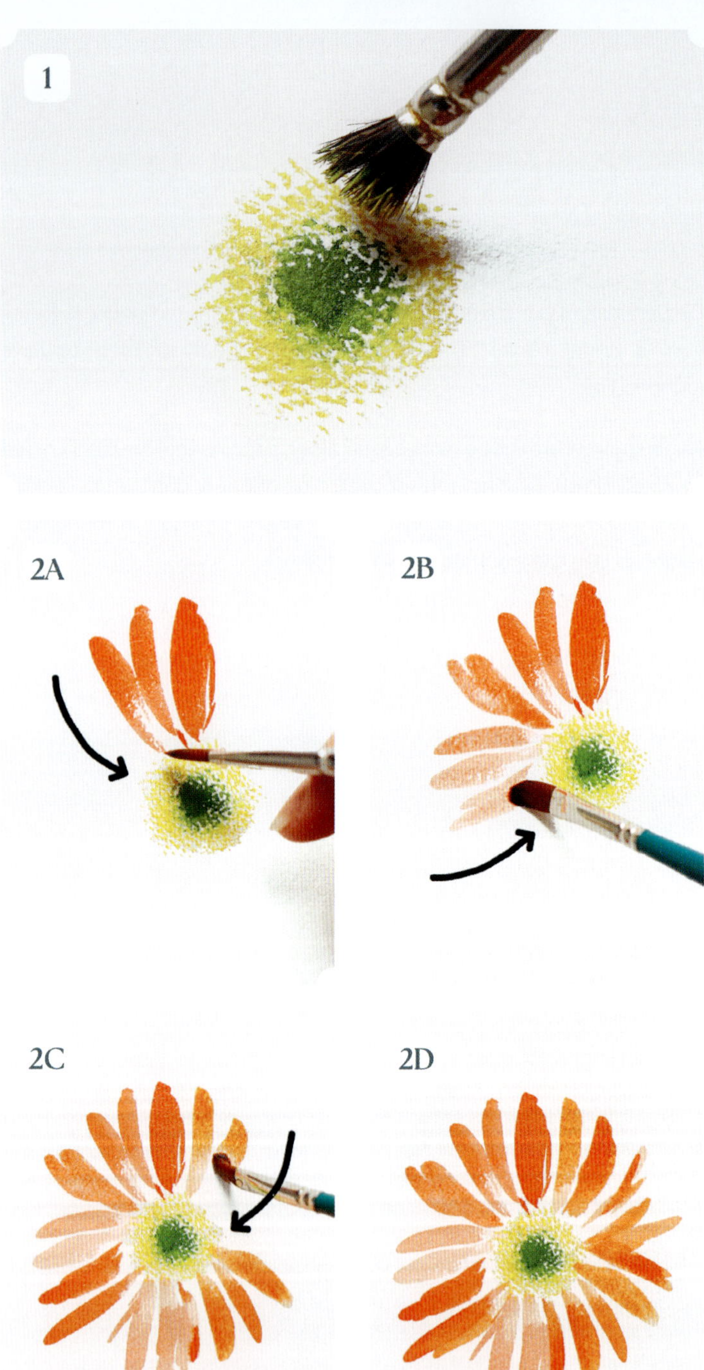

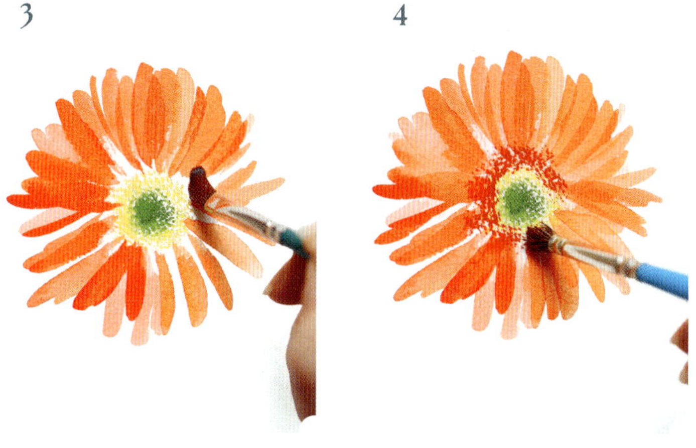

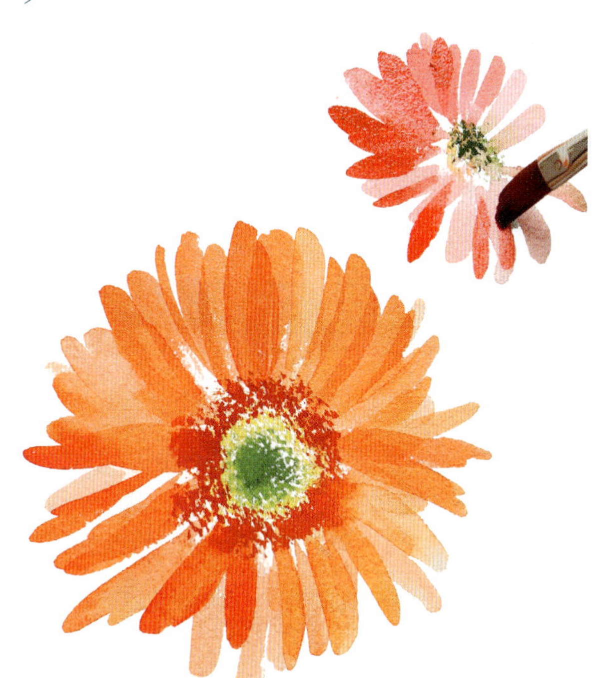

3. Add a Second Layer of Petals

When the first layer is dry, paint additional petals in the gaps to make it look fuller and layered. Play around with values—some strokes will have a light consistency of Vermilion, and some a more saturated mix. Begin at the tip, press, drag, and lift your filbert brush. Allow some petals to be shorter than the others to add variety.

4. Add More Contrast

Mix a thick consistency of equal parts of Burnt Sienna and Vermilion. Load your deerfoot brush with this mixture. Make sure your brush isn't too wet so you can see the texture on the paper. Stipple the brush around the yellow ring to add depth and texture to the flower's center.

5. Paint a Side-Facing Flower

Using a pencil, lightly sketch an oval as a guide. Stipple the center with Sap Green using a deerfoot brush. For the petals, alternate strokes of light- and medium-consistency Permanent Rose using a filbert brush. Paint elongated strokes from the tip toward the center. Once dry, add a second layer of petals and stipple a more pigmented Permanent Rose around the green center.

6. Add the Back-Facing Flower and Stems

To add variety, let's paint a flower facing toward the back, which means that we will not see the center of the flower. Feel free to use any color. I used a medium consistency of Permanent Yellow Light that works well with the other flower colors. Paint elongated strokes in a semicircle, varying the petal lengths. Once dry, add another layer to give it volume.

For the stems, mix a medium-consistency Sap Green. Paint slender stems extending downward.

7. Add Petal Details

With a size 2 round brush, mix a thick consistency of Vermilion to paint thin lines radiating along the petals of the orange flowers. Play with a few shorter strokes outside the petals for a whimsical touch.

For the other flowers, use a darker value of their base color for the details.

To deepen the centers, dab your deerfoot brush around the yellow ring using equal parts Burnt Sienna and Vermilion.

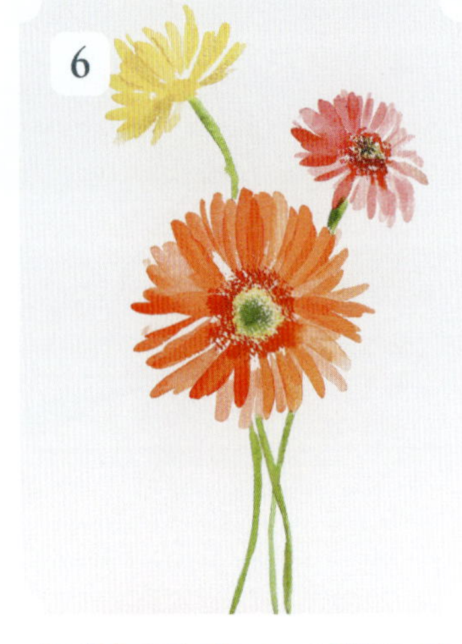

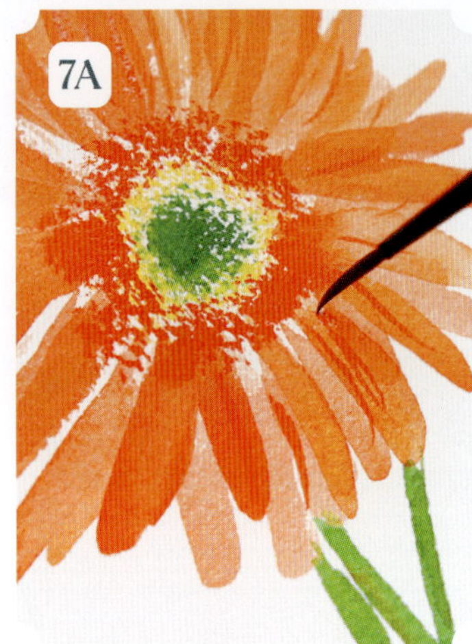

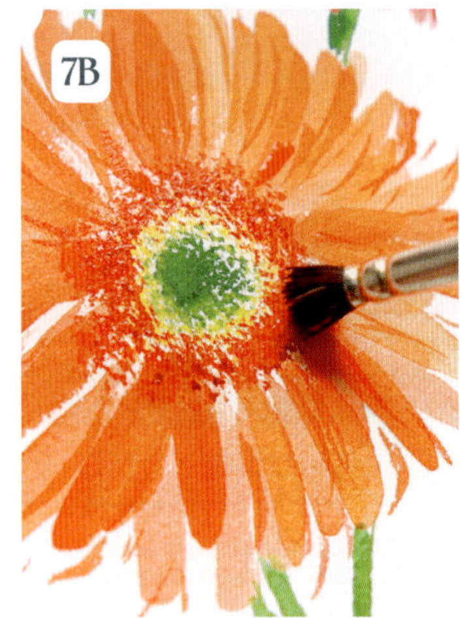

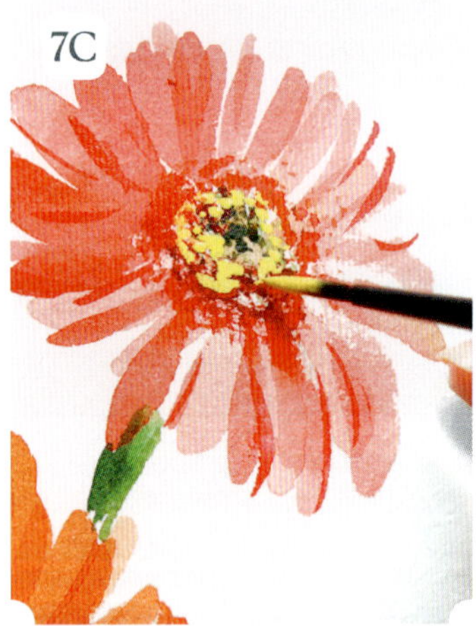

Optionally, mix equal parts white gouache and Permanent Yellow Light. With a size 2 round brush, lightly dot the mixture in the flower's center for a final highlight.

You did it! Your Gerbera looks lovely.

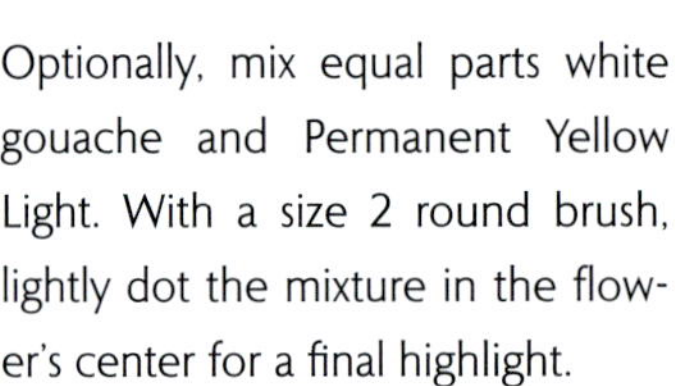

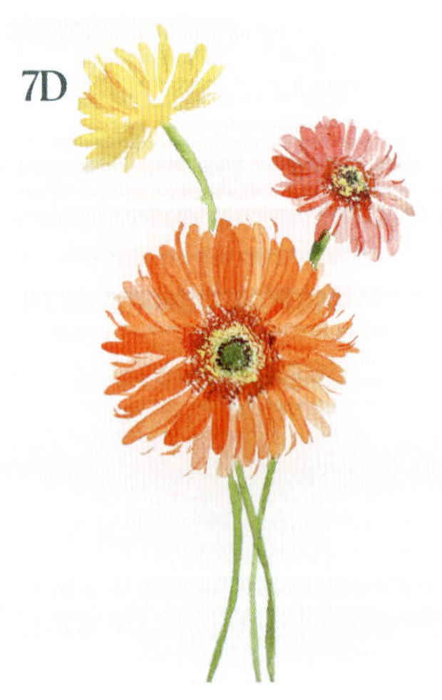

BLUSH SWEET PEA

Sweet peas are such charming flowers! They have soft, ruffled petals that look like delicate triangles. In this lesson, we will paint them in a loose and effortless style. We'll apply the wet-on-wet technique for soft blends.

The best part? These flowers don't need perfect shapes. Just let your brush dance and wiggle to create airy petals. Lastly, we'll add playful splatter in the background for a lively touch.

Colors

- Shell Pink
- Permanent Rose
- Permanent Yellow Light
- Permanent Violet
- Sap Green
- Lilac
- Indigo

Brushes

- Size 8 round brush
- Size 4 round brush
- Size 2 round brush

Other Materials

- Pencil

Floral Strokes

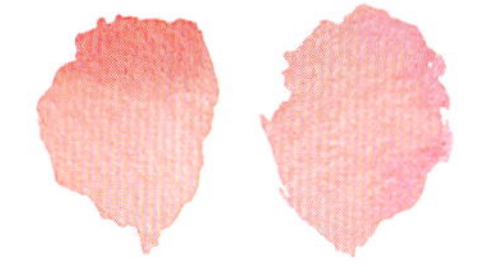

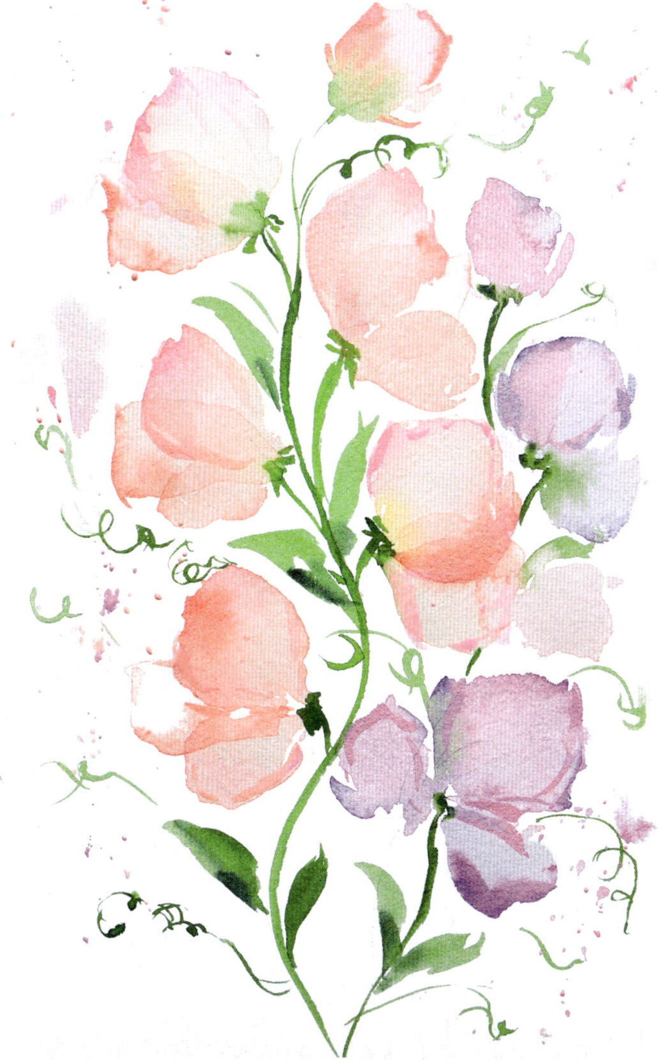

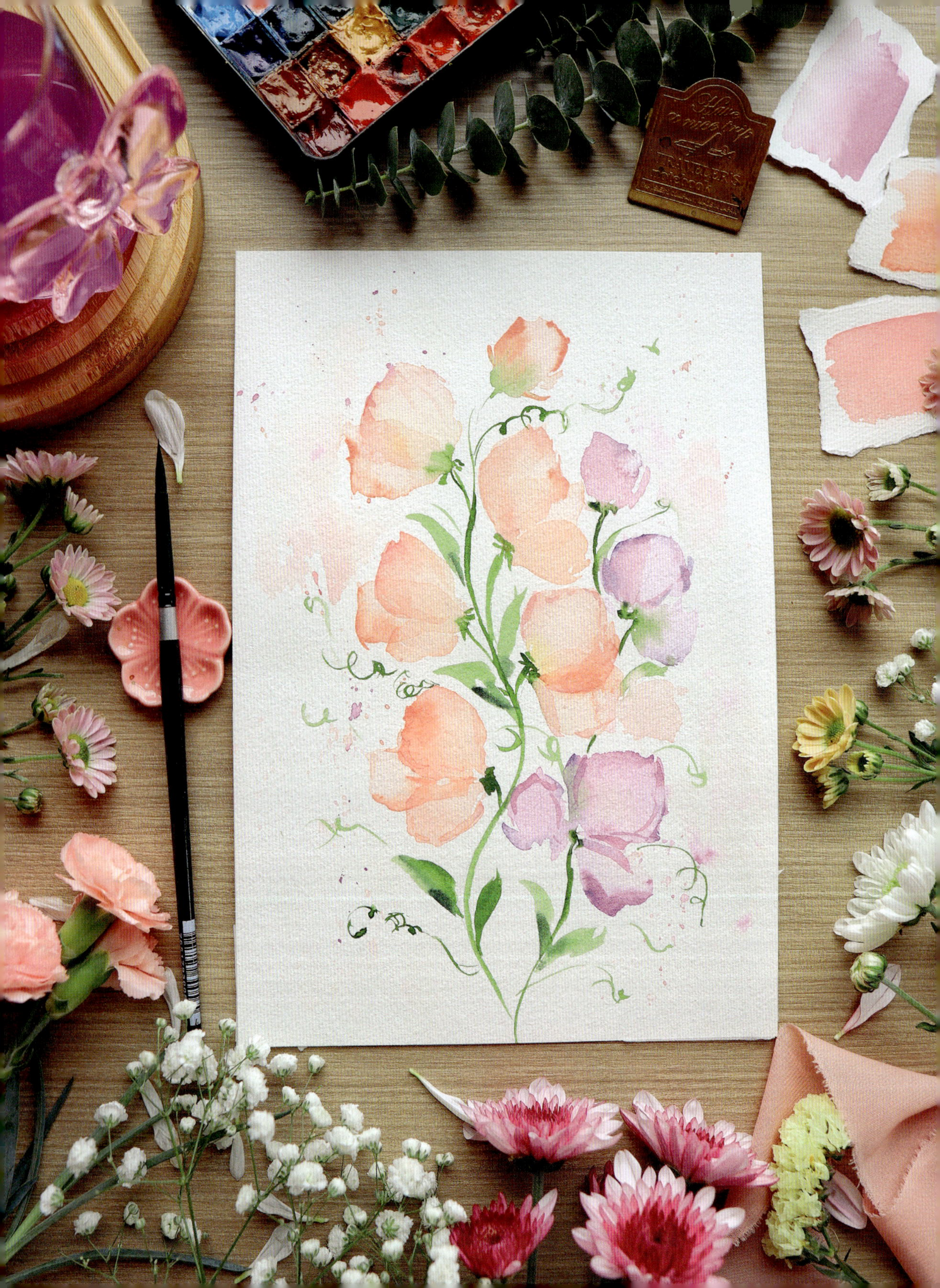
Have
a nice trip
TRAVELER'S
notebook

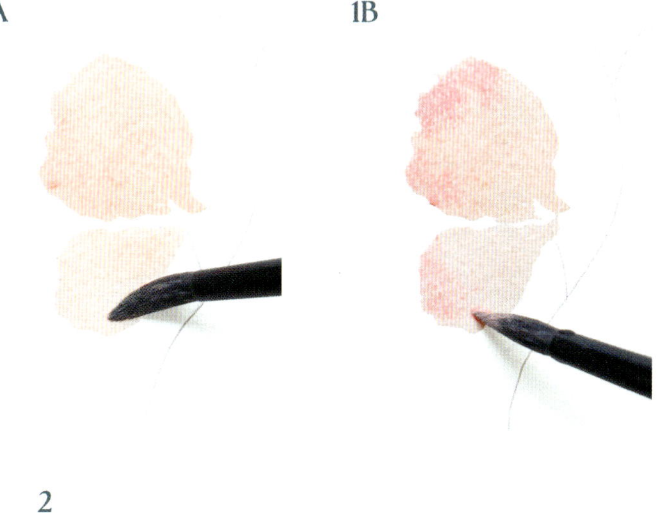

1. Paint the First Petal Shapes

Using a pencil, lightly sketch an S-shaped stem as a guide. We will add the flowers diagonally across each other along this line. Load your size 8 round brush with a very light and watery consistency of Shell Pink. Paint the first petal, imagining it as a soft, ruffled triangle. Press your brush onto the paper and wiggle it with the tip facing away from you to create fluttery edges, then pull it inward to form a pointy base.

Add a second petal below or beside the first, allowing the edges to remain irregular for a natural look.

Mix a little Permanent Rose into the Shell Pink for a more pigmented pink, and drop it along the petal edges for more depth.

2. Build the Flower Cluster

Continue adding more petals along the lightly sketched stem. Vary the angles and sizes of the petals to mimic how sweet peas naturally bloom. You may add a touch of Permanent Yellow Light or Permanent Violet for a subtle color shift. Let some petals overlap slightly and leave white gaps for an airy effect.

> **TIP:** Sweet pea petals have a fluttery look, so keep your brushstrokes gentle and irregular.

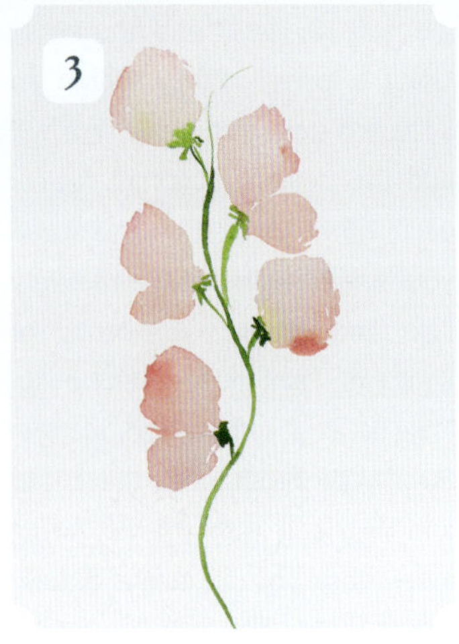

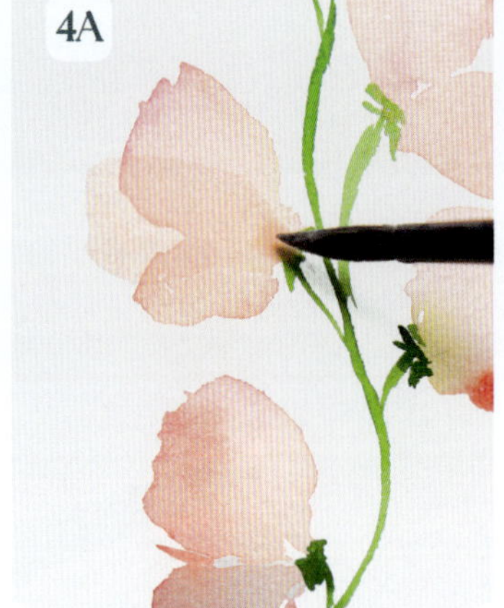

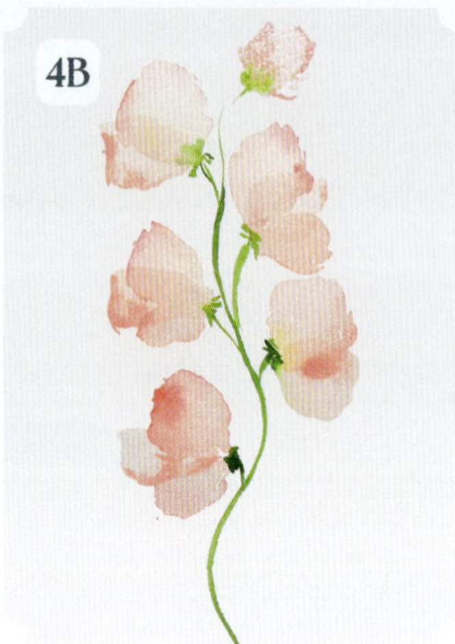

3. Add the Stem and Sepals

Switch to a size **4** round brush and load it with a medium-consistency Sap Green. At the base of each flower, paint a few short strokes to create sepals. Then, connect the flowers with a curved, flowing stem.

4. Layer the Petals

Use a hairdryer to quickly dry the first layer, allowing you to add a second layer to make the flowers look fuller.

Mix a light consistency of Shell Pink, then load your size **8** round brush with juicy paint. Add new petal shapes next to or in between the existing petals. While the paint is still damp, drop in a more pigmented pink toward the edges for more definition. Feel free to add some smaller buds at this point to make your composition more balanced.

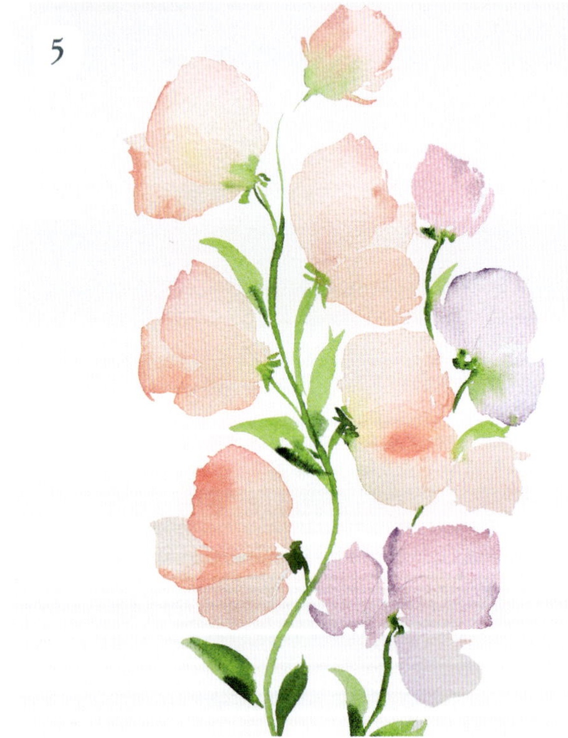

5. Add Violet Blooms

Add more flowers along new stems for color variation. Mix a light consistency of Lilac for the base petals, then drop in a light consistency of Permanent Violet. Let the colors bleed into each other. Connect them with a Sap Green stem.

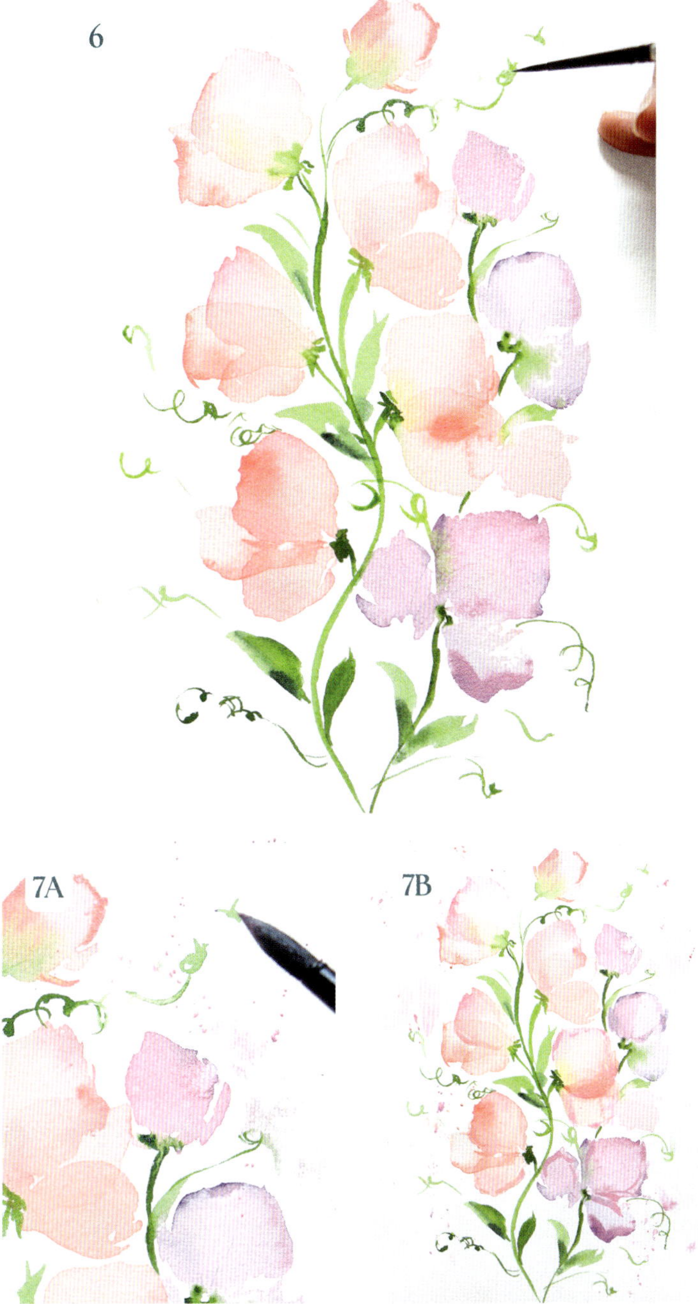

6. Add Leaves and Tendrils

Sweet peas have slender leaves and curling tendrils. With your size 4 round brush, paint the leaves using a medium-consistency Sap Green. While it's damp, drop in a thick consistency of Indigo to add contrast.

For tendrils, switch to a size 2 round brush for more precise details. Use the very tip to create thin, curling strokes, alternating between light and medium consistency of Sap Green. Let some of the lines appear broken to keep the painting loose and natural.

7. Final Touches

Finish your painting with fun splatters. Lightly wet a few areas of the background (avoiding the flowers) with clean water. Load your size 8 round brush with medium-consistency Shell Pink and Lilac, then flick it to create splatters. Those landing on wet areas will softly blur, while those on dry paper will look like small dots. Play around with other colors too! Step back and admire those beautiful splatters.

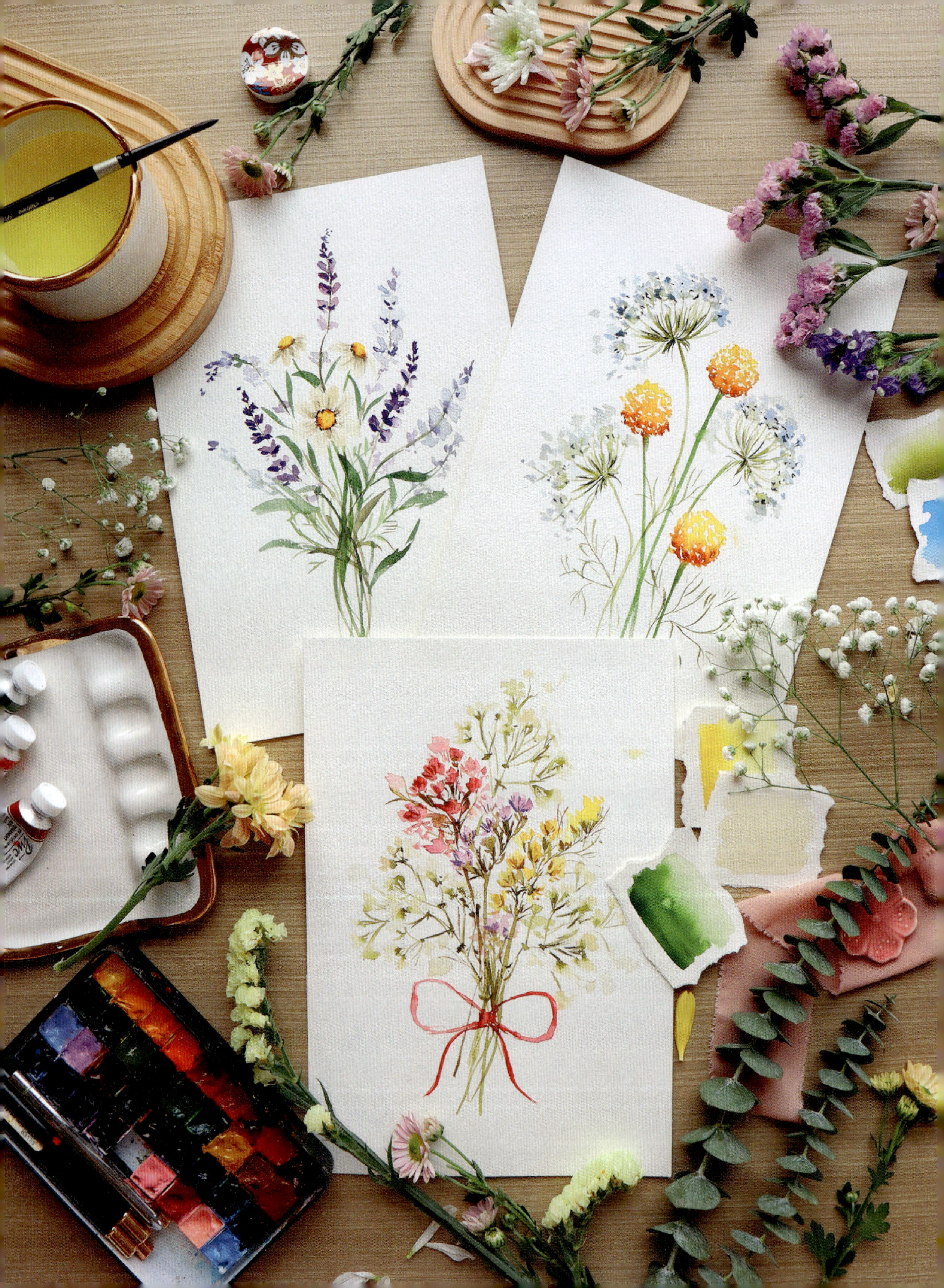

Dainty PAIRINGS

Filler flowers may be small, but they play a big role in bringing balance to a floral arrangement. They fill in the gaps, add texture, and make the focal flowers stand out.

Now that you've painted some statement florals, I encourage you to build your watercolor intuition and play with unique strokes. If you want a refresher on different types of floral brushstrokes, you can always turn to page 22, but I know you've got this! Be brave and experiment to find your own style.

In this chapter, we will paint dainty pairings of floral fillers such as Chamomile and Lavender (page 91), Buttercup and Forget-Me-Not (page 95), and Queen Anne's Lace and Craspedia (page 101).

These delicate combinations are easy to paint and versatile too! They look lovely on their own or can be seamlessly tucked into wreaths, bouquets, and other compositions.

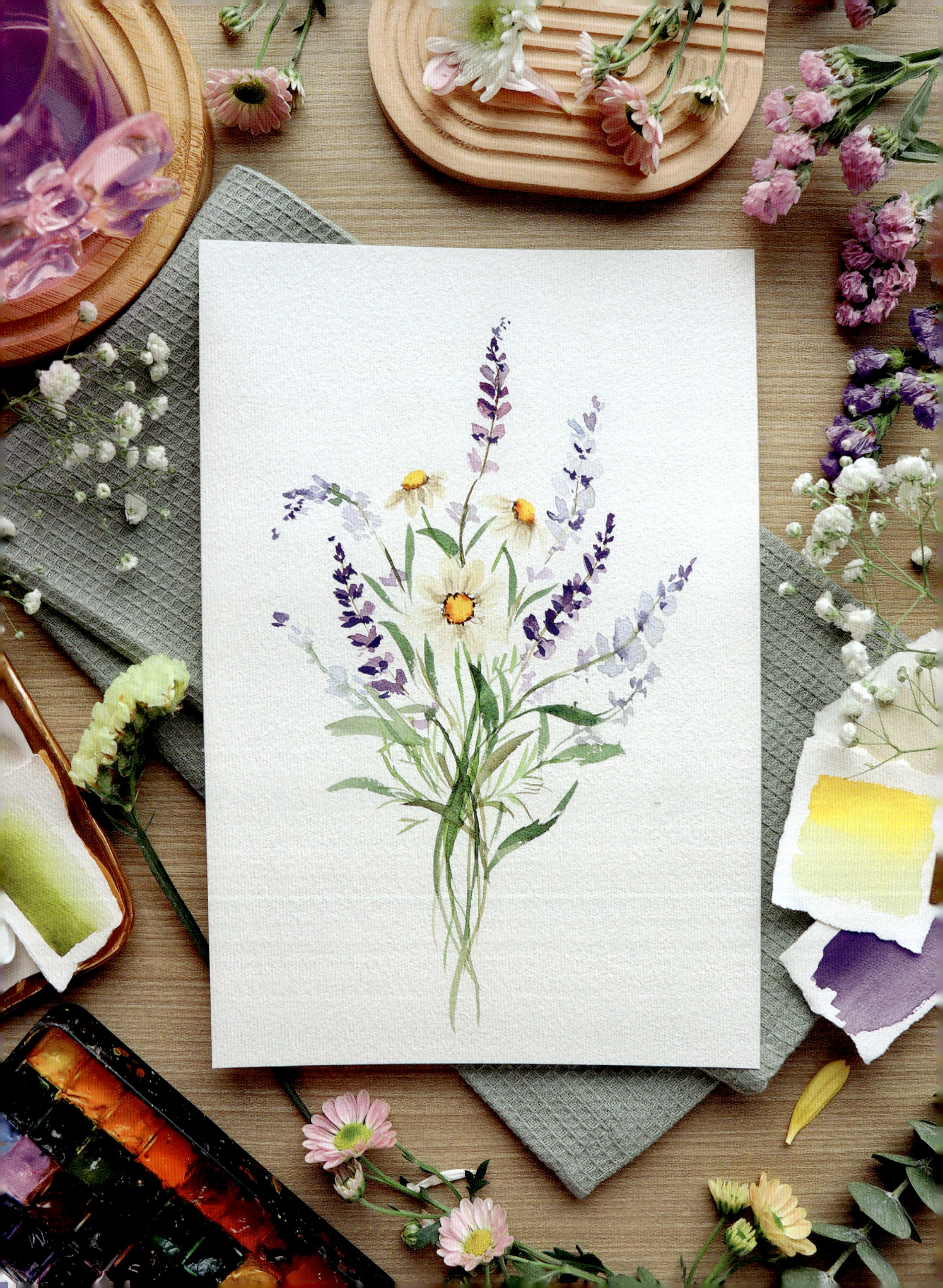

CHAMOMILE AND LAVENDER

Chamomile and lavender are such a lovely pair to paint. The combination feels like a bouquet picked straight from the garden!

Chamomile's warm white petals and sunny yellow centers bring brightness and freshness to a composition, while the lavender adds contrast with its graceful stems and tiny V-shaped purple clusters.

Together, they create a harmonious mix of round and elongated forms.

Colors

- Permanent Yellow Light
- Burnt Sienna
- Buff Titanium
- Sepia
- Sap Green
- Permanent Violet
- Mineral Violet, optional
- Ultramarine Blue
- Lavender
- Burnt Umber
- Indigo

Brushes

- Size 4 round brush
- Size 2 round brush

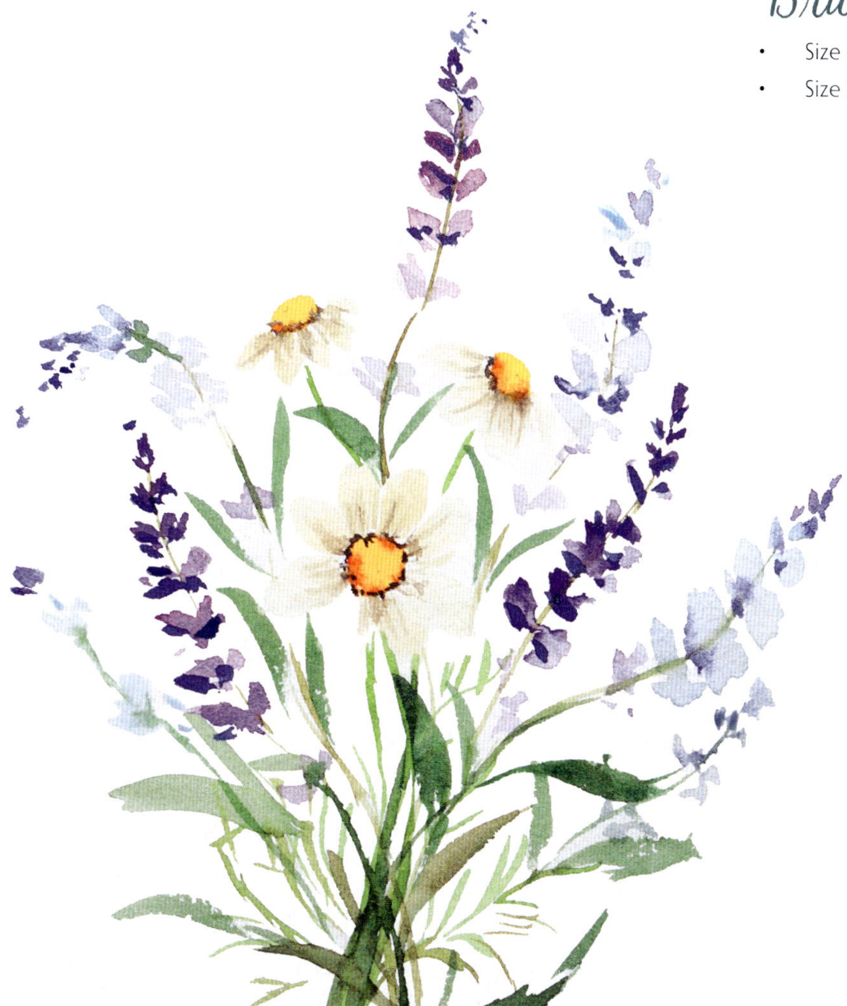

1. Paint the Chamomile Center

Mix a medium-consistency Permanent Yellow Light and load your size 4 round brush.

Since the flowers are small, using a smaller brush will give you more control. Paint the three centers: one round for a front-facing chamomile and two oval for side-facing ones. You can add more flowers if you like.

While the centers are still damp, load your brush with a medium-consistency Burnt Sienna. Dab off the excess paint on a tissue paper, then gently dab the tip of the brush around the edges of the centers to create depth. Make sure your brush isn't too wet to avoid overblending. Let the centers dry.

2. Paint the Chamomile Petals

Mix a light consistency of Buff Titanium. Using the same brush, paint small, rounded petals around the circle center. For the oval centers, add petals only along the lower half to show that they are side facing. Let them dry.

To add contrast, load your size 2 round brush with a thick consistency of Sepia. Lightly add a ring of dots around the center. Rinse your brush and blot on a tissue paper. Softly drag small strokes from the center outward.

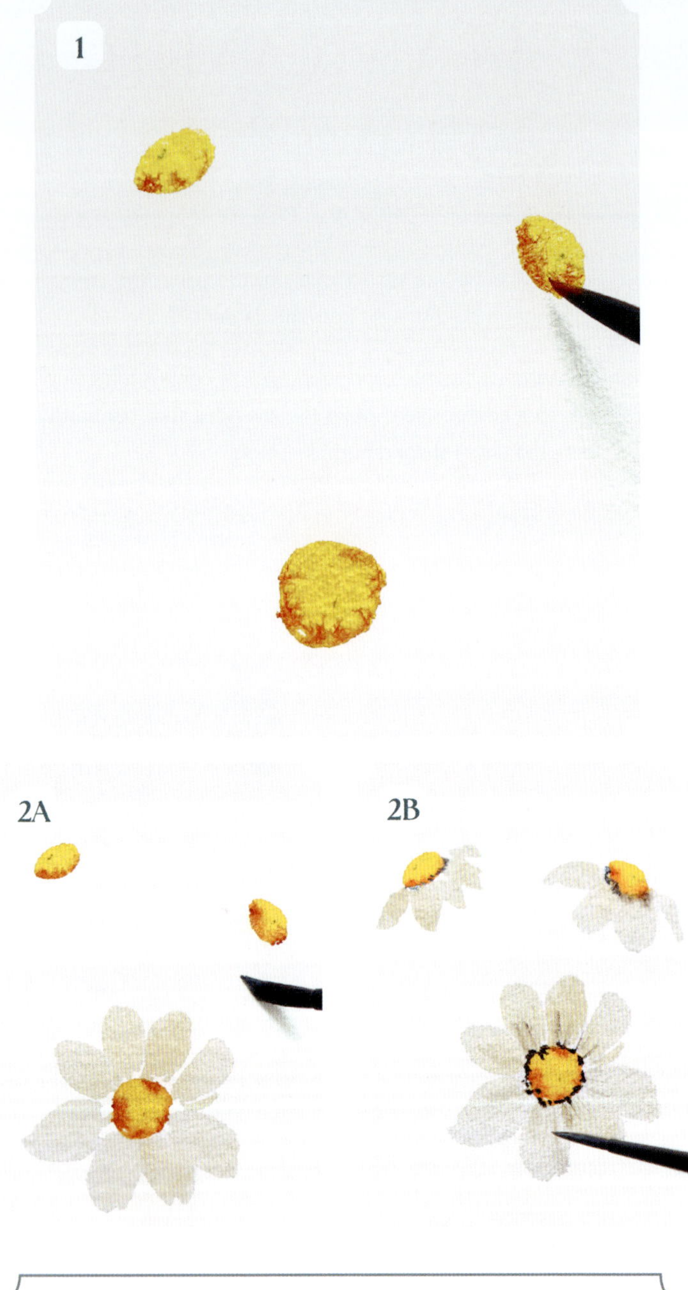

TIP: For a cooler white petal, play around with mix of Burnt Umber and Ultramarine Blue and add lots of water.

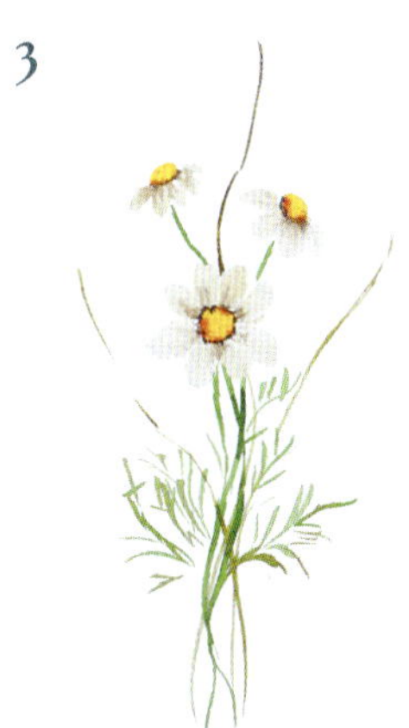

3

4A

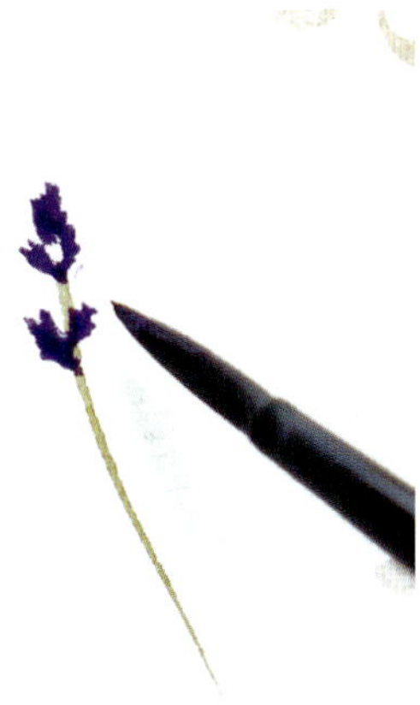

4B

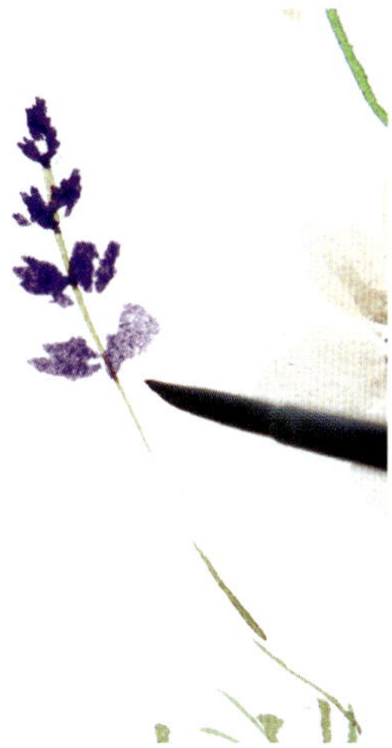

4C

3. Paint the Stems and Leaves

Using medium-consistency Sap Green, paint thin, curving stems that connect to each flower.

Keep the leaves light and feathery. Drag the brush tip to create thin, wavy strokes, then flick out tiny, curved strokes on both sides. Drop in a touch of darker green at the base of some leaves while still damp.

Prepare the lavender stalks by mixing a medium consistency of Sap Green and painting three or more tall stems between the chamomile flowers.

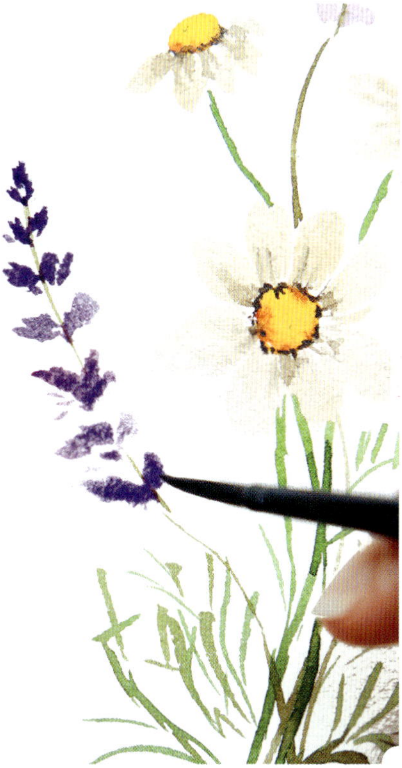

4. Paint the Lavender Flowers

Lavender flowers are made of tiny clustered petals. Using a medium-consistency Permanent Violet, load your size 4 round brush. Start at the tip of the stem that we painted earlier. Lightly dab the tip of the brush to paint the first few petals. Continue downward, adding loose V-shaped clusters along each side of the stem, spacing them irregularly. Let the clusters become slightly bigger as they go further down.

Vary the colors by using lighter or darker values. You may add Mineral Violet or Ultramarine Blue for more variation.

5. Add Volume and Leaves

If the composition feels sparse, fill the gaps with a few more lavender stalks. First, paint thin, curving stems to guide their placement. Using a light-consistency Lavender, dab and slightly wiggle your brush along each side of the stem to create the flower clusters. This way it looks looser.

For the leaves, mix two parts Sap Green and one part Burnt Umber. Paint thin, elongated, and curved strokes. It's fine if they overlap with the chamomile leaves, as this adds depth. While the leaves are damp, drop in a bit of Indigo to some of the leaves to add contrast. Let it dry.

6. Finishing Touches

To give the lavender flowers more depth, let's add another layer. Mix equal parts Permanent Violet and Ultramarine Blue into a thick consistency. Dab this mix at the base of some of the petals to give them more dimension. You can also extend some stems upward with a few extra clusters at the top to create variation in height.

Add additional lavender stalks where needed to balance the painting. And there you have it! You've just finished painting this dainty mini bouquet!

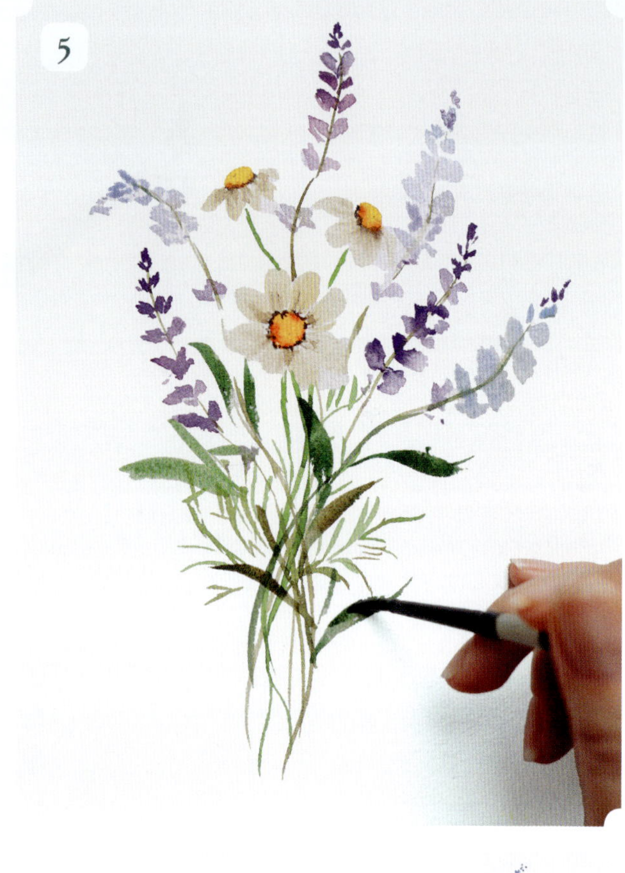

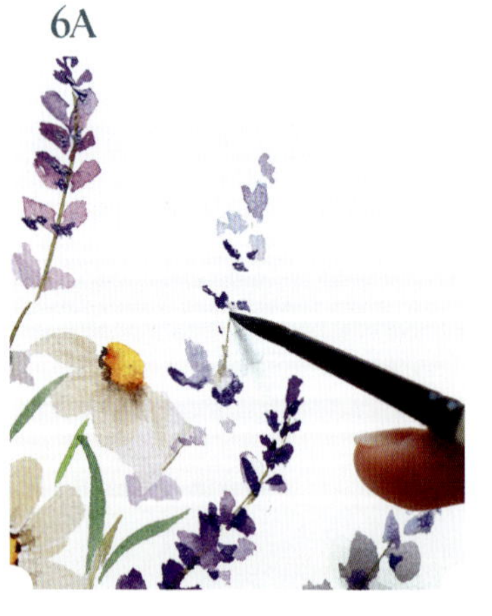

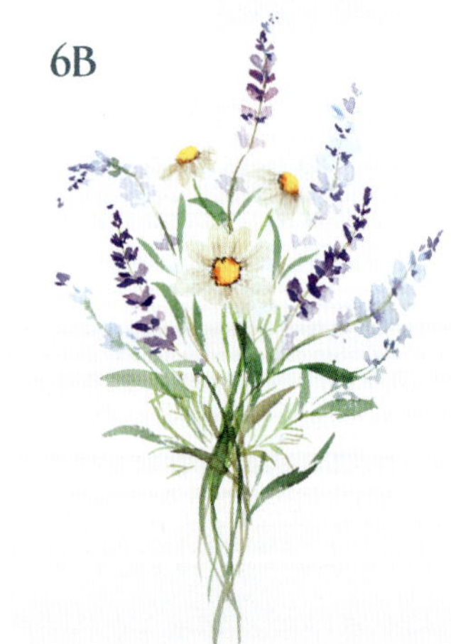

BUTTERCUP AND FORGET-ME-NOT

These two flowers are such a happy and cheerful combination to paint! Buttercups bring a dose of sunshine with their bright yellow petals, while Forget-Me-Nots add a calm and delicate touch with their pretty blue flowers. They create a bouquet that feels fresh and light.

In this lesson, I will guide you through painting the buttercup petals using a filbert brush, which makes shaping the petals so much easier. We'll also have fun playing with different blue tones to paint the tiny blooms of Forget-Me-Nots. It's a joyful project that's sure to brighten your painting session.

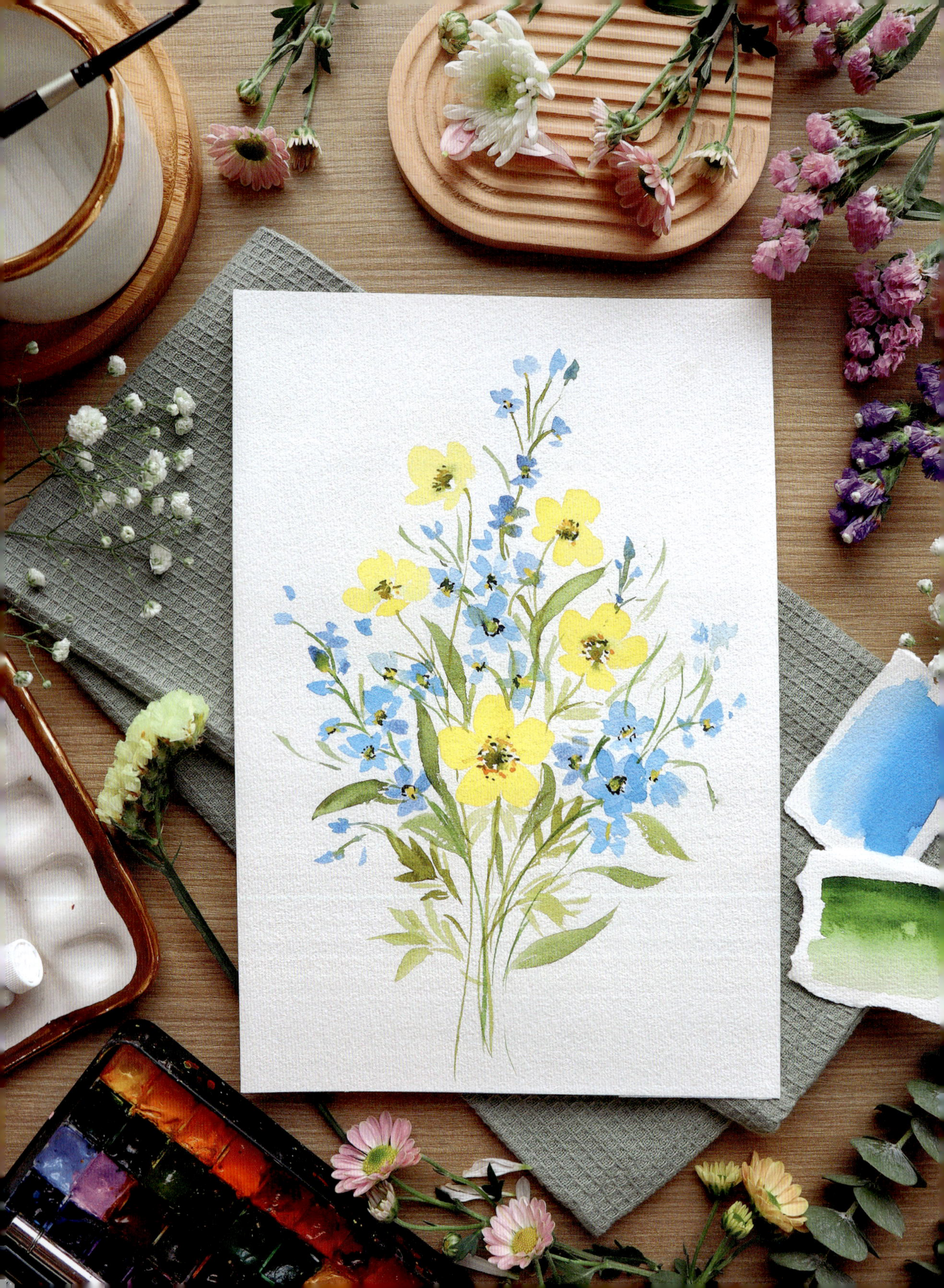

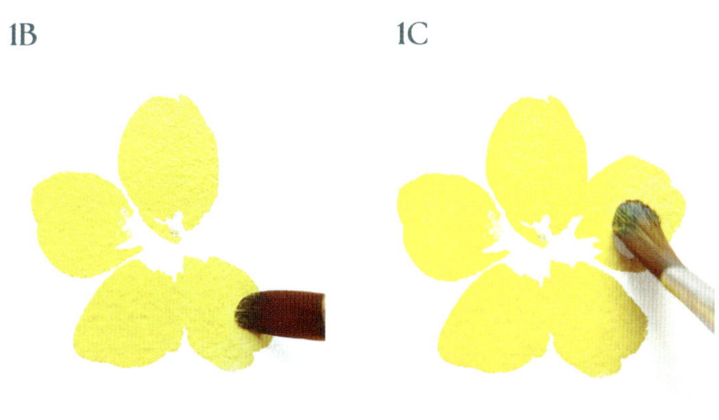

1. Paint the Buttercup Flowers

Load your ³⁄₈-inch (1-cm) filbert brush with a medium-consistency Permanent Yellow Light. For a front-facing flower, paint five rounded petals by pressing your brush on the paper, dragging slightly, and then lifting. Leave the center white.

For side-facing flowers, paint a horizontal stroke at the bottom using the side of the filbert brush, then add three to four petals above it. Vary the directions and petal lengths of the other flowers to create a natural look.

2. Add the Center

With a size 2 round brush, mix a medium-consistency Olive Green and place a small dot in the center of the flowers. It's fine if the color blends slightly into the petals. Once dry, add small dots of medium-consistency Permanent Yellow Deep and Olive Green in the center of the flower to build depth.

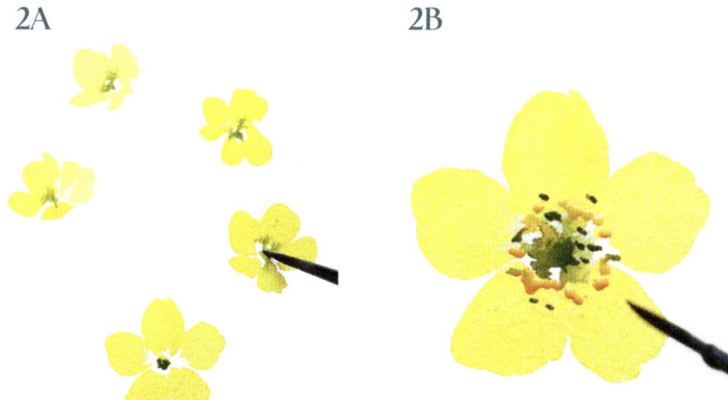

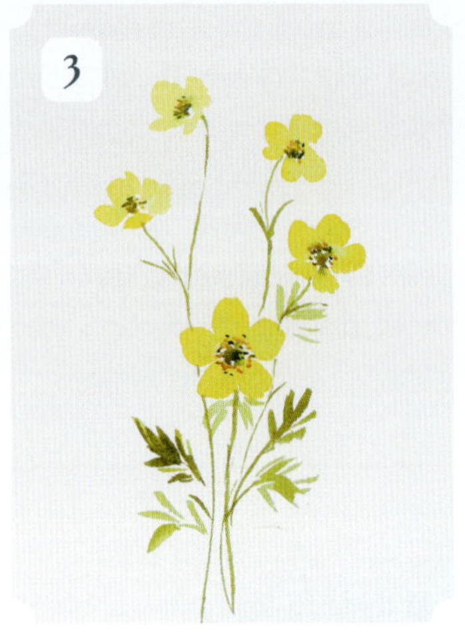

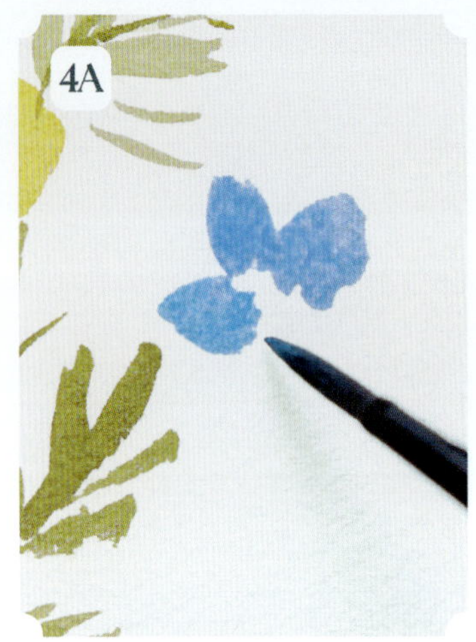

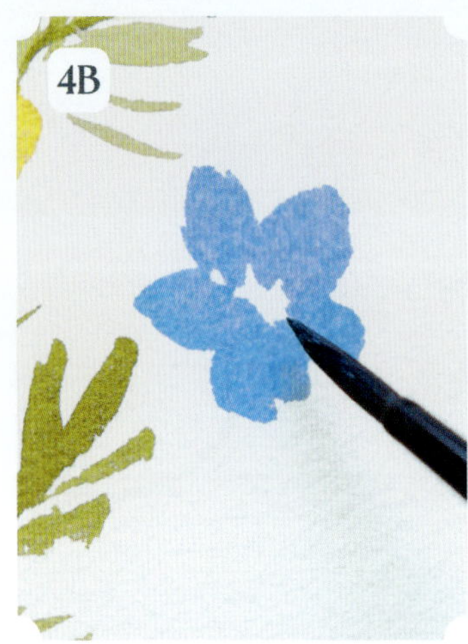

3. Paint the Stems and Leaves

Using a medium-consistency Olive Green, paint thin and curvy stems connecting to the flowers. Switch to a size 4 round brush to paint the leaves. Paint elongated strokes with a slight curve to suggest a more natural movement.

4. Paint the Forget-Me-Not Petals

Prepare light consistencies of the following: Cerulean Blue, Verditer Blue, and Ultramarine Blue.

Using a size 4 round brush, paint five small, rounded petals around an empty center. Keep the petals loose and slightly irregular to avoid a stiff look.

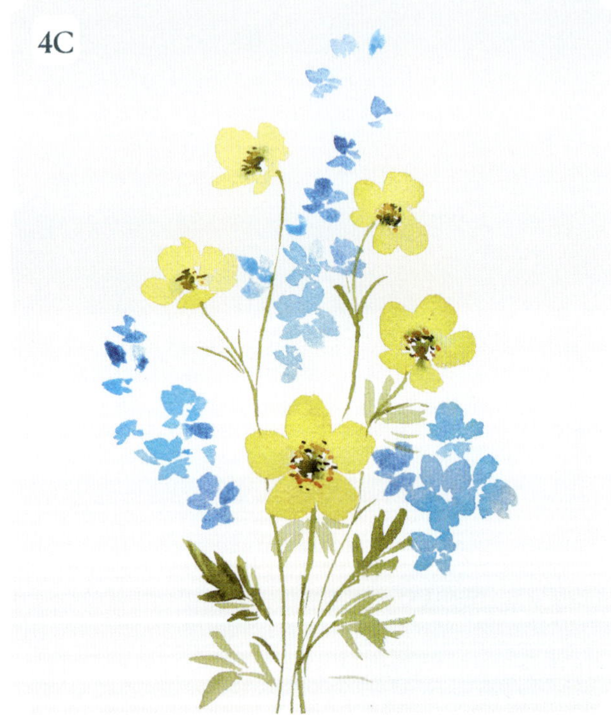

For side-facing flowers, start with a horizontal stroke and add three petals above it. Alternate the blue tones as you paint, leaving some gaps between flowers for an airy feel.

At the top of the stalk, paint smaller petals to suggest young blooms or buds. Arrange the Forget-Me-Nots in three points around the bouquet to create balance.

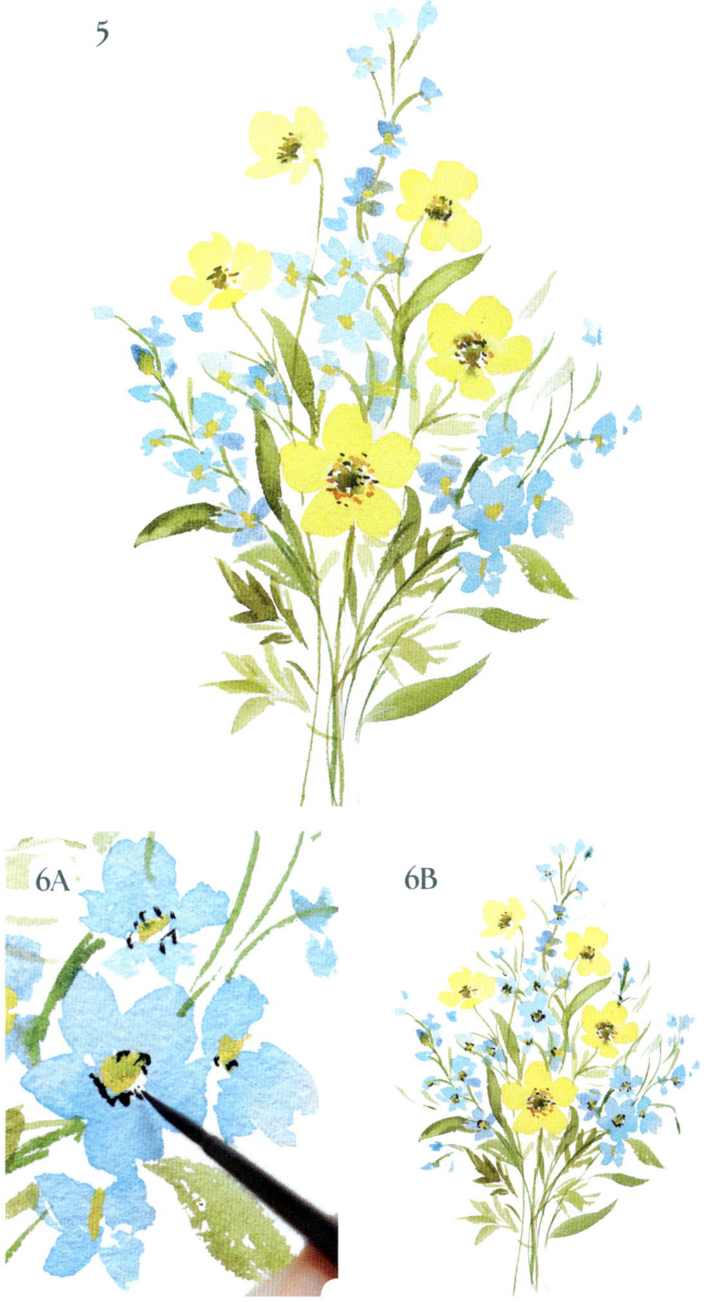

5

6A

6B

5. Paint the Stems and Leaves

Using medium-consistency Sap Green and your size 2 round brush, paint thin stems to connect all the flowers. Add a few extra stems extending into the gaps to keep the composition full.

Once the petals are dry, add small yellow dots to the centers using Permanent Yellow Light.

For the leaves, use the same green. Press your brush on the paper and slowly drag to form elongated leaves. Make them a little curvy to add movement. Overlap some leaves with stems and buttercup foliage.

6. Finishing Touches

For contrast, load a size 2 round brush with thick-consistency Indigo. Paint small dots around the yellow center to make the Forget-Me-Nots stand out. Rinse your brush and grab a light consistency of Cerulean Blue paint. Add a few extra petals at the top of the stalk or in the small white gaps. This softens the transitions and makes the bouquet look lush. Well done! Look at how your beautiful flowers shine!

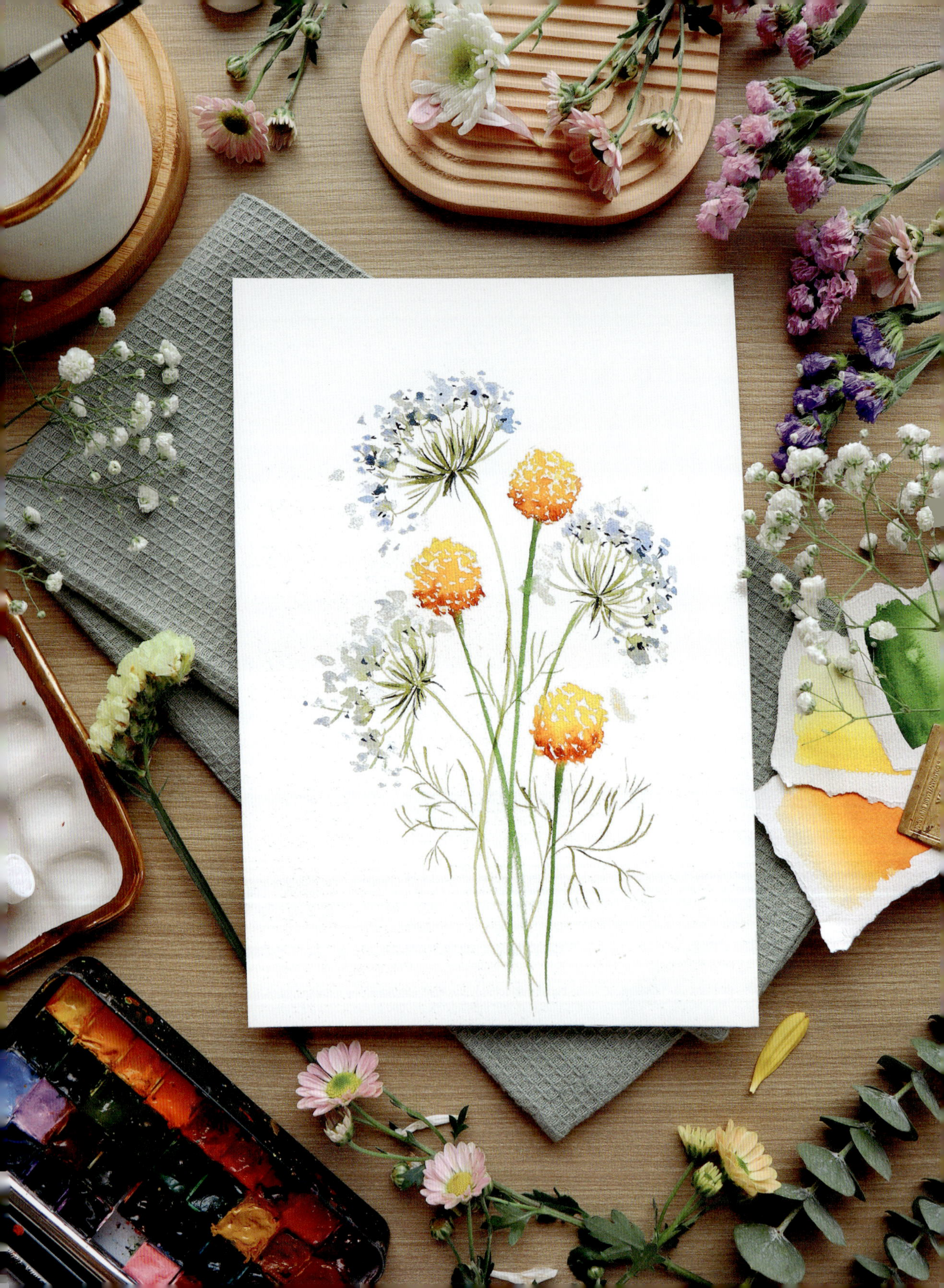

QUEEN ANNE'S LACE AND CRASPEDIA

I've always been charmed by the delicate and feathery beauty of Queen Anne's Lace. It looks so good when paired with the bright and bold Craspedia.

In this tutorial, you'll learn how to use a dotting technique to suggest the Queen Anne's Lace's airy clusters. We'll also use a small round brush to paint thin, wispy stems that keep the composition light. Then, we'll move on to Craspedia, using the same playful dotting technique to build texture while creating a smooth gradient with three colors.

By the end, you'll have a bouquet that is both soft and bursting with sunny charm!

Brushes

- Size 2 round brush
- Size 4 round brush

Other Materials

- Pencil

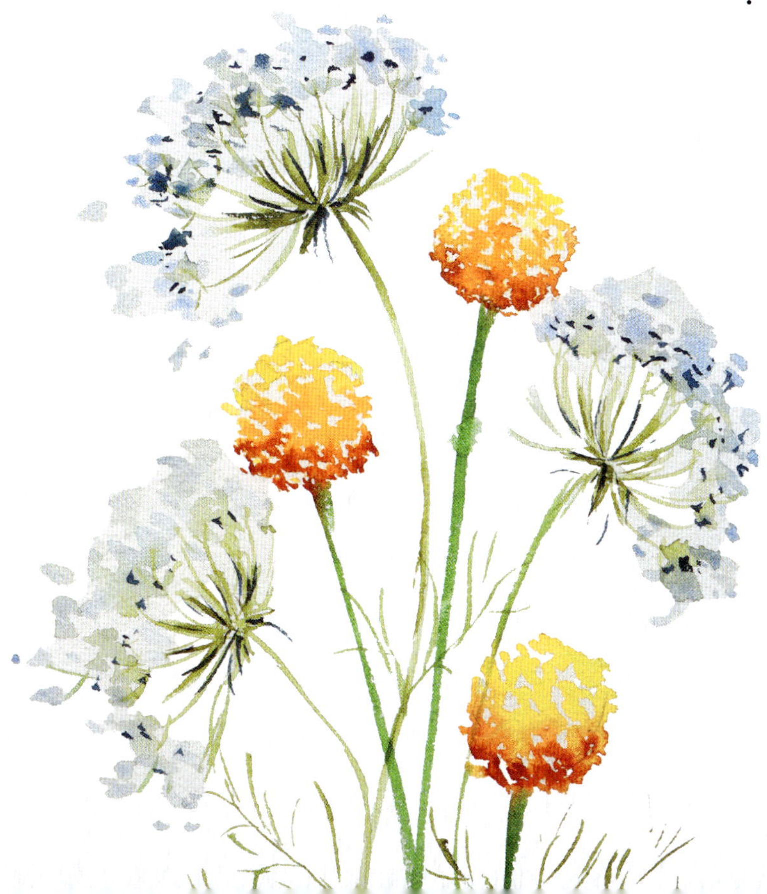

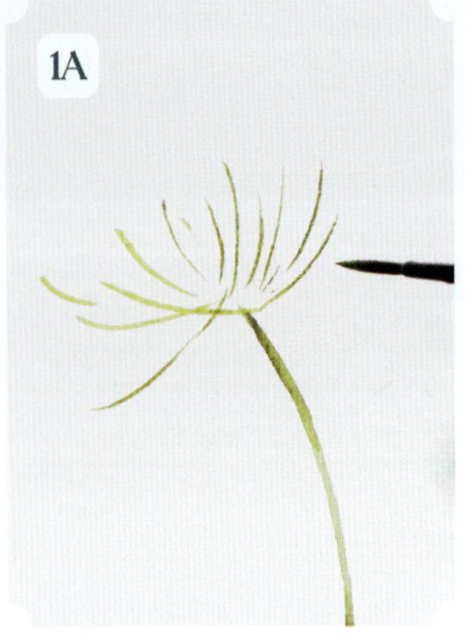

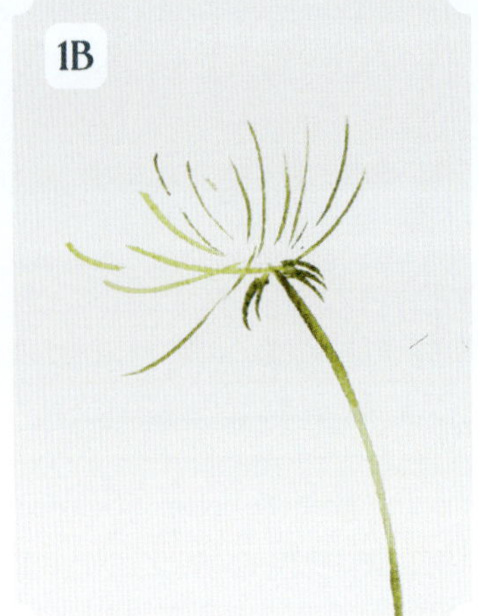

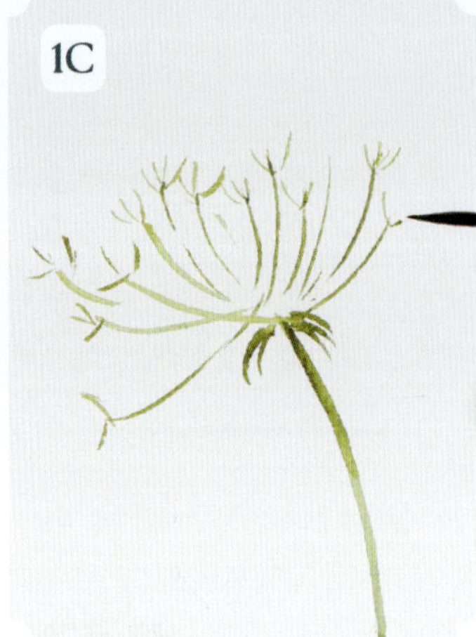

1. Paint the Queen Anne's Lace Stems

Let's start by painting three curved stems. Prepare a light-consistency Olive Green and load it into your size 2 round brush. Paint a long, curved stem in the center of the paper. While damp, drop medium-consistency Olive Green in a few spots to add variation.

At the top of the stem, use the same green to paint very thin, curved strokes that resemble an umbrella frame. Vary the lengths and angles to keep it looking natural. At the tip of each stroke, add short strokes that will hold the cluster of flowers.

Beneath this "umbrella," paint a few fine and feathery strokes too. Repeat these steps for the other two long stems.

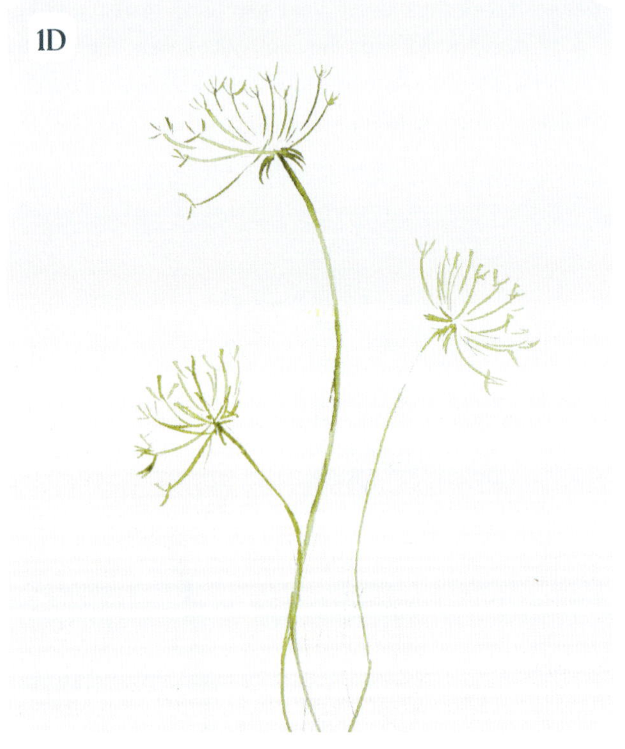

2. Paint the Flower Clusters

Mix a very light and watery consistency of Ultramarine Blue and Burnt Umber to create a muted gray. I like adding a bit more blue to the mix for a cooler tone. Gently tap the tip of your size 4 round brush to make small dots and tiny clusters at the ends of the stalk.

Leave small gaps and vary their spacing for a delicate and airy feel. Let some dots sit farther away so they look detached.

Drop in Verditer Blue on some clusters for color variation. Then add a touch of watery Olive Green to certain clusters to visually connect them to the stalks.

3. Add Contrast

Using a size 2 round brush, prepare two mixes of Olive Green: one medium consistency and one thick. Paint another layer of thin strokes on the umbrella frame, alternating between the two mixes to create contrast.

Once the flower clusters are dry, switch to thick-consistency Indigo. With your size 2 round brush, add a few small dots on top of some clusters to give them depth. Keep this minimal so it doesn't feel crowded. You can also use the Indigo to add a few extra thin strokes along the stalks for more dimension. Repeat for the other flowers.

4. Paint the Craspedia Base

Lightly sketch a circle as a guide for each Craspedia flower, placing them in between the Queen Anne's Lace stems. With a light-consistency Permanent Yellow Light, load your size 4 round brush. Gently tap the brush tip to fill in the circle with tiny dots. Leave small gaps in between the dots, and let them be slightly uneven for a more natural texture.

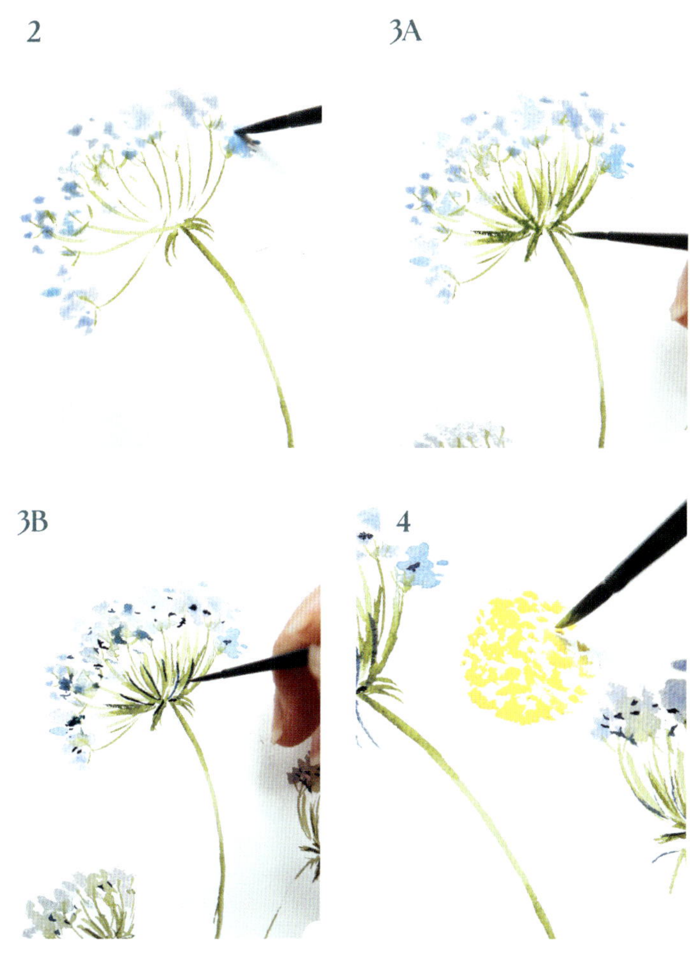

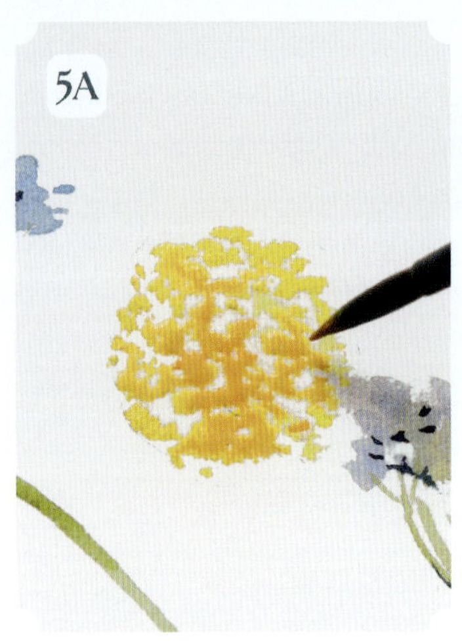

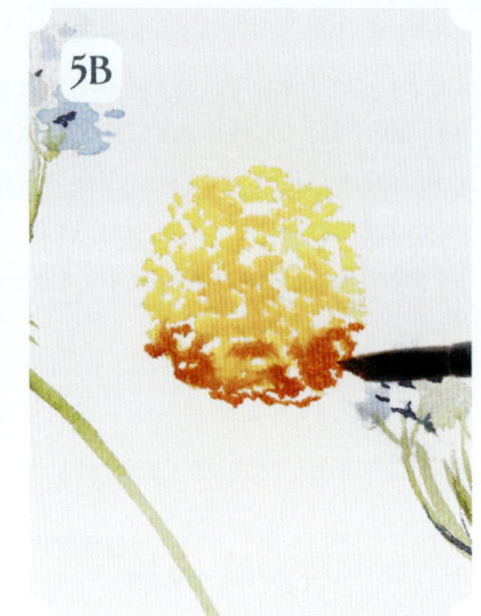

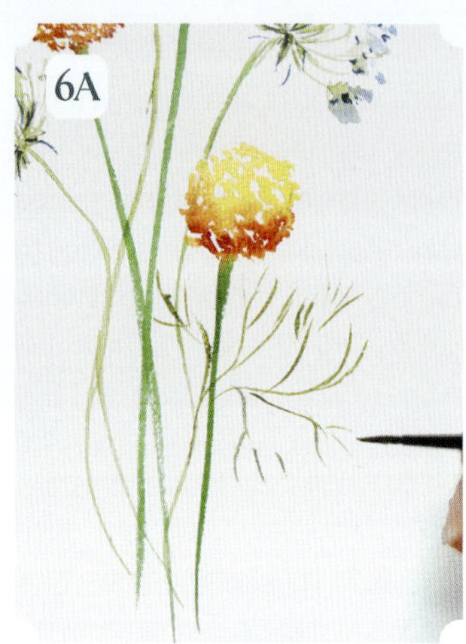

5. Add Depth and Shadow

Mix a medium-consistency Permanent Yellow Deep, and dab it over half of the Craspedia while the yellow base is still wet so the colors blend softly.

Rinse your brush and switch to a thick-consistency Burnt Sienna. Lightly dab this color at the base of the flower, blending it with the yellow to create a warm gradient. Paint two or more Craspedia blooms using the same method.

6. Add Stems and Leaves

Mix a medium-consistency Sap Green and paint the straight stems of the Craspedia.

Next, let's add the leaves of Queen Anne's Lace. They look like mini ferns. Using a size 2 round brush, load it with medium-consistency Olive Green. Paint a thin, slightly curved central stem. From this, flick your brush outward to create more thin segments on each side. From the thin segments, add secondary segments with shorter thin strokes. You may play with the green tones, keeping some lighter and others richer for depth. Add extra leaves to help balance the composition. Step back and admire your gorgeous painting!

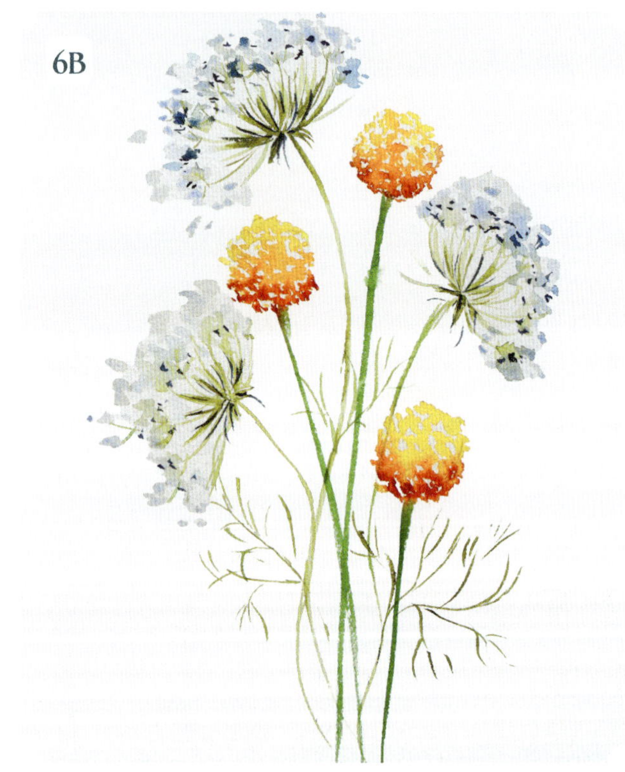

SEA LAVENDER AND BABY'S BREATH

Sea Lavender and Baby's Breath are popular filler flowers. They're like the behind-the-scenes team that makes the whole arrangement shine.

Sea Lavender adds a little pop of color with its tiny, papery blooms, while Baby's Breath brings a soft and airy feel. Together, they make a lovely pair for a dainty bouquet, or you can mix them with bigger statement flowers in other projects.

Colors

- Lilac
- Olive Green
- Burnt Umber
- Permanent Yellow Light
- Permanent Rose
- Permanent Violet
- Burnt Sienna, optional
- Buff Titanium
- Ultramarine Blue, optional

Brushes

- Size 4 round brush
- Size 2 round brush

Other Materials

- Pencil

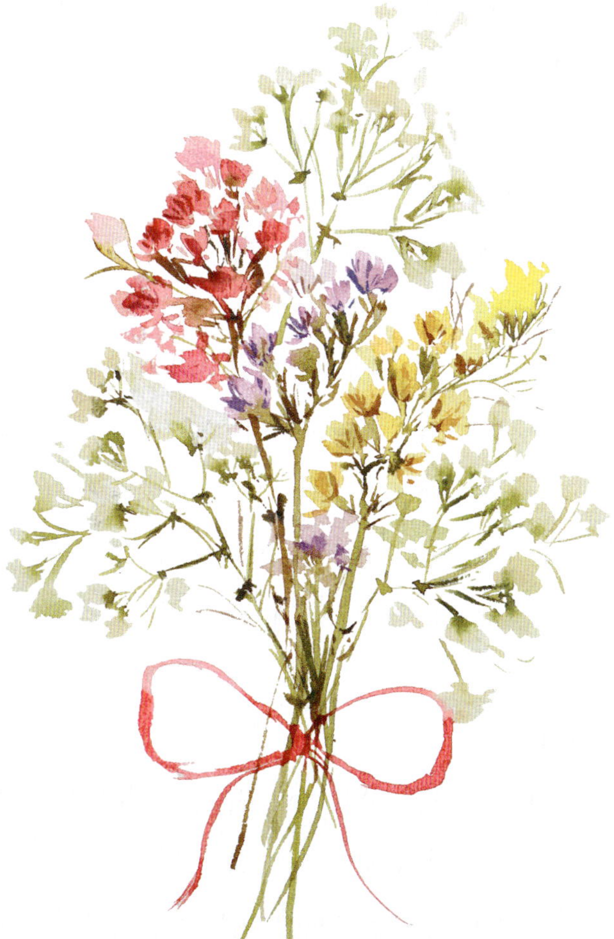

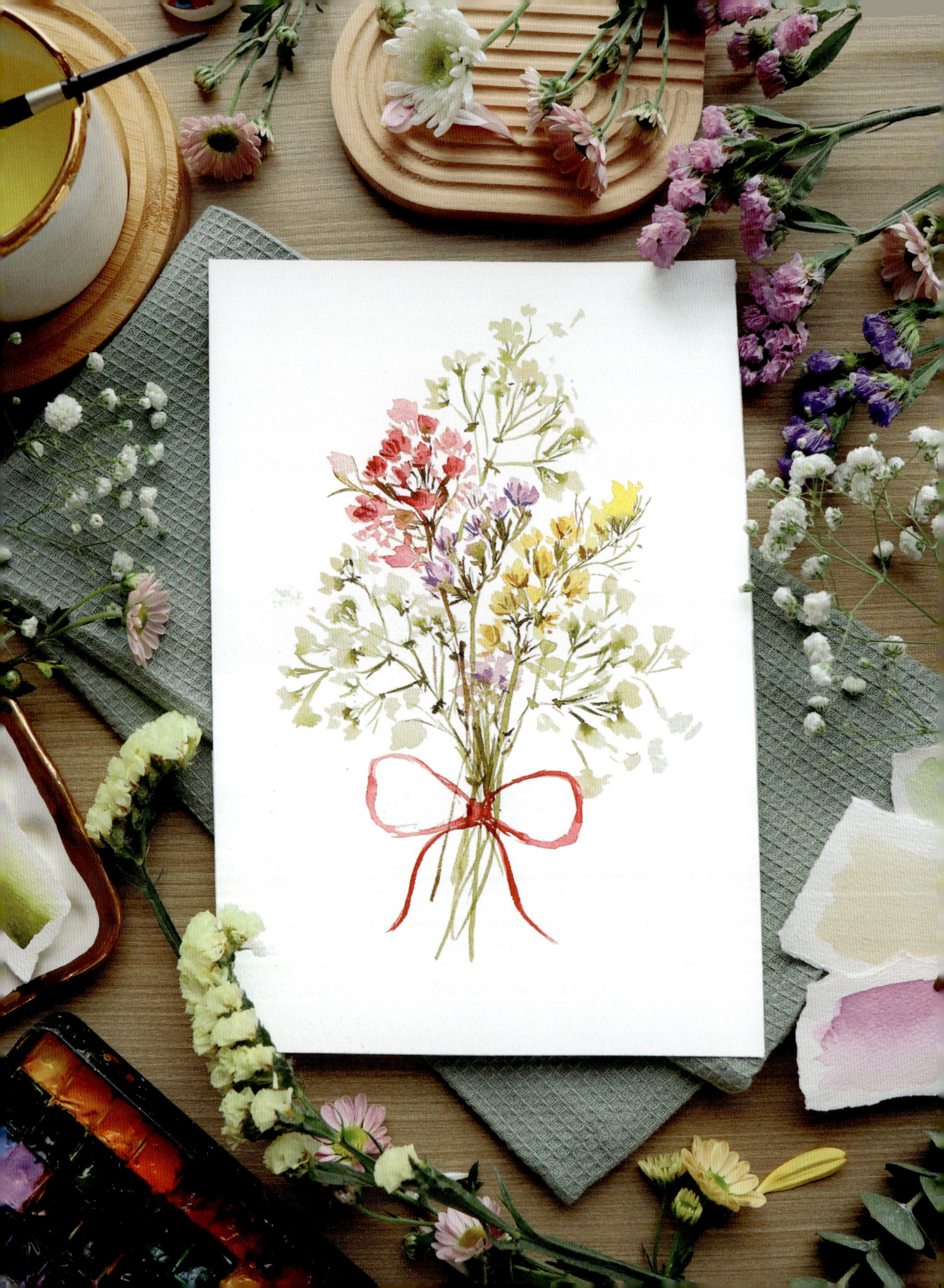

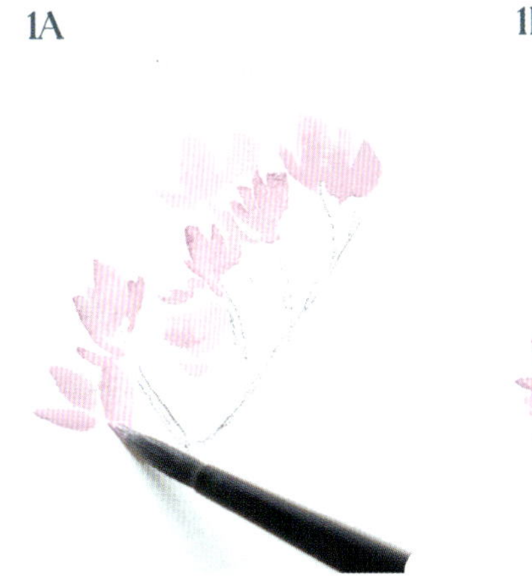

1A

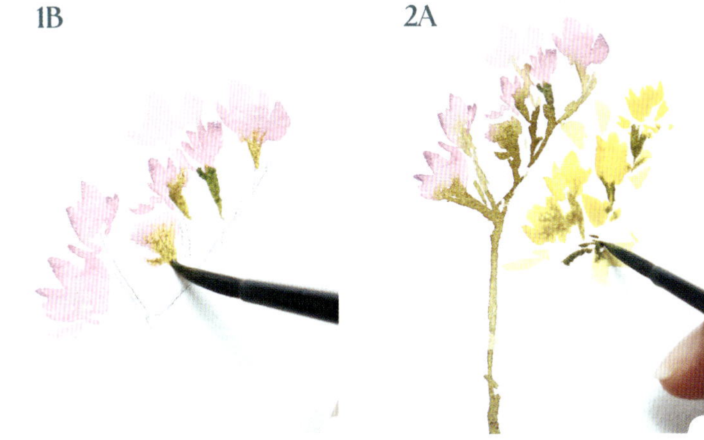

1B   2A

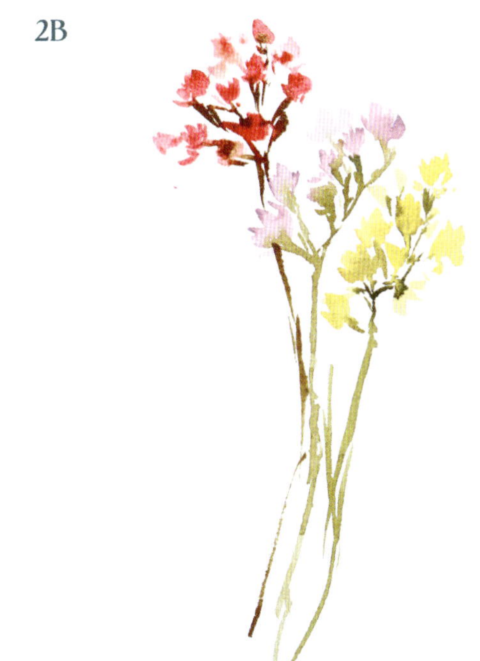

2B

1. Paint the Sea Lavender Flowers

Lightly sketch the stems and tiny branches using a pencil. Think of a wide Y shape or a candelabra.

Mix a light-consistency Lilac and load it to your size 4 round brush. At the tips of the small branches, lightly stamp your brush to create clustered petals. Vary the Lilac color—some petals should be lighter, some darker. Don't aim for perfection. It's the randomness that makes it feel natural.

Mix two parts Olive Green and one part Burnt Umber. While the flowers are still damp, paint the tiny branches to connect them to the main stem. Keep the main stem slightly crooked for a natural look.

2. Add More Flowers

Mix a light-consistency Permanent Yellow Light and load your size 4 round brush. Create another set of flowers on the right using the same stamping method. Vary the direction and pressure of your brush.

On the left, paint another stem using light- to medium-consistency Permanent Rose. Feel free to choose other colors. For now, we'll paint just three stems and add more later when finishing the bouquet.

3. Add a Second Layer

Use a hairdryer to quickly dry the first layer before adding the second layer for texture and depth.

Mix equal parts Lilac and Permanent Violet into a thick consistency. Using a size 2 round brush, go back in and dab tiny strokes on the purple flowers, focusing near the base of the flowers and in between petals.

For the yellow flowers, mix a more saturated Permanent Yellow Light or add a little bit of Burnt Sienna.

For the pink flowers, mix a thicker consistency of Permanent Rose for richer color.

To add more texture to the stems, mix a dark brownish green (two parts Olive Green and one part Burnt Umber). With your size 2 round brush, add small flicks near the branches of the flower clusters and some along the main stem to suggest breaks and shadows.

4. Paint the Baby's Breath Stem

Baby's Breath grows in a branching pattern. On the left side of the arrangement, lightly sketch a thin main stem using a pencil and branch it out to a Y shape. Split each of those branches into even smaller stems. At the tip of these smaller stems are short strokes that will hold the flowers.

With a light-consistency Olive Green, paint over the sketched stem. Switch to a thick-consistency Olive Green, and lightly dab the tip of brush along anywhere two stems meet.

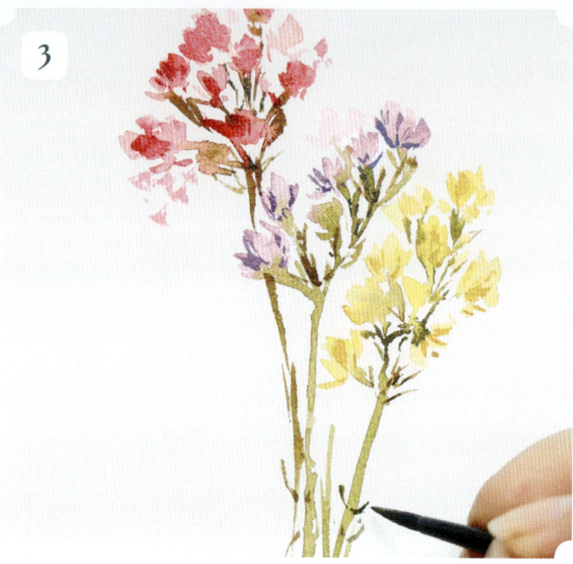

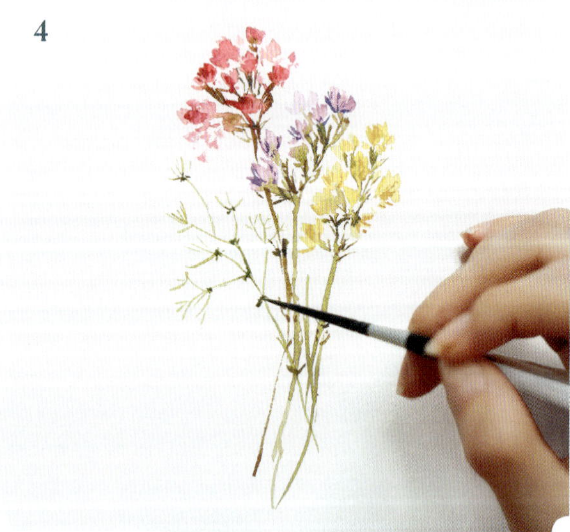

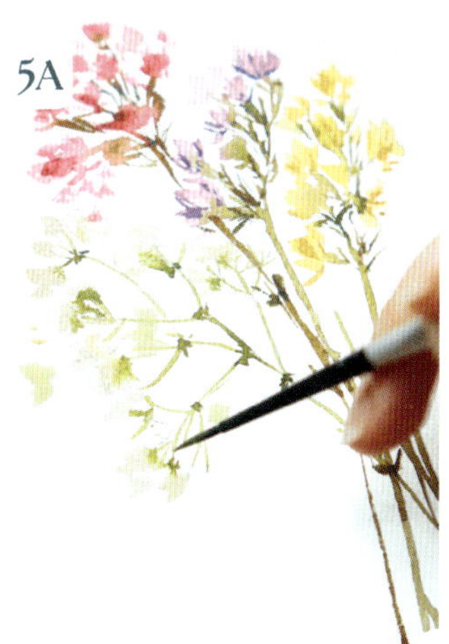

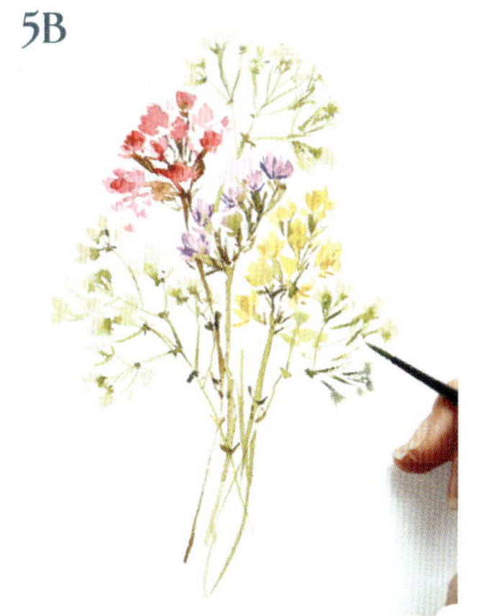

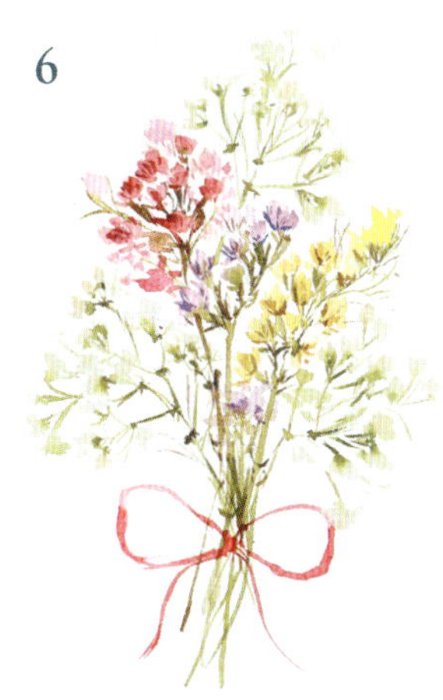

5. Paint the Baby's Breath Flowers

Mix a light-consistency Buff Titanium and load your size 2 round brush. Dab your brush along the tips of the branches to suggest tiny white flowers. Vary the size of the strokes. While the flowers are damp, drop in a light consistency of Olive Green to the base of the flowers to let them blend softly.

Add one more Baby's Breath stalk at the top and one on the right side to balance the bouquet. Vary the height for a natural look.

> **TIP:** You may also mix Burnt Umber and Ultramarine Blue into a light watery consistency to make a soft neutral color for the flowers.

6. Add Finishing Touches

Fill in the gaps by extending some Sea Lavender stems and adding a few more flower clusters.

Keep some of the stalks slightly longer for a loose and airy feel. You can introduce more colors for variety.

Step back and look at your painting from a distance. It's the easiest way to see where adjustments are needed.

Optionally, paint a thin ribbon to make it look like a hand-tied bouquet. Simply paint two loops on each side, then add S-shaped tails with some Permanent Rose.

You've just finished another delicate bouquet! Good job!

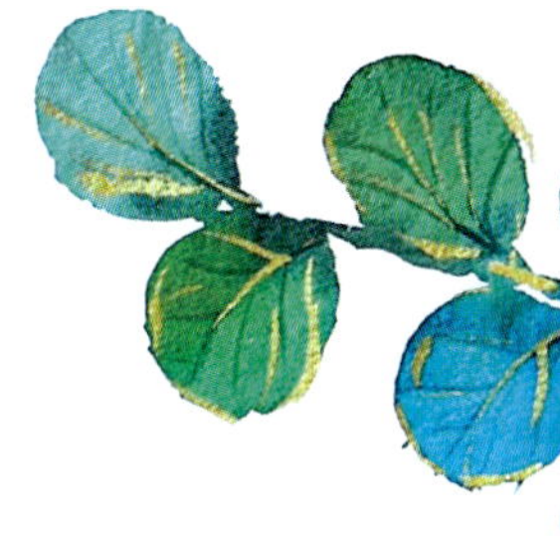

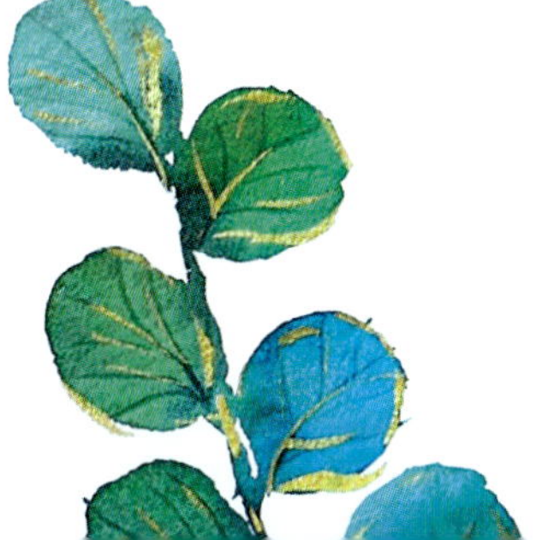

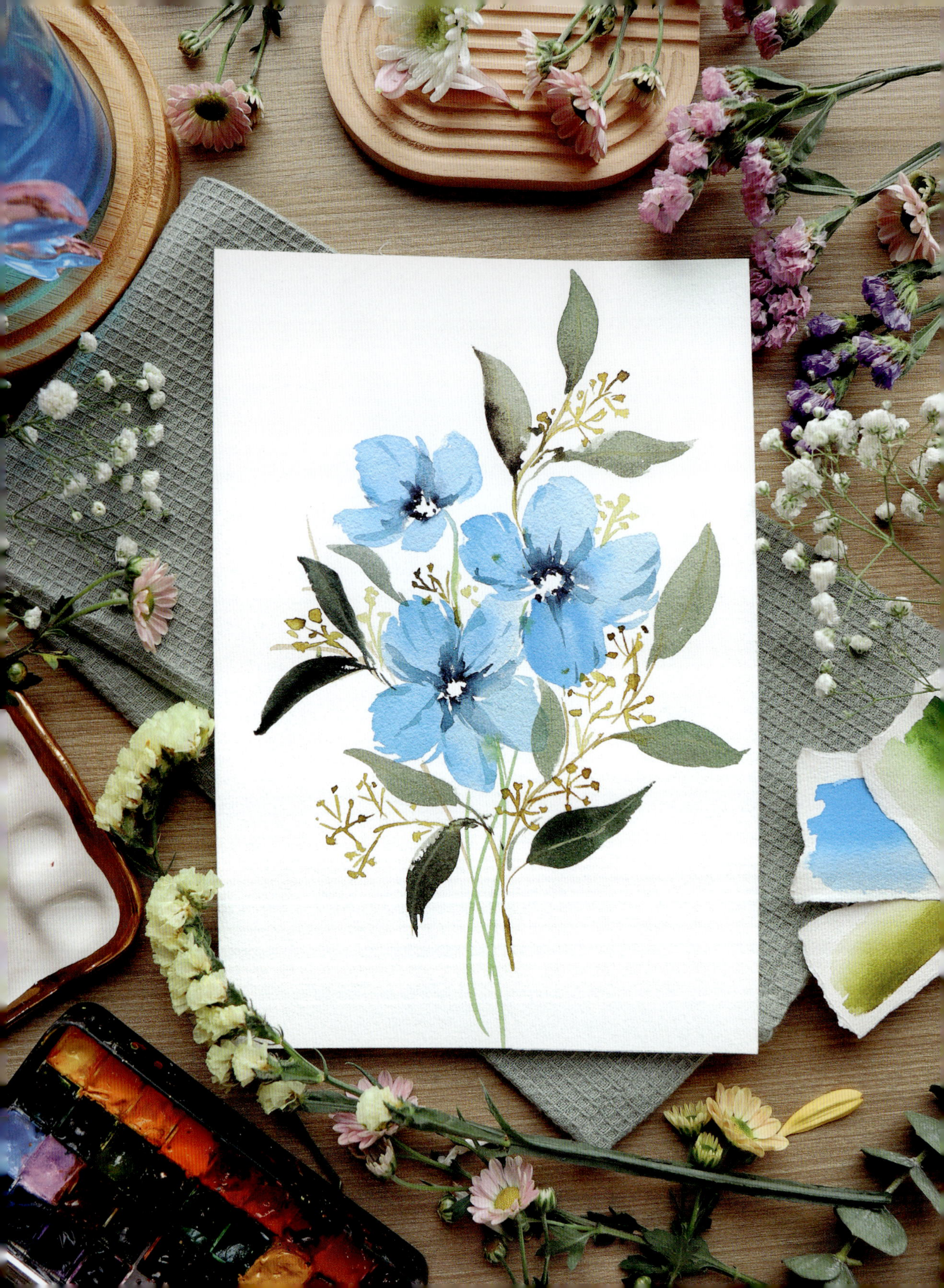

SEEDED EUCALYPTUS AND FIVE-PETAL FLOWER

I love a dainty pairing that is versatile and works in any season. The five-petal flower is a staple in loose watercolor florals. You can easily change its color to suit the mood—use soft pink for a romantic look or sunny yellow for summer. For this lesson, I have chosen blue flowers that complement the textured Seeded Eucalyptus for a bouquet that feels calming.

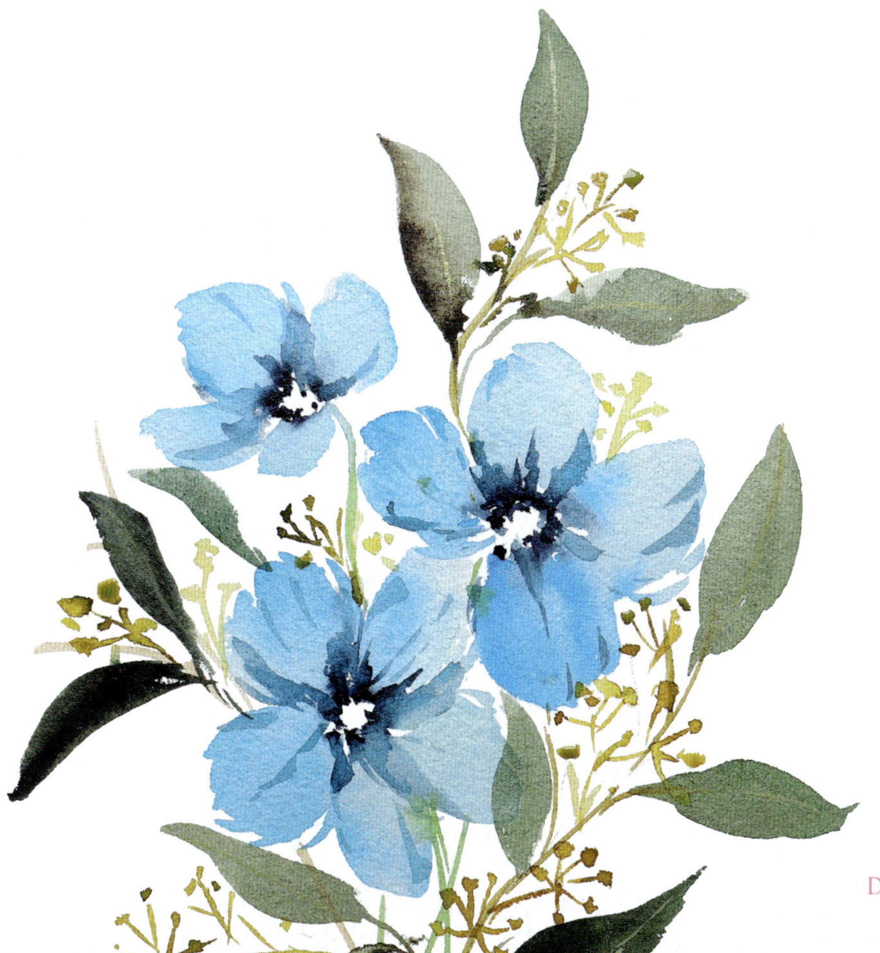

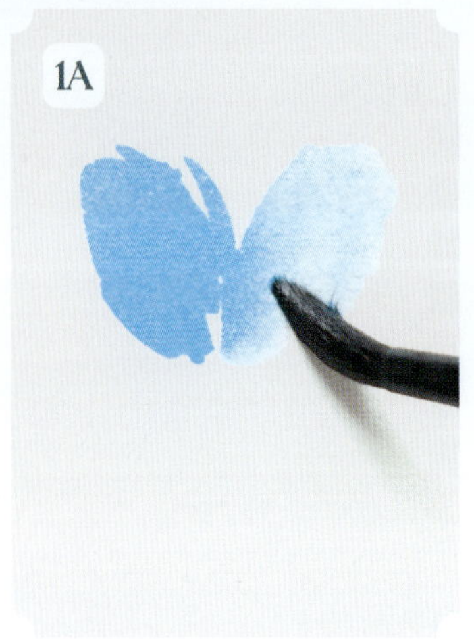

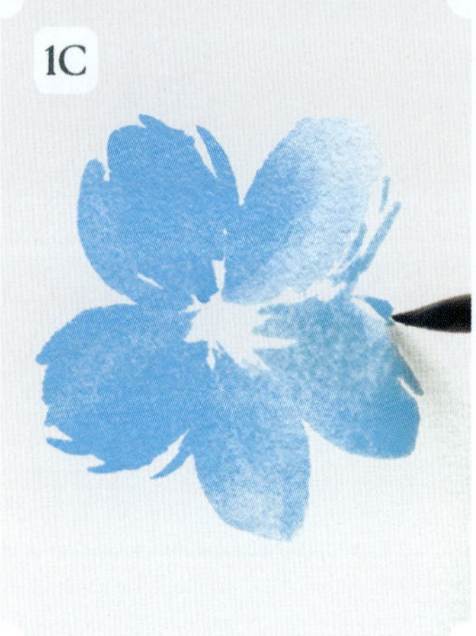

1. Paint the Five-Petal Flower

Mix a light consistency of Cerulean Blue. Load your size 8 round brush with a juicy paint and paint rounded petals. Start at the top petal. Press the full belly of the brush down, drag lightly, then lift at the tip. Overlap with another stroke to make a fuller petal. You may add thin strokes beside it for texture. Rinse your brush, make a lighter Cerulean Blue, and paint the next petal on the right.

Continue until you have all five petals, keeping the center blank.

Switch to a thick-consistency Indigo, load your brush, then blot off the excess paint in a tissue paper. While the petals are wet, add this color to the center of the flower where the petals meet so they blend softly.

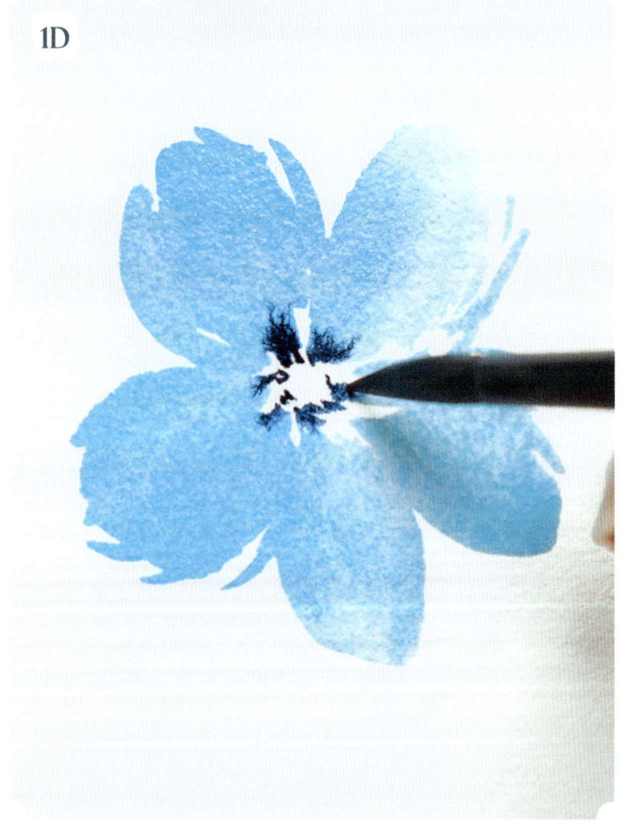

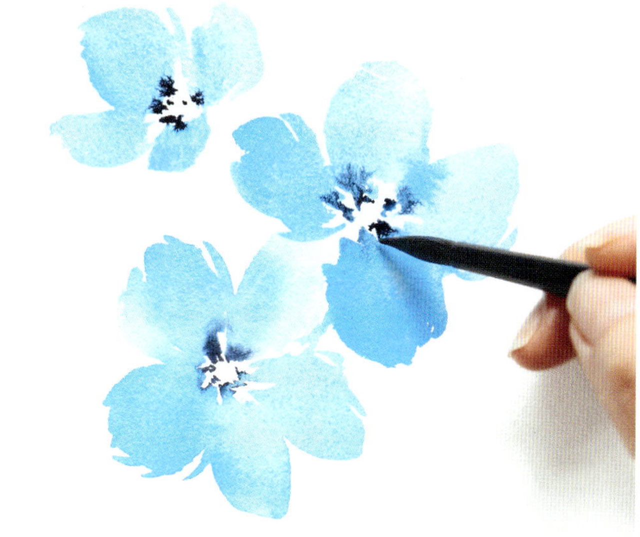

2. Add More Flowers

Repeat the same method for the other flowers. Add another flower diagonally across from the first one, but paint only four petals so it looks like one is hidden behind the first flower. Vary the pressure of your strokes to create more expressive petals. Leave white gaps to let the painting breathe, and vary the blue tones so the flower doesn't look flat.

For a side-facing flower, paint an oval base then paint three petals above it.

3. Add the Stems

Mix a medium-consistency Sap Green and paint thin, curvy stems attached to the blue flowers, letting some intertwine.

Let's paint the stem of the Seeded Eucalyptus. Mix two parts Olive Green and one part Burnt Umber, and load your size 2 round brush. Paint S stems with small branches sticking out in three points of the bouquet.

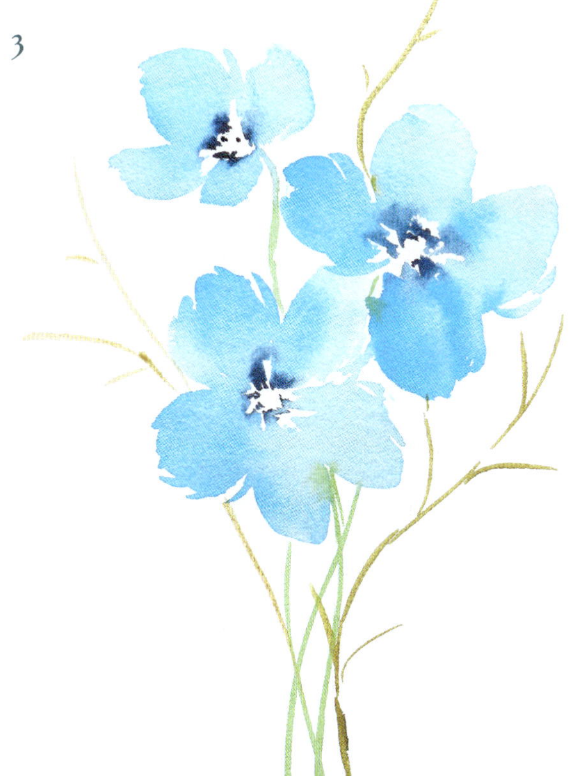

4. Paint the Eucalyptus Leaves

Seeded Eucalyptus has paired leaves along its stems. They are opposite each other but slightly staggered. Prepare two separate mixes of dark green color (we will alternate): two parts Hooker's Green and one part Indigo, and two parts Hooker's Green and one part Sepia. Alternating between two green mixtures instead of one helps prevent the leaves from looking flat and adds depth to the foliage.

Load your size 8 round brush. Start at one of the branches sticking out. We'll paint a two-stroke leaf. Press your brush, drag, and lift for the top half. Repeat the same for the bottom half. The leaf should be slightly elongated.

Let some leaves face different directions for a natural look. You don't need to put a leaf on all the branches sticking out. Place the lighter-toned leaves at the top, and while they are still damp, drop in a darker green (the thick-consistency mixture of two parts Hooker's Green and one part Sepia) at the base for depth.

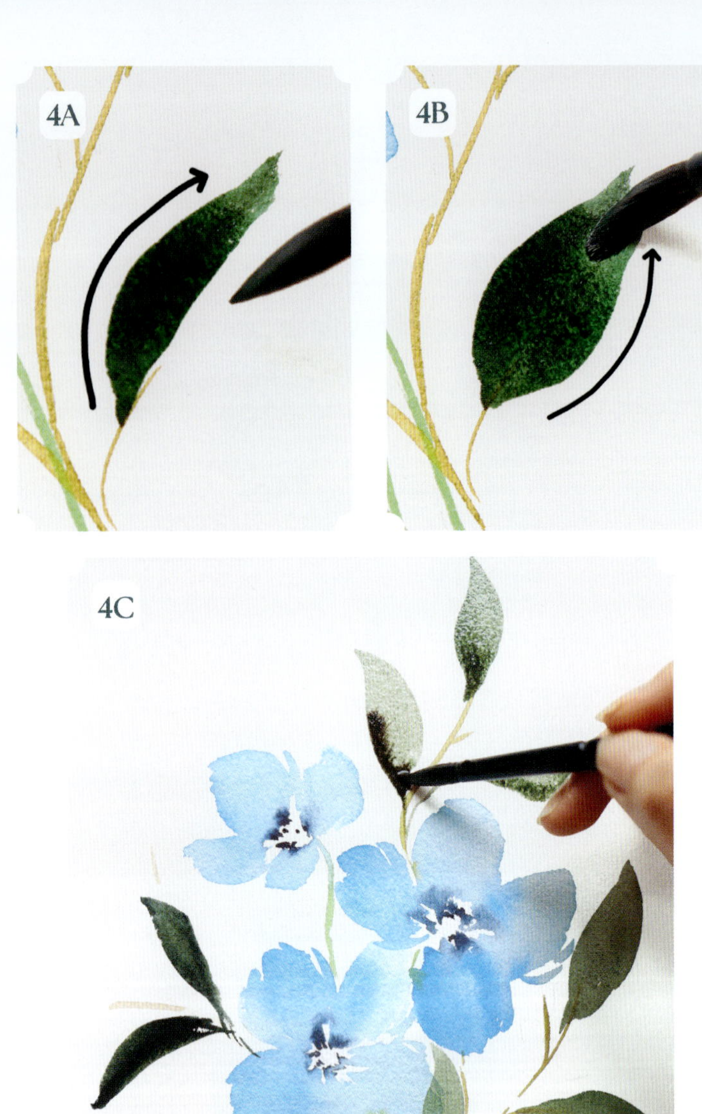

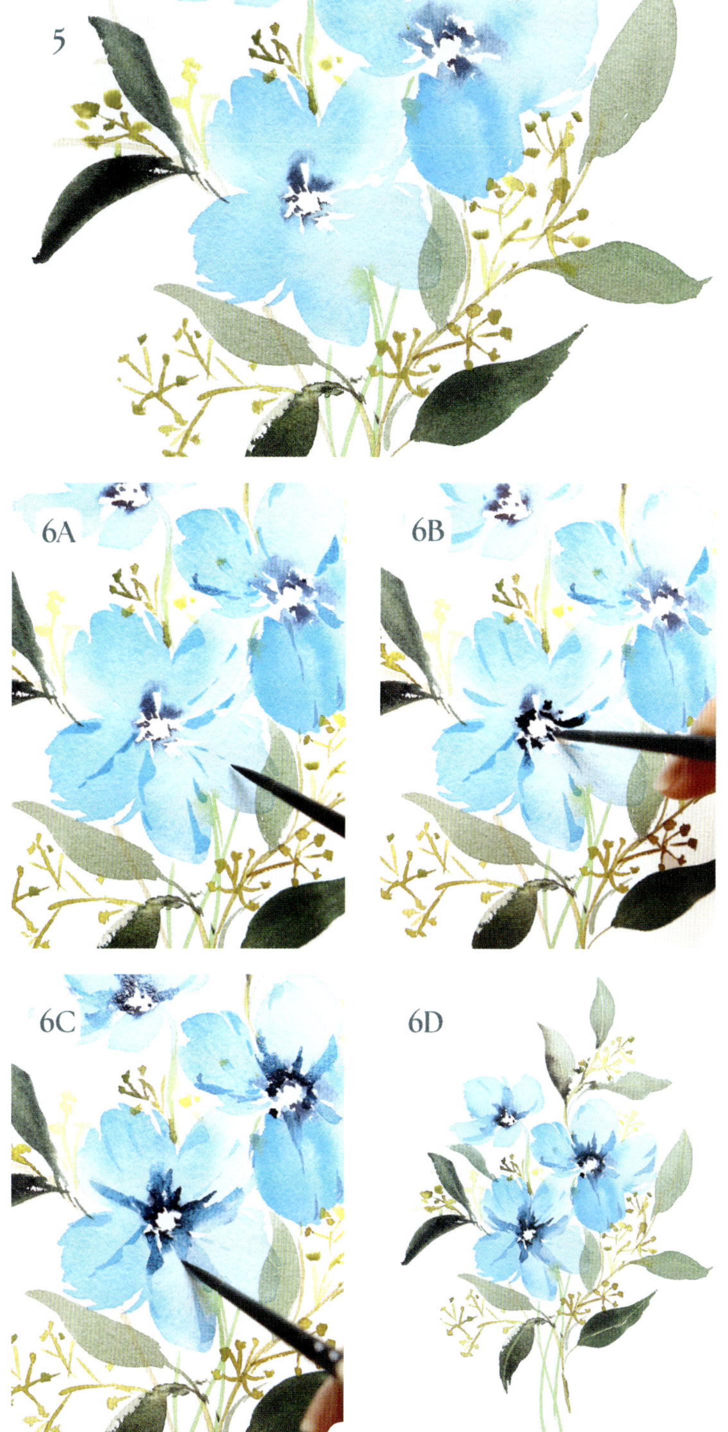

5. Paint the Seeds

Load your size 2 round brush with light-consistency Greenish Yellow. Paint small round shapes in clustered groups of three to six, then connect them with thin stems. Place them near the leaves or at branch tips. For variety, you may switch between Olive Green and Greenish Yellow, and use both light and medium consistencies.

6. Add the Finishing Touches

Let's add more details to the five-petal flowers. Mix three parts Cerulean Blue and one part Indigo into a light consistency, just enough to make it slightly darker than the base color of the petals. Use a size 2 round brush and paint a few delicate, vein-like strokes on the petals of the five-petal flower.

Rinse your brush, then switch to thick-consistency Indigo. Add a few dots to the centers of the flowers. Using a clean, damp brush, gently pull some of this color into the veins so it softens and flows into the petals for a dramatic effect.

Lastly, you may add a vein along the center of the leaves using thick-consistency Greenish Yellow. It's looking gorgeous!

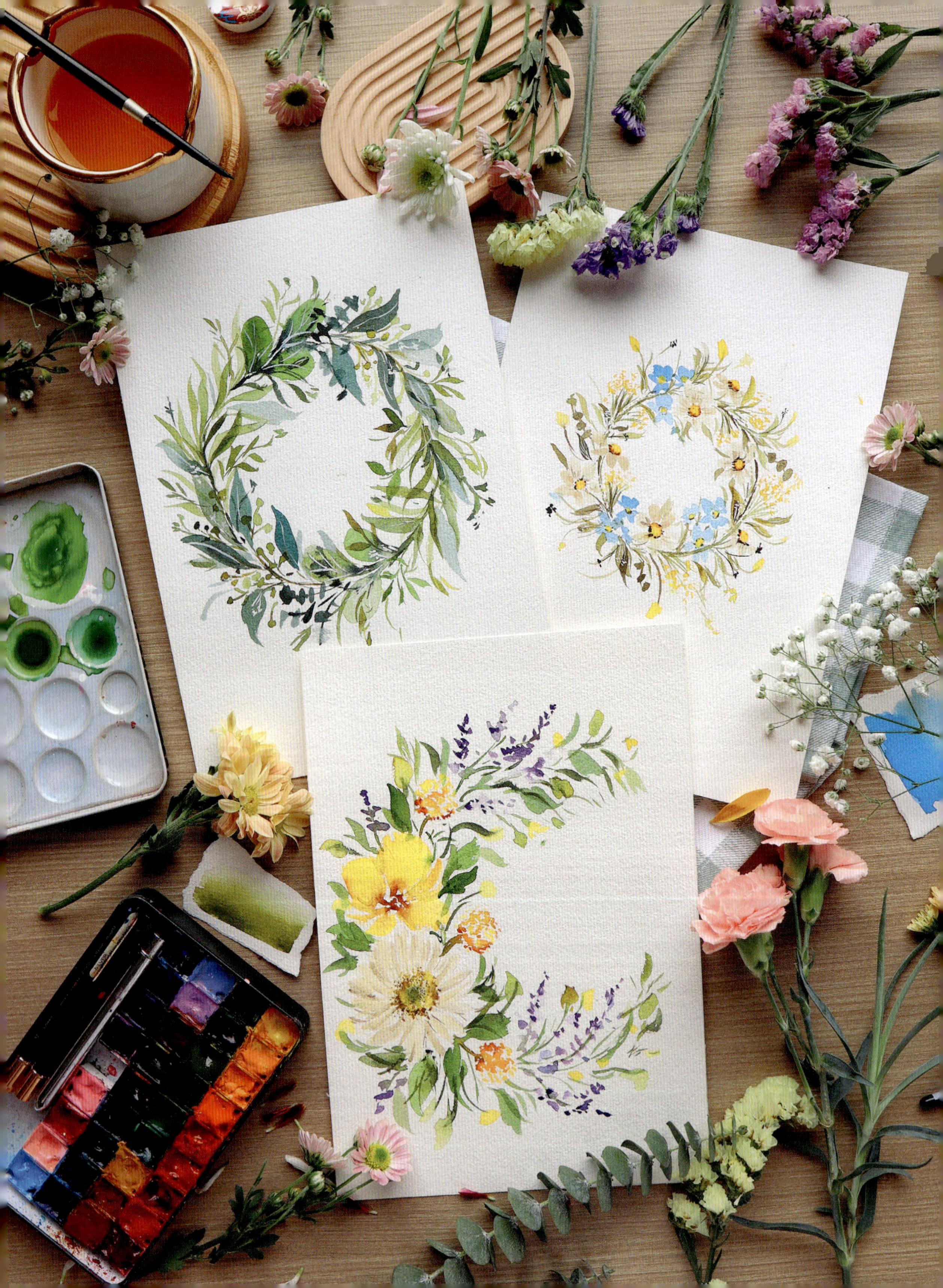

Easy and Elegant
WREATHS

Wreaths are one of my favorite compositions because they are simple to create, yet have endless possibilities for variation. You can keep them light and dainty or rustic or even add a touch of gold for elegance.

In this chapter, we will explore different styles of wreaths that you can easily customize with your favorite flowers and foliage. You can write personal messages in the middle, gift them to loved ones, use them for your wedding invitations, or display them in your own home.

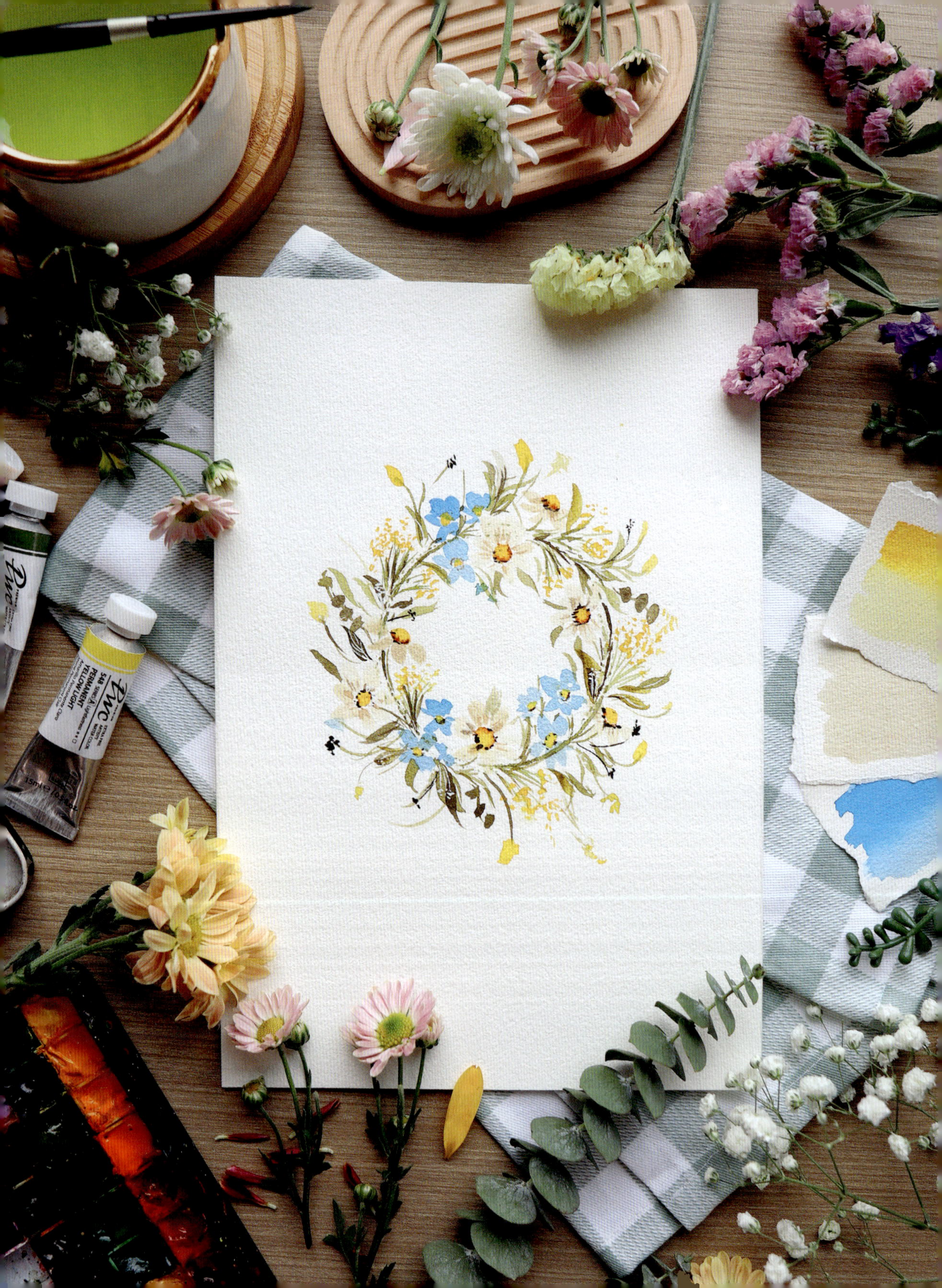

DAINTY FLORAL WREATH

During one of my in-person workshops, a student was struggling with painting larger flowers and asked, "Can I just use fillers to make a wreath instead?" I smiled and said, "Yes, of course!" This is a wonderful reminder that you don't always need big blooms to create something special.

There is also something soothing about painting a dainty wreath filled with small flowers, leaves, and other tiny elements. It invites you to slow down and enjoy the quiet rhythm of adding each filler with a small round brush.

By the end, you'll have a joyful wreath that you can turn into a card with a quote in the center or frame as a keepsake.

Colors

- Sap Green
- Permanent Yellow Light
- Burnt Sienna
- Buff Titanium
- Cerulean Blue
- Verditer Blue
- Burnt Umber
- Sepia

Brushes

- Size 4 round brush
- Size 2 round brush

Other Materials

- Small jar
- White gouache, optional

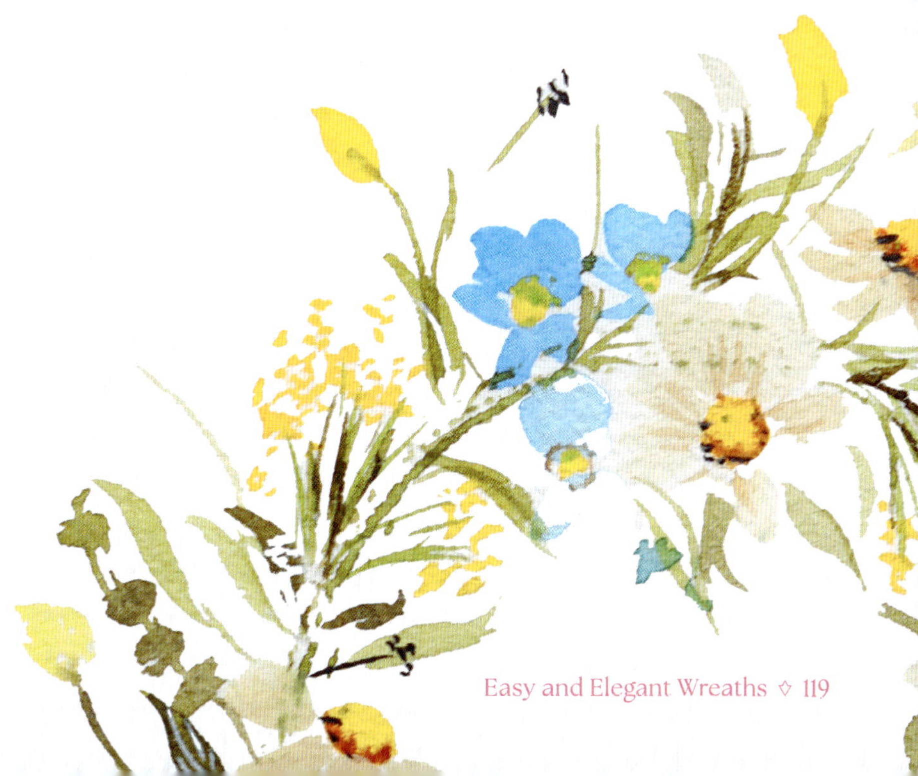

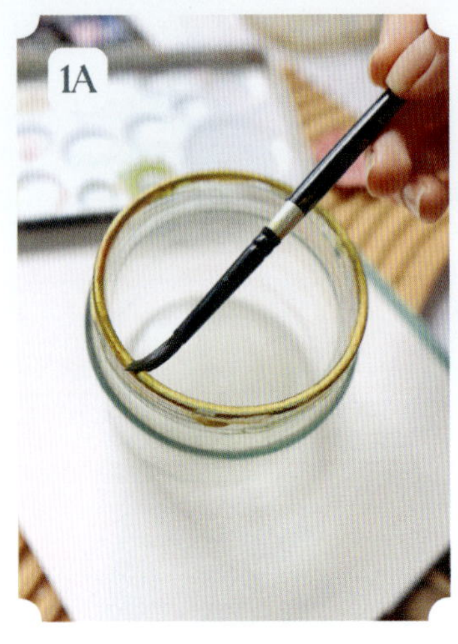

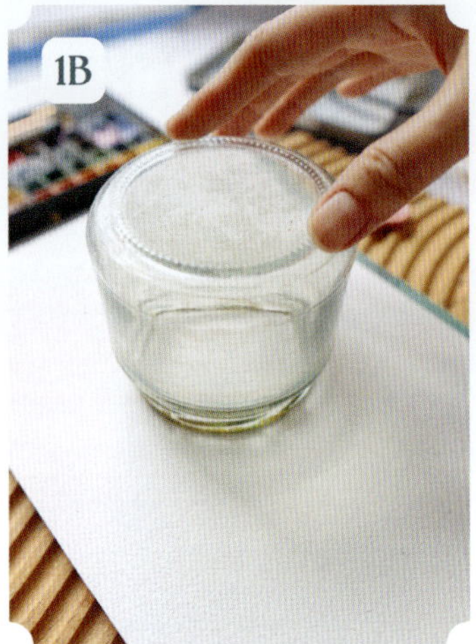

1. Create the Wreath Base

Let's start with the base of the wreath. Find a jar or any round object with a 4- to 5-inch (10- to 12.5-cm) diameter, like a mason jar. Using any round brush, mix a light consistency of Sap Green on a palette. Paint onto the rim of the jar. The mixture might not stick on the entire surface of the rim, as the glass is shiny, but that's perfectly fine. Stamp the rim of the jar onto the paper to create an imperfect circle. Don't worry if it's patchy— that unevenness adds to the charm. You can add color to the rim again and stamp it once or twice more if you'd like a slightly more defined or rustic outline.

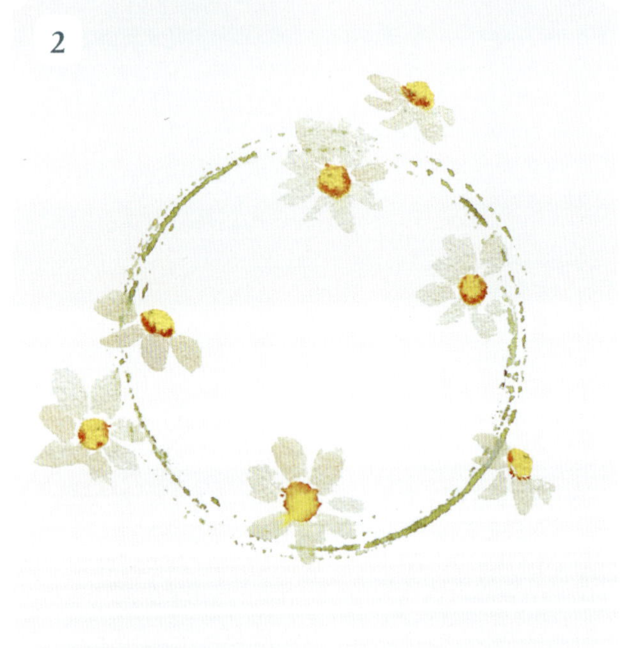

2. Add the Chamomile Centers

Let's place the bases of our Chamomile (page 91) using a size 4 round brush. Using Permanent Yellow Light, create small round shapes for front-facing flowers and oval shapes for side-facing ones. While the yellow center is still damp, add a touch of Burnt Sienna around the edges to create depth. Scatter them around the wreath, leaving space in between. Once dry, you'll come back to add the petals using Buff Titanium.

3

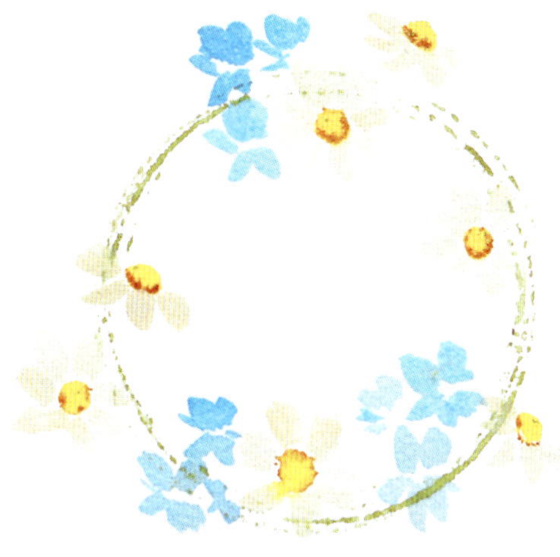

3. Paint Forget-Me-Nots

Next, with a size **4** round brush, add clusters of Forget-Me-Nots using Cerulean Blue and Verditer Blue (page 95). These tiny blue blooms will bring a soft pop of color. I like placing them in three points around the wreath to keep things visually balanced, especially near the chamomile flowers.

4. Add Filler Stems and Dots

Let's add some thin fillers. Mix two parts Sap Green and one part Burnt Umber to create a medium-consistency earthy green color. Using a size 2 round brush, paint thin strokes in varying lengths. Add them in areas that feel empty.

Rinse your brush and mix a thick consistency of Permanent Yellow Light. Lightly tap some dots at the end of the thin filler stems. Vary the sizes of the dots. Let some touch each other and others float a bit farther away to keep it light and airy. Feel free to experiment with color here; for example, add a second color for the dots. Once the Forget-Me-Not petals are dry, you can also add a Permanent Yellow Light dot at their centers.

4A   4B

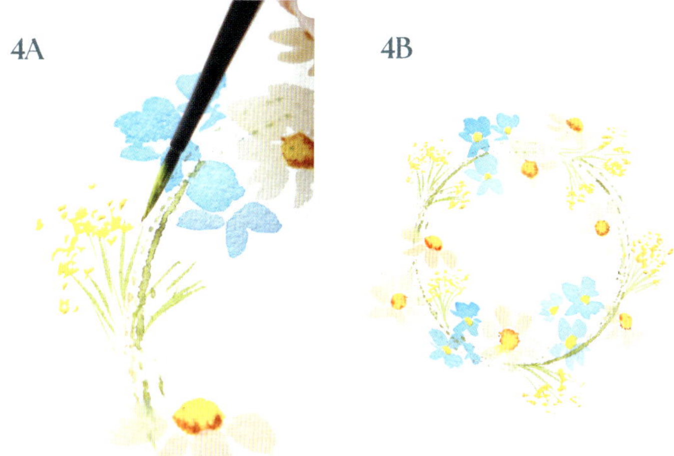

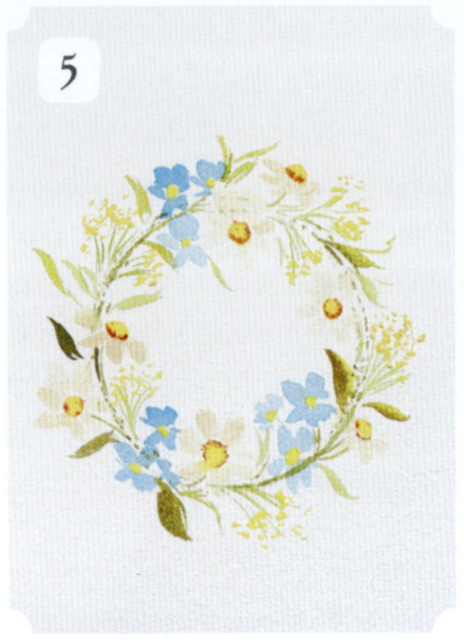

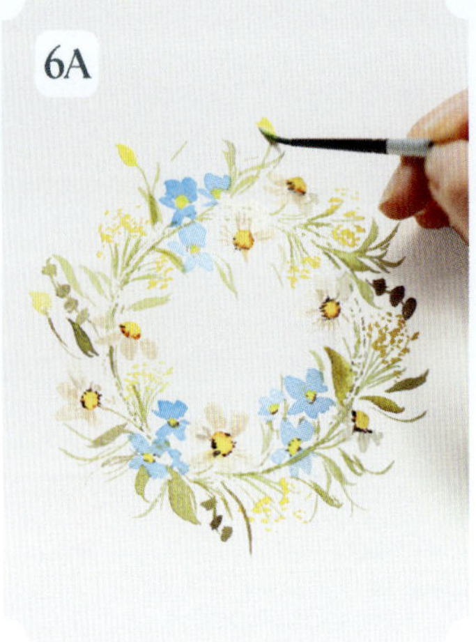

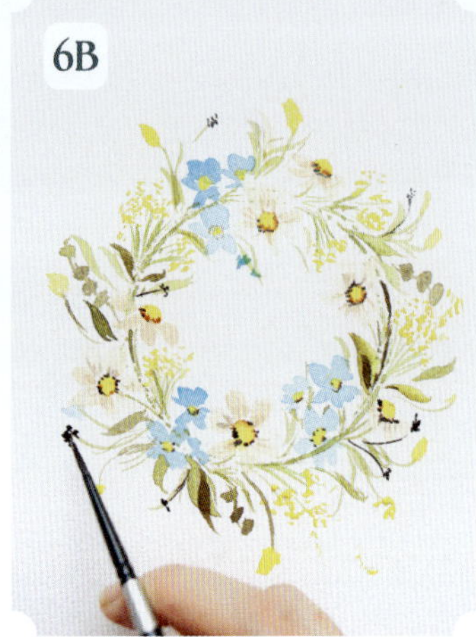

5. Paint the Leaves

Let's prep two green mixes: two parts Sap Green with one part Burnt Umber, and two parts Sap Green with one part Burnt Sienna.

Use both light and medium consistencies to give your leaves variety. Begin by adding small leaves between flowers and in empty spaces. Vary their size and direction as this gives your wreath a natural, flowing feel. You can also add a few Eucalyptus-style leaves (page 111).

6. Adding Final Details

Now that the wreath base is dry, it's time to bring everything together with some final touches.

Start by adding detail to the chamomile centers. Using a size 2 round brush and a thick mixture of Sepia, paint a ring of tiny dots in the middle of each flower. You can also add fine lines on the petals with a light consistency of Sepia to suggest delicate veins and soft shadows.

Next, paint buds and loose stems to add movement and lightness to the composition. With a size 2 round brush and medium-consistency green paint, lightly drag the tip to create thin, curved stems that peek out from the wreath. At the tip of each stem, gently stamp a bud using a medium yellow consistency.

For variation, you may tap gestural dots in small clusters using any dark color, like Sepia, at the end of the loose stems. These subtle accents add contrast and visual interest. Once the first layer of leaves has dried, you can also layer in more leaves to create a fuller look. Just be careful not to overfill, as we want to keep that delicate, airy feel.

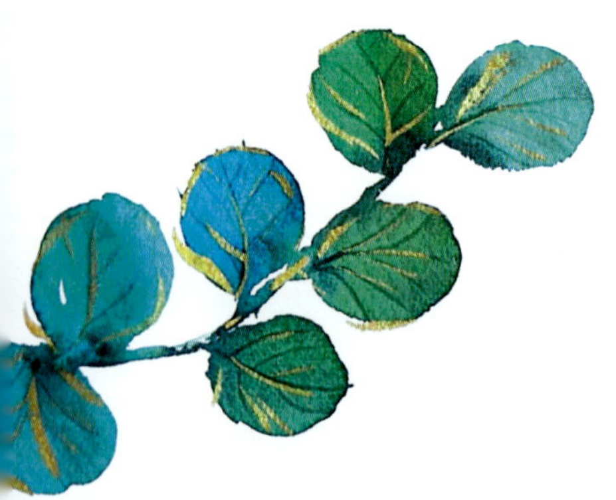

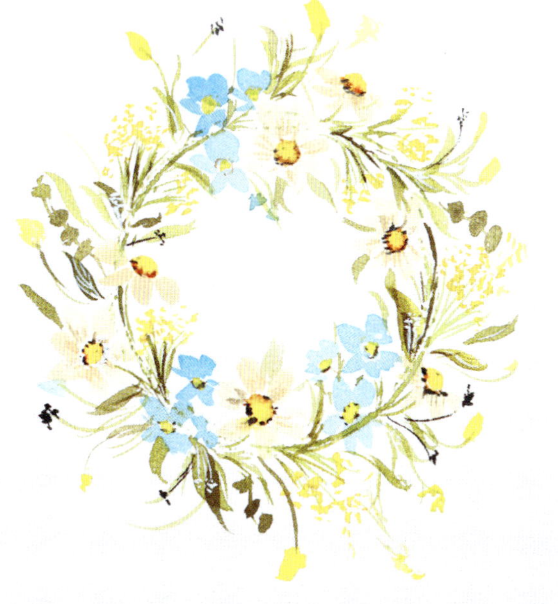

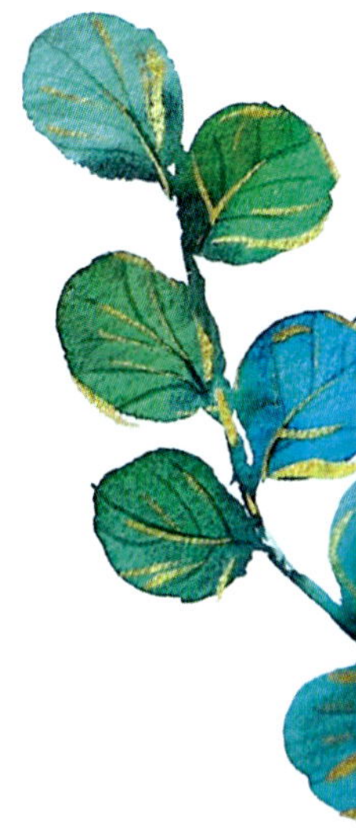

7. Adding White Gouache

If you'd like to add some highlights, squeeze out a small amount of white gouache and mix in a drop of water to create a creamy consistency. Use a size 2 round brush to paint delicate white veins on the leaves or tiny dotted accents. Just be sure to paint these over darker areas so the white really stands out. That's it! Your wreath turned out lovely!

> **TIP:** You may use this wreath pattern and replace the flowers with your favorite ones. Just remember to start with the base flowers first and then start adding the smaller flowers and foliage.

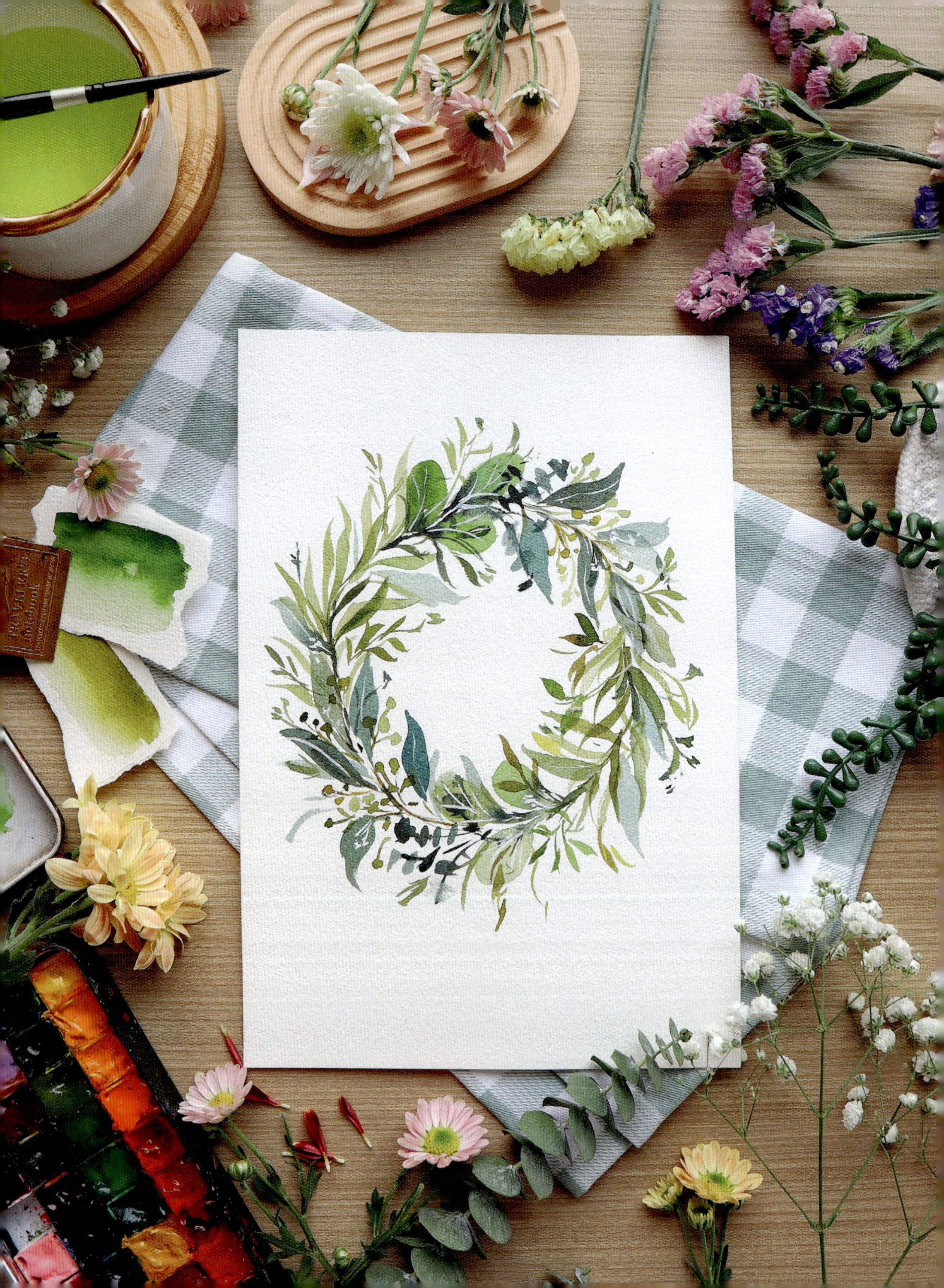

LUSH GREEN WREATH

If you are looking for a relaxing project, then a leafy wreath is the perfect start! It's forgiving, flexible, and so much fun to build up layer by layer. The magic of an eye-catching wreath comes from adding variety to the leaf shapes, sizes, shades of green, and directions. Play around and let your brush dance around the circle. Begin with two main leaf clusters at different anchor points, and slowly add more leaves for a fuller look.

Colors

- Olive Green
- Hooker's Green
- Indigo
- Sap Green
- Burnt Umber
- Shadow Green
- Greenish Yellow
- Prussian Blue, optional

Brushes

- Size 8 round brush
- Size 6 round brush
- ⅜-inch (1-cm) filbert brush
- Size 2 round brush

Other Materials

- Pencil
- White gouache

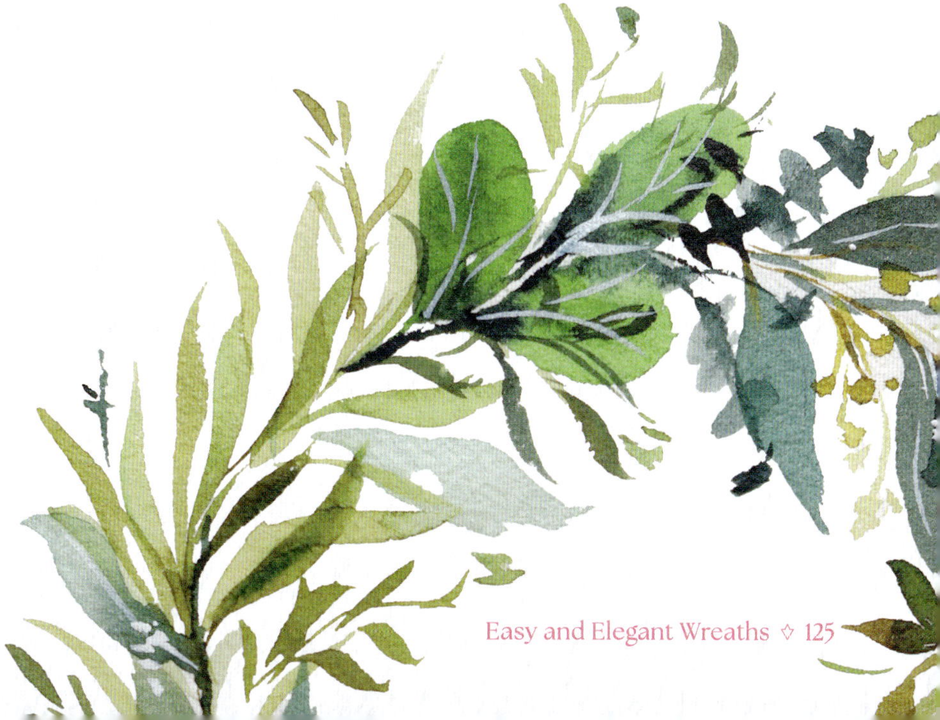

1. Start with the Base

With a pencil, lightly sketch a circle as a guide. Begin with two sets of Seeded Eucalyptus (page 111) placed diagonally across from each other. Paint the stems first with medium-consistency Olive Green. Then, mix a medium consistency of two parts Hooker's Green and one part Indigo for a rich, deep green. Load your size 8 round brush with plenty of paint, press the brush down, and gently drag it to form elongated leaves. Paint three to five leaves per section, adding more later if needed. Let them face in different directions for a natural look.

2. Add the Slender and Rounded Leaves

Following your circle outline, add two sets of long, slender leaves near the Seeded Eucalyptus. Load your size 6 round brush with a mix of two parts Sap Green and one part Burnt Umber. Prepare a light and medium consistency. Press, drag, and slightly wiggle your brush to create movement. Alternate the green tones for variety.

Next, let's add the rounded leaves using Sap Green. Add about three on each side. You may add more if it feels right. While still wet, drop in a thick consistency of Indigo at the leaf bases to create contrast.

3. Add the Seeds and the Baby Eucalyptus

Beside the rounded leaves, let's add the baby eucalyptus. Paint short, thin stems first using a medium-consistency Shadow Green. Next, grab your ³⁄₈-inch (1-cm) filbert brush and load it with the same Shadow Green. Start stamping the side of the brush on the stems to create flat, oval-shaped leaves. Alternate lighter and darker green leaves. A round brush also works if you don't have a filbert.

For the seeds, load your size 2 round brush with light-consistency Greenish Yellow. Paint small round shapes in clustered groups of three to six, then connect them with thin stems. Place these near the Seeded Eucalyptus leaves.

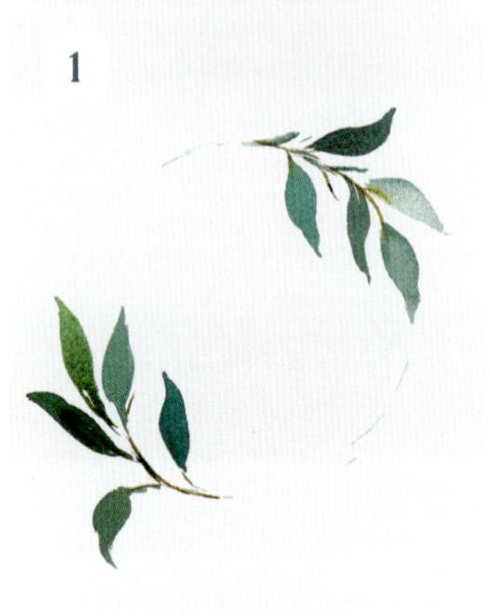

1

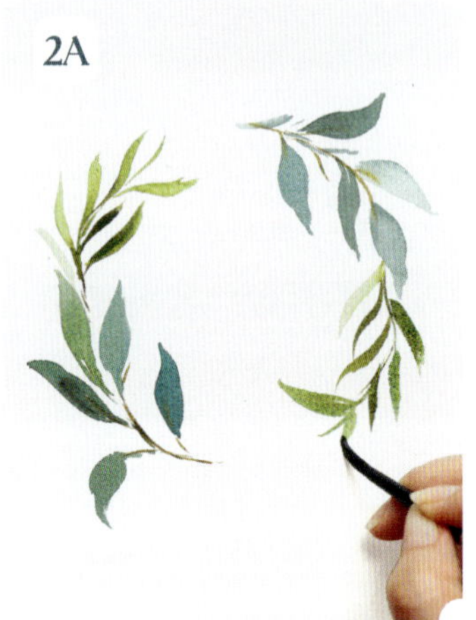

2A

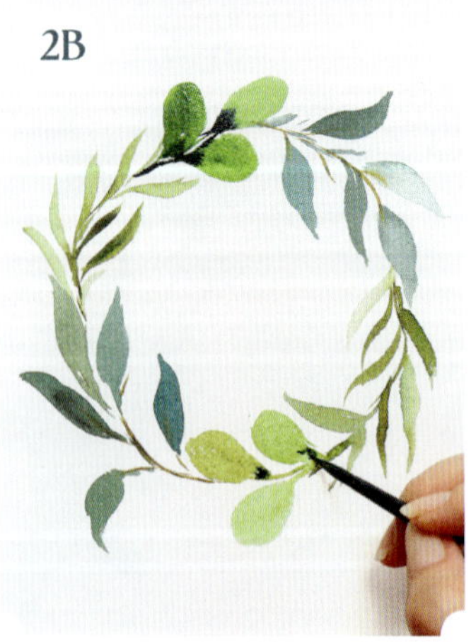

2B

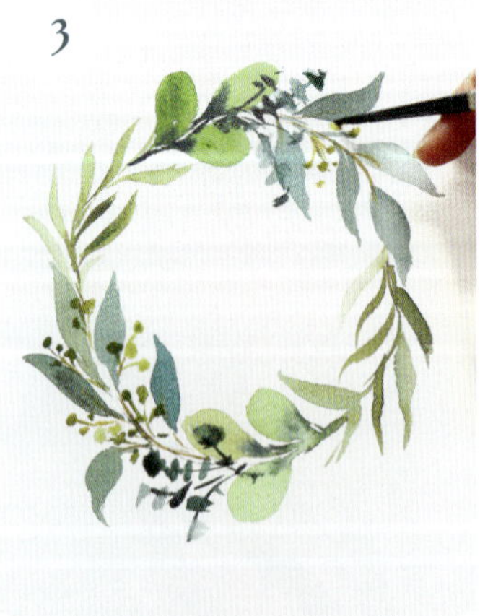

3

4. Layer the Leaves

Use a hairdryer to quickly dry the first layer. Then, let's add another layer of leaves to create depth and fill in the gaps. With a light mix of Sap Green and Burnt Umber, load your size 6 round brush. Paint a few slender leaves on top of the existing ones, overlapping some so they look intertwined.

Start adding smaller leaves all around the wreath with a size 2 round brush, alternating between Sap Green and Olive Green. Vary the leaf direction.

5. Add Shadow Leaves and Thin, Wispy Foliage

Shadow leaves are very light, almost translucent. Try mixing Sap Green with a touch of Prussian Blue or Indigo. Add this in odd gaps to fill in the spaces without making the wreath feel heavy.

For wispy foliage, use a size 2 round brush to make quick flicks and curved strokes for small sprigs or to connect larger leaves together. Vary the tones, and consider using a medium-consistency Indigo for contrast. Feel free to add it where it feels right.

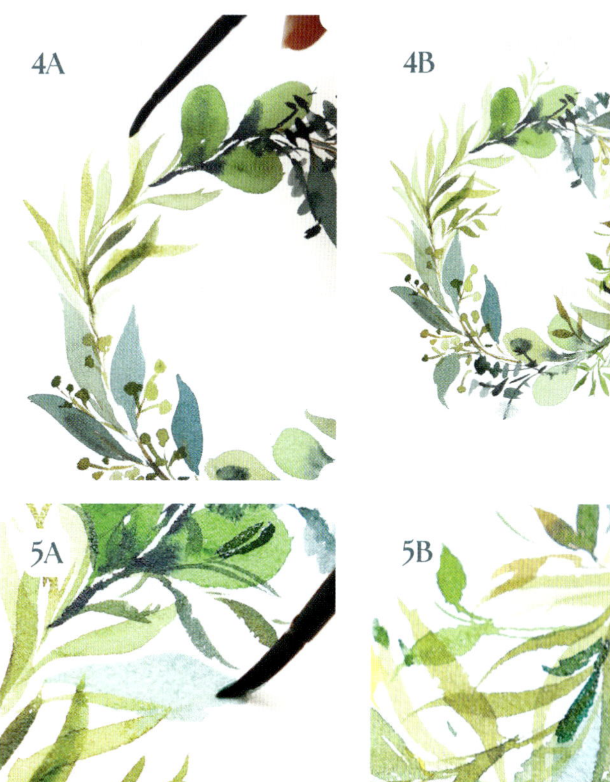

6. Adding White Gouache

Mix a creamy consistency of white gouache and load your size 2 round brush. Use this to add veins on the leaves or cover patchy spots. You can also add small white berries or flowers. Well done! You've just created a beautiful, elegant wreath!

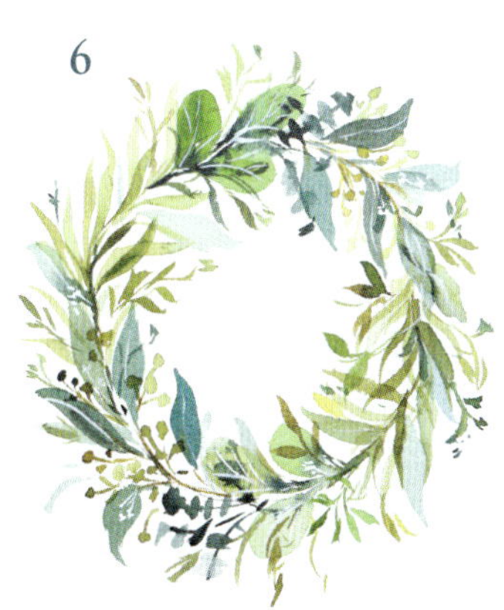

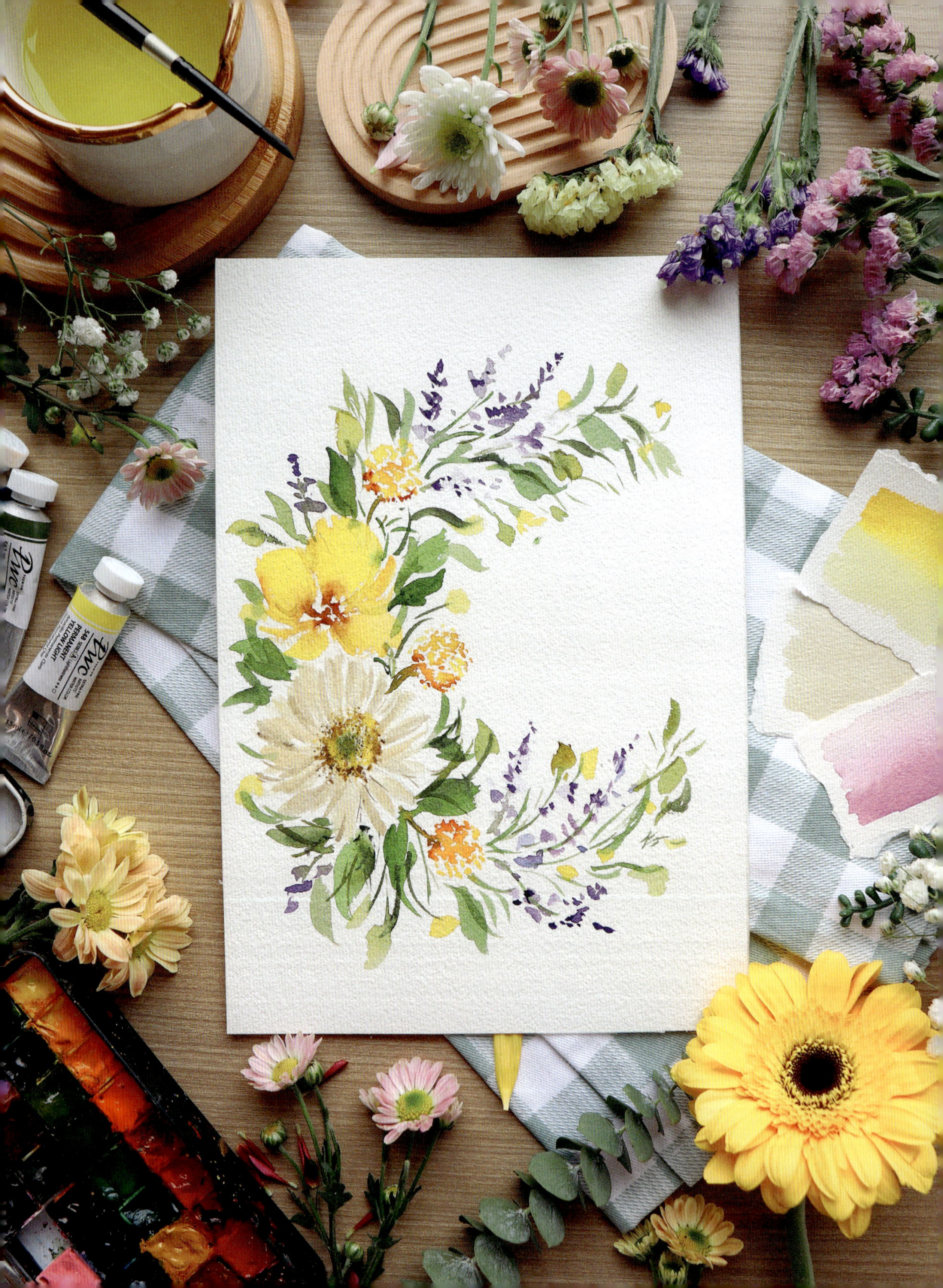

HALF MOON WREATH

The Half Moon Wreath is such a fun composition to paint! It features flowers and foliage flowing along one curve while the other side stays open, giving it an airy feel. You can let the curve sweep upward or tilt it sideways like a letter C. Either way, it creates a beautiful sense of balance.

In this lesson, you will learn how to combine different floral shapes, such as a Gerbera (page 79) and Craspedia (page 101). We'll use yellow and violet, which are complementary colors that will make this composition pop. To soften the look, we'll use Buff Titanium for the Gerbera, then incorporate fillers like Lavender (page 91) to bring movement and flow to the wreath.

Colors

- Sap Green
- Permanent Yellow Light
- Buff Titanium
- Burnt Sienna
- Permanent Yellow Deep
- Permanent Violet
- Mineral Violet, optional
- Lavender, optional
- Burnt Umber
- Indigo, optional
- Greenish Yellow

Brushes

- Size 2.5 surikomi brush or ¼-inch deerfoot brush
- ⅜-inch (1-cm) filbert brush
- Size 4 round brush
- Size 2 round brush

Other Materials

- Pencil

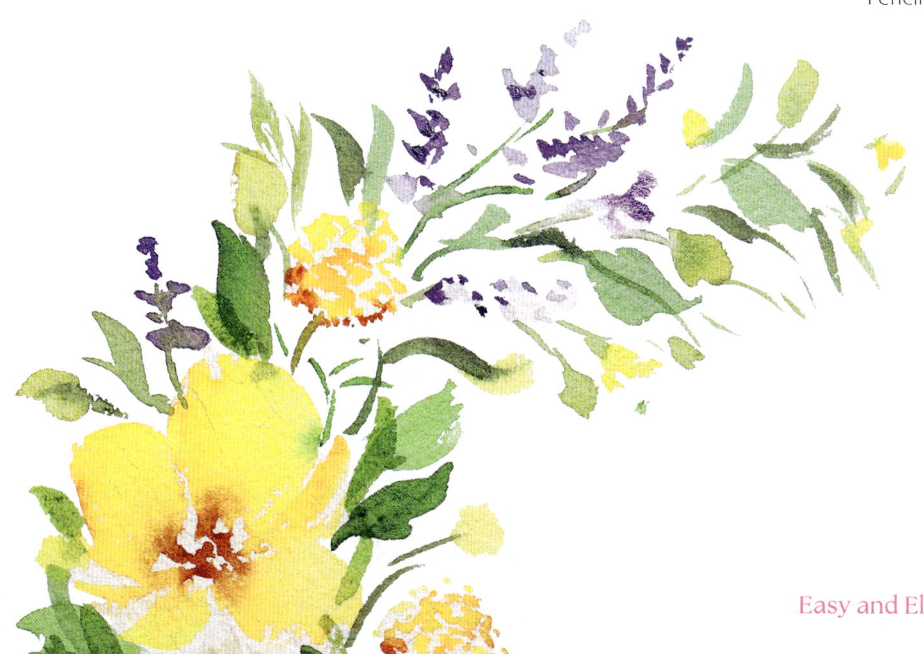

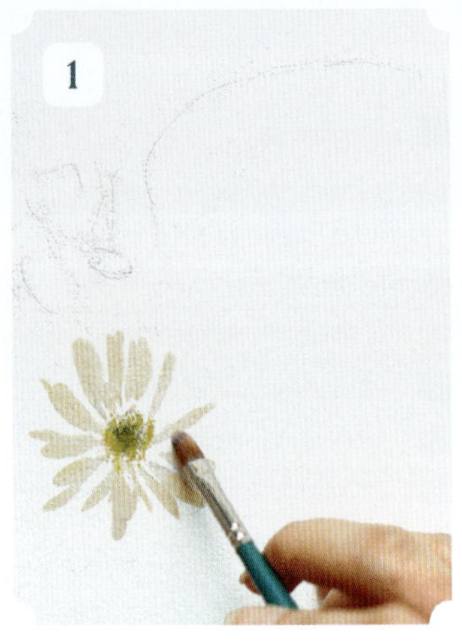

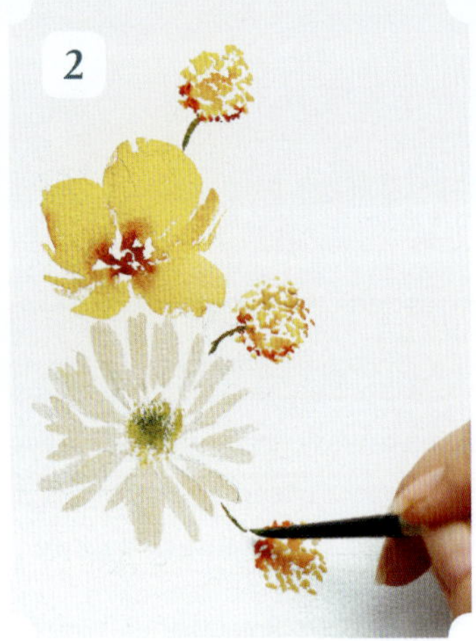

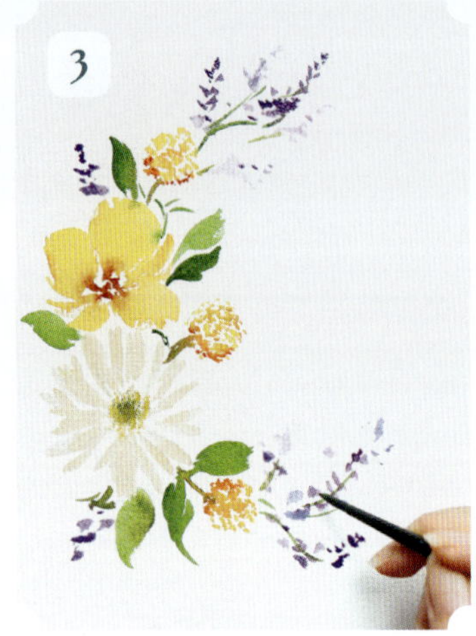

1. Paint the White Gerbera

Using a pencil, lightly sketch a C shape as a guide for the wreath. Begin with a Gerbera (page 79) on the lower-left curve. Using a suri-komi or deerfoot brush, dab the flower center with thick-consistency Sap Green. Then, dab a ring around it using Permanent Yellow Light.

To paint the petals, switch to a ³⁄₈-inch (1-cm) filbert brush and load it with light-consistency Buff Titanium. Pull the petals from the tip to the center, using the flat side for broad strokes and the edge for thinner ones. Continue around the center, making sure to leave white spaces in between.

2. Add the Supporting Flowers

Above the Gerbera, paint a simple four-petal flower with medium-consistency Permanent Yellow Light. Press, drag, and lift your brush to create a petal, then add thin strokes beside it for character. Paint three petals in a fan shape, then a shorter petal tucked below to suggest it's behind the Gerbera. Drop Burnt Sienna into the center while the petals are damp.

Next, add three Craspedia flowers (page 101) at three different points of the wreath.

3. Paint the Lavender

With a medium-consistency Sap Green, paint thin, curvy stems on each side of the wreath to help define the half-moon shape. Along the stems, dab Lavender flowers (page 91) with a size 4 round brush with Permanent Violet. You may use Mineral Violet and Lavender for variation. Leave space between strokes to create an airy feel. Add a few Sap Green leaves near the main flowers to frame them and make them pop.

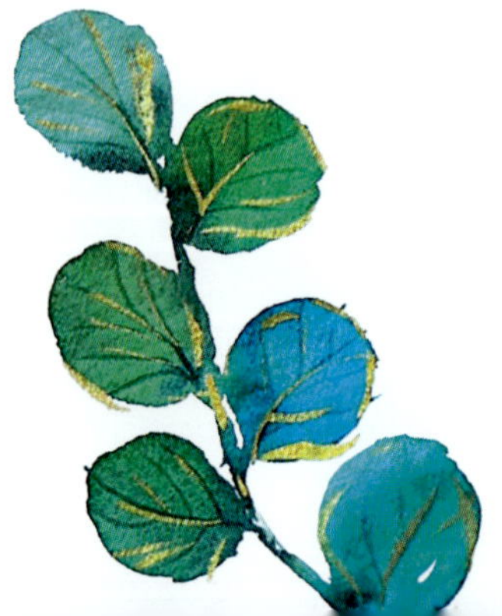

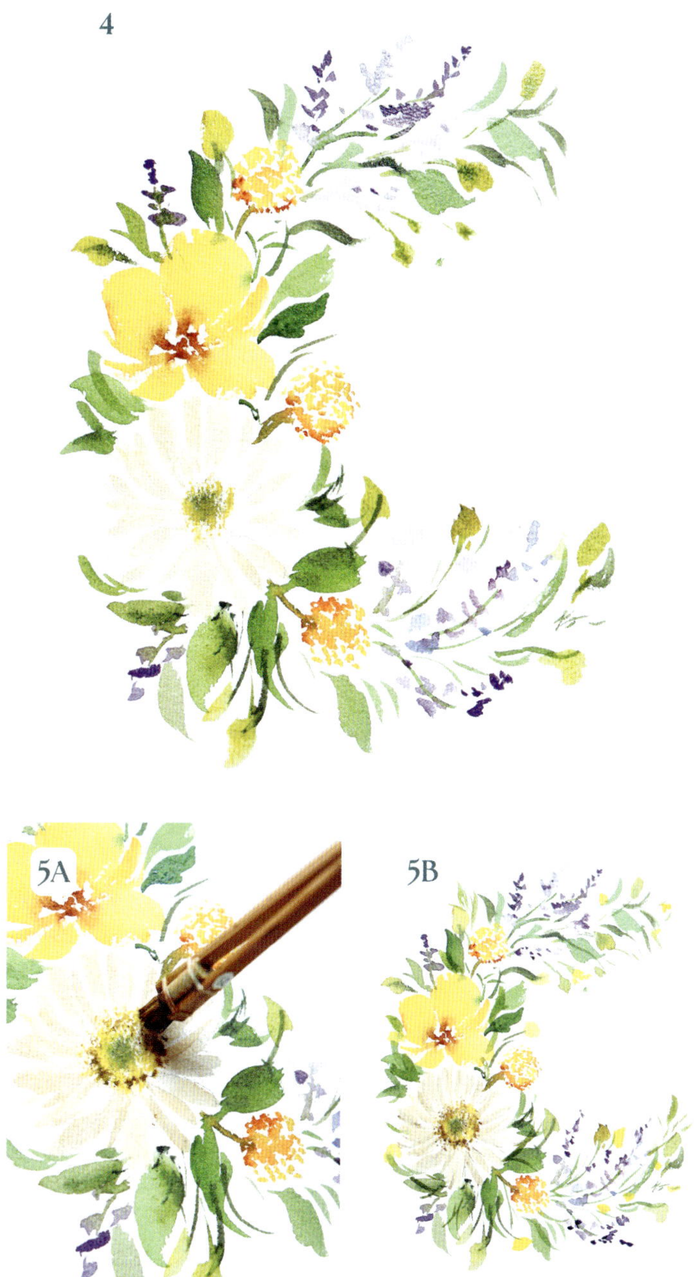

4. Add More Foliage

Prepare your greens. Mix two parts Sap Green and one part Burnt Umber (or add Indigo for variety.) Fill the wreath with leaves near the fillers. Use a size 2 round brush to add wispy leaves near each end of the wreath so it looks a little tapered and airy.

For a fresh accent, dab small buds using Greenish Yellow all around the wreath.

5. Add More Depth

Deepen the Gerbera by layering additional petals on top of the base petals using a ³⁄₈-inch (1-cm) filbert brush. Use a medium consistency of four parts Buff Titanium and one part Burnt Umber. The color should be one to two shades deeper than the base flower. Be careful not to overcrowd. You can switch to a size 2 round brush for thin strokes in between the petals.

For the center, prepare a thick-consistency Burnt Umber. Using a surikomi brush or a deerfoot brush, lightly dab the brush to add texture around the yellow ring. A round brush also works.

Finally, sprinkle in a few small yellow buds using Permanent Yellow Light along the wreath for extra color. You've added such lovely depth!

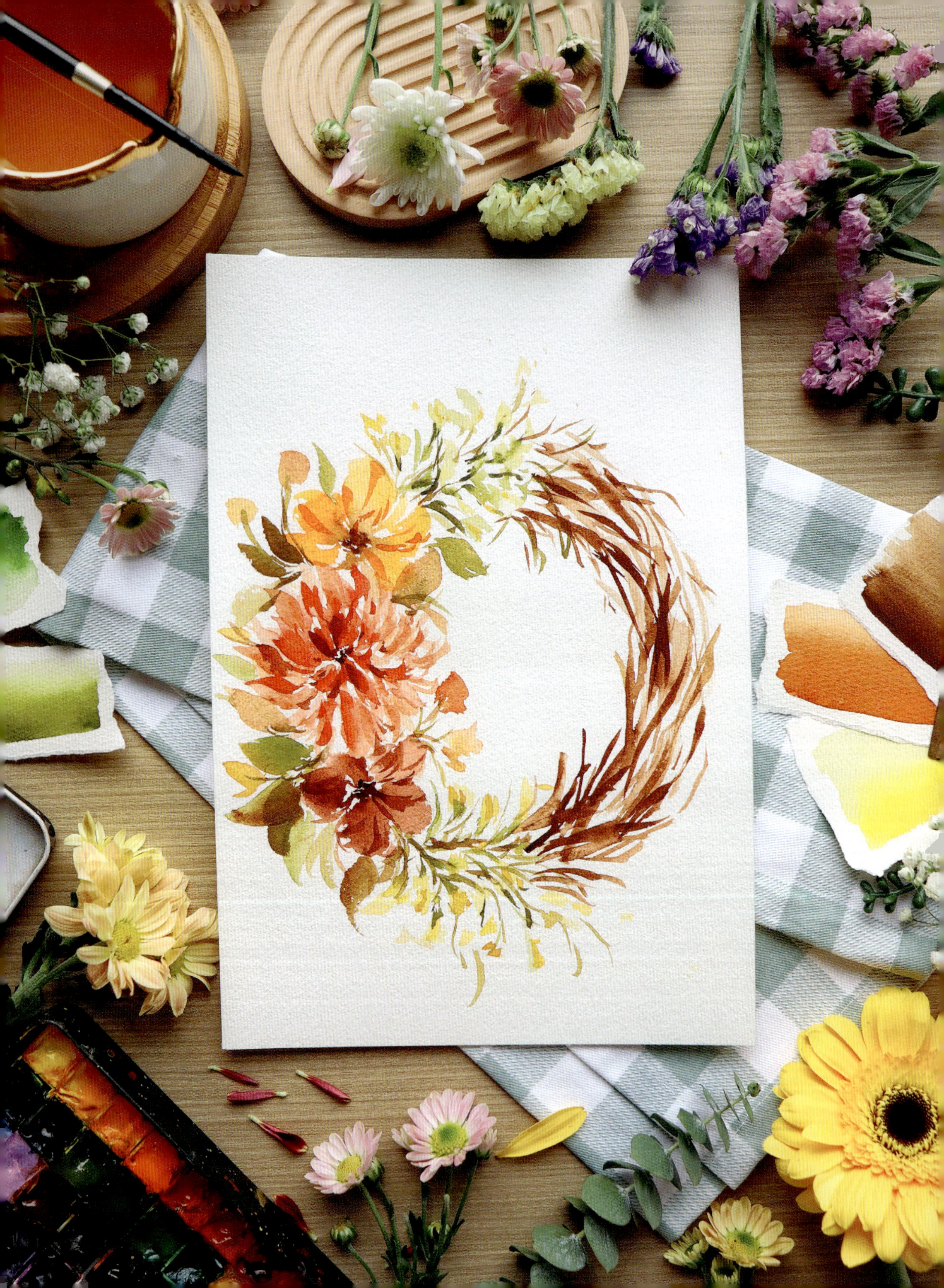

RUSTIC FLORAL WREATH

There's something warm and inviting about a rustic wreath, which is why I chose a palette inspired by autumn colors. In this project, we'll learn how to paint easy, earthy twigs with dimension, then pair them with a Dahlia (page 57) and warm orange Five-Petal Flowers (page 111). We'll also paint Sea Lavender (page 105), which adds to the rustic charm with its papery petals. Feel free to add more flowers that suit your style. You can also add some Sunset Orange Gerberas (page 79) and Romantic Pink Roses (page 37).

Colors

- Permanent Rose
- Burnt Sienna
- Yellow Orange
- Burnt Umber
- Brown Red
- Olive Green
- Permanent Yellow Light

Brush

- Size 6 round brush

Other Materials

- Pencil
- Small bowl or jar, optional

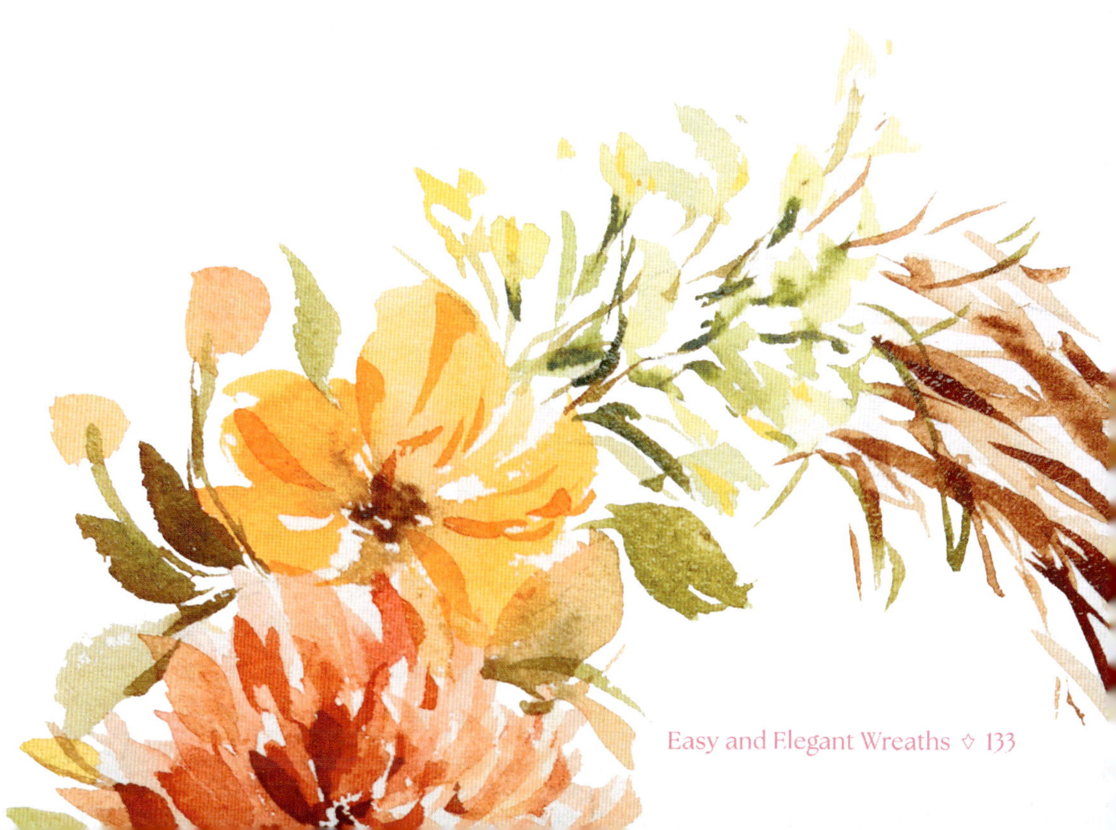

1. Paint the Main Flower

With a pencil, lightly sketch a circle to serve as a guide for the wreath shape. You may use a small bowl or jar to trace the circle. On the left side, sketch three circles, one large for the main flower and two medium for the secondary flowers.

Let's start with the Dahlia (page 57) in a warm orange-brown color. Mix equal parts Permanent Rose and Burnt Sienna. Paint the base layer first, varying the consistency for depth. Use a thicker consistency for the strokes in the center.

2. Add the Secondary Flowers

We'll paint simple Five-Petal Flowers (page 111) to complement the Dahlia. The size will be a little bit smaller than the Dahlia. Load your size 6 round brush with medium-consistency Yellow Orange. Paint four petals in a fan shape, leaving the bottom petal out so the flowers appear behind the Dahlia. While the petals are still damp, drop in a thick-consistency Burnt Umber at the center.

For the bottom flower, repeat the steps using Brown Red.

3. Add Leaves and Sea Lavender

Paint leaves between the main flowers, using different mixes of Olive Green and Burnt Sienna. You can also mix some of the main flower color into your greens. Here, I added a touch of Yellow Orange to make the palette more cohesive. Vary the shape, size, and direction to make it more natural.

Next, paint Sea Lavender (page 105) on each side of the wreath near the Five-Petal Flowers using Permanent Yellow Light. Keep it loose, as we can always add more later on.

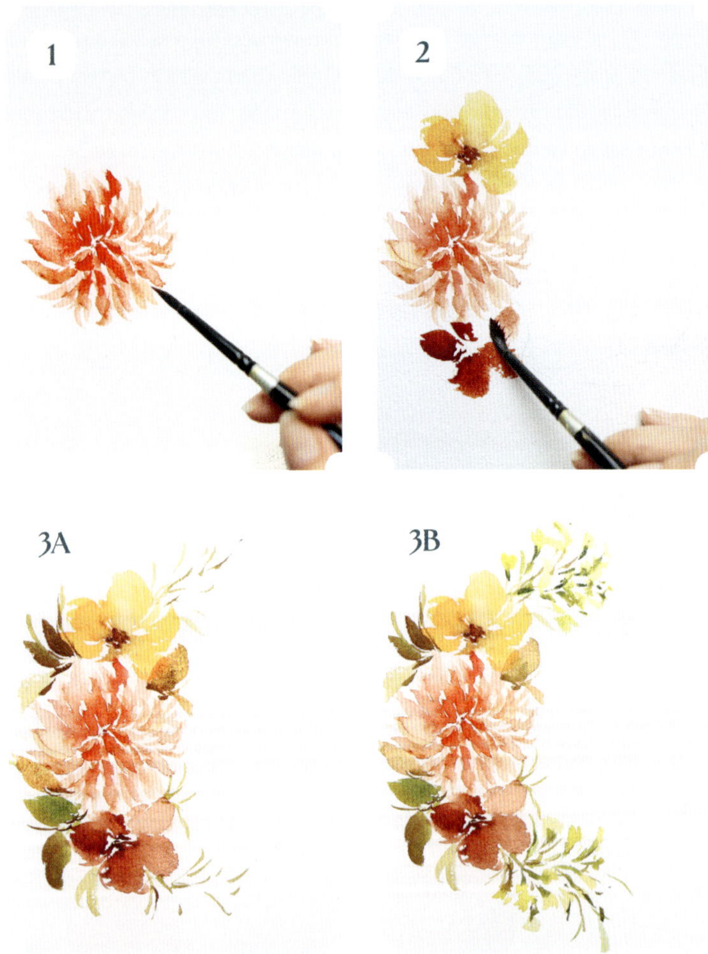

4. Paint the Twigs

For the twigs on the right side of the wreath, mix a light consistency of Burnt Umber and load it onto your size 6 round brush. Using the tip of the brush, paint in broken, uneven lines instead of one continuous stroke. Let some parts skip small sections or fade out. Vary the pressure so the twigs look loose and organic. The irregularity will give them that rustic, natural feel.

While the first layer is still damp, mix a medium-consistency Burnt Umber. Paint a second layer of twigs, overlapping the first. Let the darker strokes bleed into the lighter ones and let some twigs stick out.

5. Paint the Second Layer for the Flowers

Use a hairdryer to quickly dry the first layer. Paint more curved petals on the Dahlia using a thick consistency of Permanent Rose and Burnt Sienna.

For the Five-Petal Flowers, use a thick consistency of the same color as the base layer. Paint a few thin veins on the petals, just enough to add texture without overcrowding.

6. Add Finishing Touches

Fill any gaps with small buds using the main flower color. Lightly dab your brush to create a petal shape and attach it to a green stem.

Paint wispy foliage using a medium-consistency Olive Green around the wreath using the tip of the brush. You may also add more Sea Lavender to make the wreath look fuller.

Mix equal parts of Permanent Rose, Burnt Sienna, and Brown Red. Using a size 6 round brush, paint thin, curvy strokes, concentrating more in the center of the Dahlia. Lastly, use thick-consistency Burnt Umber to layer in a few more twigs for extra depth.

Wonderful work! Your rustic floral wreath looks warm and natural!

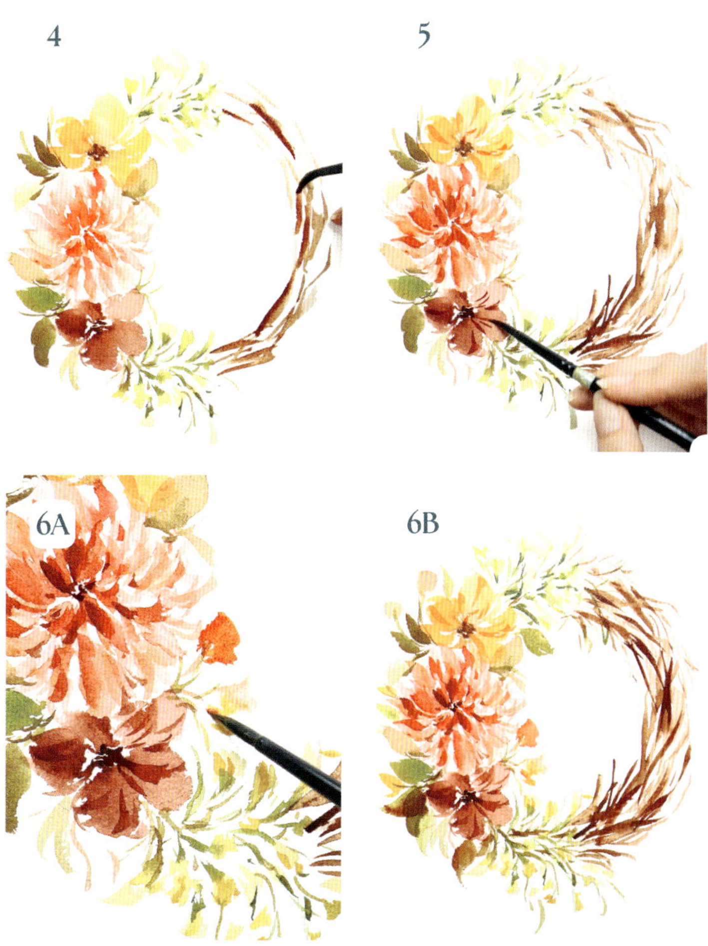

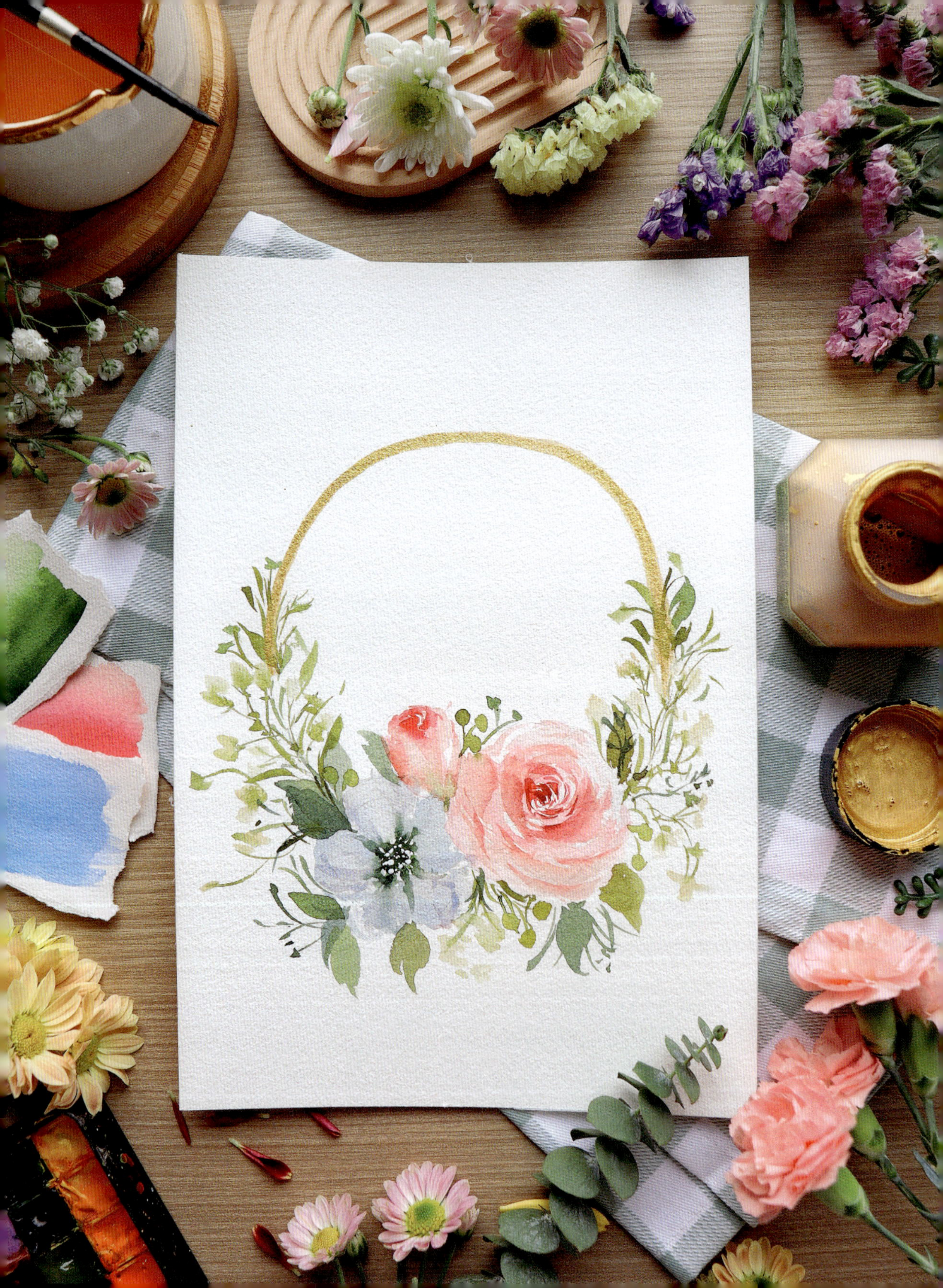

GOLD RING FLORAL WREATH

Adding a touch of gold to my paintings is one of my favorite things to do! It instantly brings elegance and a little sparkle to the page. The gold ring transforms a simple floral cluster into something refined and modern.

In this lesson, you will learn how to combine a Rose (page 37) and Scabiosa (page 69) into a cluster, then taper the design with fillers like Baby's Breath (page 105), green berries, and other leaves so it flows naturally into the gold ring. This wreath is both quick and fun to paint since you only need to fill in the lower half with flowers, and let the gold ring do the rest!

Colors

- Permanent Rose
- Sap Green
- Ultramarine Blue
- Burnt Umber
- Olive Green
- Buff Titanium
- Greenish Yellow
- Indigo

Brushes

- Size 4 round brush
- Size 2 round brush
- ⅜-inch (1-cm) filbert brush

Other Materials

- Pencil
- Small bowl or jar, optional
- Kuretake Gold Mica

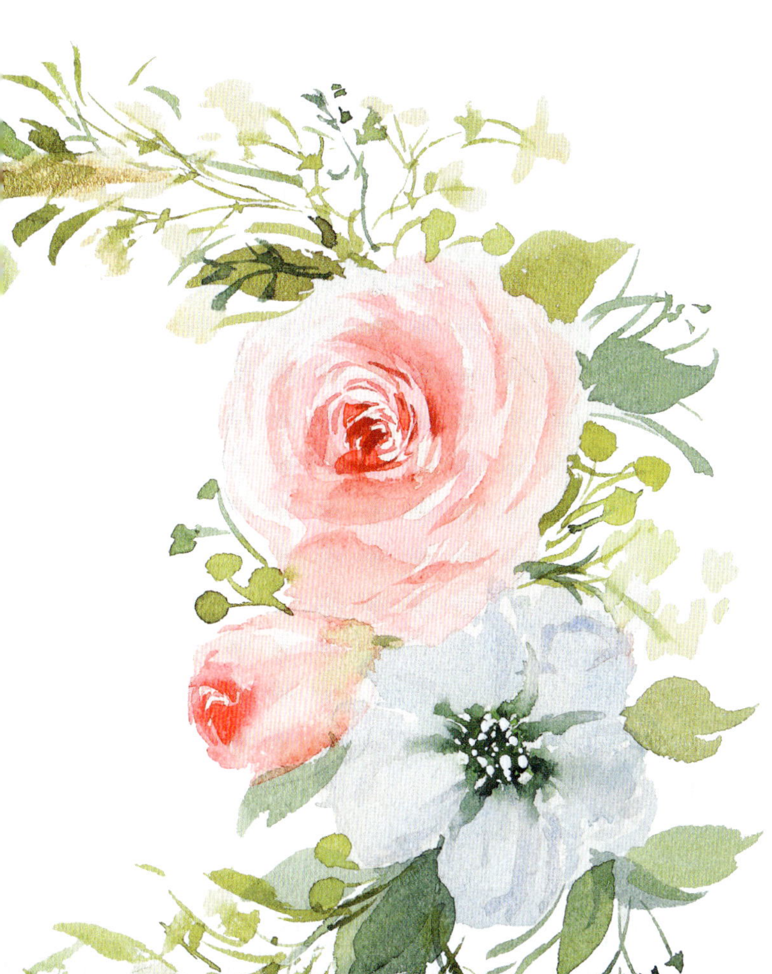

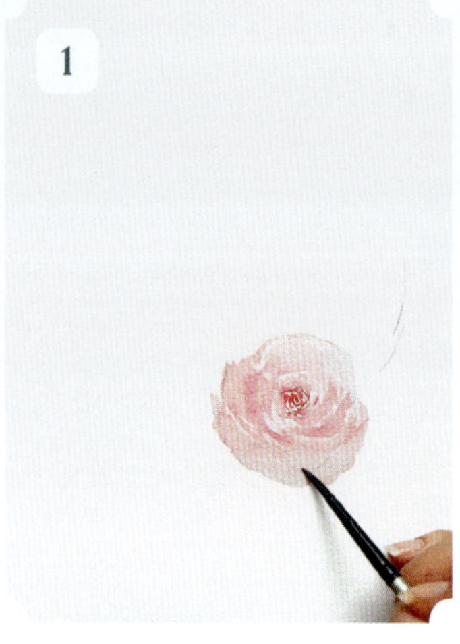

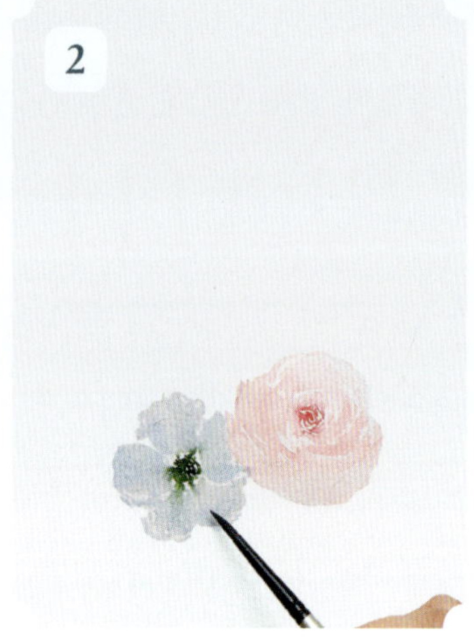

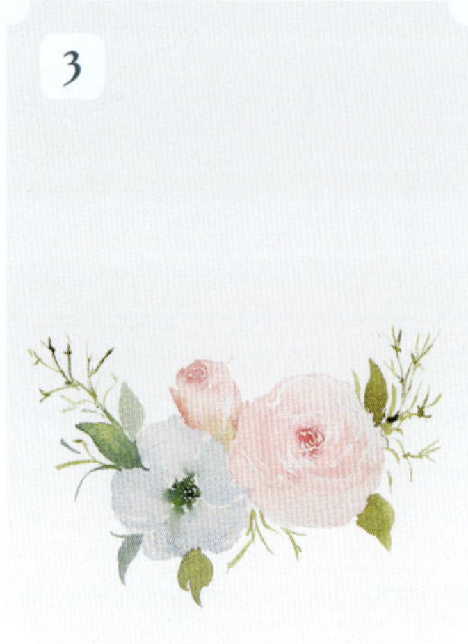

1. Paint the Main Flowers

Using a pencil, lightly sketch a large circle as a guide for the shape of the wreath. You may use a bowl or a jar to trace the circle. At the bottom, draw two medium circles diagonally across from each other and one smaller circle between them. Using a size 4 round brush, begin with a Rose (page 37) on the lower-right side using the color Permanent Rose.

2. Add White Scabiosa

For the center of the Scabiosa (page 69), use thick-consistency Sap Green and paint small dots until you form a small circle.

To create neutral white petals, mix equal parts Ultramarine Blue and Burnt Umber with lots of water. Adjust the ratio depending on whether you want a cooler or warmer color. With a size 4 round brush, press, wiggle, drag, and lift to shape the petals. Add five or six around the center.

3. Add a Rosebud, Stems, and Leaves

Paint a rosebud between the main flowers, angled slightly for a natural look. Starting with thick-consistency Permanent Rose, paint short strokes at the top of the rosebud. Rinse your brush and pull the color down to form the bud.

For the greenery, prepare two parts Sap Green and one part Burnt Umber. Add leaves between the flowers, varying the hues by dropping in a touch of blue.

With medium-consistency Olive Green and your size 2 round brush, paint Baby's Breath stems (page 105) extending on each side of the main flowers.

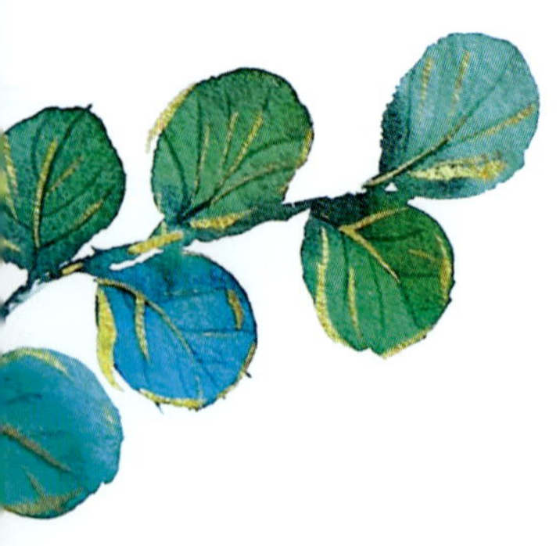

4. Paint the Baby's Breath Flower and Other Fillers

Dab tiny blooms along the Baby's Breath stems using Buff Titanium. You can drop in a little bit of Greenish Yellow for a pop of color.

Add more leaves for dimension, overlapping the first layer. Using a size 2 round brush, paint wispy leaves using a mix of two parts Sap Green and one part Indigo to add contrast. Next, paint small green berries between the flowers using Greenish Yellow for a lively accent. Add more Baby's Breath if you need more volume in your wreath.

5. Add More Depth

Deepen the rose by layering the petals in one to two shades darker than your base. Paint more C-shaped strokes to make it fuller. For the Scabiosa, refine the petals by adding light veins using Ultramarine Blue, then place a few Indigo dots in the center for contrast.

6. Paint the Gold Ring

Dip a ³⁄₈-inch (1-cm) filbert brush into the gold paint and tap off the excess. Use the side of the brush to paint the upper half of the circle by following the pencil outline. A flat or round brush also works.

Once you complete the gold ring, the part where the ring meets the floral section might look bare. Soften this area by adding a few overlapping leaves with a medium-consistency Olive Green to seamlessly connect the gold ring and lower floral half. Great job! You've just painted an elegant wreath.

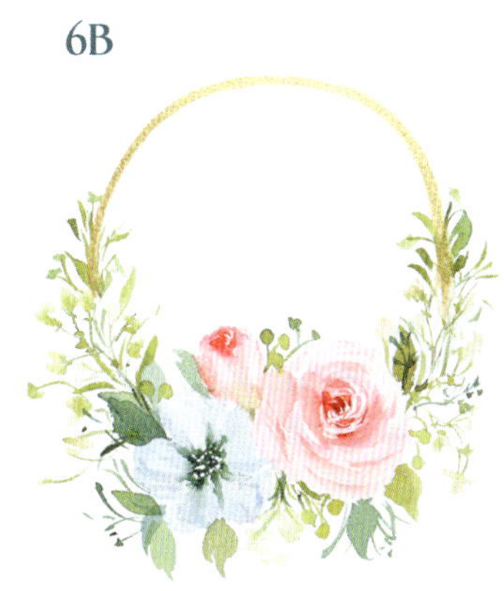

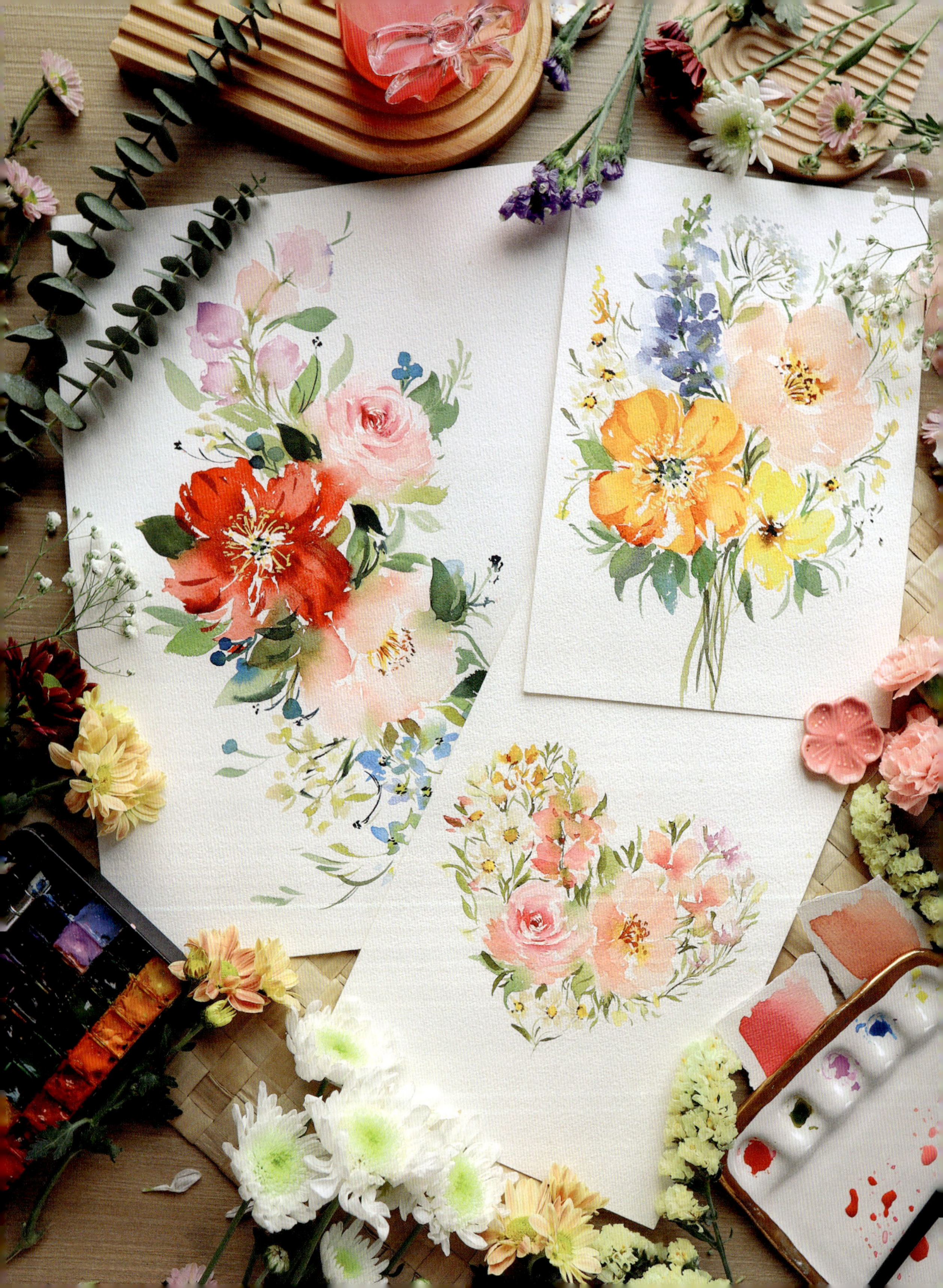

Dreamy and Charming
BOUQUETS

Painting bouquets is a great way to bring together everything you've learned so far. Unlike wreaths, which form a circle, bouquets let you play with flow and direction.

In this section, we will experiment with different ways of arranging blooms, such as the S curve, which guides our viewers' eyes across the page. We'll also paint a Loose Hand-Tied Bouquet (page 143), learning how to combine focal flowers, secondary flowers, and fillers. For something a little more playful, we'll create a Heart-Shaped Bouquet (page 157) that's perfect for special occasions like Mother's Day or Valentine's Day.

Each bouquet will give you a chance to practice movement, balance, and composition, while still leaving plenty of room for your own style.

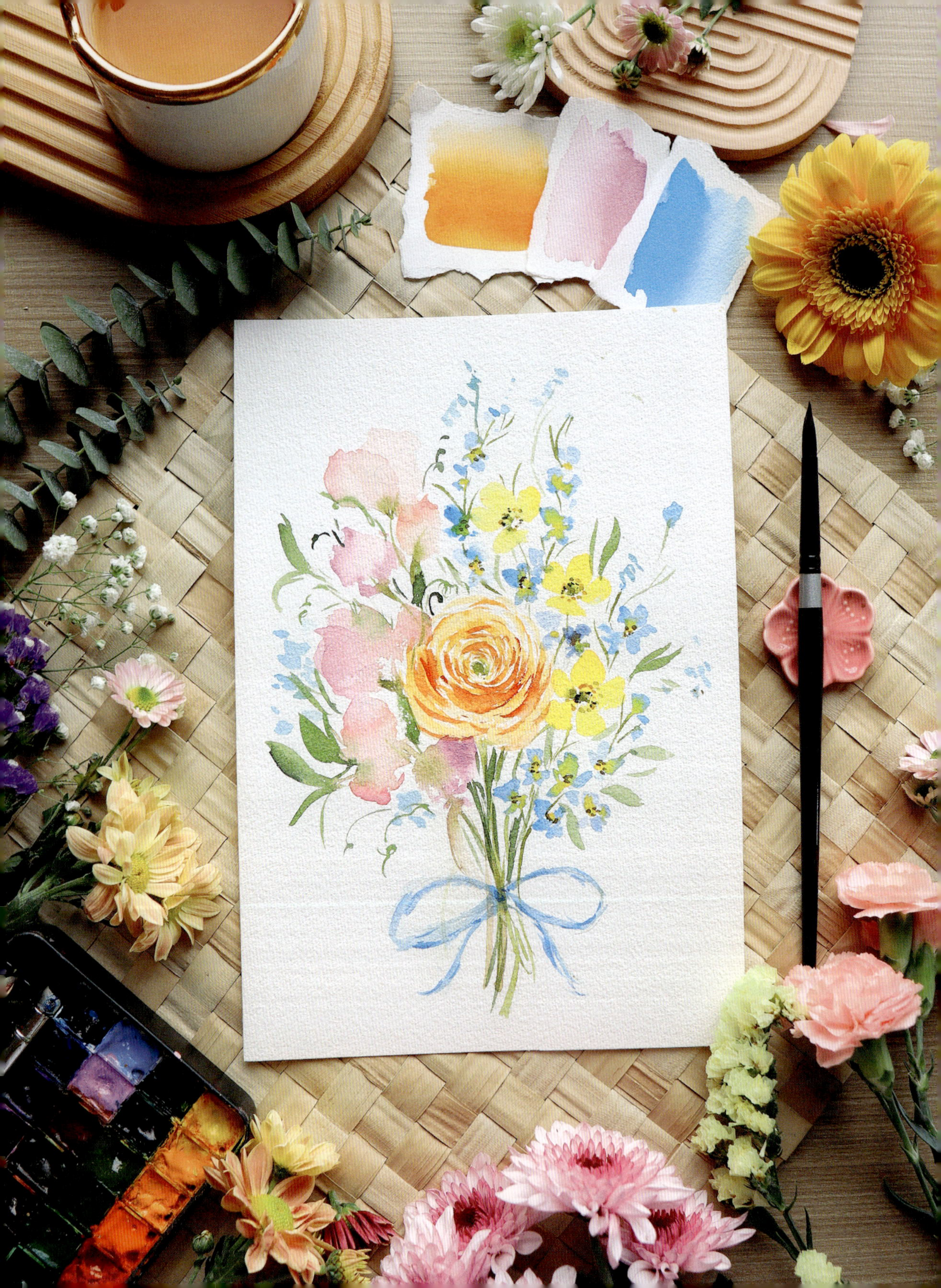

LOOSE HAND-TIED BOUQUET

In this lesson, we'll paint a cheerful hand-tied bouquet that feels fresh and balanced. We'll begin with the vibrant orange Ranunculus (page 53) as the focal flower with its round, layered petals. The soft pink Sweet Peas (page 83) add a gentle movement to one side while yellow Buttercups (page 95) bring a pop of color. Small blue Forget-Me-Nots (page 95) act as delicate fillers, tying the entire arrangement together. By mixing flowers of different sizes, we'll create a loose bouquet that feels natural.

Colors

- Sap Green
- Yellow Orange
- Olive Green
- Permanent Yellow Light
- Permanent Yellow Deep
- Verditer Blue
- Cerulean Blue
- Permanent Rose
- Lilac
- Burnt Umber
- Permanent Red
- Indigo

Brushes

- Size 4 round brush
- Size 8 round brush
- Size 2 round brush

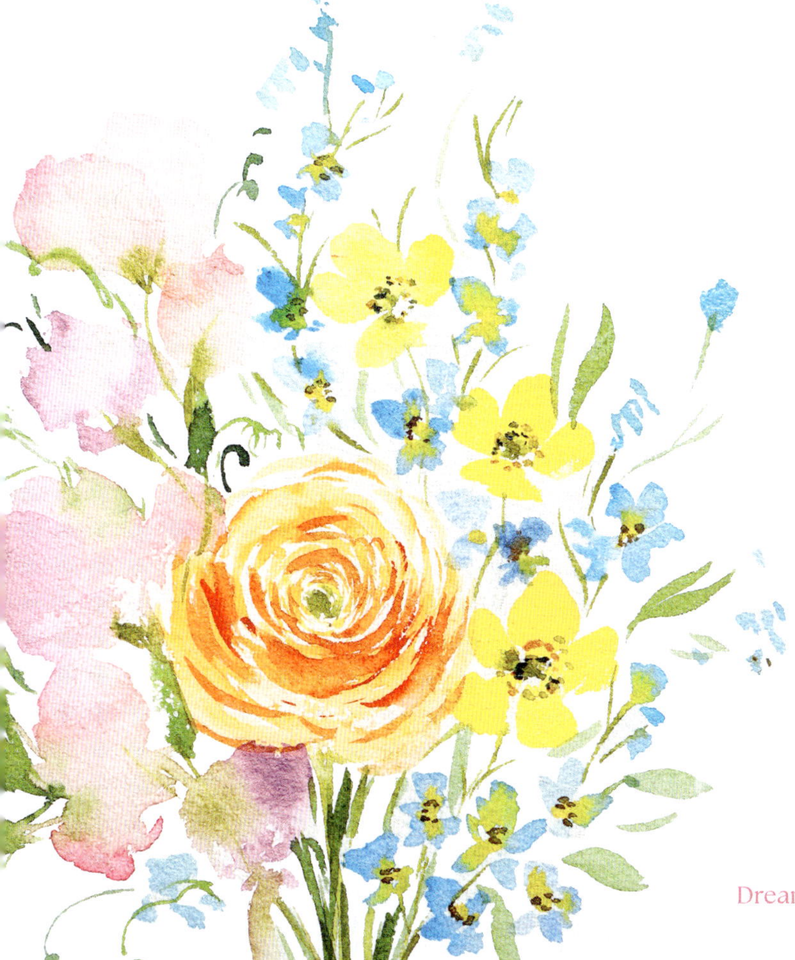

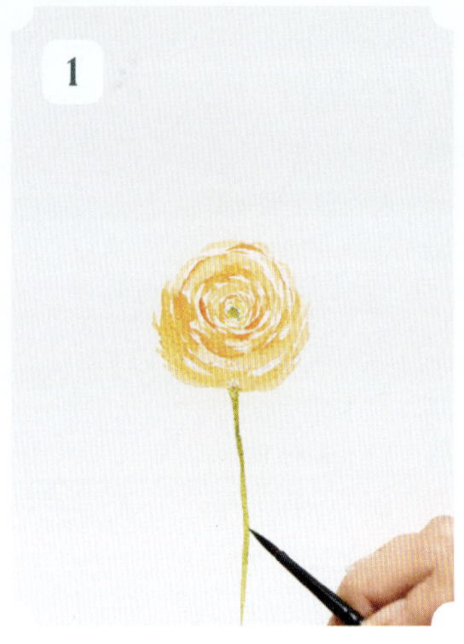

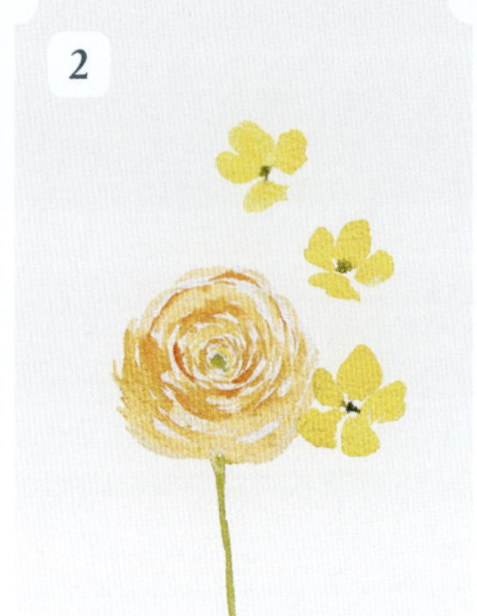

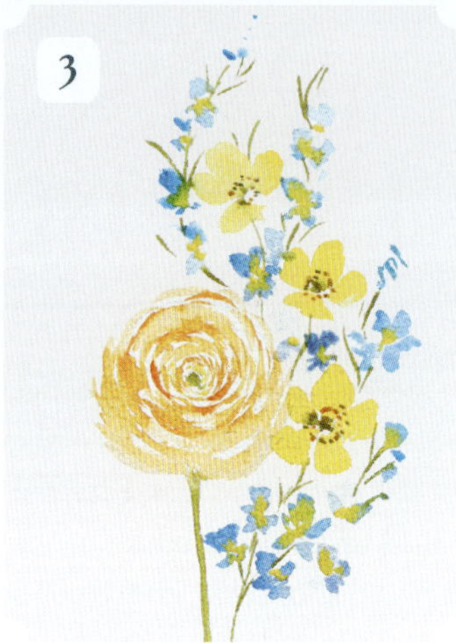

1. Start with Main Flower

Begin with a Sunlit Yellow Orange Ranunculus (page 53) in the center of the bouquet using a size 4 round brush. Paint a Sap Green comma stroke, then layer it with thin C strokes using Yellow Orange and add an Olive Green stem.

2. Add Buttercup Flowers

On the right side, paint three or more Buttercups (page 95) using Permanent Yellow Light, then add Olive Green in the center of the flower. Once dry, add small dots of Permanent Yellow Deep and Olive Green around the flower center.

3. Add Forget-Me-Nots

For the Forget-Me-Nots (page 95), alternate Verditer Blue and Cerulean Blue to paint small clusters of four to five petals using a size 4 round brush. Stamp the brush lightly for a loose look and add tiny buds at the top of the stems. Place them around the Ranunculus and Buttercups. Keep them playful and imperfect!

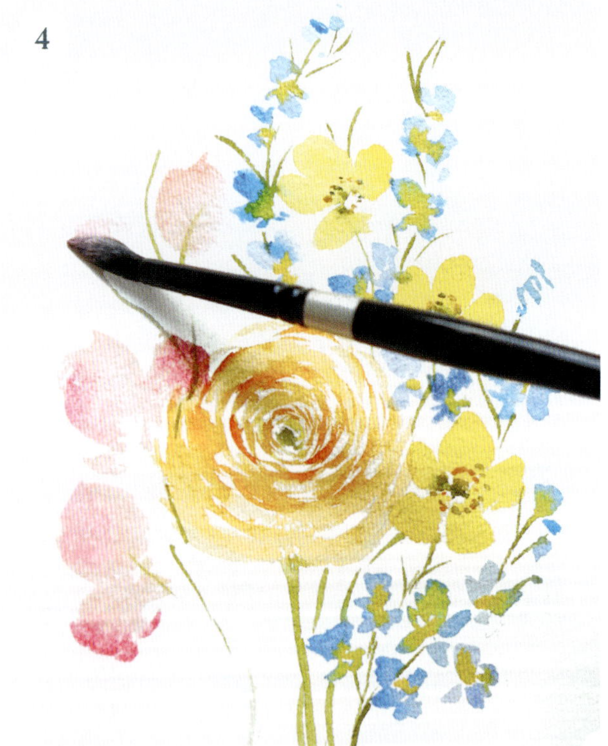

4. Paint the Sweet Peas

Using a size 8 round brush, begin with a thin, Sap Green, curvy stem of Blush Sweet Peas (page 83), using the left side of the Ranunculus as your guide. Alternate the color of the petals with light-consistency Permanent Rose and Lilac.

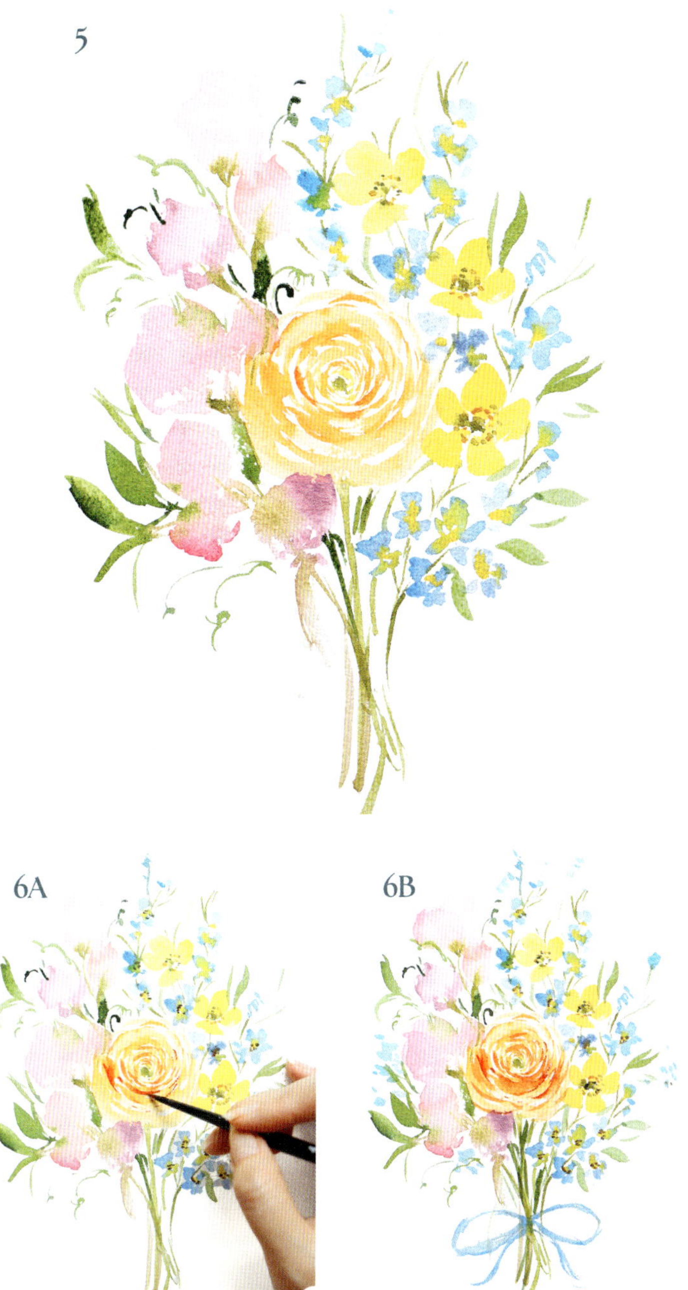

6A 6B

5. Add the Leaves and Tendrils

Add leaves in between the flowers using a size 4 round brush. Mix two parts Sap Green and one part Burnt Umber to make a rich, earthy green. Play with the light and dark tones to make it interesting. Using a size 2 round brush, paint the curly tendrils of the Sweet Peas with Sap Green to add movement.

6. Add Depth and a Ribbon

Using a size 4 round brush, start adding more depth to the Ranunculus by layering thin C strokes, using a mixture of one part Yellow Orange and one part Permanent Red for tighter looking petals. Next, add a ring of tiny Indigo dots around the center of the Forget-Me-Nots.

For the Sweet Peas, mix a light consistency of the base color and overlap more petals on some of the existing ones.

Feel free to add more Forget-Me-Nots on the left side of the bouquet for balance.

Lastly, paint a thin blue ribbon to hold the bouquet together using light-consistency Cerulean Blue. Hooray for your first bouquet! This turned out so radiant.

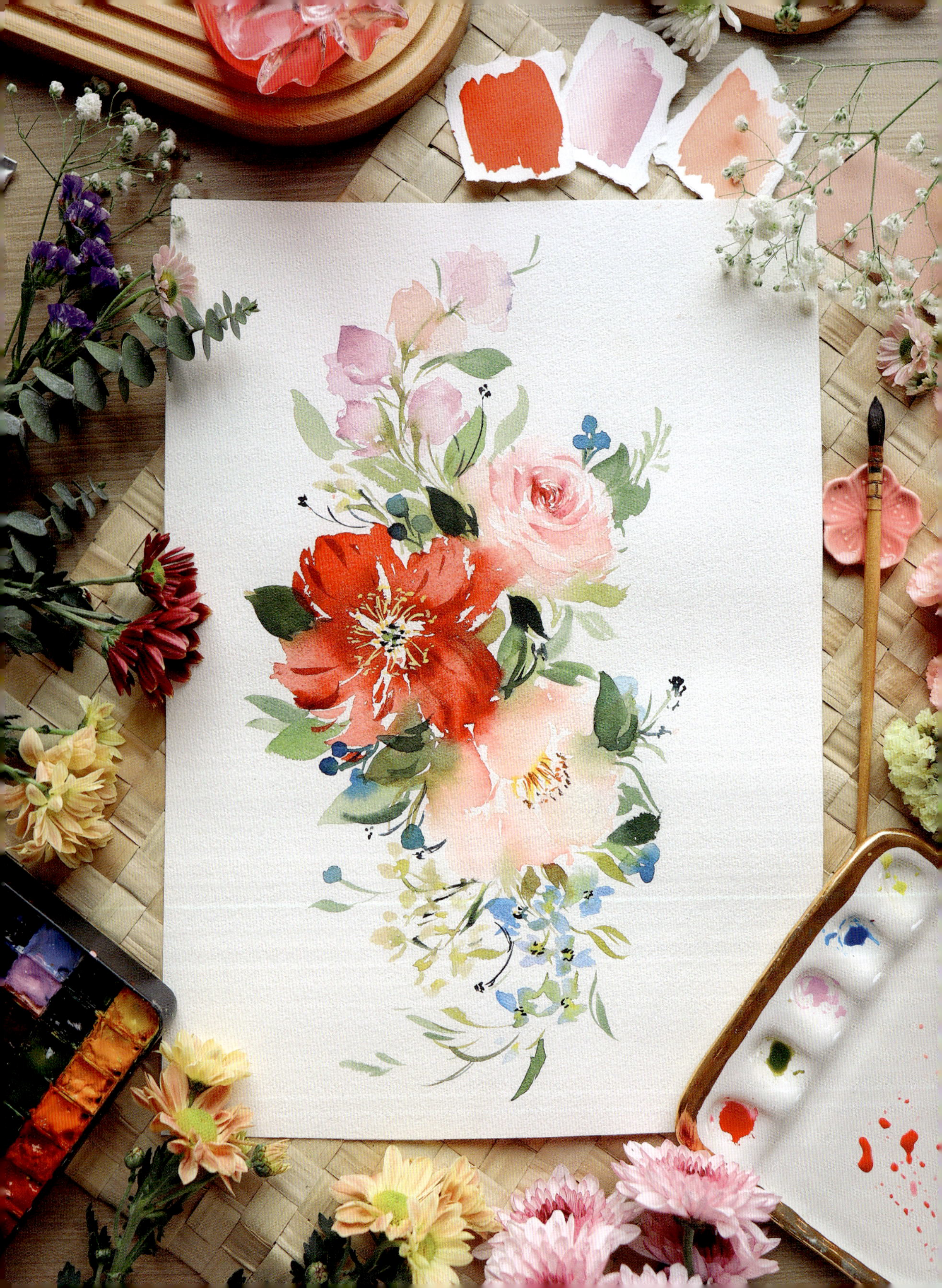

DIAGONAL BLOOM SPRAY

This cheerful yet romantic bouquet dances across the page in a graceful diagonal composition. Its sweep guides the eye from one end to the other, giving the painting a sense of movement and harmony.

In this lesson, you'll learn how to mix focal flowers with supporting flowers, letting the colors blend naturally. We'll play with bold and soft colors using pinks and reds, then add light filler flowers to create an airy, spontaneous feel.

Colors

- Permanent Rose
- Olive Green
- Permanent Yellow Light
- Permanent Red
- Hooker's Green
- Brilliant Pink
- Lilac
- Shell Pink
- Verditer Blue
- Buff Titanium
- Sap Green
- Indigo
- Prussian Blue
- Burnt Sienna

Brushes

- Size 6 round brush
- Size 2 round brush
- Size 0 mop brush
- Size 8 round brush

Other Materials

- Pencil
- Kneaded eraser
- White gouache

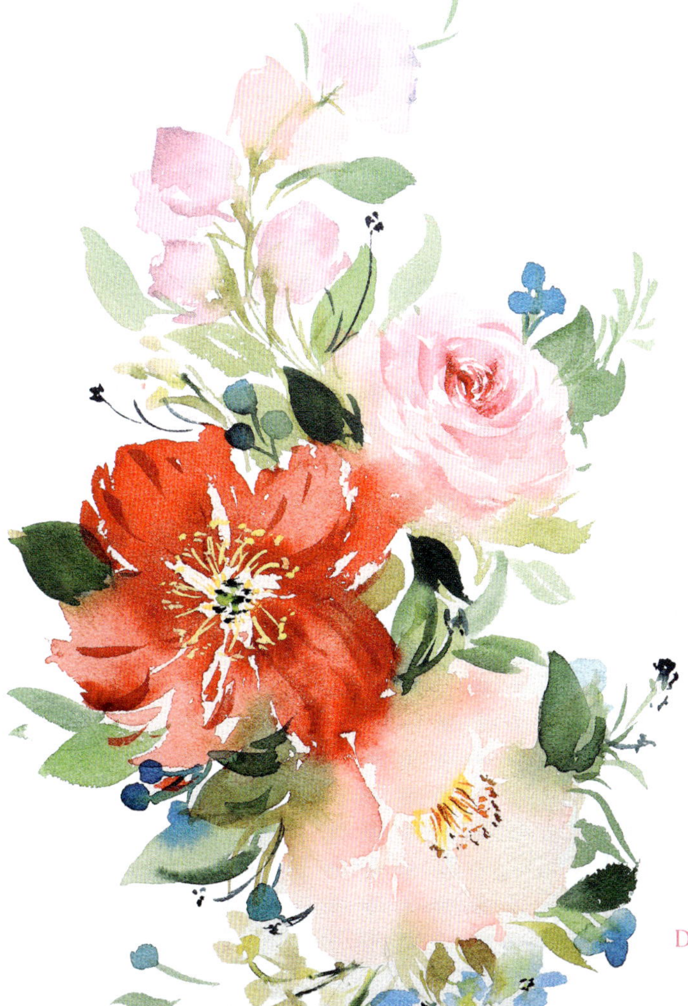

1. Sketch the Shape

Start by sketching either a simple diagonal across your paper or an S curve if you want more movement. Then draw three circles in the center that will represent the main flowers as shown in the photo. Use a kneaded eraser to gently lighten your sketch before painting.

2. Paint a Rose

Begin with the top circle. Using a size 6 round brush, paint the base of the Romantic Pink Rose (page 37) using the color Permanent Rose. Add more petals at the bottom part to suggest that the flower is at an angle. While still damp, paint a few Olive Green leaves around it so they blend softly.

3. Add a Red Poppy

Diagonally below the rose, begin with the Poppy (page 47) with a medium-consistency Permanent Yellow Light. Using a size 2 round brush, paint short strokes to form a small circle. Paint the petals with a size 0 mop brush using Permanent Red. While still damp, drop in a deeper red mixture (three parts Permanent Red and one part Hooker's Green), at the base of the petals near the center for more depth. Let some of its petals touch the rose so the colors blend gently. Work quickly here because both flowers need to be damp to create that soft connection.

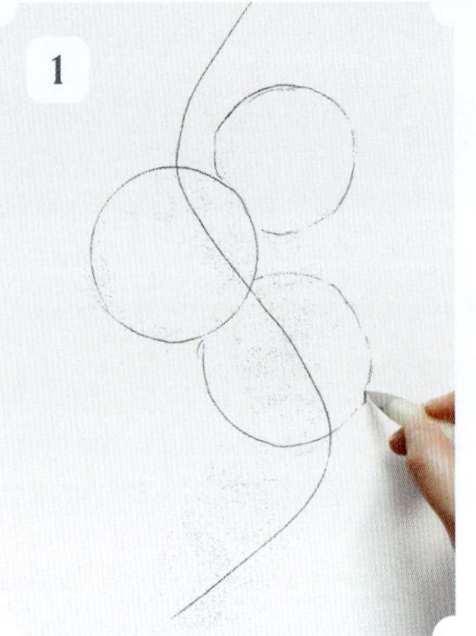

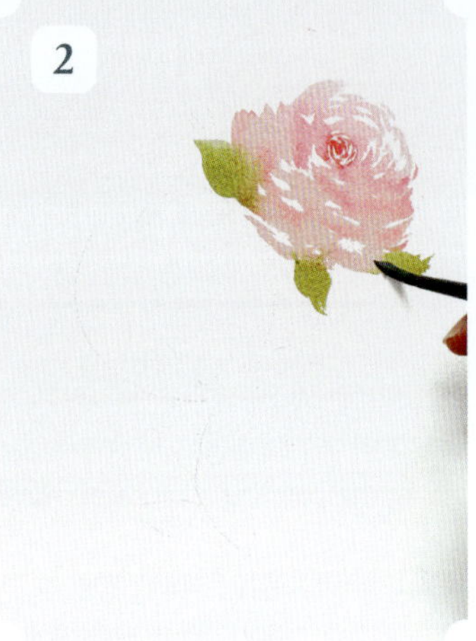

3

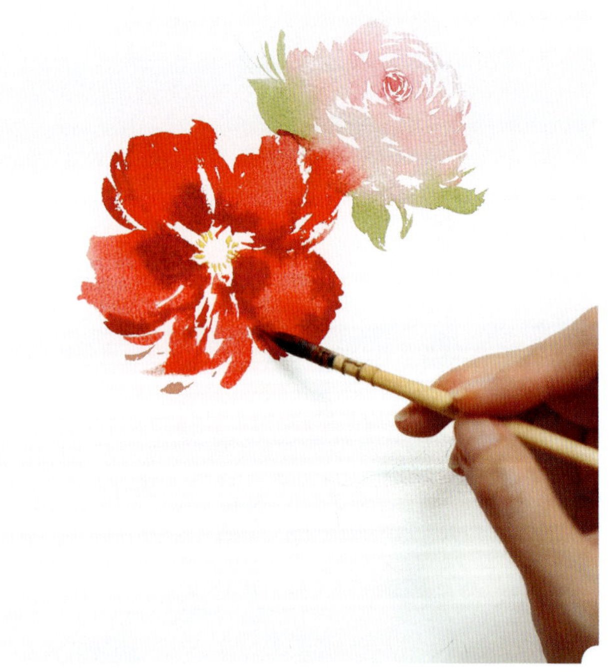

4

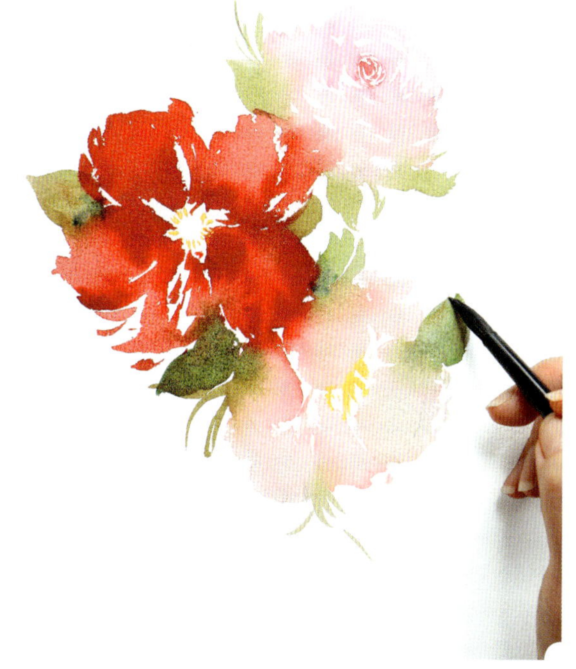

4. Paint a Peony

With a size **8** round brush, prepare a Brilliant Pink color for the Lush Pink Peony (page 43). Place this flower diagonally below the Poppy, letting some petals blend together. With a size **2** round brush, paint the stamen with short, thin strokes using medium-consistency Permanent Yellow Light. Add more leaves in varying green tones around the flowers while they are still damp.

5. Paint the Supporting Flowers

To add variety, paint Blush Sweet Peas (page 83) using a size **8** round brush, following the top curve of the S shape. Use Lilac and Shell Pink for a soft effect. If you prefer a diagonal line instead of an S shape, simply follow that line as you add more flowers.

At the bottom curve of the S shape, scatter small clusters of Forget-Me-Nots (page 95) using Verditer Blue and Baby's Breath (page 105) using Buff Titanium. You can paint these smaller flowers throughout the bouquet too. To add movement, paint wispy leaves with a size **2** round brush to fill any gaps.

5A 5B

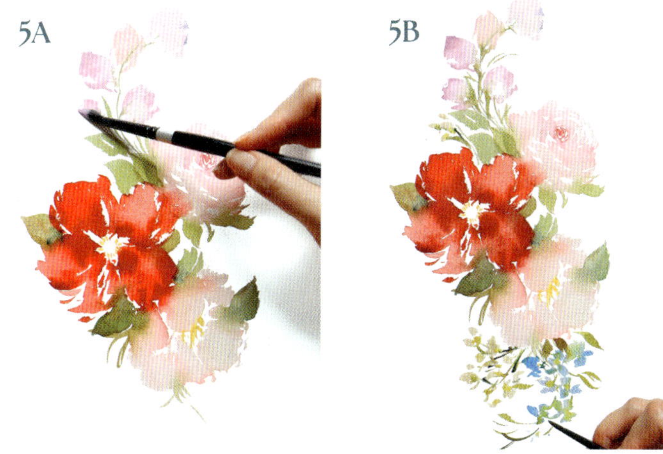

6. Paint Botanical Fillers

Deepen the greens by layering darker leaves on top. Mix two parts Sap Green and one part Indigo for a deep green color. Place these leaves near the main flowers to frame the shapes and create contrast.

For extra detail and contrast, add small berries in Prussian Blue. You may also paint thin stems extending outward with tiny Indigo dots at the tips for more texture.

7. Add Finishing Touches

Use a hairdryer to quickly dry the first layer, and add second-layer details to the flowers. Paint the stamens of the Peony using Burnt Sienna. For the stamens of the Red Poppy, mix one part white gouache and one part Permanent Yellow Light, then go back and add second-layer details. To add an airy feel, use your size 2 round brush to paint loose, elongated leaves around the bouquet. Keep them a little detached from the main cluster because this creates movement and makes the bouquet feel light. Take a moment to celebrate your work! This is a lovely, romantic bouquet.

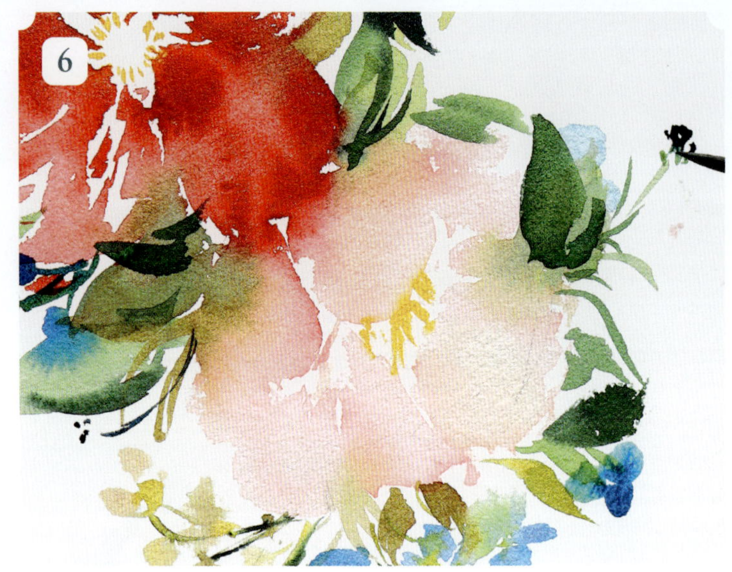

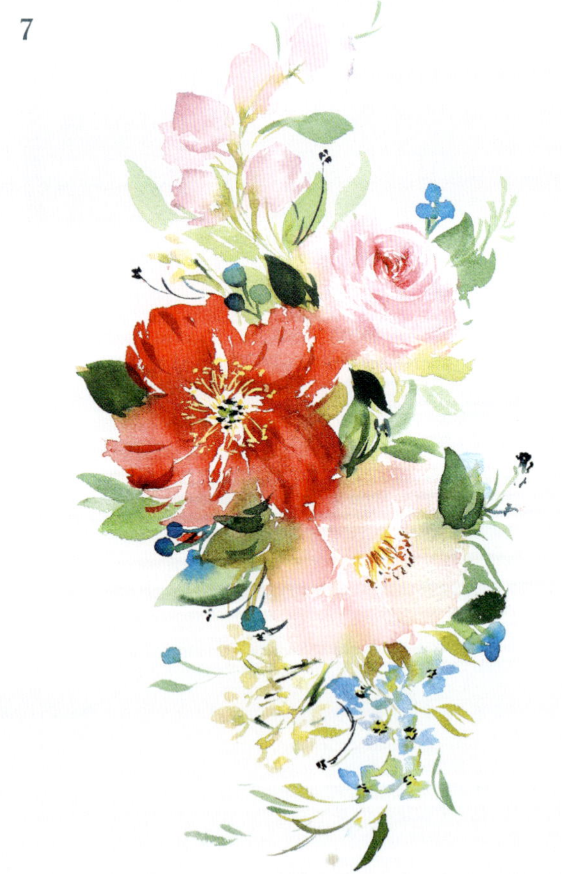

SPRING GARDEN BOUQUET

When I think of spring, I imagine cheerful and dainty colors. The bold orange Poppy (page 47) pairs beautifully with the soft blush Peony (page 43). Both act as focal flowers, giving the bouquet weight and drawing the attention of the viewer. To balance the strong shapes, airy flowers such as Queen Anne's Lace (page 101) add lightness to the bouquet.

The blue-violet Stock (page 73) brings height and complements the warm tones of the orange Poppy. Chamomile (page 91) and wispy foliage softly fill the gaps to keep the composition fresh.

Colors

- Permanent Yellow Light
- Yellow Orange
- Shell Pink
- Permanent Violet
- Cerulean Blue
- Greenish Yellow
- Olive Green
- Burnt Sienna
- Ultramarine Blue
- Burnt Umber
- Buff Titanium
- Sap Green
- Indigo
- Vermilion
- Sepia

Brushes

- Size 2 round brush
- Size 0 mop brush
- Size 4 round brush

Other Materials

- White gouache

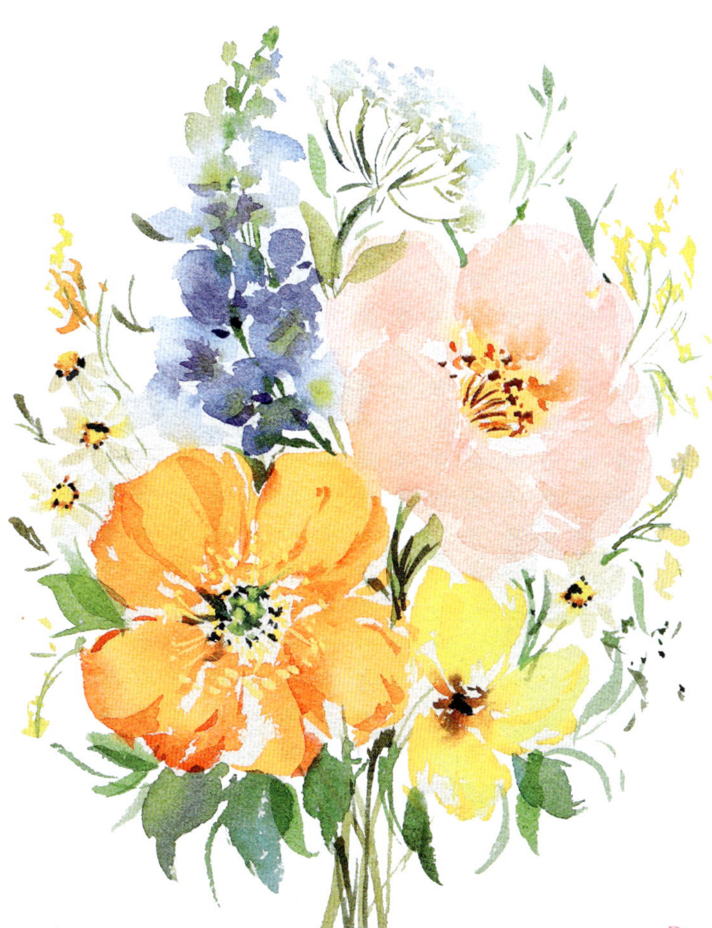

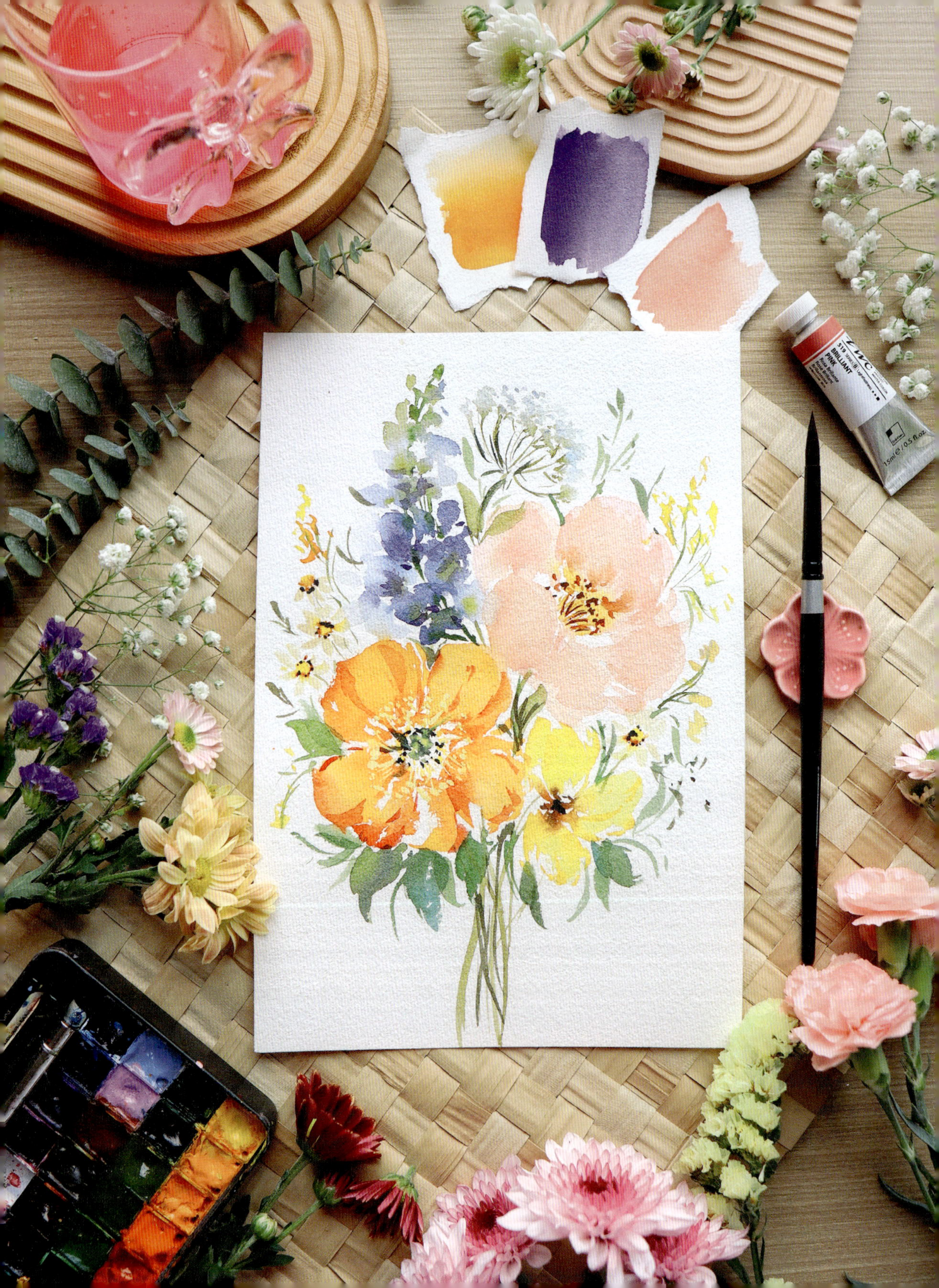

1. Start with the Icelandic Poppy

Begin with a Fiery Icelandic Poppy (page 47) on the lower-left side of the bouquet. Using a size 2 round brush, paint the center with short, thin strokes that form a circle using Permanent Yellow Light. Next, load your size 0 mop brush with medium-consistency Yellow Orange for the petals. Drop in more pigment between the petals and tips for more contrast.

2. Add the Pink Peony

To paint a soft Lush Pink Peony (page 43) at an angle, mix a light-consistency Shell Pink. Load your size 0 mop brush and paint two rounded petals first in front as a guide. Then add three more petals above in a fan shape. While damp, use Permanent Yellow Light to paint thin strokes for stamens and let them blend softly into the petals.

3. Paint the Blue-Violet Stock

Mix two parts Permanent Violet and one part Cerulean Blue for the Stormy Violet Stock flower (page 73). Start painting four-petal flowers, using a size 4 round brush and varying the tones to create visual contrast. Slowly build the clusters from the bottom up, tapering toward the top. Add small Greenish Yellow buds at the tip and connect with thin stems in Olive Green. To keep it loose, lightly stamp your brush on the sides of the flowers for a few airy petals using light-consistency Permanent Violet.

1

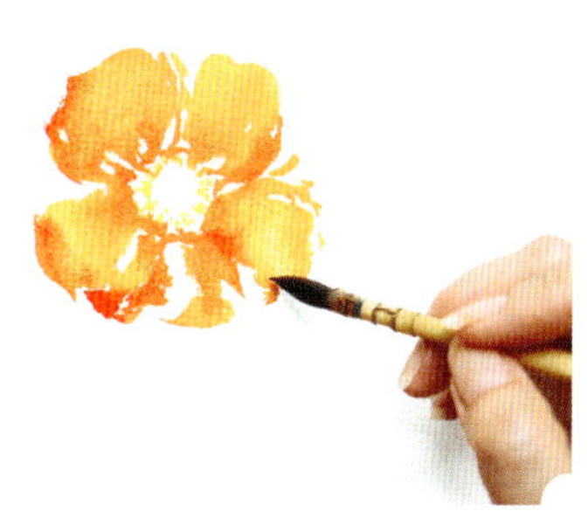

2

3A

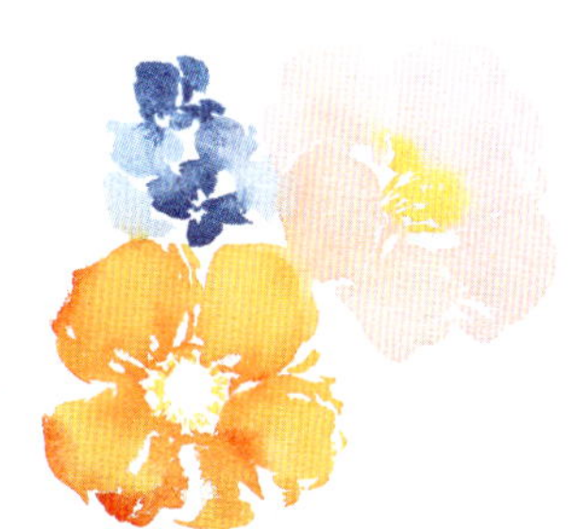

3B

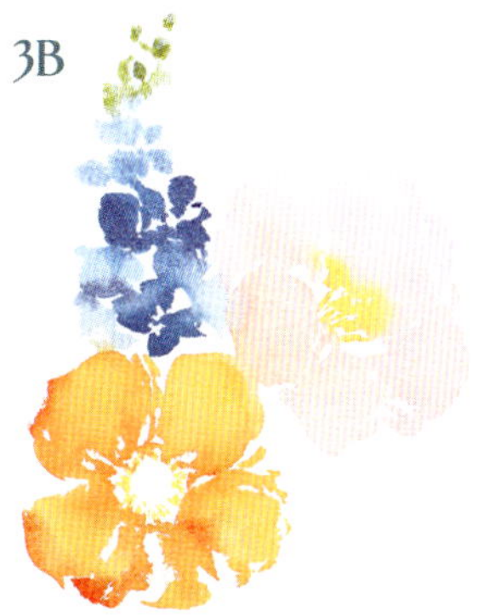

3C

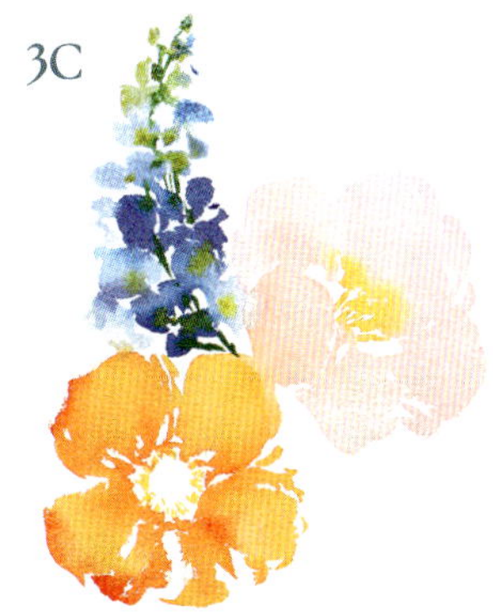

4. Add the Filler Flowers

On the lower right, using a size 4 round brush, paint a three-petal flower using medium-consistency Permanent Yellow Light to bring a pop of color. While damp, drop Burnt Sienna in the center for contrast.

To add height and texture, paint the stem of Queen Anne's Lace (page 101) using Olive Green in between the Stock and Peony. Mix one part Ultramarine Blue and one part Burnt Umber in a very light consistency for the delicate flowers.

5. Add Chamomile and Yellow Fillers

Fill in white gaps with small Chamomile flowers (page 91) using a size 4 round brush, painting them in odd numbers for balance. Start with Permanent Yellow Light for the centers, add Burnt Sienna around the edges of the centers, then paint the petals with Buff Titanium. Then, add thin Sap Green stems with a size 2 round brush. Start dabbing along these stems using Permanent Yellow Light to suggest tiny florals. Place these near the outer edges so they look light and airy. Add a few leaves in varying green tones to frame the main flowers.

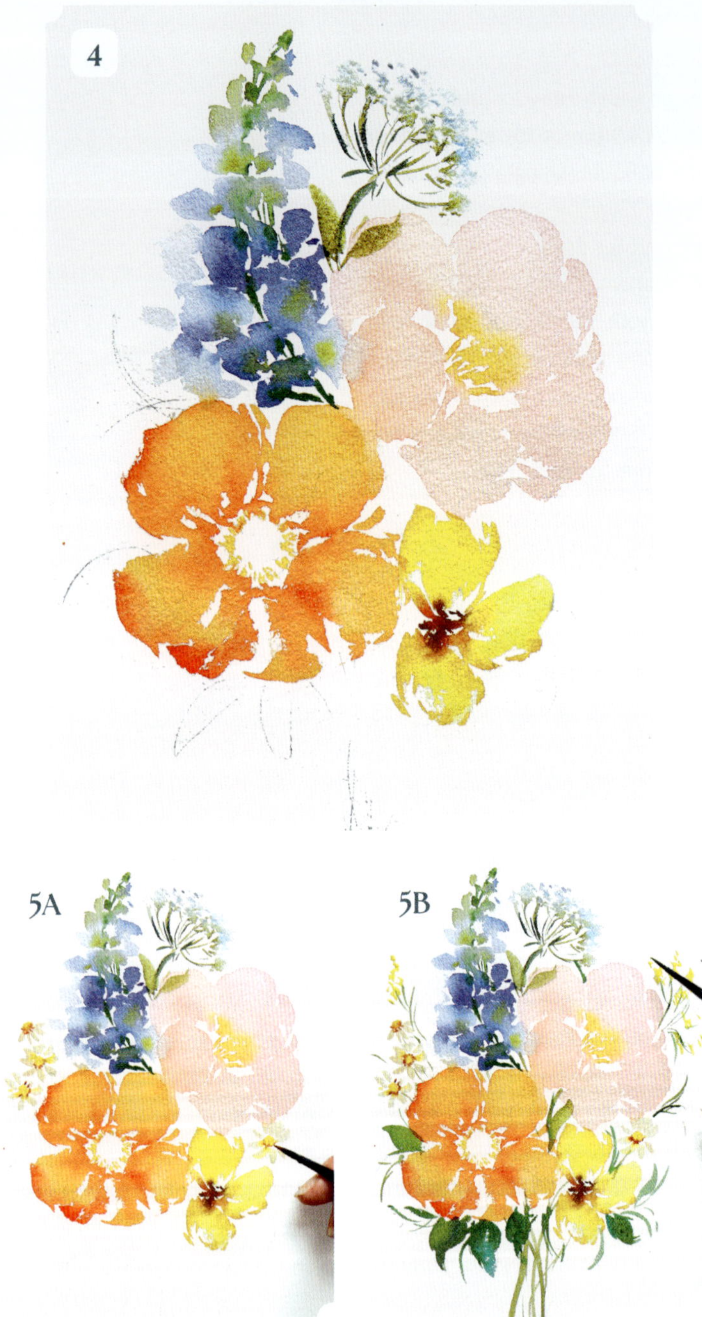

6A

Use a hairdryer to quickly dry the first layer before adding the second-layer details. Using a size 2 round brush, paint thin strokes and dots using Burnt Sienna to define the Peony stamens.

On the Poppy petals, add a few delicate, vein-like strokes using one part Vermilion and one part Yellow Orange, then paint the Sap Green center with tiny Indigo dots. Paint the opaque yellow stamens using a mix of white gouache and Permanent Yellow Light watercolor.

For the Stock, deepen the florals by layering a second round of flowers using a thicker consistency of the base flower (two parts Permanent Violet and one part Cerulean Blue). Add dots to the center of the Chamomile using Sepia, and add a few wispy green stems around the bouquet to keep it light. Step back and admire your spring bouquet!

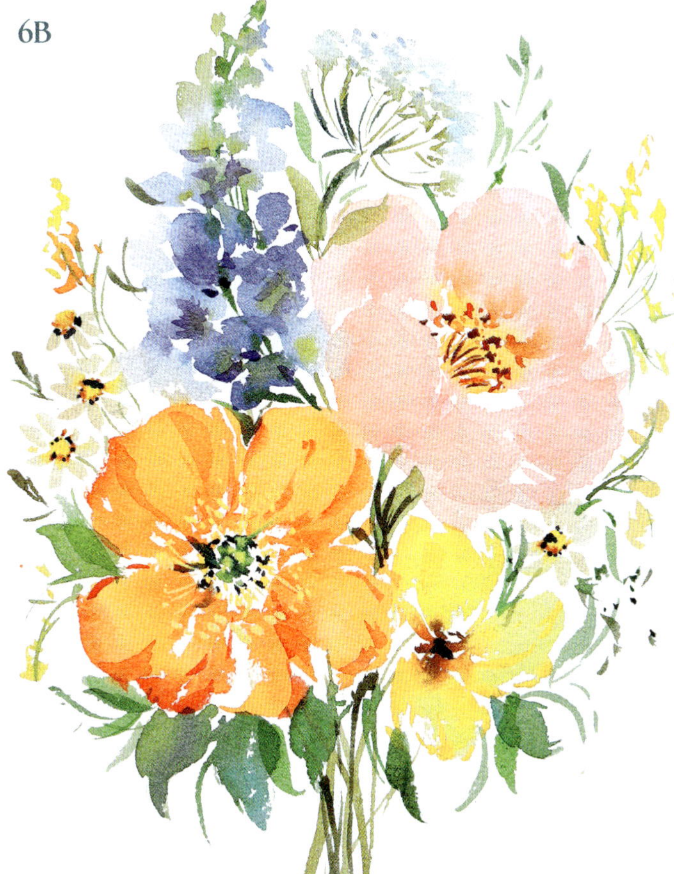

6B

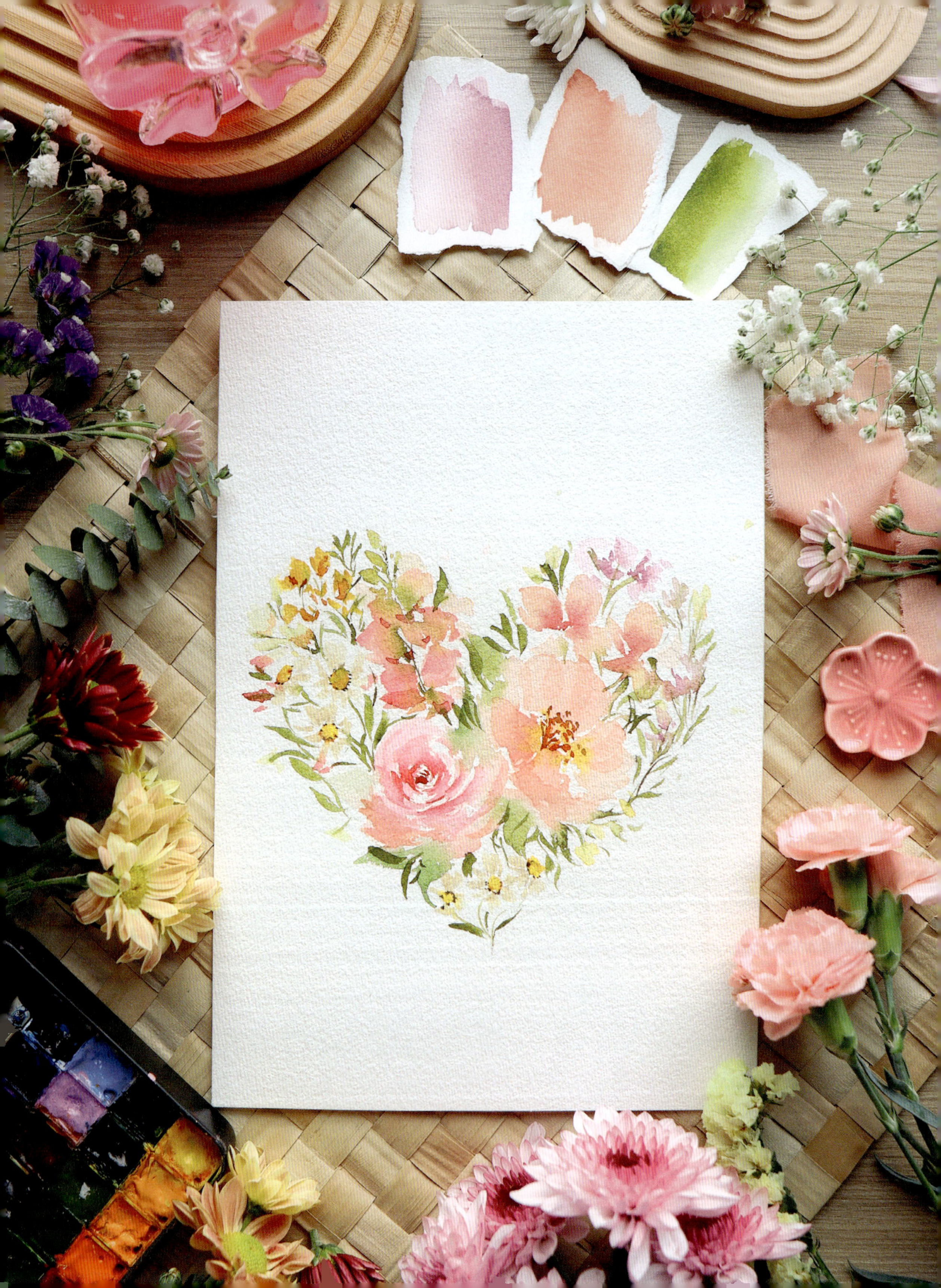

HEART-SHAPED BOUQUET

This project may look intricate but it's actually very easy! You'll simply fill in the heart-shaped silhouette with loose flowers and greenery. I enjoy painting this because it feels like piecing together a puzzle by mixing and matching flowers until the shape comes alive. In this lesson, we'll start by choosing a few main flowers as anchors, then add fillers and leaves to complete the arrangement.

This creative bouquet is ideal for occasions like Valentine's Day or Mother's Day or as a heartfelt gift for someone special.

Colors

- Permanent Rose
- Olive Green
- Shell Pink
- Permanent Yellow Light
- Brilliant Pink
- Burnt Sienna
- Buff Titanium
- Sepia
- Lilac
- Sap Green
- Indigo

Brushes

- Size 6 round brush
- Size 4 round brush
- Size 2 round brush

Other Materials

- Pencil

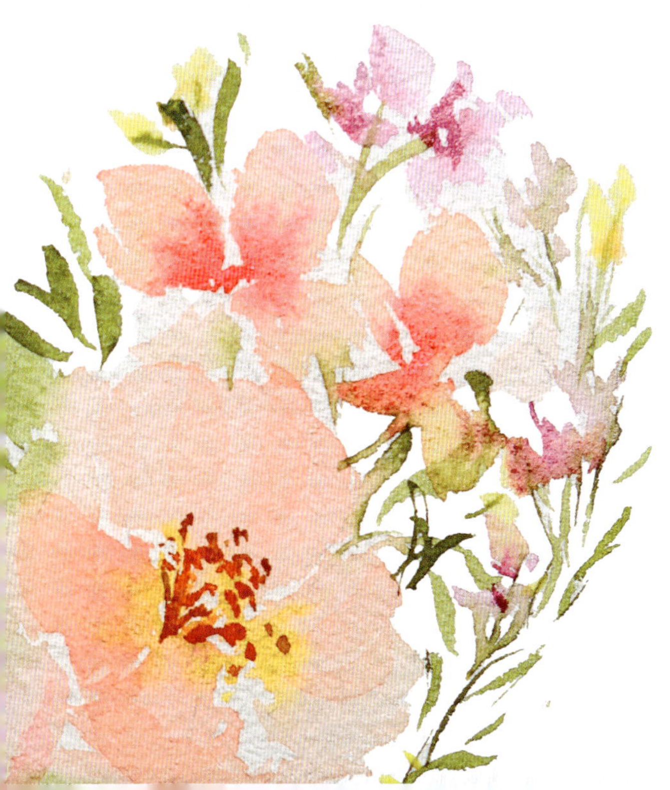

1. Plan the Bouquet

Using a pencil, lightly draw a heart shape as a guide. Begin by placing the main flowers diagonally across from each other. You can position them anywhere within the heart, but starting near the center makes it easier to fill in the space naturally.

2. Paint the Main Flowers

Using a size 6 round brush, start with a Rose (page 37) using the color Permanent Rose. While the petals are damp, add a few Olive Green leaves nearby so the colors blend softly, framing the flower.

Next, paint a Peony (page 43) using a size 6 round brush diagonally across from the Rose. Use Shell Pink or mix two parts Permanent Rose with one part Permanent Yellow Light plus plenty of water to create a soft peach tone. Let the Peony touch the edge of the rose and add a few leaves around it.

3. Paint Secondary Flowers

For variety, paint a Stock flower (page 73) with a size 6 round brush above the Rose using the color Brilliant Pink. Use Olive Green for the stem. To add a lighter, neutral accent, add small clusters of Chamomile flowers (page 91) using a size 4 round brush. Start with Permanent Yellow Light for the centers, add Burnt Sienna around the edges, then paint the petals with Buff Titanium. For more depth, paint small dots of Sepia when the flowers are dry. Scatter them around the main flowers to fill in the space and balance the bouquet.

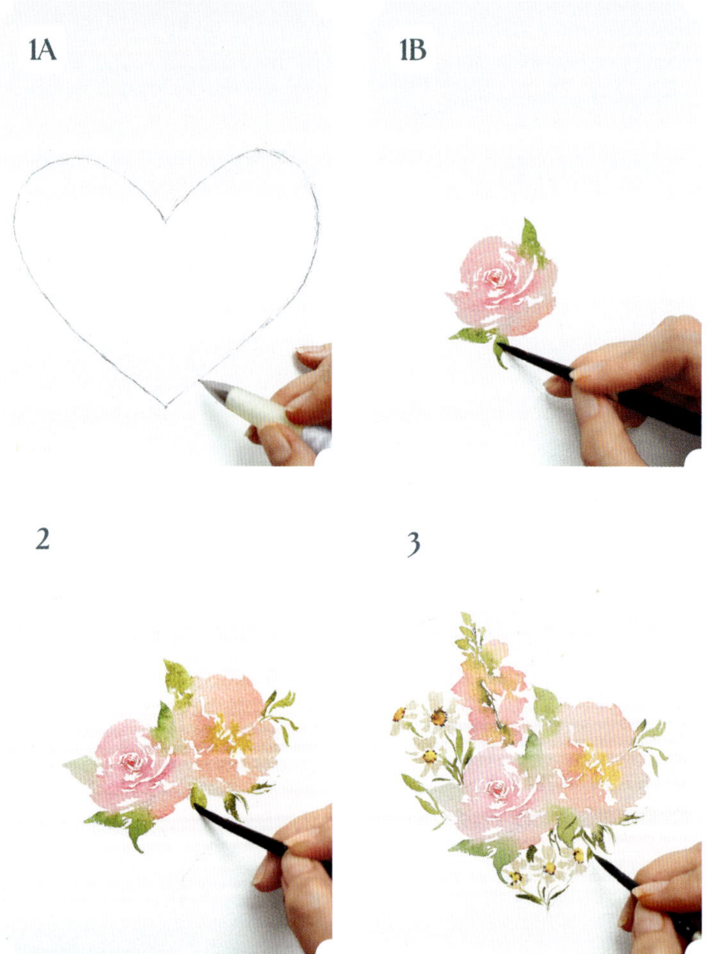

4. Add Filler Flowers

To keep the bouquet light, add smaller flowers at the top part of the heart. Paint a few four- or five-petal flowers (page 111) on the right side using light-consistency Brilliant Pink to fill the large white space. Drop in a medium-consistency Permanent Rose in the center while the flower is still damp. For the remaining space, using a size 4 round brush, paint Sea Lavender (page 105) in Permanent Yellow Light, Brilliant Pink, and Lilac.

Add small leaves in different green tones of Olive Green and Sap Green. Use a size 2 round brush for delicate details.

5. Add Finishing Touches

Use a hairdryer to quickly dry the first layer, then start to deepen the details of the Rose and Peony with a second layer. Mix a more pigmented Permanent Rose and add more C-shaped strokes on the Rose. For the Peony, add the stamens using Burnt Sienna. Paint a ring of dots using Sepia in the center of the Chamomile flowers.

Mix two parts Sap Green and one part Indigo to create a rich, deep green. Load your size 2 round brush and paint more leaves, layering some on top of the others to add depth and dimension. What a lovely piece! It will bring so much joy to the person who receives it.

4A **4B**

5A **5B**

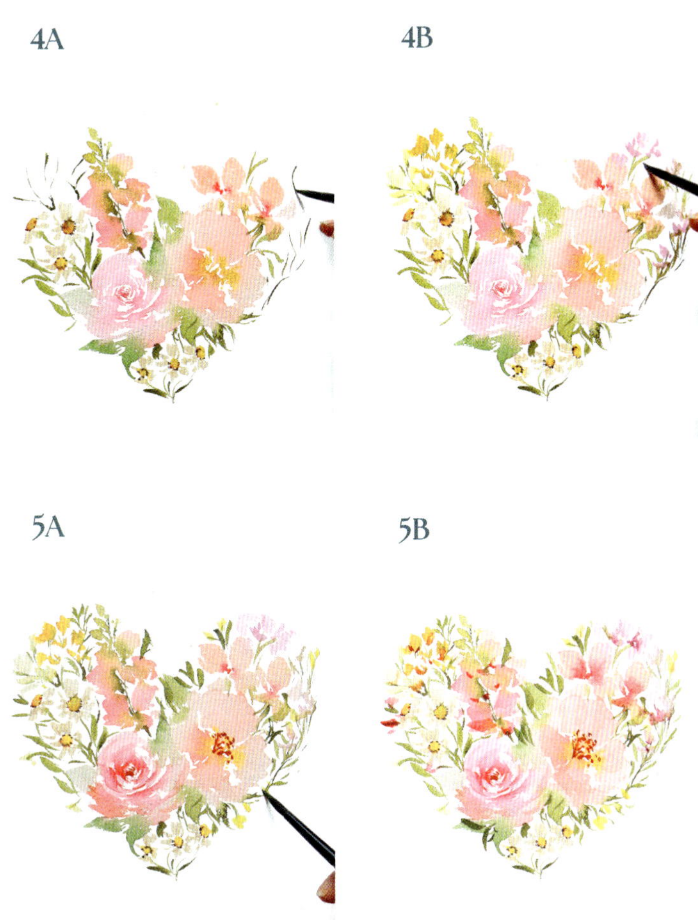

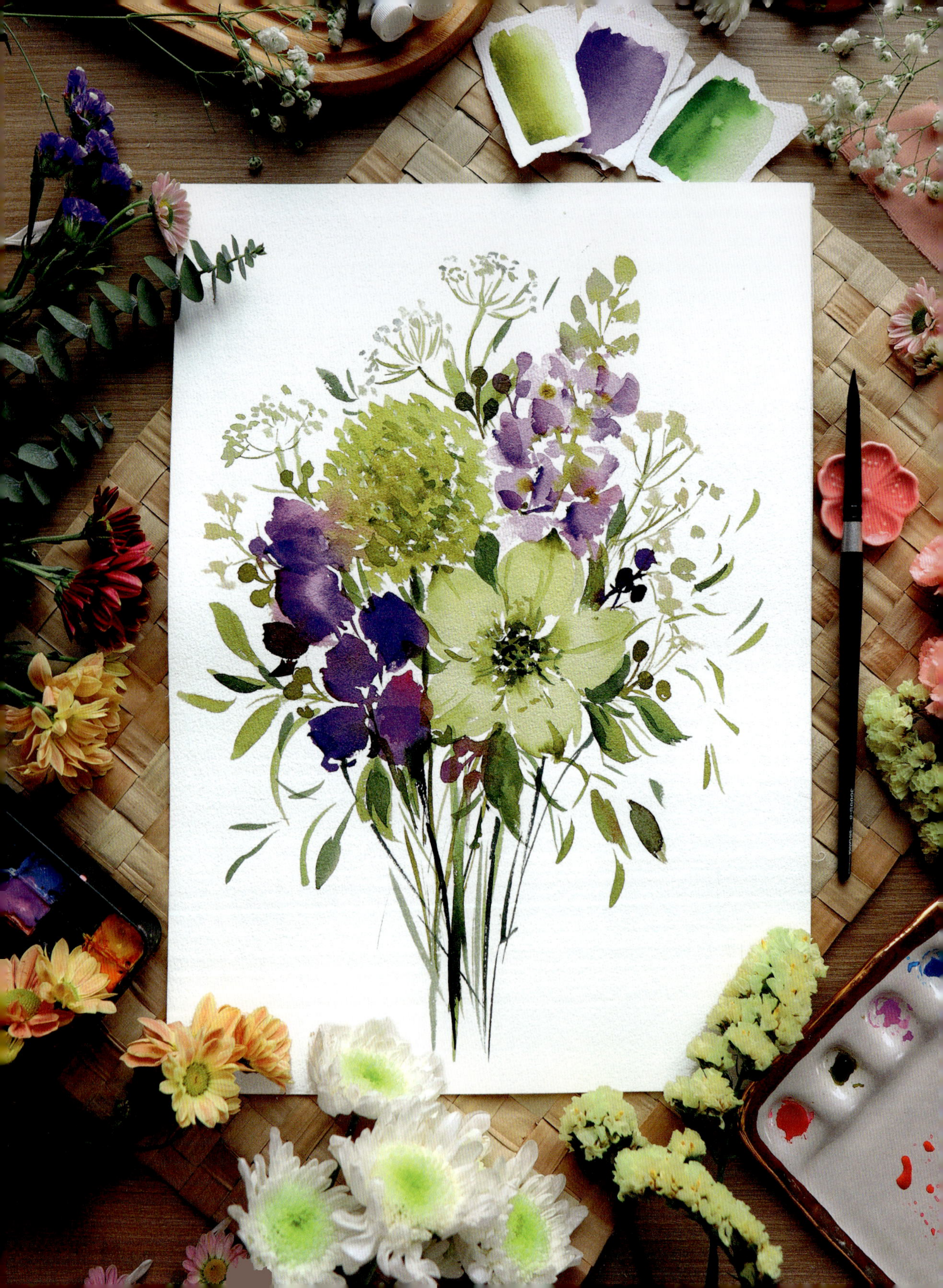

COLOR ACCENT BOUQUET

Using color accents in a bouquet is a great way to add interest to your composition. Pops of contrasting or complementary colors create a vibrant combination. You can even explore accents through playful elements like fruits or berries.

In this project, let's challenge ourselves by using colors that we don't usually reach for. Pink is my go-to color for flowers, but in this project, I challenged myself to mix Greenish Yellow and Violet. Greenish Yellow florals such as Hellebores (page 63) serve as the base color, while Sweet Pea (page 83) and Stock (page 73) are the violet accents. Since these colors feel heavy, I added light, feathery fillers to make the composition airy.

Colors

- Greenish Yellow
- Olive Green
- Sap Green
- Permanent Violet
- Mineral Violet
- Bright Rose
- Cerulean Blue
- Buff Titanium
- Burnt Umber

Brushes

- Size 8 round brush
- Size 6 round brush
- Size 2 round brush

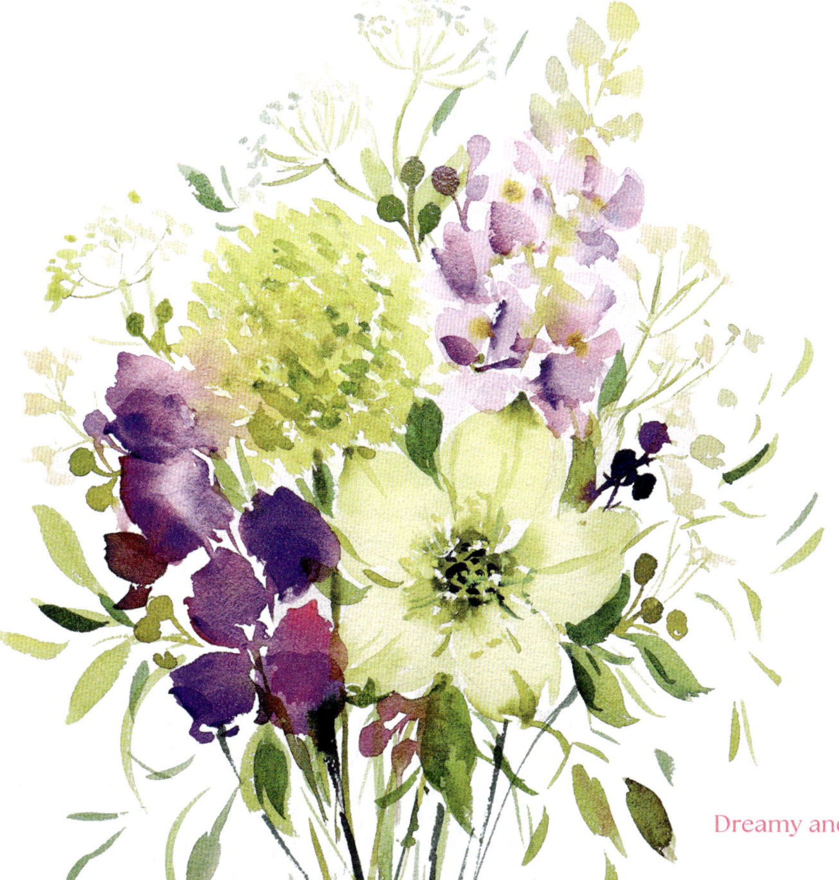

1. Paint the Main Flowers

Using a size 8 round brush, start with the two main flowers placed diagonally across from each other. On the lower-right side, paint the base of a Hellebore flower (page 63) using Greenish Yellow and deepen the center and petal tips with Olive Green.

On the upper-left side, let's paint a Greenish Yellow clustered flower using the stamping technique. While damp, drop in medium-consistency Olive Green toward the bottom half of the sphere to suggest there's a shadow. Paint green stems using Sap Green.

2. Add the Color Accent

Using a size 8 round brush, paint a Sweet Pea stalk (page 83) on the left side of the bouquet. Use deep and rich colors such as Permanent Violet, Mineral Violet, and Bright Rose in medium and thick consistency. Paint the stem in Sap Green.

On the upper-right side, use a size 6 round brush to add height by painting a Stock flower (page 73) using light-consistency Permanent Violet. You can play around and add purple and pink tones on the petals.

3. Add Feathery Details

To balance the bold flowers, paint Queen Anne's Lace (page 101) with an Olive Green stem and the delicate flowers in a light consistency of Cerulean Blue at the top of the bouquet. Add them in varying heights so they don't look flat.

On the sides, paint Baby's Breath flowers (page 105) using Buff Titanium for an airy texture.

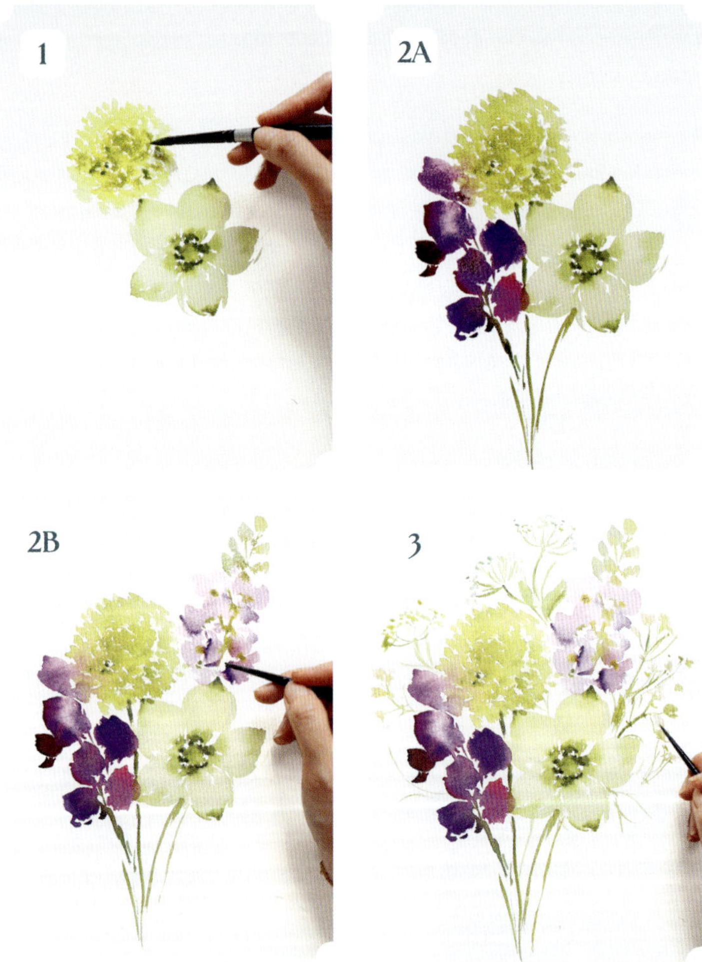

4. Add Leaves and Dark Berries

Mix two parts Sap Green and one part Burnt Umber to make an earthy green color. Use your size 8 brush to paint leaves in different sizes near the main flowers, with a few extending a bit further to add looseness. Add a few wispy leaves using a size 2 round brush.

To add contrast, use a thick-consistency Permanent Violet and place some berries near the Greenish Yellow flowers. Let some of the colors bleed into the leaves. Near the violet flowers, add berries in Olive Green for variation. Paint extra stems in mixed green tones to tie everything together.

5. Add a Second Layer

Use a hairdryer to quickly dry the first layer. Continue layering the details on the flowers as needed, following the referenced tutorials. For the green clustered flower, mix medium-consistency Olive Green and load it to your size 6 round brush. Start stamping petals on the flower to add more depth. Make sure to leave spaces in between your strokes so we can still see the base color. Mix a light-consistency Olive Green. Using a size 2 round brush, add delicate vein details on the Hellebore petals by dragging the tip of the brush on the paper. Keep the lines soft and slightly broken to create a more natural look.

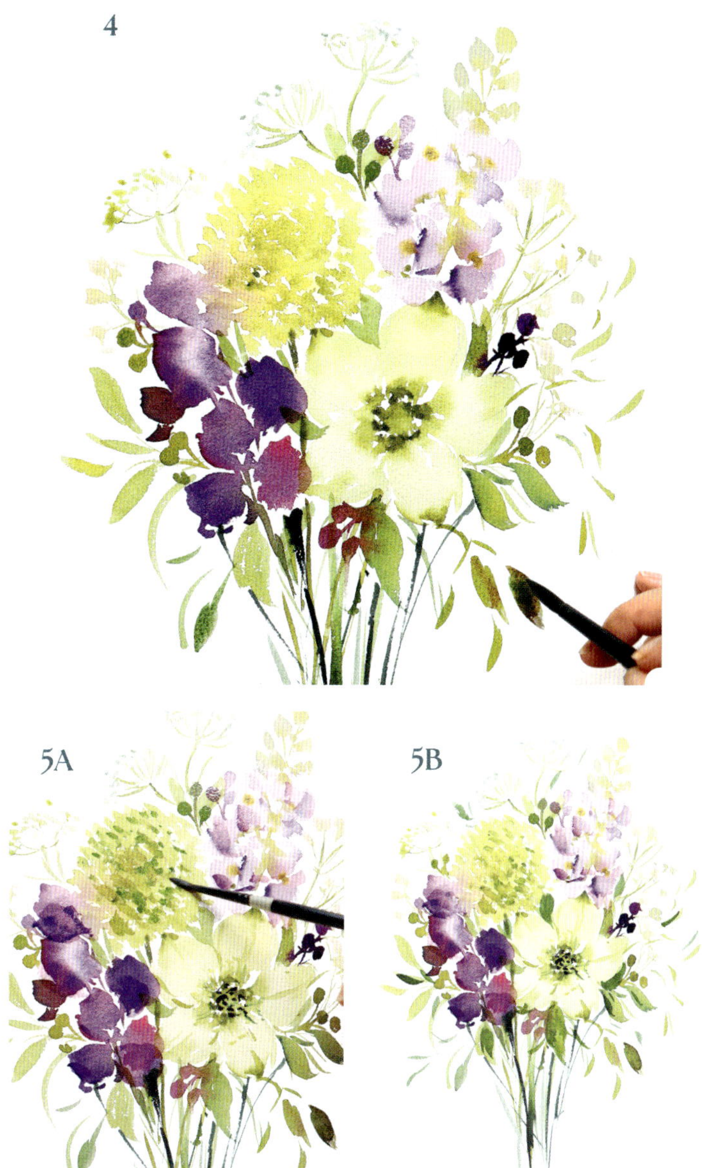

Step back and check if you need to add more color accents to the bouquet. Well done!

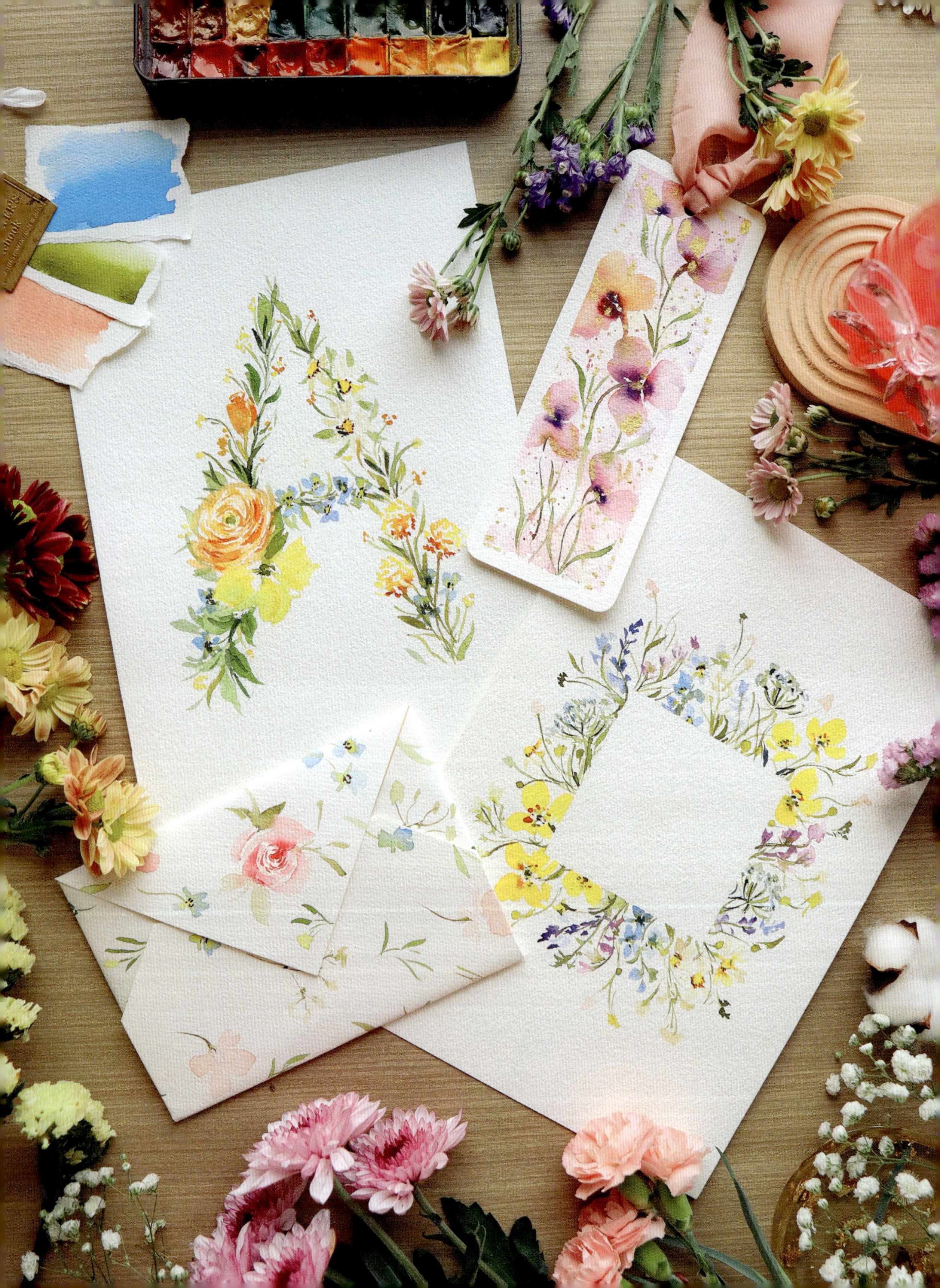

Creative PROJECTS

I absolutely love finding unique ways to bring watercolor florals into everyday projects. This must be my second-favorite chapter in the book! We'll explore fun and practical ideas that you can create for yourself or give as a gift.

With the help of washi tape, we'll create clean borders for a Whimsical Botanical Bookmark (page 171) and a Wildflower Frame (page 177).

We'll also be making a Personalized Floral Monogram (page 167), which is great to give as a gift because you can customize the flowers and colors.

And one of the most special projects to me is Hand-Painted Envelopes (page 185) because I personally painted my own wedding invitation envelopes. We'll take it a step further by making our own envelopes from scratch. Don't worry, it's very easy to do!

These projects are all about enjoying the process and creating something that feels personal.

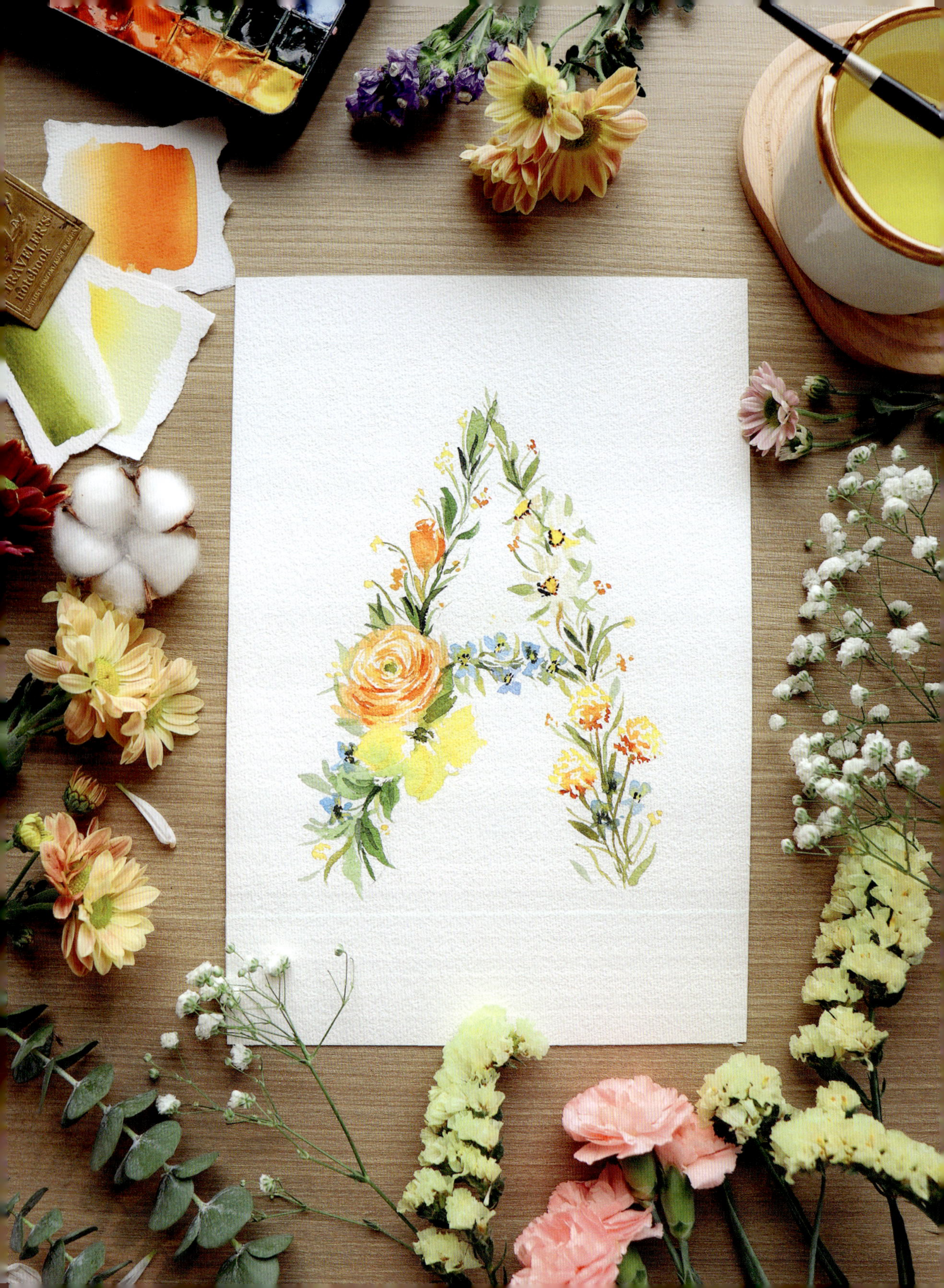

PERSONALIZED FLORAL MONOGRAM

Letters can be written in flowers too! In this fun project, we'll transform a simple letter into a garden by arranging the flowers and leaves along its shape. The result is a piece that feels personal.

You can paint the first letter of your name, a loved one's initial, or even a number that feels special to you. This project makes a thoughtful gift or a beautiful display for your home. When painting, think of the person's favorite colors or flowers to help guide your composition.

Colors

- Sap Green
- Yellow Orange
- Permanent Yellow Light
- Olive Green
- Permanent Yellow Deep
- Burnt Sienna
- Buff Titanium
- Verditer Blue
- Indigo
- Sepia

Brushes

- Size 6 round brush
- Size 4 round brush
- Size 2 round brush

Other Materials

- Pencil
- Kneaded eraser

1. Sketch the Letter

Using a pencil, sketch the letter you've chosen. Draw two to three circles on one side of the letter as the guide for the main flowers. Placing your focal blooms on one side helps create a balanced composition. Just be sure your guides don't obstruct the shape of the letter—you still want it to read clearly. In this lesson, we will put two main flowers on the left side of the letter "A."

> **TIP:** Before you begin to paint, gently lighten your pencil sketch using a kneaded eraser. Once watercolor is applied, the pencil outline underneath can no longer be erased, so keeping the sketch light will ensure a clean finish.

2. Paint the Main Flowers

Place a Sunlit Yellow Orange Ranunculus (page 53) in the upper-left circle using a size 6 round brush. In the lower-left circle, paint a flower with three to four petals using Permanent Yellow Light. While the petals are still wet, drop in Olive Green at the center for depth.

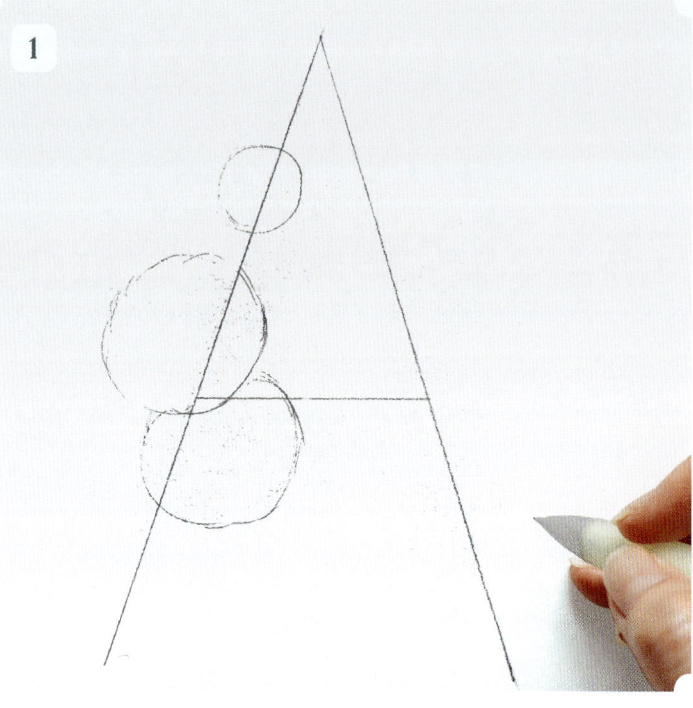

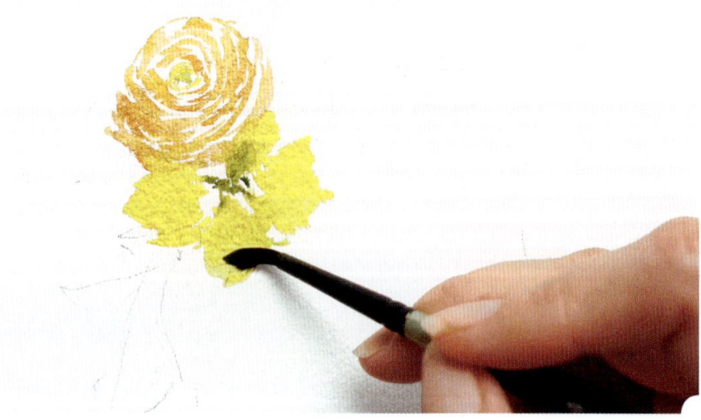

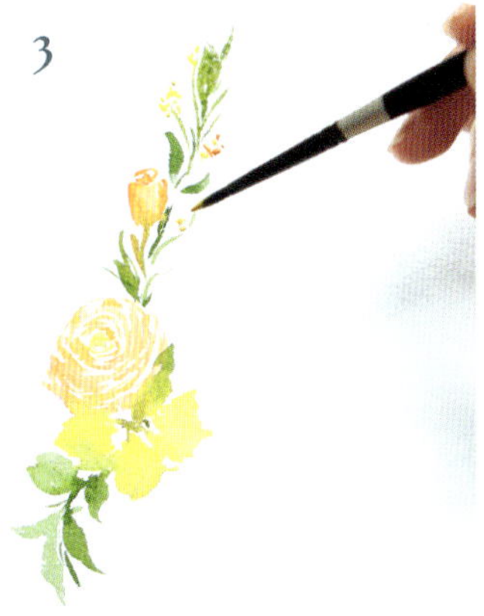

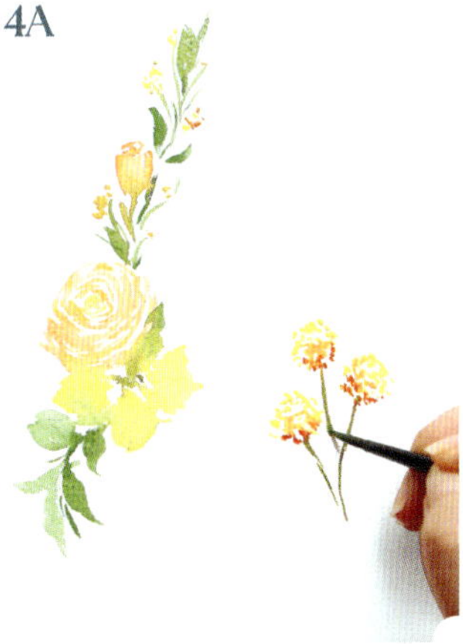

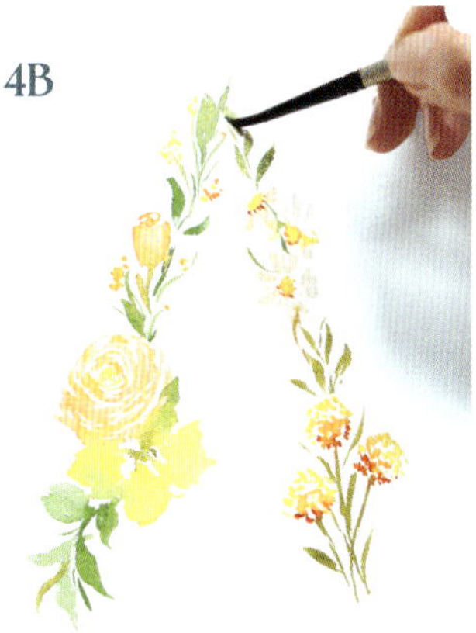

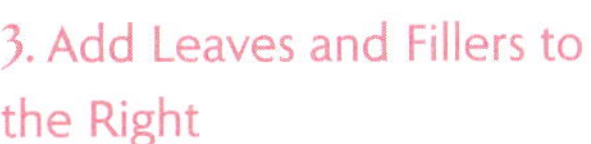

3. Add Leaves and Fillers to the Right

Add larger leaves in varying green tones toward the lower part of the letter. Next, paint a small orange bud to support the main flowers. With a size 4 round brush, add smaller leaves that climb up toward the tip of the letter. Extend a few thin stems using a size 2 round brush and place tiny orange and yellow dot fillers at their tips for a dainty touch.

4. Form the Right Side

On the lower right, paint three Craspedia stalks (page 101) in varying heights using Permanent Yellow Light, Permanent Yellow Deep, and Burnt Sienna. Above them, add a few leaves and then place three Buff Titanium Chamomile flowers (page 91). Vary the angles to add movement. Adding the leaves in between these two different flowers gives the composition a little break.

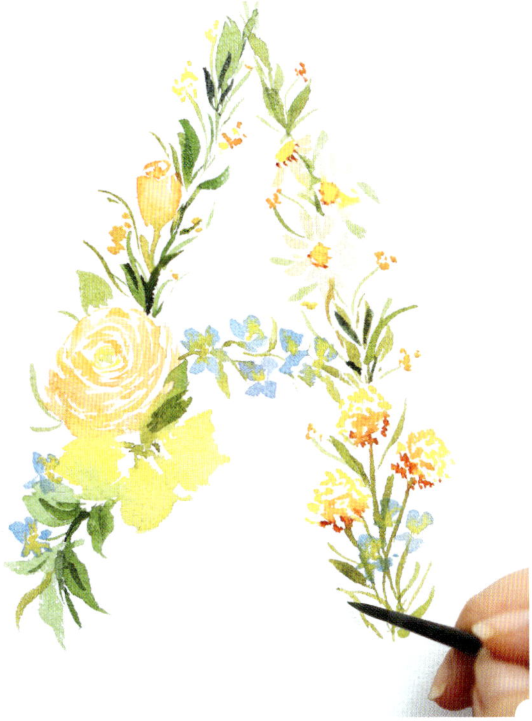

5. Paint the Forget-Me-Nots

Place Verditer Blue Forget-Me-Nots (page 95) along the center line of the letter. Stagger the flowers diagonally from each other rather than in a straight line to create movement.

Next, scatter a few more clusters near the bottom part of the letter to complement the yellow flowers.

6. Add Finishing Touches

Once everything is dry (use a hair-dryer to speed up drying), mix a deep green color using two parts Sap Green and one part Indigo. Paint thin leaves overlapping the existing ones to create depth.

Add the second layer details of the flowers (Ranunculus [page 53], Craspedia [page 101], Chamomile [page 91], Forget-Me-Nots [page 95]).

Using a size 2 round brush, paint more orange and yellow dots throughout the letter to bring a pop of color. Extend a few stems outward to give the composition extra visual interest.

All done! You've just finished painting a charming floral letter.

TIP: If you don't have much time to paint, try grouping the flowers together by putting them on one side or placing them in a corner. Then, paint the rest of the letter using one solid color or even gold for a sparkly effect. Here are some examples:

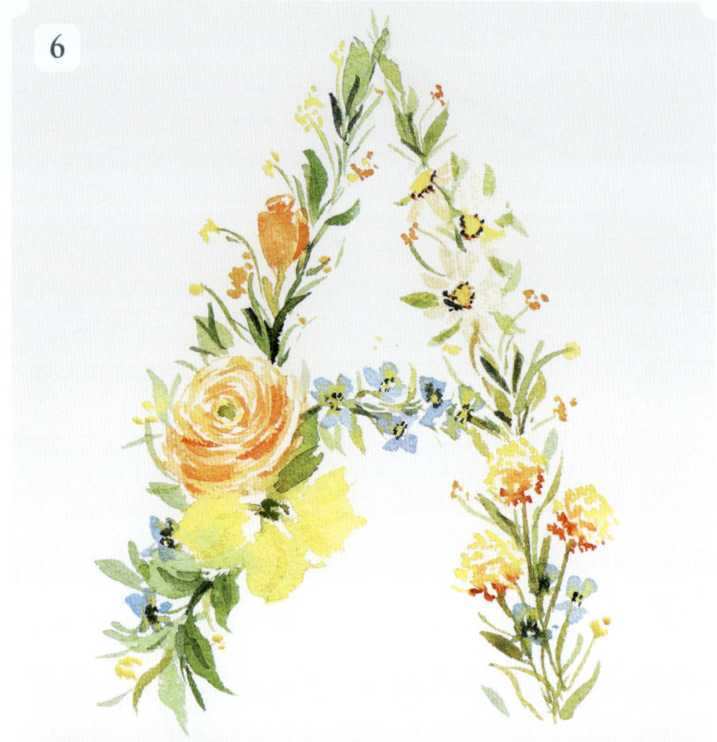

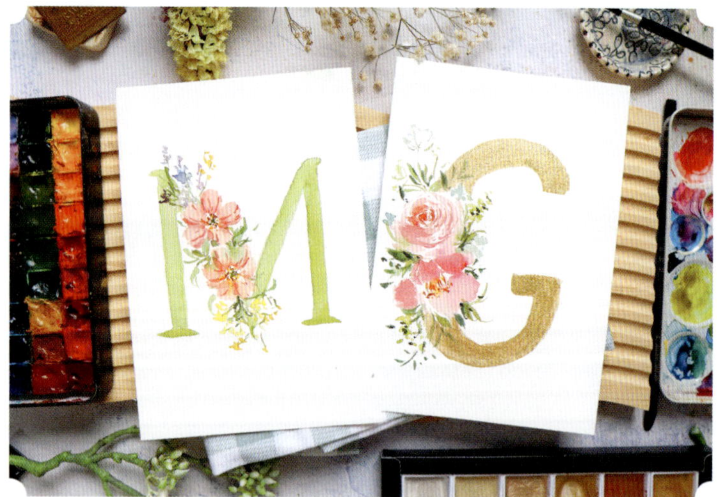

WHIMSICAL BOTANICAL B∞KMARK

This lesson is all about embracing the natural flow of watercolor. We'll have fun with painting splatters on wet paper to create a soft, dreamy background. Once dry, you'll transform simple concentrated dots into delicate petals, forming light and airy flowers. We'll finish the design with playful splatters of gold paint for a sparkly effect that makes this bookmark feel extra special!

Colors

- Permanent Rose
- Permanent Violet
- Permanent Yellow Light
- Sap Green

Brushes

- Size 8 round brush
- Size 4 round brush
- Size 2 round brush

Other Materials

- Washi tape
- Kuretake Gold Mica
- Hole punch
- Ribbon

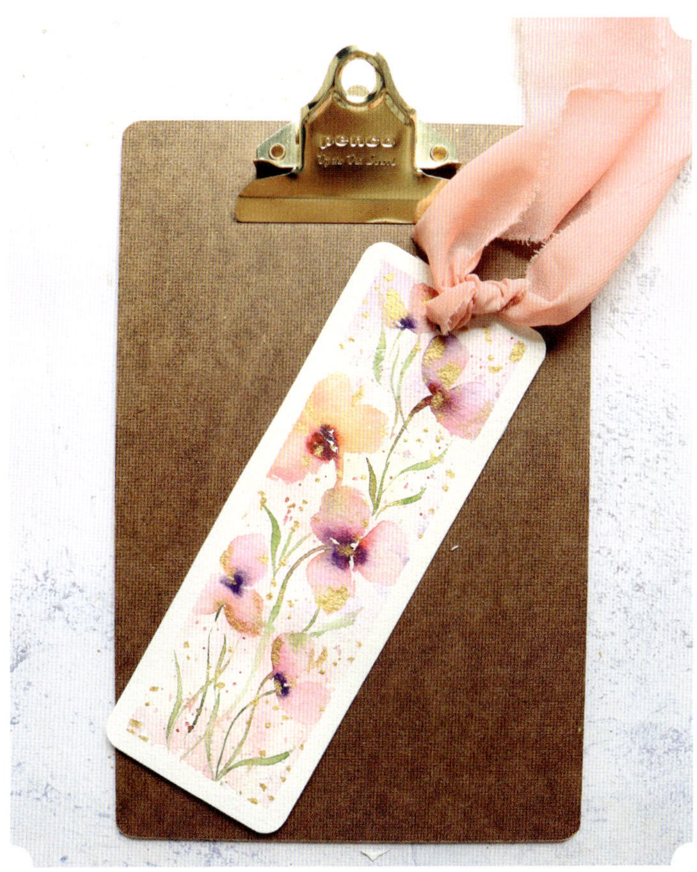

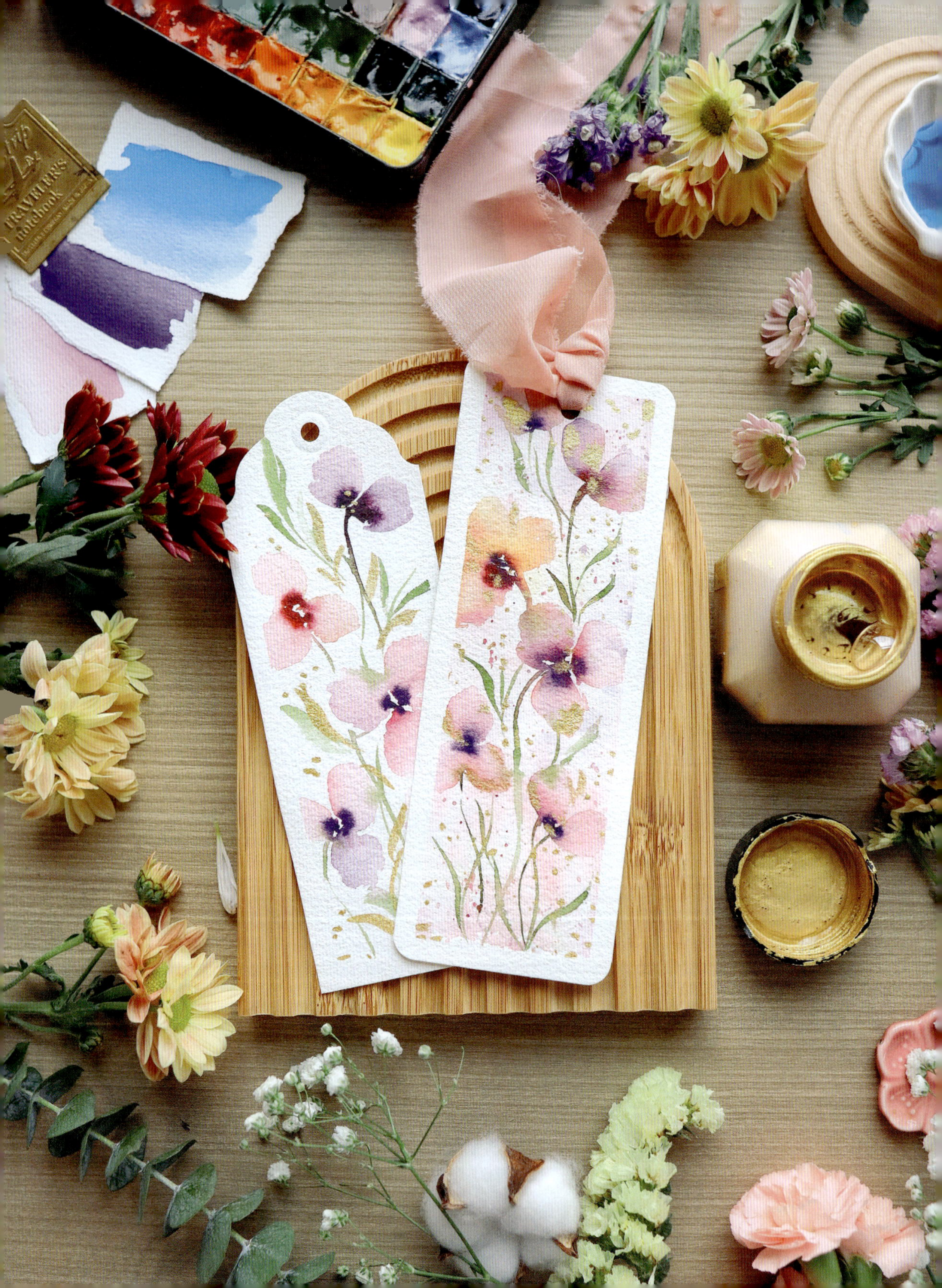

1. Prepare the Bookmark

Cut a piece of watercolor paper to your desired bookmark size. For this project, I cut my paper to 2.5 x 7 inches (6 x 18 cm). Next, tape the sides of the paper using washi tape for a nice thin, white border when it's finished.

2. Paint the Background

Using a size 8 round brush, wet the entire surface with clean water, making sure it's even without puddles. Next, load your size 4 round brush with light-consistency Permanent Rose and flick your brush onto the wet paper to create soft blooms. Repeat this with Permanent Violet and Permanent Yellow Light. Don't cover the whole paper with splatters as we are aiming for a light and dreamy background. Leave some white spaces too. Use a hairdryer to quickly dry it completely.

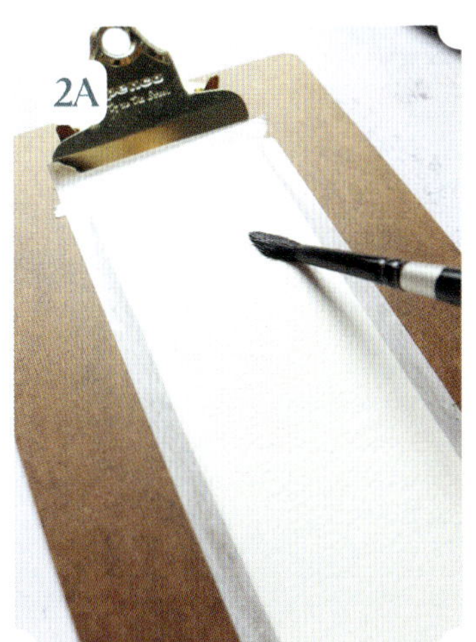

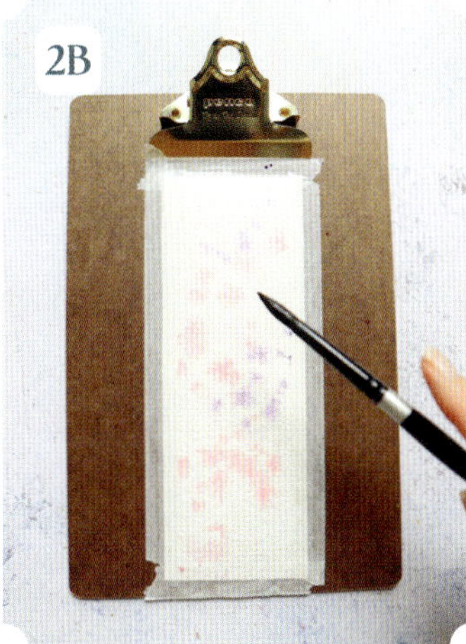

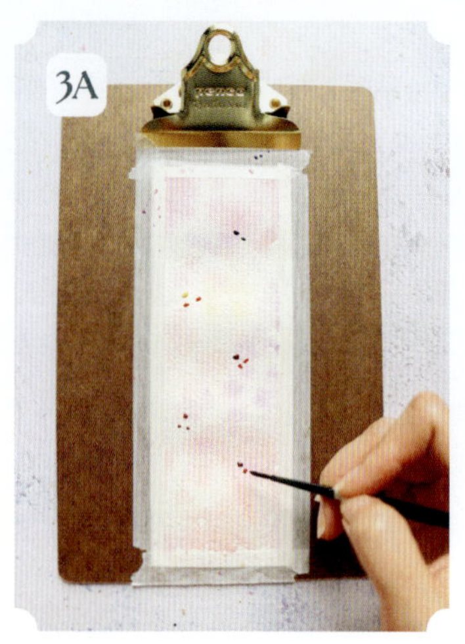

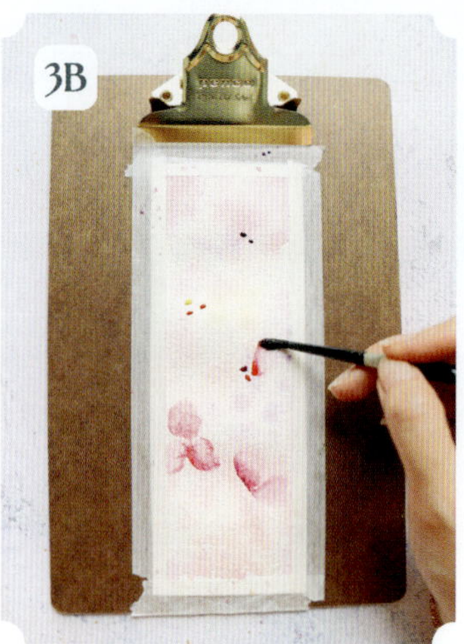

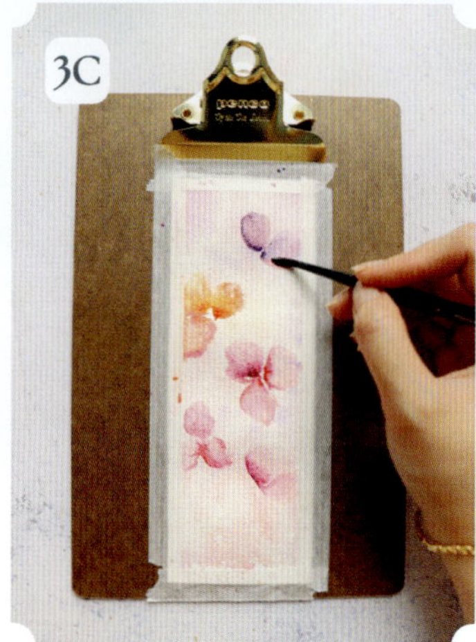

3. Paint the Flowers

Place small clusters of concentrated dots diagonally across from one another using Permanent Rose, Permanent Violet, and Permanent Yellow Light. These will become our flowers.

Rinse your size 4 round brush, touch the edge of a dot, and pull your brush outward to form a petal. Repeat this with the other dots. Keep them varied, with some flowers having two or three loose petals. It's fine if they look imperfect because we are aiming for a whimsical look.

While the petals are damp, drop in a thick-consistency Permanent Violet to the center of the flowers to give contrast.

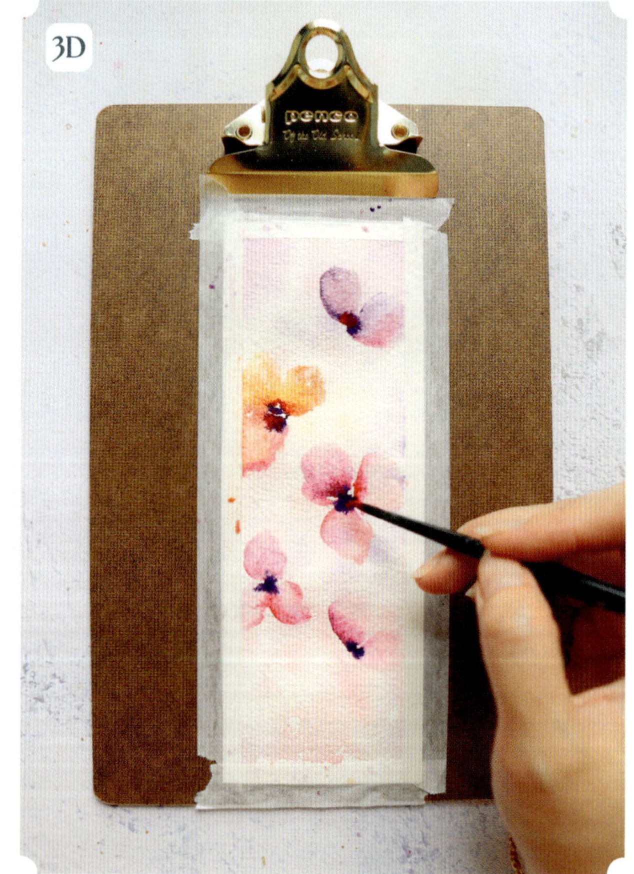

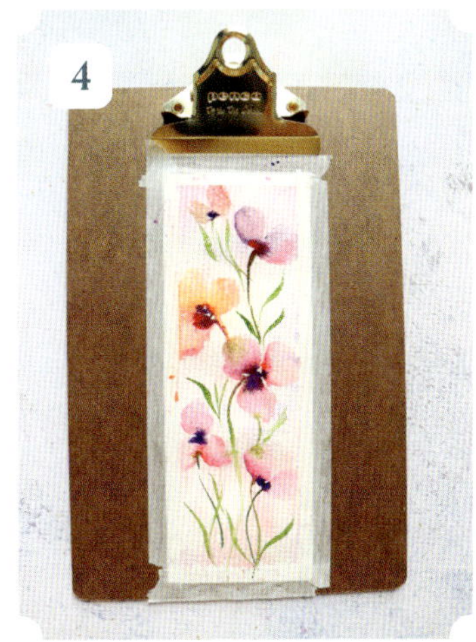

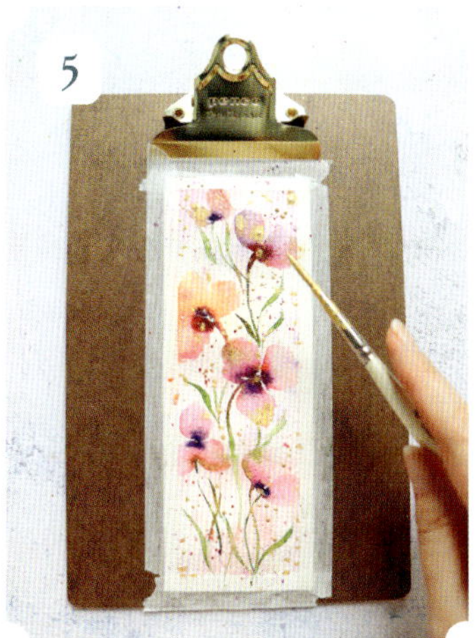

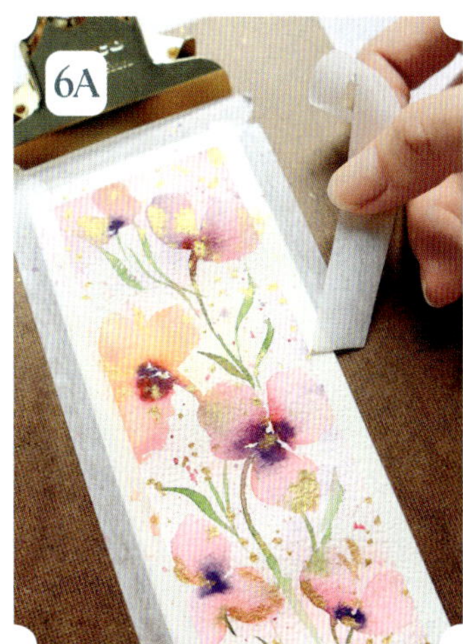

4. Add Stems and Leaves

Load your size 2 round brush with medium-consistency Sap Green and paint thin, curvy stems connected to the flowers. Add thin, wispy leaves that look like they are swaying.

5. Add Splatters

While the flowers are damp, add splatters. Load your brush with medium-consistency paint in the same colors as the flowers and flick to create splatters. For a sparkly effect, flick in some gold paint. Let a few larger splatters land on the damp petals to create beautiful blends.

6. Peel the Tape

Once everything is dry, carefully peel off the tape at an angle close to the surface to prevent any tearing on the paper. You may trim the corners of the bookmark for a rounded look. Next, punch a hole at the top and insert a ribbon. All done! Your bookmark looks magical!

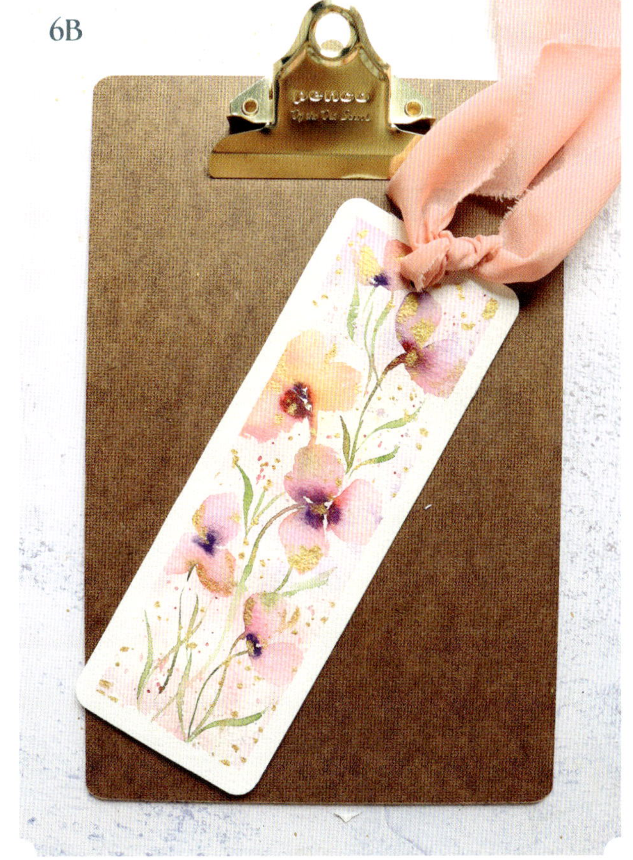

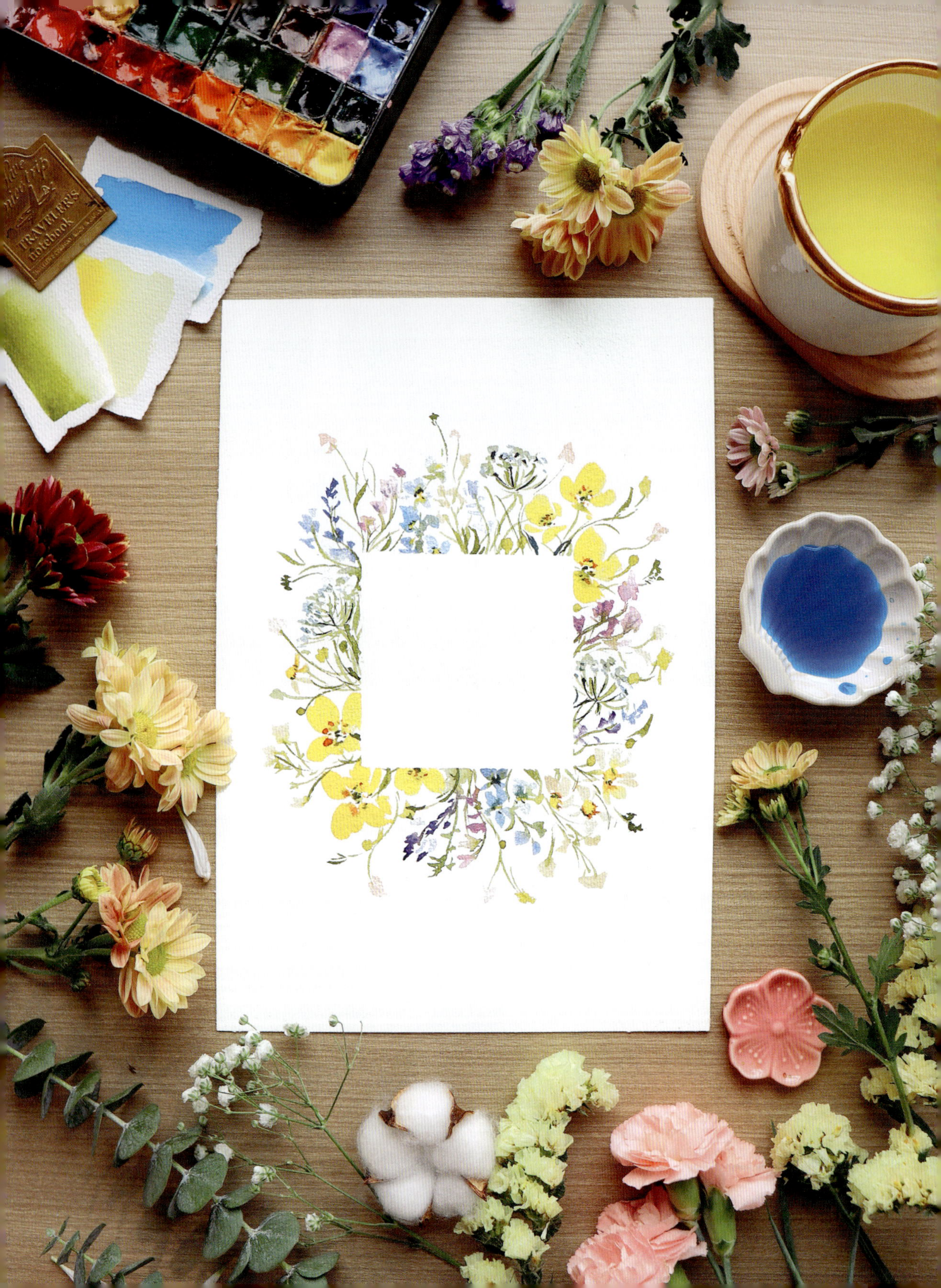

WILDFLOWER FRAME

Sometimes the simplest ideas lead to the most exciting art! In this project, we'll use washi tape to mask the center of the paper to create a beautiful floral frame. You can keep the middle blank or fill it later with a favorite quote or message.

This design is all about having fun, mixing colors, and experimenting with flower combinations. Painting tiny, delicate flowers gives the frame a dainty and minimalist look. Choose flowers that you love and let them dance around the border.

Colors

- Permanent Yellow Light
- Olive Green
- Permanent Yellow Deep
- Ultramarine Blue
- Burnt Umber
- Burnt Sienna
- Buff Titanium
- Sepia
- Permanent Violet
- Lavender
- Verditer Blue
- Sap Green
- Lilac
- Indigo
- Brilliant Pink

Brushes

- Size 4 round brush
- Size 2 round brush

Other Materials

- Pencil
- Washi tape

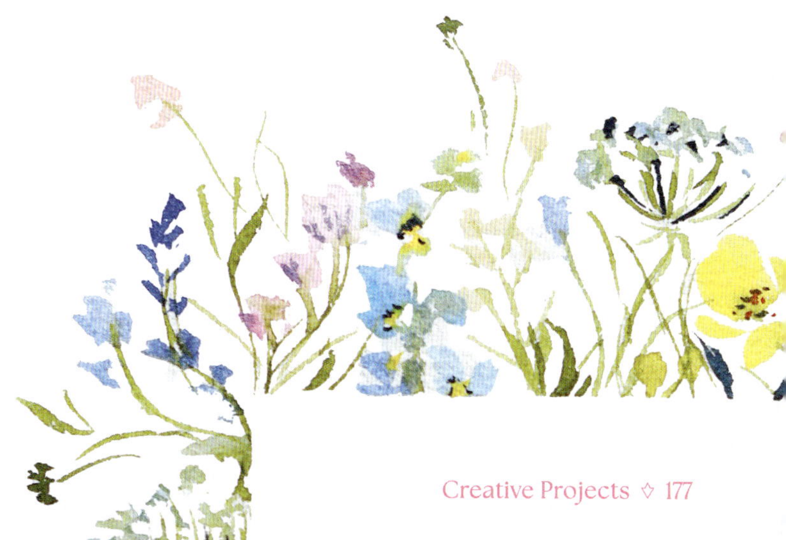

1. Prepare the Frame

Lightly sketch a square or any shape you prefer in the center of your paper. Keep in mind that you may want to write a quote or message inside later. Next, line the inside edges of the shape with washi tape. Press firmly to prevent watercolor from seeping through.

2. Choose the Main Flowers

Start with the boldest flowers as anchors. Paint a cluster of Permanent Yellow Light Buttercups (page 95) using a size 4 round brush in two corners diagonally across from each other. Let some overlap the tape so parts of the flowers appear tucked behind the frame. Using a size 2 round brush, add Olive Green and Permanent Yellow Deep dots in the flower center. Then, paint the stems in Olive Green.

3. Paint the Queen Anne's Lace and Chamomile

Using a size 2 round brush, add Queen Anne's Lace (page 101) using a light mixture of Ultramarine Blue and Burnt Umber, with more blue in the ratio. Vary the height of the flowers for a more natural look. Extend the Olive Green stems out as guides for some flowers later on.

Next, paint the Chamomile flowers (page 91), carefully distributing them around the frame with Olive Green stems. Begin by adding Permanent Yellow Light center with a ring of Burnt Sienna around it. Add the petals using Buff Titanium. Once dry, paint a ring of small dots in the center using Sepia. It is better to start with a few flowers and add some more later on rather than overdo it now. The key to this project is to layer it gradually.

4. Add Blues and Purples

For a color contrast with the yellow Buttercups, add Lavender (page 91) using Permanent Violet and Lavender, then add Verditer Blue Forget-Me-Nots (page 95). Use Sap Green for their stems. Paint them loosely on opposite sides of the frame for balance. Let some thin, curvy stems extend outward as guides for future fillers.

To fill in small gaps, paint clusters of Sea Lavender (page 105) in the color Lilac at three or more different points.

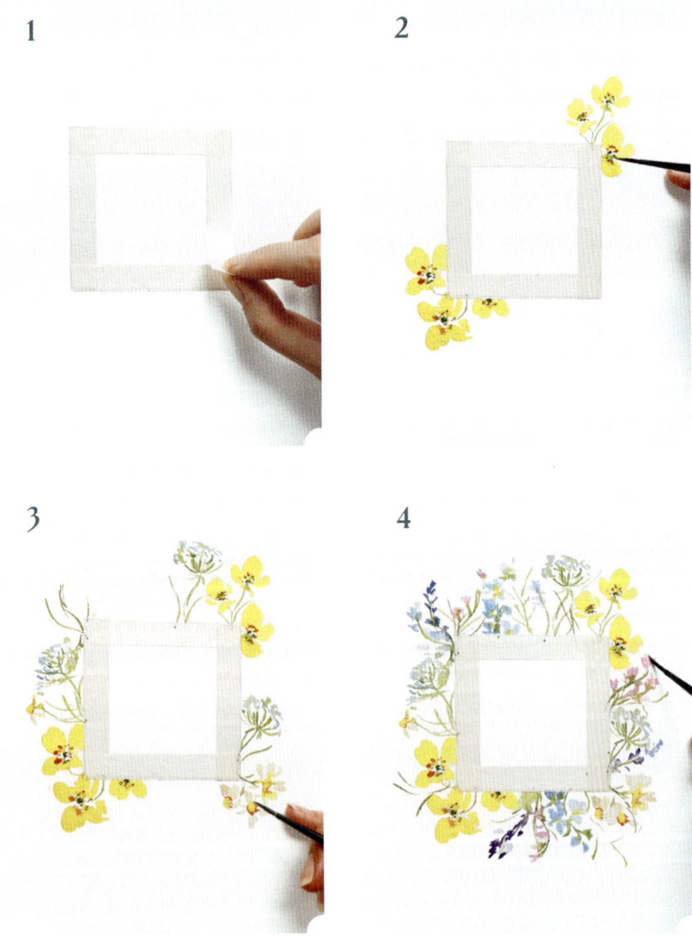

5. Paint Baby's Breath and Fillers

To add a neutral color, scatter Baby's Breath (page 105) around the frame. Paint the Olive Green stems first, then add the delicate Buff Titanium flowers while the stems are still wet to let them blend softly. Next, add fillers by painting small Indigo dots at the tips of the loose stems to add contrast. Using the same color, you can also paint over the stems of the Queen Anne's Lace and add a delicate ring of dots to the Forget-Me-Nots. To spread pops of color throughout the frame, dab tiny Brilliant Pink buds at ends of the other stems using the belly of your brush.

6. Add Depth and Peel the Tape

Mix a deep green color using two parts Sap Green and one part Indigo. With a size 2 round brush, paint small leaves close to the taped edge to ensure a crisp and clean border.

Once everything is dry (use a hair-dryer to speed up drying), carefully peel off the tape at a low angle close to the surface of the paper to minimize the chance of tearing the paper.

For the finishing touch, you may write your favorite quote or word in the center. Start by penciling it in as a guide, then go over it with a pen or paint the letters using a small round brush. Don't worry about perfection! Your personal touch is what makes it beautiful!

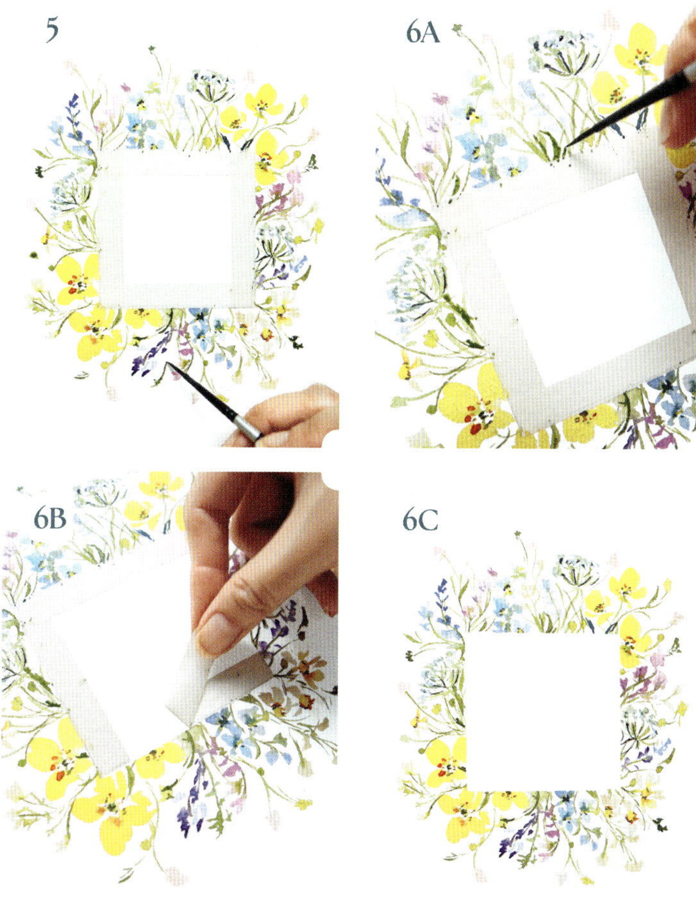

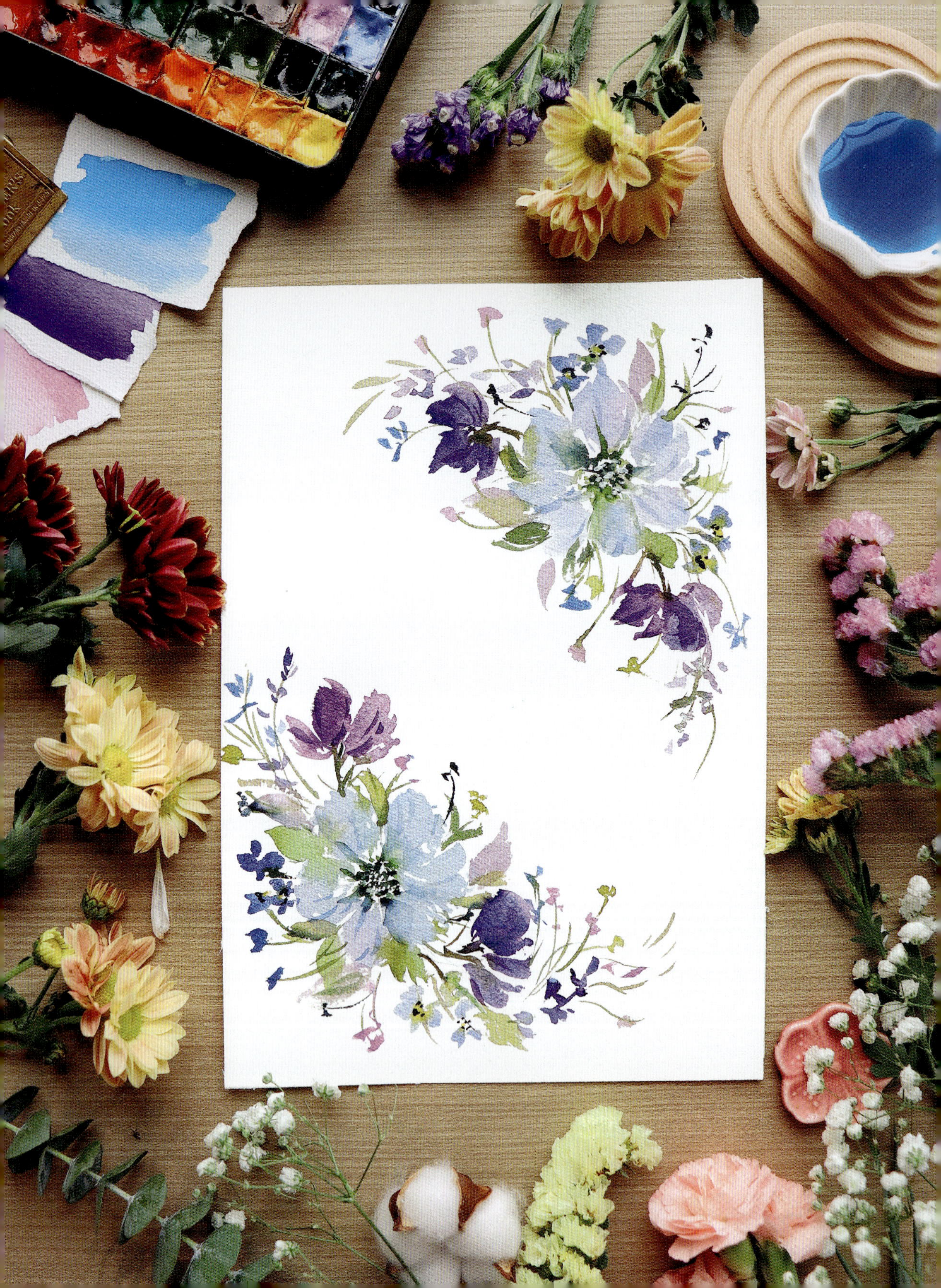

CORNER FLORALS

In this project, we will explore painting florals that naturally flow from two opposite corners, leaving the center open. This arrangement works beautifully for greeting cards and invitations, or you can simply frame it with your favorite quote in the center.

If you'd like extra space for your writing, you can keep the design on just one corner. That's the beauty of this composition: It is simple, versatile, and easy to make your own.

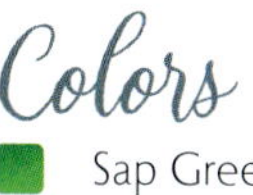

Colors

- Sap Green
- Indigo
- Verditer Blue
- Permanent Violet
- Olive Green
- Mineral Violet
- Cerulean Blue
- Ultramarine Blue
- Permanent Yellow Light
- Lilac

Brushes

- Size 6 round brush
- Size 4 round brush
- Size 2 round brush

Other Materials

- Pencil
- Kuretake Gold Mica, optional

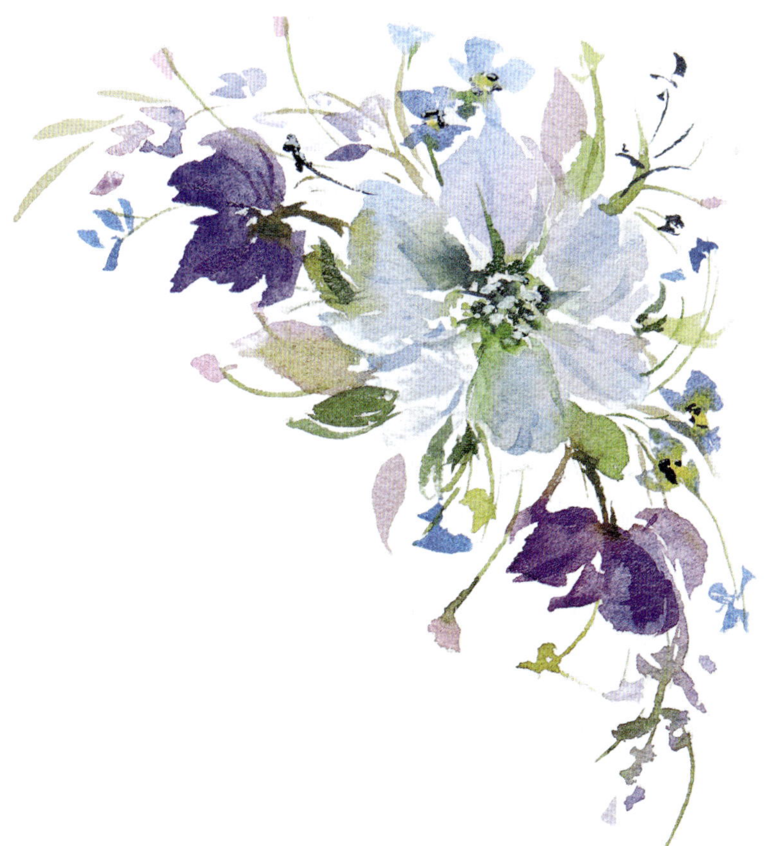

1. Start with the Main Flower

Lightly sketch a circle on two corners of the paper as a guide for the placement of the main flowers. These will serve as anchors for the composition so you can paint more flowers from there.

Using a size 6 round brush, paint the Scabiosa (page 69) where the circles are. Aside from Verditer Blue, drop in a light-consistency Permanent Violet on some petals. Then, while the petals are damp, add a few Olive Green leaves.

2. Paint Supporting Flowers

Next to each Scabiosa, paint a flower with three petals forming a fan shape. Leave small gaps in between the petals. Choose a color that is darker than the Scabiosa to add contrast to the arrangement. Permanent Violet and Mineral Violet work beautifully here. Add thin stems extending outward to help guide the fillers later on.

3. Add Forget-Me-Nots and Lavender

Using a size 4 round brush, paint tiny clusters of Forget-Me-Nots (page 95) near the main flowers. Prepare the blue tones using Cerulean Blue, Verditer Blue, and Ultramarine Blue. Use these varied blues to make it visually more interesting. Once the petals are in place, add the Permanent Yellow Light centers.

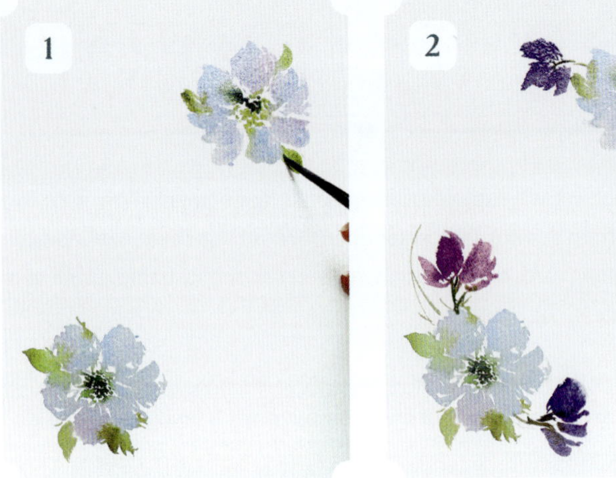

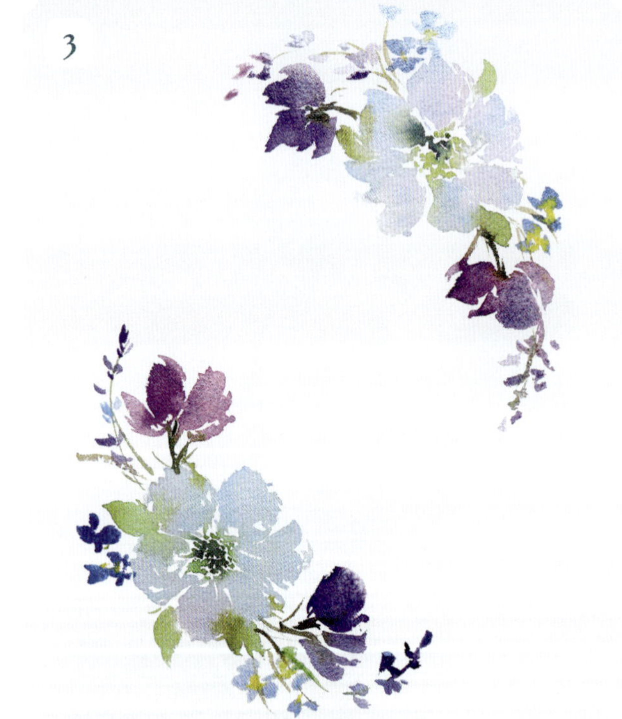

Next, to extend the composition, paint Lavender stalks (page 91) on each side of the corners, curving them slightly to create movement. Alternate between Permanent Violet and Mineral Violet for the V-shaped clusters. Vary the colors by using both lighter and darker values to add depth.

4

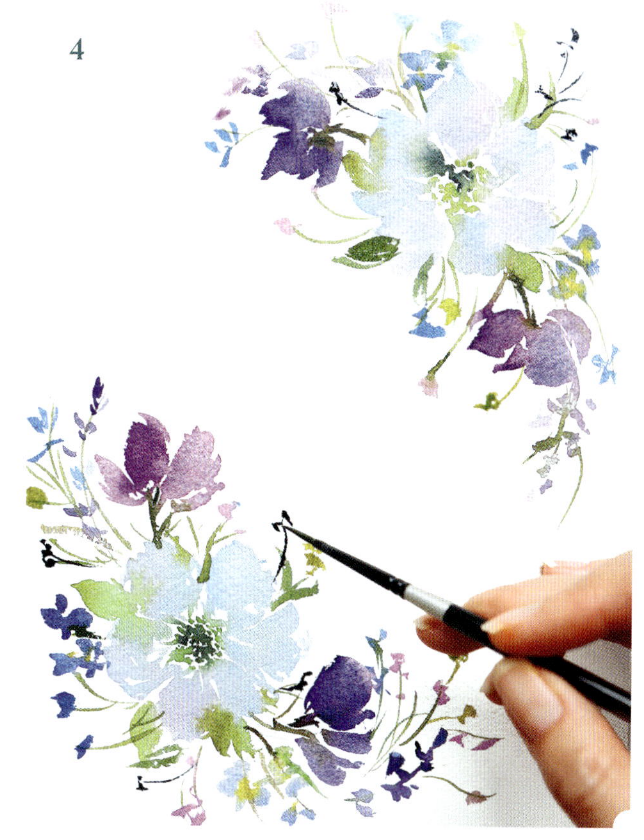

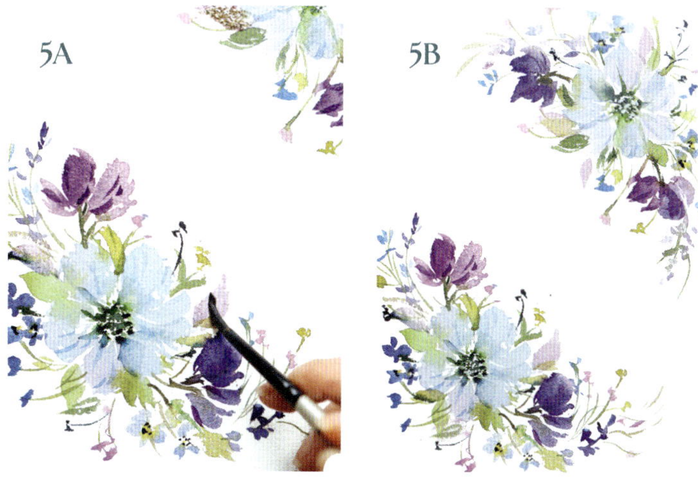

5A

5B

4. Add Filler Flowers

Add wispy leaves and stems using a size 2 round brush using Sap Green. At the tips of the stems, dab your brush with the color Lilac to suggest small, irregular petals. Use colors from the flowers to keep the palette harmonious. For contrast, add small Indigo dots at the ends of a few stems.

5. Add Finishing Touches

Use a hairdryer to speed up drying the first layer, then paint the second layer to deepen the details (Scabiosa [page 69], Forget-Me-Nots [page 95], Lavender [page 91]). For a whimsical look, add a few colored leaves throughout the arrangement.

If you would like to write a quote in the center, start by penciling it in. Then, go over it with a pen or paint the letters using a small round brush. You may even use gold paint for an elegant touch!

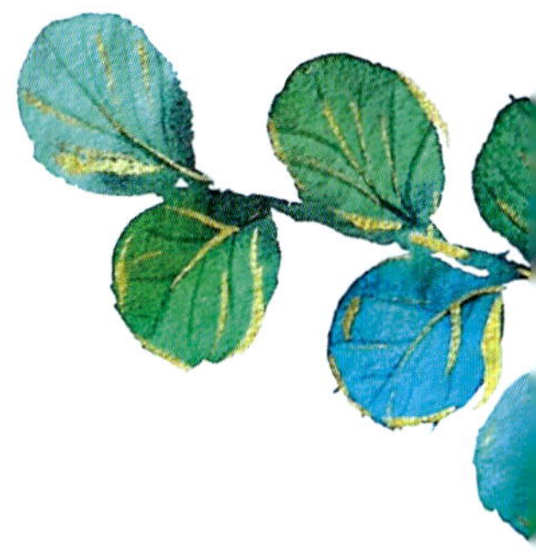

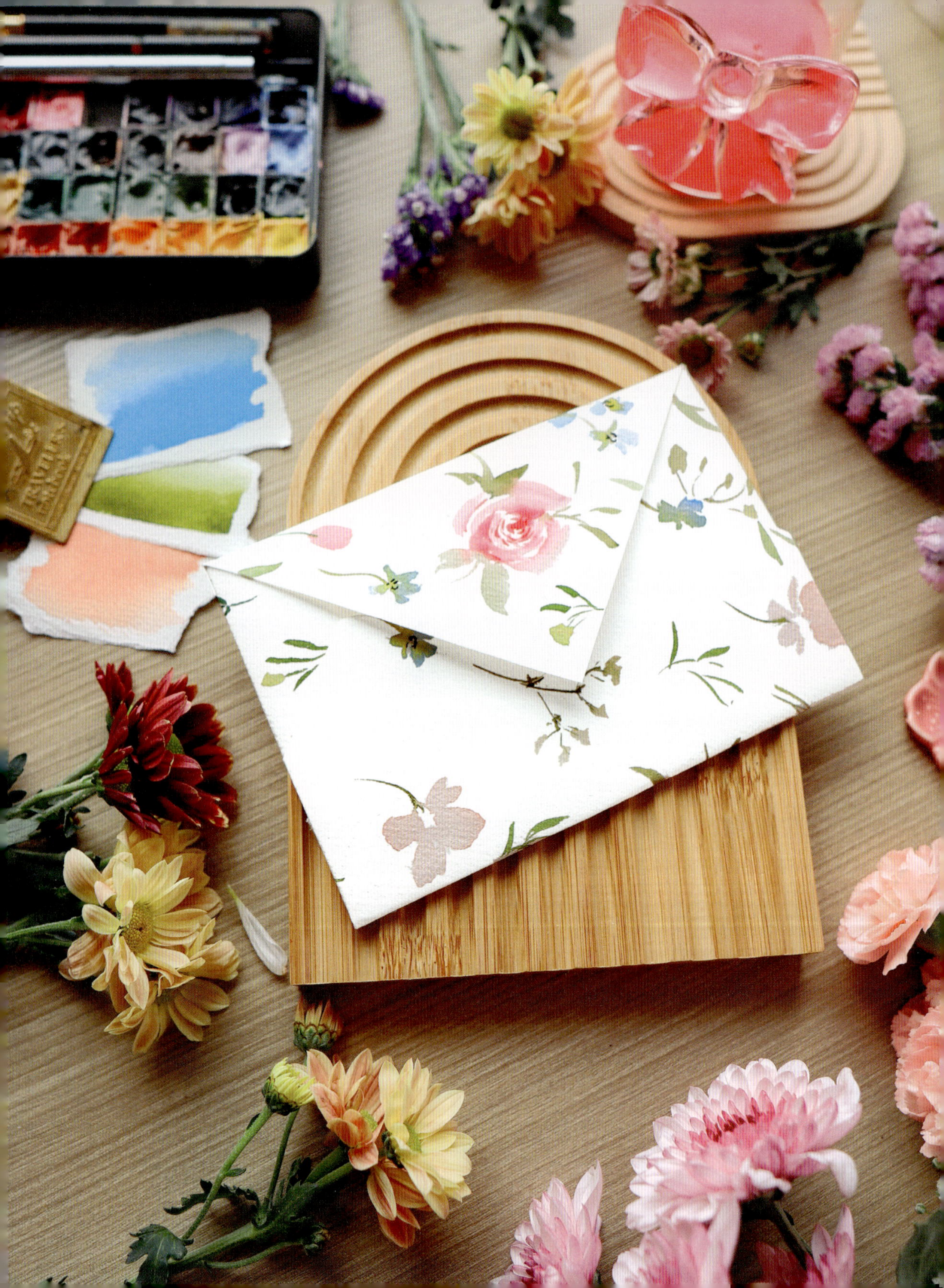

HAND-PAINTED ENVELOPE

This project is truly special to me! For my own wedding, I hand-painted all 200 envelopes for my invitations. At that time, I used pre-made envelopes made of regular paper, which still worked well. I just had to lessen the amount of water in my brush to avoid creating puddles. If you choose to paint on a pre-made envelope, make sure it's matte, not glossy. You want a surface that can absorb watercolor. Glossy paper will cause the paint to sit on top and may not give the best results.

In this lesson, we'll take it a step further. Not only will you paint floral patterns, but you'll also learn how to make an envelope from scratch using watercolor paper!

For this tutorial, we'll choose smaller flowers for a minimalist feel. You'll discover how a few simple blossoms and leaves can transform plain watercolor paper into a charming hand-painted envelope.

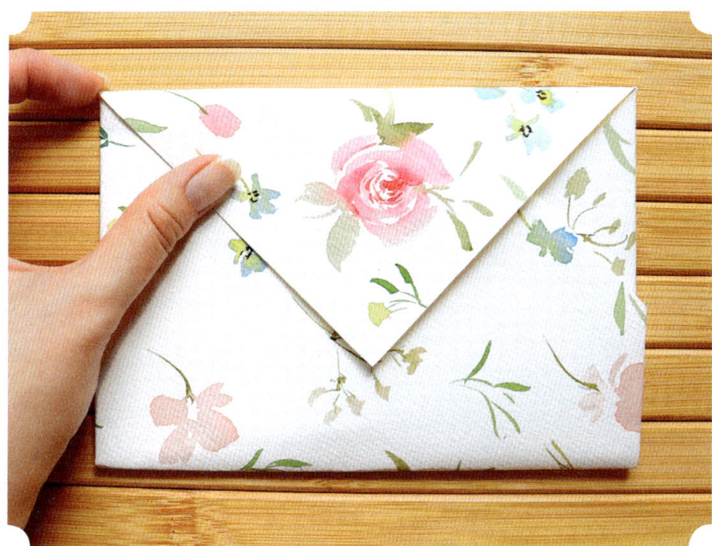

Colors

- Permanent Rose
- Olive Green
- Brilliant Pink
- Buff Titanium
- Verditer Blue
- Permanent Yellow Light
- Sap Green
- Burnt Umber
- Indigo

Brushes

- Size 6 round brush
- Size 2 round brush

Paper

- 9 x 9-inch (23 x 23-cm) sheet of Baohong Academy Cold Pressed Paper, 200 gsm

Other Materials

- Pencil
- Double-sided tape, optional
- Kuretake Gold Mica, optional

1. Start with the Main Flowers

Prepare a 9 x 9-inch (23 x 23-cm) sheet of watercolor paper. Choose a thin paper like 200 gsm so it's easier to fold. Using a size 6 round brush, paint a Rose (page 37) in the center using Permanent Rose with Olive Green leaves and small buds around it. Next, scatter more small roses across the paper in a loose, zigzag way so the eye travels around the page. Let your brush wander and enjoy making a pattern that feels uniquely yours.

2. Paint Small Flowers and Buds

Paint small four-petal flowers in Brilliant Pink and other buds with stems around or in between the Roses. Angle the buds in different directions to add movement and keep the pattern playful. To soften any heavy areas, add Buff Titanium Baby's Breath (page 105) in the gaps.

3. Add a Pop of Color

Scatter Verditer Blue Forget-Me-Nots (page 95) in empty spaces to create contrast. You can create small clusters or single flowers.

Add a few Permanent Yellow Light buds where you feel the composition needs brightness. Finally, fill in awkward gaps with tiny, wispy leaves using a size 2 round brush in varying green tones, using a mixture of Sap Green and Burnt Umber.

4. Add Finishing Touches

Use a hairdryer to quickly dry the first layer, then go back and add second-layer details to the flowers (Rose [page 37], Baby's Breath [page 105], Forget-Me-Nots [page 95]).

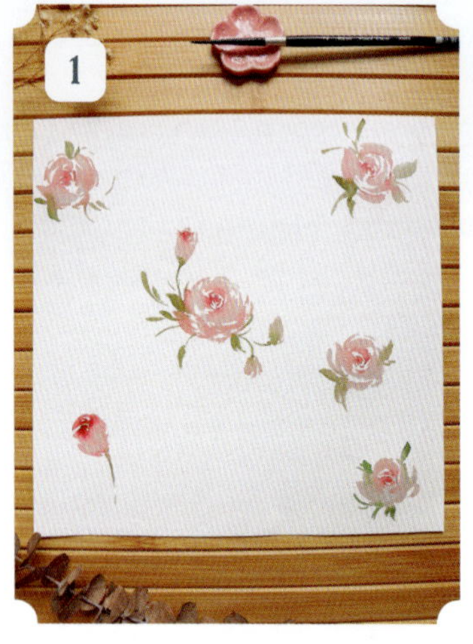

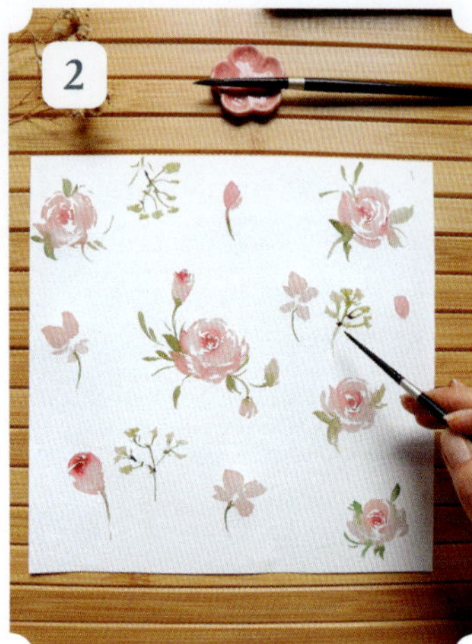

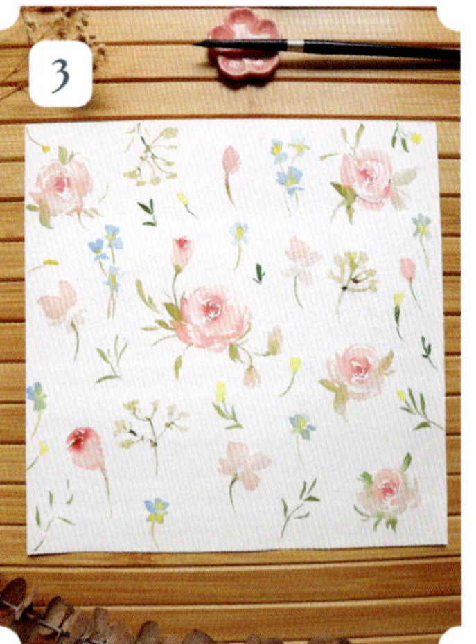

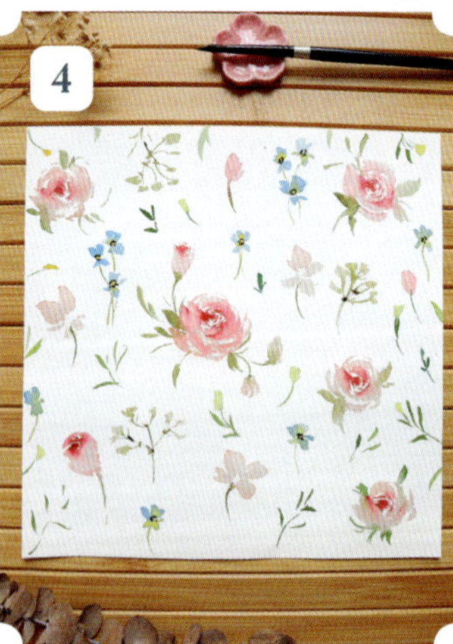

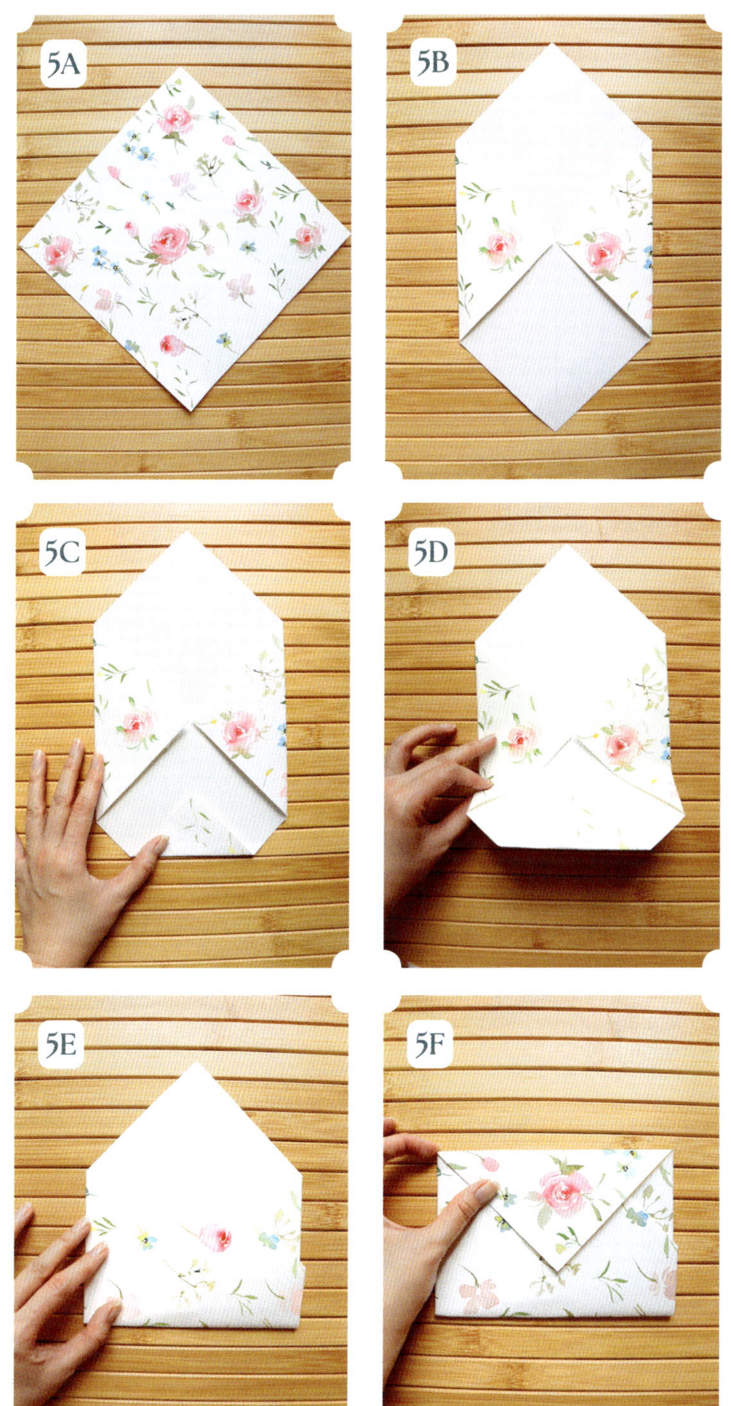

5. Turn It into an Envelope

Once it is completely dry, rotate your painting into a diamond position, then flip it so that the blank side is facing up.

Fold the left corner to the center and crease it. Repeat with the right corner, aligning the corners neatly in the middle. You can draw a pencil mark in the middle as a guide so that you know where the center is.

About 1½ inches (3.75 cm) from the bottom, fold the bottom corner up into a small triangle. Then, fold the bottom flap up toward the center, overlapping the side flaps. Press firmly to crease. You can use double-sided tape to keep this in place.

Fold the top corner down toward the center to form the envelope's closing flap. Your envelope is now complete!

> **TIP:** Add some gold paint for a touch of elegance.

CREATE YOUR OWN SIGNATURE FLORAL PIECE

You've learned the basics, painted the individual flowers, and explored different compositions. Now it's time to create your own signature floral piece.

It's your turn to combine the flowers, colors, and techniques you have enjoyed the most. Choose a few favorites and play with a color palette that excites you, and arrange the flowers in a free-flowing design.

Remember, your unique style shows up in the little things: the way you hold your brush, the colors you mix, and even the happy accidents along the way. Don't worry about perfection—instead, celebrate your growth and progress.

Your signature floral piece is more than a final project. It's a reflection of your watercolor journey.

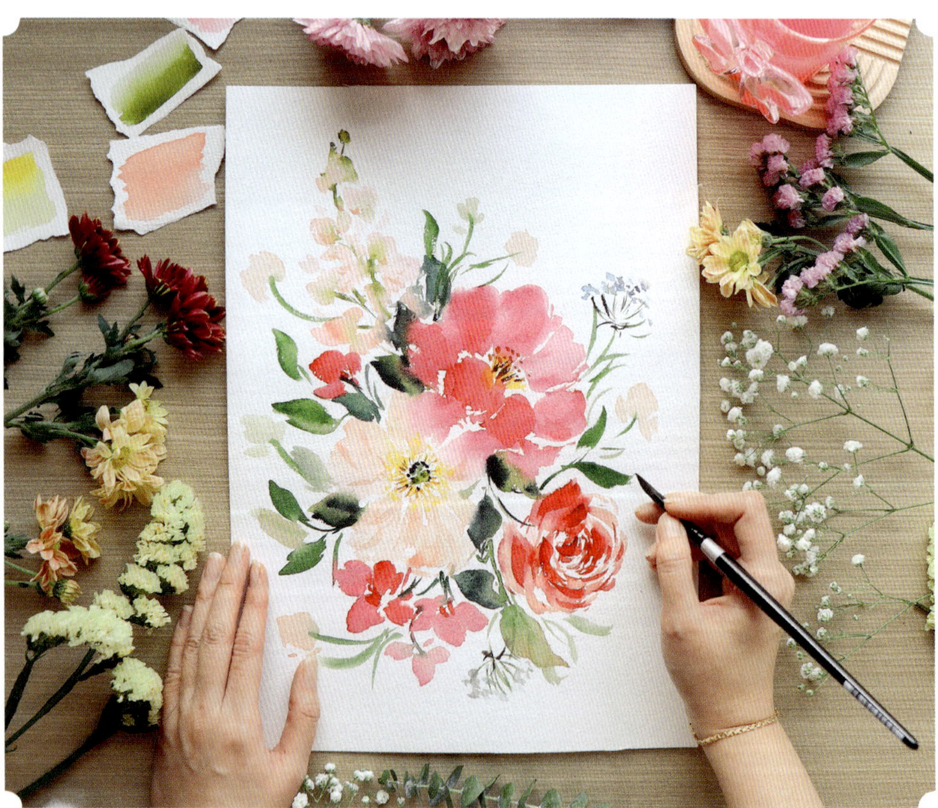

ACKNOWLEDGMENTS

I would like to thank my family and my husband, Lennart, for their love and continuous support throughout my painting journey. To my son, Avery, thank you for being my inspiration and for showing me every day the simple joys of life.

To my students and creative community around the world, thank you for painting along with me and for reminding me every day why I love to share art.

I am also deeply grateful to the Page Street Publishing team for believing in me and guiding me in creating this book, especially to my editor, Krystle Green, who has been patient and encouraging throughout the process.

This book is for all of you who believe in the joy of creating.

ABOUT THE AUTHOR

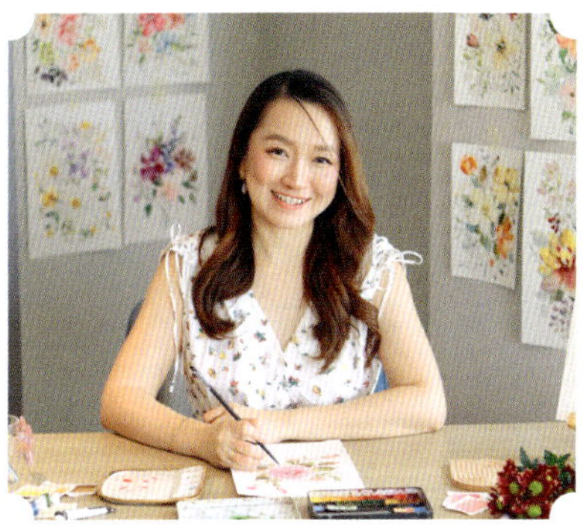

Joly Poa is a self-taught watercolor artist based in Metro Manila, Philippines. She is known for "dancing with her brush" and creating soft and expressive florals with graceful strokes.

Since discovering her love for watercolor in 2013, Joly has inspired thousands of students worldwide through in-person workshops and online classes. Her step-by-step lessons make watercolor approachable, breaking down complex techniques into easy and approachable lessons.

With a growing community of more than a million followers across Instagram, Facebook, and You-Tube, Joly continues to inspire both beginners and watercolor enthusiasts through her calming floral videos, helpful tutorials, and creative insights.

She believes that painting is about finding joy in the process, embracing mistakes and learning from them, and remembering that every brushstroke is uniquely yours, a reflection of your own creative journey.

Website: www.jolypoa.com — **Instagram:** @jolypoa — **Facebook:** @jolypoawatercolorist —
YouTube: @jolypoa — **TikTok:** @jolypoa

INDEX